PREFACE

THIS volume has been compiled from war diaries, private diaries, letters and interviews. War diaries, however, of necessity concise, have little regard to the demands of the historian, as the needs of the moment require a ready weapon rather than a profuse pen. A soldier in the forefront of a battle sees as it were through blinkers ; it is difficult, in fact, for the uninitiated to realise the remarkable restriction of his field of vision. Moreover, he has deeper concerns than writing. As regards the other sources of information, these too are subject to the limitations and immediate outlook of the individual concerned. Undue or insufficient space—as the case may be—may seem to have been devoted to certain aspects of the war, whilst here and there the doings of one or other of the battalions may be considered to obtrude themselves. But owing to the caprices of fortune, history clings to one battalion rather than another, and in many cases a detailed account of the actions and vicissitudes of a single battalion would fill a volume of its own. Some of the disbanded units remained in existence longer than others ; some again, owing to casualties, to lapse of time, or force of circumstances, can furnish little if any information. These considerations will, it is hoped, account for the fact that some battalions are treated at greater length than others. Nevertheless, an equitable, rather than an equal, allocation of space has been the object in view.

Unfortunately, the scope of this volume only admits of the inclusion of a limited number of the honours and awards gained by the regiment.

The thanks of the Regimental History Committee are due to Major A. B. Wright, M.C., who contributed most of the earlier history of the 11th Battalion; to Major E. R. Cooper for his article on the Suffolk Volunteers; to Colonel F. W. Jarvis, D.S.O., for information regarding the Suffolk Yeomanry; to Mr. T. O'H. Horsman, J.P., Littlehampton, for his valuable assistance and advice; and to the proprietors of the *Cambridge Chronicle* and the *East Anglian Daily Times* for their courteous permission to use articles which appeared in their respective journals.

C. C. R. M.

LITTLEHAMPTON
2nd March, 1928

THE HISTORY OF THE SUFFOLK REGIMENT
1914-1927

BY THE SAME AUTHOR

STORIES AND ADVENTURES
THE GAZETTEER OF ARABIA
ROUTES IN ARABIA
OPERATIONS IN WAZIRISTAN
SOLDIERS OF THE PROPHET
ETC.

Photo by] [*W. Burke*

MAJOR-GENERAL SIR JOHN PONSONBY,
K.C.B., C.M.G., D.S.O.

THE HISTORY OF THE SUFFOLK REGIMENT

1914–1927

by

LIEUT.-COLONEL C. C. R. MURPHY

(*Late* THE SUFFOLK REGIMENT)

WITH NUMEROUS PORTRAITS, ILLUSTRATIONS
MAPS AND PLANS

HUTCHINSON & CO. (Publishers) LTD.
34–36 Paternoster Row, London, E.C.4

Printed and bound by Antony Rowe Ltd, Eastbourne

CONTENTS

BEFORE THE GREAT WAR

CHAPTER PAGE

I. Introductory Remarks—The Suffolk Regiment in 1914 15

THE GREAT WAR

II. The Declaration of War—The 2nd Battalion goes to France with the original British Expeditionary Force—The Retreat from Mons 21

III. The Battle of Le Cateau, with a Foreword by General Sir Horace Smith-Dorrien 28

IV. The German Invasion—The Entry of the Territorial Army—The 4th Battalion lands in France—The 2nd and 4th Battalions to the end of 1914—The Marne—The Aisne—La Bassée—Givenchy 39

V. The First Winter—Summer Operations, 1915—Neuve Chapelle—The 1st, 2nd, and 4th Battalions, to the Battles of Ypres, 1915 49

VI. The Battles of Ypres, 1915—Gravenstafel—The Gas Attack—St. Julien—Aubers 64

VII. The Battles of Ypres, 1915 (*contd.*)—Frezenberg—Bellewaarde—Hooge—The 1st, 2nd, and 4th Battalions, to the Battle of Loos 75

VIII. The Service Battalions of the New Army; their Formation and Early History—The 7th, 8th, and 9th Battalions, to the Battle of Loos—The 11th and 12th Battalions, to their Arrival in France . . . 88

IX. The 5th Battalion—Its Origin and Early History—The Gallipoli Campaign—Egypt 99

X. The Suffolk Yeomanry (The Duke of York's Own Loyal Suffolk Hussars) 111

XI. The Battle of Loos; to the eve of the Battles of the Somme, 1916 120

XII. The 1st Battalion in Macedonia 155

Contents

CHAPTER		PAGE
XIII.	The Battles of the Somme, 1916, to the eve of the Battles of Arras, 1917	165
XIV.	The 5th and 15th Battalions in Palestine, to the Fall of Jerusalem	201
XV.	The Allied Offensives, to the Eve of the German Offensive	219
XVI.	The great German Offensive—The First Battles of the Somme, 1918, and the Battles of the Lys	260
XVII.	The Advance to Victory	287
XVIII.	The 1st Battalion, to the Armistice with Germany	303
XIX.	The 5th Battalion in Palestine and Syria, and the 15th Battalion in Palestine and France, to the Armistice with Germany	311
XX.	The 3rd Battalion	322
XXI.	Battalions of the Second and Third Lines, and those not proceeding overseas integrally	332
XXII.	The Great Dispersal	346
XXIII.	The Suffolk Volunteers	360

AFTER THE GREAT WAR

XXIV.	The 1st Battalion to 1927	380
XXV.	The 2nd Battalion, to 1927	391
XXVI.	The 4th Battalion, to 1927	396
	Appendices	399
	Index	405

INDEX BY BATTALIONS

		PAGES
1st Battalion		
January—August, 1914	Sudan	16–18
August, 1914—April, 1915	England and France	49–56
April—May, 1915	France and Flanders	64–70
May—September, 1915	Do.	75–81
September—October, 1915	Do.	126–129
October, 1915—December, 1916	Macedonia	155–164
January, 1917—November, 1918	Do.	303–310
November, 1918—December, 1927	Various	380–390
2nd Battalion		
January—August, 1914	Ireland	18–20
August, 1914	France and Flanders	21–27
August—September, 1914	France	31–38
September—December, 1914	Do.	39–44
January, 1915—April, 1915	Flanders	56–60
April—June, 1915	Do.	72–74
June—September, 1915	Do.	82–85
September, 1915—June, 1916	Do.	133–142
July, 1916—April, 1917	France	182–189
April, 1917—March, 1918	Do.	219–225
March—June, 1918	Do.	260–268
July—November, 1918	Do.	287–293
November, 1918—December, 1927	Various	391–395
3rd Battalion		
August, 1914—July, 1919		322–331
4th Battalion		
July—December, 1914	Home and France	44–48
January—April, 1915	France	60–63
April—May, 1915	Do.	70–72
May—September, 1915	Do.	85–87
September, 1915—July, 1916	Do.	142–146
July, 1916—April, 1917	Do.	189–194
April, 1917—March, 1918	Do.	225–232
March—June, 1918	Do.	268–272
August—November, 1918	Do.	293–296
November, 1918—December, 1927	France and Home	396–398
2/4th and 3/4th Battalions		332–334

5TH BATTALION

		PAGES
1859—1915	Various. Gallipoli	99–110
January, 1916—December, 1917	Egypt and Palestine	201–211
December, 1917—November, 1918	Palestine and Syria	311–318
November, 1918—December, 1921	Egypt and Home	349–352

2/5TH AND 3/5TH BATTALIONS 332–334

1/6TH AND 2/6TH BATTALIONS 334–338

CAMBRIDGE AND SUFFOLK (RESERVE) BATTALION 338–339

7TH BATTALION

August, 1914—September, 1915	Home and France	88–91
September, 1915—July, 1916	France	129–133
July, 1916—April, 1917	Do.	177–181
April, 1917—February, 1918	Do.	232–238
March—May, 1918	Do.	272–277
May, 1918—July, 1919	France and Home	352–353

8TH BATTALION

September, 1914—September, 1915	Home and France	91–92
September, 1915—July, 1916	France	146–150
July, 1916—April, 1917	Do.	165–172
April, 1917—February, 1918	Do.	238–243

9TH BATTALION

September, 1914—September, 1915	Home and France	92–94
September, 1915—July, 1916	France	120–126
August, 1916—April, 1917	Do.	194–199
April, 1917—February, 1918	Do.	243–249

10TH BATTALION 339–341

11TH BATTALION

September, 1914—January, 1916	Home	94–97
January—June, 1916	France	150–154
July, 1916—April, 1917	Do.	172–177
April, 1917—March, 1918	Do.	249–255
March—June, 1918	Do.	277–282
July—November, 1918	Do.	296–300
November, 1918—December, 1919	France, Germany, Home	353–356

12TH BATTALION

June, 1915—June, 1916	Home	97–98
June, 1916—March, 1917	France	199–200
April, 1917—March, 1918	Do.	255–259
March—June, 1918	Do.	282–286
June—November, 1918	Home and France	300–302
November, 1918—July, 1919	France and Home	356–357

		PAGES
13TH BATTALION		341–342
14TH BATTALION		342–343
15TH BATTALION		
1667—August, 1914	Home	111–119
August, 1914—December, 1917	Gallipoli ; E.E.F.	211–218
December, 1917—November, 1918	E.E.F. and France	318–321
November, 1918—December, 1927	France and Home	357–359
1ST GARRISON BATTALION		343–344
2ND GARRISON BATTALION		343–345
THE SUFFOLK VOLUNTEERS		360–379

PORTRAITS

Major-General Sir John Ponsonby, K.C.B., C.M.G., D.S.O. *Frontispiece*

FACING PAGE

Lieut.-Colonel C. A. H. Brett, D.S.O. 34

Lieut.-Colonel W. M. Armes, T.D. 104

Sgt. A. F. Saunders, V.C. 124

Lieut.-Colonel H. W. Cruddas, D.S.O. 144

Brig.-General. H. F. H. Clifford, D.S.O. 186

Lieut.-Colonel A. P. Mack 196

Cpl. S. J. Day, V.C. 252

Lieut.-Colonel T. Eardley-Wilmot, D.S.O. 284

Lieut.-Colonel F. H. A. Wollaston, D.S.O. 314

ILLUSTRATIONS

The 4th Battalion at Neuve Chapelle 60

Sanctuary Wood 84

The Chalk Caves at Arras, Easter Sunday, 1917 220

Courcelles-le-Comte 288

The Cenotaph of the Suffolk Regiment, St. Mary's Church, Bury St. Edmunds 350

The Unveiling of the Le Cateau Memorial by General Sir Horace Smith-Dorrien, G.C.B., G.C.M.G., D.S.O. 394

MAPS

PAGE

Malabar 383

The Western Front . . . . *End paper*

THE HISTORY OF THE SUFFOLK REGIMENT, 1914-1927

CHAPTER I

Introductory—The 1st Battalion in Cairo—Goes to Khartoum—The 2nd Battalion at the Curragh—The Ulster Crisis—The Curragh Incident

THE history of the 12th (Suffolk) Regiment, published in 1914, is a chronicle wrested from the past with great labour. It constitutes a complete record of the regiment from 1685 to the end of 1913, describing its evolution from the company of foot soldiers, stationed at Windsor and commanded by Henry, seventh Duke of Norfolk, Constable and Governor of Windsor Castle, to its six battalions of 1914.

The present volume has no such archæological pretensions; it merely carries the story a little further down the pathway of time. But in doing so it records the growth of the regiment from its more modest proportions of 1914 to a size approaching that of an army corps. It follows the fortunes of a number of Suffolk battalions the like of which may not be witnessed again, and watches them emerge victorious from the greatest war the world has ever seen. During that war, battalions of the Suffolk Regiment served in France and Flanders, Gallipoli, Macedonia, Egypt and Palestine, and at home. Altogether nearly seven thousand officers and men made the supreme sacrifice, seventeen battalions out of an aggregate of twenty-three, together with the depot, contributing to the casualty lists.

The history of a line regiment may be likened to the records of an ancient family; that of a service battalion, to the crowded hour of a young, adventurous life. These service battalions of the new army sprang suddenly into being, won great fame, and as suddenly disappeared. They came into existence in the days closely following the declaration of war, amid scenes of the wildest enthusiasm, unparalleled and indescribable. Men from all corners of the Empire and all parts of the world, from almost every race, every grade of society, and every walk in life, flocked to enlist in their tens of thousands. Day and night they streamed into countless barracks, billets, and camps. A battalion returning from a route march would find itself stronger than when it started. No one knew whence the new arrivals came. Alongside one another in the ranks stood the man of fashion and the tatterdemalion.

These new units followed the line battalions into the midst of the great adventure. They fought the same battles, shared the same hardships, and in the short span of their existence rendered services to their country which will never be forgotten. Many of these battalions, like those of the regular army and the territorial force, were reduplicated over and over again. But as fresh officers and men joined they at once became imbued with pride and interest in the traditions of their regiment, striving with double zeal, like converts to a new faith, to live up to those traditions, to carry them on, and honourably to fill the places of those who had gone before.

On January 1, 1914, from which the present volume dates, the Suffolk Regiment consisted of the 1st and 2nd Battalions; the 3rd (Special Reserve) Battalion, and the 4th, 5th, and 6th (Cyclist) Battalions of the Territorial Force. To meet the dire necessities of the Great War, sixteen other battalions were raised and added, and the Suffolk Yeomanry converted in 1917 into the 15th Battalion, making a grand total of twenty-three. The doings of the ten battalions which proceeded overseas are all woven together into the general story of this book, those of the remaining thirteen battalions forming the subject-matter of separate chapters.

1st Battalion

When the memorable year of 1914 opened the 1st Battalion was stationed in Cairo, where they had arrived from Alexandria, on January 23, 1912. They were, however, under orders for Khartoum. On New Year's Day they furnished a guard of honour, composed of fifty non-commissioned officers and men, with band and drums and the regimental colour, under Captain Jourdain and Lieutenants J. A. Campbell and Bolton, on the occasion of the arrival in Cairo of General Sir Ian Hamilton, Inspector General of the Overseas Forces. An interesting fitness characterised the event, for this distinguished soldier, like Wolfe, Picton, and Wolseley before him, had once held a commission in the 12th Foot. On the day after this visit Lieut. D. V. M. Balders took over the adjutancy from Captain F. S. Cooper, the appointment dating officially from December 31.

On January 8 Captain Wood-Martin and 2nd Lieut. C. F. B. Smith left Cairo with an advance party to take over barracks in Khartoum prior to the move of the battalion. On the 13th Major d'Arch Smith and Lieut. Leach left for Alexandria with a half-company to embark for Cyprus, where they relieved a corresponding number of the 1st Welch Regiment. Two days later the remainder of the company, under Captain Jourdain and Lieuts. Leith-Hay-Clark and Bolton, followed as far as Alexandria, where they were quartered in the Ras-el-Tin barracks. The advance party for Cyprus, consisting of Lieut. Moysey and two sergeants, had left Cairo on the 6th. On January 19 a large party, including a number of women and children, left the 1st Battalion and were attached to the 2nd Devon Regiment at Abbasia, Cairo, prior to embarking in the H.M.T. *Soudan* at Alexandria for Southampton for discharge or transfer. They did not sail, however, till February 6.

On January 22 battalion headquarters, with the band and drums and three companies, left Cairo for Suez. On the following day they embarked in the H.M.T. *Rewa* for Port Sudan, reached two days later, and on the 27th arrived in Khartoum, being joined shortly afterwards by the remainder of the battalion. Half of "B" Company was then formed into the British camel corps company, under the command of Captain Thomas, the other officers being 2nd Lieuts. Forbes and C. F. B. Smith.

On January 24 a large draft from the 2nd Battalion, under 2nd Lieuts. Wood and Hunt, left Southampton in the H.M.T. *Soudan*, reaching Alexandria on February 5. With the exception of the first-named officer, who remained behind temporarily in hospital, and also of one sergeant and three men, this draft reached Khartoum on the 17th. The hot weather of 1914 passed uneventfully, and at the outbreak of the great war the 1st Battalion was still in Khartoum.

2nd Battalion

New Year's Day of 1914 found the 2nd Battalion at the Curragh, having arrived there from Aldershot on September 28, 1913. On January 11 Major C. R. Fryer, attaining the age limit, retired from the army after more than twenty-eight years' service in the Suffolk Regiment. His time, both as subaltern and captain, had been spent in the 1st Battalion, and only the last six years in the 2nd Battalion.

The annual inspection report on the battalion for 1912–13 was extremely good, the opinion of the G.O.C.-in-C., Aldershot Command (Lieut.-General Sir Douglas Haig), being that they were a fine battalion, well commanded, and thoroughly deserving the very satisfactory report which had been given them by the G.O.C. 2nd Division. On February 1 Lieut. G. C. Stubbs was appointed an officer of a company of gentlemen cadets at the Royal Military College, Sandhurst. On the 19th the draft, which had left Alexandria on February 6, disembarked at Southampton. A few days later Lieut.-Colonel C. H. C. Van Straubenzee was placed on half-pay on completion of his period in command of the battalion, being succeeded by Lieut.-Colonel C. A. H. Brett, D.S.O. In April Major Barnardiston rejoined from service under the Colonial Office, and Captain Walford was attached to the General Staff, being graded as a brigade-major.

During the previous month the battalion had passed through a critical and anxious time, generally referred to as the Ulster crisis, the circumstances of which, so far as they affected the 2nd Battalion only, were briefly as follows. On March 20 Lieut.-Colonel Brett, suddenly summoning the officers together, announced that in accordance with instructions received by the G.O.C.-in-C. from the War Office, he had been ordered to ask each officer individually whether (1) he was prepared to proceed against Ulster, or whether (2) he wished to resign his commission, forfeiting his pension. The commanding officer added that the answers were to be reported to the brigade commander at once.

As may be readily supposed, this announcement, clearly portending action against Ulster, caused the utmost consternation. The officers submitted that it was impossible to come to so momentous a decision within the space of a few minutes, but agreed to send in their answers the following morning. That evening the officers of the battalion met and resolved unanimously to exercise their option and resign their commissions rather than take any action against loyal Ulster.

On March 21 the 2nd Battalion was ordered to parade in the garrison gymnasium at the Curragh. The officers were then told to fall out and to assemble in the fencing-room. Here they were addressed by the G.O.C. 5th Division, who was accompanied by the G.O.C. 14th Infantry Brigade. The divisional commander, after making certain introductory remarks, declared that so far the only order impending was one contemplating the despatch of troops to Ulster. He maintained that there would be no justification for officers to refuse duty or to resign their commissions in a body at that stage. It would be a different matter if, on arrival in Ulster, orders were given raising the questions of legality or conscience, when officers would have to decide for themselves. But in the meantime it was their duty to avoid all appearance of political leaning and to remember the interests of duty and discipline. He appealed to them to keep their heads and, whatever line others might follow, to take no extreme steps until the necessity arose. At this juncture an officer rose and pointed out that as the War Office instructions offered a choice between two courses of action there could in no case be any question of mutiny.

The divisional commander then left the fencing-room and addressed the battalion in the gymnasium. Shortly afterwards Lieut.-Colonel Brett held a meeting of officers at which it was decided to proceed to Ulster if required. In arriving at such a decision, most distasteful to themselves as soldiers, they felt they were doing their utmost to carry out their orders in a situation with which they should never in any circumstances have been confronted.

From the foregoing statement it is clear that no officer belonging to the Suffolk Regiment was in the least degree guilty of mutiny, either in fact or intention. News of the Curragh incident soon travelled to Westminster, and heated discussions in Parliament followed. To sum up, the Cabinet's proposals to employ the army against Ulster met with such a storm of protest that the matter was shelved and, the great war intervening, this unfortunate and distasteful episode came to an end.

CHAPTER II

The declaration of war—The 2nd Battalion arrives in France—The advance into Belgium—First contact with the enemy—The retreat from Mons—The Via Dolorosa

ENGLAND declared war against Germany on Tuesday, August 4, 1914, and on the following day the mobilisation of regulars, Special Reserve, and Territorials was ordered. That of the 5th Division at the Curragh and Dublin was on the whole carried through rapidly, and by the 10th the division was ready to embark.

The 5th Division, under the command of Major-General Sir Charles Fergusson, Bart., C.B., M.V.O., D.S.O., consisted of the 13th, 14th, and 15th Infantry Brigades as follows :—

13TH INFANTRY BRIGADE

Brig.-General G. J. Cuthbert, C.B.

2nd Battalion K.O. Scottish Borderers.
2nd Battalion D. of W. West Riding Regiment.
1st Battalion Royal West Kent Regiment.
2nd Battalion K.O. Yorkshire L.I.

14TH INFANTRY BRIGADE

Brig.-General S. P. Rolt, C.B.

2nd Battalion Suffolk Regiment.
1st Battalion East Surrey Regiment.
1st Battalion D.C.L.I.
2nd Battalion Manchester Regiment.

15TH INFANTRY BRIGADE

Brig.-General Count Gleichen, K.C.V.O., C.B., C.M.G., D.S.O.

1st Battalion Norfolk Regiment.
1st Battalion Bedford Regiment.
1st Battalion Cheshire Regiment.
1st Battalion Dorset Regiment.

The troops were accorded a splendid send-off from Ireland, leaving amidst tumultuous cheering and patriotic enthusiasm. The 2nd Battalion, which mustered all told nearly a thousand strong, including twenty-six officers and a medical officer, did not, however, proceed to France as a whole. The right half left Dublin in the s.s. *Lanfranc* on August 13. The left half were not so fortunate ; there was no ship ready for them, and so they remained in barracks in Dublin for the night. On the following day they embarked in s.s. *Poland*, a small tramp steamer with only sufficient accommodation for two companies. On disembarking at Havre the battalion, having reassembled, left in one long troop train at three o'clock in the morning of August 17. The officers landing in France with the 2nd Battalion were : Lieut.-Colonel C. A. H. Brett, D.S.O., in command ; Major E. C. Doughty, second-in-command ; Majors A. S. Peebles, D.S.O., F. T. D. Wilson, and S. J. B. Barnardiston, D.S.O. ; Captains E. E. Orford, E. E. Pearson, E. H. Reid, W. M. Campbell, A. M. Cutbill (Adjutant), and L. F. Hepworth ; Lieuts. N. A. Bittleston (M.G.O.), T. W. Reynolds (attd. 5th Division Cyclists), and N. B. Oakes (T.O.) ; 2nd Lieuts. J. B. Morgan, F. V. C. Pereira, E. H. W. Backhouse, R. G. C. Harvey ; Captain W. Blackwell (Quartermaster) ; Captain E. C. Phelan, R.A.M.C. (Medical Officer) ; and the following second lieutenants from the 3rd Battalion : T. L. George, P. C. Nicholls, V. M. G. Phillips, F. C. Berril,l P. R. W. Carthew, H. P. James, G. H. Payne, and E. G. Myddleton.

The next evening the battalion detrained at Le Cateau, noteworthy as the first general headquarters of the British Army in France, and marched on to Landrecies, a distance of about eight miles. The weather was hot and still, and this march—after a tense fortnight of unusual bustle and racket—proved, though sufficiently short, a tiring one.

The original British Expeditionary Force consisted of the Ist Army Corps (1st and 2nd Divisions), under Lieut.-General Sir Douglas Haig ; the IInd Army Corps (3rd and 5th Divisions), under Lieut.-General Sir James Grierson ; and the Cavalry Division, under Major-General Allenby. In addition, there was the 19th Infantry Brigade, employed at first on the lines of communication. The 4th Division landed later and joined the main force during the retreat from Mons, detraining at Le Cateau on the eve of that battle. During the journey by rail to Le Cateau the 2nd Battalion heard with great regret of the sudden death of their corps commander, Sir James Grierson. He was succeeded by General Sir Horace Smith-Dorrien, under whom the 1st Battalion had served in the South African war, and the 2nd Battalion in Karachi and Aldershot.

On August 20 a message from His Majesty King George V to his troops was read out on parade at Landrecies, and later on in the day the battalion was drawn up in a hollow square and addressed by its divisional commander, Major-General Sir Charles Fergusson, who made a stirring speech. In the afternoon orders to advance northwards into Belgium were received, and on the following morning the whole division set out along the western edge of the Mormal forest. The 14th Brigade formed the centre of three columns and marched through Pont à Vaches to Bavai, a hot and dusty journey of seventeen miles. The weather was brilliant, the countryside looked peaceful and prosperous, the farmsteads were tidy and trim, and all the orchards laden with fruit. Only a few villages were passed through, but on all sides the soldiers of Great Britain were welcomed with wild enthusiasm. Our men were offered cigars, cigarettes, eggs, bread, fruit, and many other gifts; it seemed, indeed, as if the inhabitants, in the access of their gratitude, wished to press upon them everything they possessed. The troops, bedecked with flowers, swung merrily along, ready to "greet the unseen with a cheer." Few realised what was in store for them.

Since the declaration of war a hurricane of events had swept by. Now the situation was changing almost every moment. It was therefore impossible that the troops could have any but the vaguest idea of what was happening. There was practically no information available as to the whereabouts of the French or the enemy; even the movements of the other British divisions were not known precisely, though it was understood that the 3rd Division were on the right of the 5th Division and that Haig's Corps were still further to the east.

On the night of August 21–22 the 5th Division billeted in and around Bavai and Bermeries, the 2nd Battalion being located in St. Waast. Here Major Peebles was told off to command a section of the outposts, held by his own company and one from the 2nd Manchester Regiment under Captain Knox. Early that evening a French cavalry patrol passed through on their way to Lille. This was the first the battalion had seen of the French Army at the front.

On the 22nd the battalion had another long march in the heat. This time their route lay through a succession of villages, and then across the frontier into Belgium at Hamin, where they had to wait some time before settling down in their billets. "A" and "B" Companies, under Major Doughty, which had furnished the advance guard that day, were pushed on as far as the Mons–Condé canal, being relieved later by the 1st D.C.L.I. It was on this day, soon after dawn, that the British Army in France and Flanders fired its first shot in the great war.

Sunday morning, August 23, found the inhabitants of the quaint old town of Mons going to Mass as usual. As an illustration of how little the inhabitants anticipated the impending storm and its sudden outburst, an old man came up to Major Peebles in St. Waast and asked whether it was safe to leave his cows out in a meadow on the south side of the canal. Major Peebles reassured him, and the old man went away contented. A moment later an orderly came in with a message ordering "C" and "D" Companies, under Major Doughty, to proceed at once to the canal to reinforce the 1st East Surrey Regiment, and as these two companies marched through Haine they came under the enemy's artillery fire. On arrival at the canal Major Doughty reported to Lieut.-Colonel Longley, commanding the 1st East Surrey Regiment, who ordered two platoons ("C" Company, under Captain Hepworth) to push across the canal and reinforce Captain Benson's (1st East Surrey Regiment) company holding the bridgehead. At this point there was some sharp fighting, Captain Benson and a number of his men being killed. Cpl. G. M. Page and Ptes. W. Flack and S. G. Goddard of the 2nd Battalion were killed, the first representatives of the Suffolk Regiment to give their lives in the great war. 2nd Lieut. V. M. G. Phillips, who was wounded, fell into the hands of the enemy with many other wounded a few days later. All four casualties belonged to "C" Company.

The IInd Corps were now holding the dead straight reach

of the Mons–Condé canal, running due west from Mons. The left of the 5th Division rested on the Pommerœuil–Thulin road, and the right at Mariette in touch with the 3rd Division. The 13th Brigade were on the right, the 14th on the left, and the 15th in reserve about Wasmes. Thus at noon on August 23 the 14th Brigade were on the extreme left flank of the British line. Shortly afterwards, however, the 19th Brigade were sent up to prolong the line to the left. During the afternoon Major Peebles' company built a bridge over the waterway connecting the Mons–Condé canal with the river Haine. While the work was in progress his men were worried by a German sniper, who had boldly crossed over to the south side of the canal and concealed himself. Fortunately, however, he was a poor shot.

Meanwhile the Germans in great strength were advancing rapidly, and owing to their enormous preponderance in artillery, were able to drive in a wedge between the 3rd and 5th Divisions. Crossing the canal they penetrated as far as Wasmes. Here they were held in check by the 15th Brigade, but the position was still precarious, and in response to an appeal by the IInd Corps the 5th Infantry Brigade (2nd Division) was sent to reinforce them. That evening the troops along the canal were ordered to retire, and did so after destroying as many of the bridges as was humanly possible in the time. The 2nd Battalion, crossing the Haine by an iron footbridge, fell back as far as Hamin. As soon as it was dark the Germans sounded bugle-calls all along the line, presumably to convey the impression that they were retiring.

Though it was not yet generally known, Sir John French had already decided temporarily to abandon the offensive. This retirement was the beginning of the strategic movement that will go down in history as the Retreat from Mons.

Hamin was reached about ten o'clock that night. After a halt there of about an hour and a half a further retirement was ordered, the battalion being kept on the march for practically the remainder of the night. On reaching Dour they were turned about and sent northwards to Bois de Boussu. "A" and "B" Companies were detailed for outpost duty near Cornet Halte, but soon afterwards rejoined the battalion at Bois de Boussu, where a position, prepared by the 1st

Norfolk Regiment on the north side of the railway, was occupied. The 1st D.C.L.I. prolonged the line to the right.

At noon on the 24th the retirement was resumed. The route lay through Dour, Athis, Houdain, and Prefeuillet, where there was a general deployment followed by a short halt. The march was then continued through a succession of streets, with the ever-present danger of being shelled in a confined space. Different, indeed, was the aspect now. Instead of the gay cheering crowds which had greeted the troops but two days before there were only deserted streets and shuttered houses, with never a smiling face to be seen.

All this time the German artillery fire was increasing. They appeared to possess vast quantities of shells. Allenby's cavalry division, in endeavouring to prevent the enemy from outflanking the British, had some hard fighting marked by many a gallant deed. The 1st Norfolk and 1st Cheshire Regiments, with the 119th Battery, were told off as a flank guard. They were violently attacked near Elouges, but offered the most stubborn resistance, the 1st Cheshire Regiment alone losing nearly five hundred men. At last, after what had seemed an almost endless march, the battalion struggled into St. Waast about seven o'clock in the evening.

Before dawn on August 25 the retirement was again resumed, the 5th Division moving down the long straight road which runs by the Mormal forest, and retracing their steps of the 21st. It was a hot day, just as on the former occasion, and the tall forest trees seemed to shut out every breath of air. With the disheartening effect of retreat upon them as well, it was only by dint of determination that many of the men managed to carry on at all.

The scenes along the edge of the forest were heartrending. The road was a mass of panic-stricken women and children, all flying in terror from the vengeance of the invaders. Some were struggling with perambulators or push-carts, some carrying bundles representing all they had been able to save of their worldly goods, others sitting by the roadside utterly exhausted and unable to move. All were broken and helpless. Their plight was pitiful to behold.

The cavalry division covered, as best it could, the retreat of the IInd Corps to Le Cateau. About five o'clock in the evening the battalion halted just outside Montay. It was raining heavily. After a while they moved on again, but were held up in the little town itself to allow the 3rd Cavalry Brigade to pass through. This did not improve matters, as troublesome rumours of the enemy's strength and proximity were circulated. At ten o'clock that night the battalion reached Pont des Quatre Vaux, at the cross-roads half a mile to the west of Le Cateau, where they flung themselves down to rest.

FOREWORD TO CHAPTER III

AS the commander of the British troops who fought in the glorious battle of Le Cateau on August 26, 1914, I have been asked to write a foreword to the chapter in the *History of the Suffolk Regiment* which deals with that eventful day.

It is not easy in a few words to express the depth of gratitude I feel to this gallant regiment for their noble self-sacrifice on that occasion.

The situation was this :

The British Expeditionary Force was in retreat, in close touch with an overwhelming force of an enemy with whom they had been in strenuous and continuous action for the previous three successive days, whilst marching during the same time some forty miles in very hot weather on paved roads. Either the retreat had to be continued with the danger of our own weary troops being overwhelmed and beaten in detail, for they were very much scattered, or a battle had to be fought of a nature so determined as to deal the Germans a blow serious enough to cripple them temporarily, so that our troops could break away from them and continue retiring under shadow of the night.

It was a choice of evils, but I, feeling sure that if I adopted the first course disaster was almost a certainty, decided on the second.

I had absolute confidence in our magnificent troops, with their perfect discipline, undaunted fighting spirit, and unrivalled standard of training, and felt sure that if we turned to fight we should stand a great chance of so maiming the enemy as to be able to retreat under cover of the coming night.

Under instructions from the commander-in-chief I had issued orders for the retirement to continue, and the 14th Brigade, to which the 2nd Battalion of the Suffolks belonged, had been detailed as rearguard to the 5th Division.

Thus, when in the small hours of the 26th I was able to

gauge the situation from the accumulating reports of the scattered positions of the troops in my area, I learned that many of them were still on the march, that more than one whole division would not have reached the line we had taken up until after daylight, and further, that all were exhausted and foot-sore, and therefore issued orders to stand and fight. The 14th Brigade automatically became the troops who would have to meet the first attack of the enemy. There was no time to choose, much less adequately to entrench a position, so they had to fight where they were, practically in a salient, fully exposed to the enemy's fire, and with their right flank *en l'air,* owing to the failure of the Ist Corps to come into their place in the line on the previous evening.

Some one, certainly not I, ordered that on no account were the Suffolks to retire. Such an order was enough for the Suffolks. For nine hours they fought with desperate losses, their C.O., Lieut.-Colonel Brett, being killed comparatively early in the day; but no thought of retirement entered their heads, for had they not been told to fight to the last? I was not surprised when I heard of their grand behaviour, for I had had previous experience of this magnificent regiment, especially in the Boer war, but it was never my intention that any troops should have been called on to fight to the last. My intention was to fight a serious rearguard action and, when the pressure became too great, to order a general retirement by divisions, and this I actually did about 2 p.m. It may be some satisfaction to the regiment to feel that their gallant adherence to the letter of the order they got materially helped the remainder of their comrades in the 5th Division to fall back practically unpursued; in fact, had not the Suffolks and other intrepid troops refused to budge, there would have been nothing to prevent the enemy sweeping on to the scattered units of the division before they had had time to get on the road allotted for their retirement. Had this happened, the safety of the whole force fighting at Le Cateau, and indeed of the whole B.E.F., would have been jeopardised. It is being more and more appreciated by the world as facts become known and the history of the war is studied that it was the blow to the Germans delivered on the field of Le Cateau which upset their plans and prevented their descent on Paris.

The Suffolks were one of the units which made that blow possible. I thank them, and the whole nation should be grateful to them.

H. L. Smith-Dorrien

General.

25th Nov. 1927.

CHAPTER III

The battle of Le Cateau—The Commander-in-Chief congratulates the 2nd Battalion—The 5th Division reaches Tournan

DURING the night of August 25–26 corps orders were issued to continue the retirement at seven o'clock the next morning, and at 3.30 a.m. the 5th Division stood to arms. They were then in touch with the 3rd Division on their left, but there was no sign of Haig's Corps on their right. A French corps was said to be marching from the west to the assistance of Smith-Dorrien's Corps. The 19th Brigade, which had been placed at the disposal of the latter commander, was put in reserve in the centre, but, like the rest of the troops, was in a state of physical exhaustion. The 3rd Cavalry Brigade, with parts of two others, to a certain extent covered the right flank of the division.

Shortly after 4 a.m. Brig.-General Rolt informed Lieut.-Colonel Brett that at 3 a.m. he had received orders for the retirement to be continued, with the 14th Brigade as rear-guard. The battalion then moved off in artillery formation along the open ground on the east side of the long, straight Roman road running south-west towards Reumont. Soon afterwards Lieut.-Colonel Brett and Major Doughty were called away by Brig.-General Rolt. When the two leading companies (" A " and " B," Majors Wilson and Barnardiston) had reached the cross-roads south-west of Pont des Quatre Vaux, Lord Douglas Malise Graham, A.D.C. to the Divisional Commander, came up and asked for the brigadier. On being directed, he remarked to Major Peebles, who was the senior officer present, " You are going to fight it out here."

As soon as the decision of the General Officer Commanding IInd Corps to stand and fight at Le Cateau became known, the adjutant, Captain Cutbill, rode off after the transport and recovered the regimental tools. These were handed over to " A " and " B " Companies, who took up a line in some stubble on which the corn stooks were still standing. In the mean-time positions were allotted to the various battalions.

" C " Company's (Captain Orford) trenches were represented by a few scratches in the ground; " D " Company's (Major Peebles) position was totally unprepared. Lieut. Bittleston, in charge of the two Suffolk machine-guns, chose a position in " A " Company's (Major Wilson) line.

The official history of the war says: " The Suffolks in particular, who lay immediately to the west of Le Cateau, were badly placed for a general action: there was much dead ground on every side; the field of fire was for the most part limited and could nowhere be called good; and small valleys and sunken roads at sundry points gave hostile infantry every opportunity of concealing their approach. The battalion, in common with the other troops of the 5th Division, made shift to throw up such entrenchments as it could with its ' grubbers,' no better tools being obtainable."

Lieut.-Colonel Brett, in discussing this state of affairs with his company commanders, explained that he had had nothing whatever to do with the selection of the position; they were committed to it, and everyone must do the best he could. He then impressed upon them that there was to be no retirement.

About six o'clock in the morning No. 15 Platoon opened fire. Major Peebles went over to find out what they had been firing at and was informed that a Uhlan patrol had been seen, and on going forward to make a personal reconnaissance he found the dead body of a Uhlan officer. More enemy patrols and some scouts now began to appear. Brig.-General Rolt then went up to the advanced position and explained that the 1st East Surrey Regiment and the 1st D.C.L.I. were out on the right, beyond the St. Quentin–Le Cateau–Landrecies railway, and that the French might be expected to come up on that flank. The brigadier handed over a party of thirty-four details, under the command of Captain Williams and 2nd Lieut. Burnand, both of the Dorset Regiment, to the 2nd Battalion. Before leaving he remarked: " You understand, there is to be no thought of retirement."

One and a half battalions of the 14th Brigade, who had not heard that the orders to continue the retirement had been cancelled, and who were marching to join up from the north-east of Le Cateau, were surprised in the town itself, but extricated themselves skilfully.

The corn stooks had scarcely been flattened down, and the shallowest of trenches dug, when one of the enemy's guns opened fire. The second shell landed in the middle of No. 15 Platoon, killing 2nd Lieut. Myddleton and Sgt. Molineaux. Major Peebles, finding his company enfiladed, withdrew them to the main position. About this time Lieut.-Colonel Brett fell mortally wounded.

The enemy's infantry did not show up much at first, but it became immediately evident that their artillery was in vastly superior force to that of the British. Some German skirmishers, who had crept up on to the knoll of the Montay spur, now opened fire on the British gunners. " Upon these," says the official history, " and also upon a concealed German machine-gun on the Cambrai road the left company of the Suffolks opened fire; but there was some doubt as to the situation, for it never occurred to any of the officers that the high ground immediately to the east and west of Le Cateau would be left open to free occupation by the enemy."

It was not, however, till about ten o'clock that the German infantry began to offer a target. In spite of the losses they sustained from rapid individual and machine-gun fire they continued to advance steadily for some time, but were eventually checked. The machine-guns, under Lieut. Bittleston, did very good work, and Sgt. Spriggs (machine-gun sergeant) was subsequently awarded the D.C.M. for his behaviour on this occasion.

By this time the hostile artillery fire had increased to a pitch of tremendous severity. The deafening storm of high-explosive shells, combined with the roar of the British guns, which on the right were less than a hundred yards behind the battalion, rendered communication between units well-nigh impossible. German aeroplanes, circling overhead, dropped smoke-bombs of various colours to direct their artillery. The enemy were already seeking to turn our right and enfilade us, and two battalions of the 19th Brigade were therefore sent to reinforce that flank.

Early in the day the enemy had succeeded in getting a number of machine-guns into the cutting on the Le Cateau–Cambrai road, immediately in front of the 2nd Suffolk Regiment. By 11 a.m. the fire from these guns had increased to such an extent that the position of the battalion became critical. Before noon two heroic attempts were made by the 2nd Manchester Regiment and the 2nd Argyll and Sutherland Highlanders to reinforce them, but only a few of these splendid men managed to reach the trenches. The Suffolk machine-guns were now rapidly running short of ammunition, so Major Doughty (who had succeeded to the command of the battalion when Lieut.-Colonel Brett fell) and L/Sgt. C. A. Gates brought up a few bandoliers ; but Major Doughty was at once severely wounded in three places. Almost at the same time Captain and Adjutant Cutbill was badly wounded in the head.

The official history says : " The Suffolks and the Yorkshire Light Infantry, the front line of the 14th and 13th Infantry Brigades, were also assailed by an unceasing storm of shrapnel and high-explosive shell, but vied with the artillery in steadiness. . . . The last gun of the 11th Battery was silenced and the Suffolks, together with their reinforcement of Highlanders, were in a worse plight than ever. Nevertheless, after nearly six hours of incessant and overwhelming fire the right of the British line, which rested on Le Cateau, still held firm."

By this time the Germans had worked so far round our flank that 2nd Lieuts. George and Burnand had to turn their men about, facing their original rear. To quote the official history once more : " Between 2.30 and 2.45 the end came. The Germans had by this time accumulated an overwhelming force in the shelter of the Cambrai road, and they now fell upon the Suffolks from the front, right flank, and right rear. The turning movement, however, did not at once make itself felt, and the Suffolks and Argylls opened rapid fire to their front with terrific effect, two officers of the Highlanders in particular bringing down man after man and counting their scores aloud as if at a competition. The Germans kept sounding the British " Cease Fire " and gesticulating to persuade the men to surrender, but in vain. At length a rush of enemy from the rear bore down all resistance and the Suffolks and their Highland comrades were overwhelmed. They had for nine hours been under an incessant bombardment which had pitted the whole of the ground with craters, and they had fought to the very last, covering themselves with undying glory."

Photo by] [*A. Debenham*

LIEUTENANT-COLONEL C. A. H. BRETT, D.S.O.

The casualties in the 2nd Battalion in killed, wounded, and missing amounted to about 720 of all ranks, including the following officers—*Killed :* Lieut.-Colonel C. A. H. Brett, D.S.O. ; Captain E. H. Reid ; 2nd Lieuts. G. H. Payne and E. G. Myddleton. *Severely wounded :* Major E. C. Doughty, Captain E. E. Orford, Captain and Adjutant A. M. Cutbill ; 2nd Lieuts. J. B. Morgan, E. H. W. Backhouse, and F. C. Berrill. *Slightly wounded :* Lieut. T. L. George ; 2nd Lieuts. F. V. C. Pereira and H. P. James.

The following appointments, awards, and mentions, all in connection with the battle of Le Cateau, appeared in various issues of the *London Gazette*—*D.S.O. :* Major E. C. Doughty. *M.C.:* Captain (now Major) A. M. Cutbill, Captain E. C. Phelan, R.A.M.C. (attd. 2nd Battn.) ; Lieut. (now Captain) T. L. George. *D.C.M. :* Sgt. H. Spriggs ; Pte. W. Bridges. *M.M. :* Sgts. H. Blanks, J. Argent, and P. R. Raymond ; Pte. (L/Cpl.) C. T. Baker. *Mentions :* Major E. C. Doughty ; Major (now Lieut.-Colonel) A. S. Peebles, D.S.O. ; Lieut. (now Captain) P. R. W. Carthew ; C.S.M. C. Carter ; L/Cpl. S. Fayers ; Sgt. W. Laws ; and L/Cpl. E. Rumbelow.

The cavalry on the right made a gradual fighting retirement towards the south-west. Throughout the battle there was no sign either of Haig's Corps or the French. The 2nd Battalion at Le Cateau could not have supposed that they were intended merely to fight a delaying action for a time and then to slip away under cover of a rearguard. On the contrary, all ranks were repeatedly told that on no account whatever was there to be any retirement. Their orders on this point, communicated by word of mouth, were absolutely clear and unequivocal.

Major-General Sir Charles Fergusson, who rode all over the ground and saw the rearguards away before he himself left the battlefield, wrote to an officer of the regiment present at the battle and commented on the stand made by the 2nd Suffolk Regiment in the following terms : " Anybody who held out to the end under the circumstances deserves all the honour that can be given, and did his duty nobly, and no words can express the value to the division and corps of such self-sacrifice."

From a historical point of view the battle of Le Cateau showed what strange things lie within reach of the long arm of coincidence. One of the German regiments opposed to the 2nd Suffolk Regiment in that battle wore the name "Gibraltar" inscribed on a scroll on their badges. This was none other than Hardenberg's Regiment, who were with the 12th Foot in the siege of Gibraltar. Nor was this all, for in immediate support of the 2nd Suffolk Regiment at Le Cateau was No. 11 Battery, R.F.A. All three of these units had fought together at the battle of Minden in the year 1759.

In referring to the excellent work done by the British artillery at Le Cateau, and especially by those four batteries under Lieut.-Colonel C. F. Stevens, which were supporting the 2nd Suffolk Regiment, Major Doughty says: "Their behaviour throughout was magnificent, and the moral effect on us was great. All behaved with the greatest coolness under the most trying circumstances. From my trench I could see Major Birley giving his orders as if it were an ordinary field-day."

The C.R.A., 5th Division, says: "That the help thus afforded by the artillery was appreciated by their comrades of the infantry was touchingly shown next morning. Exhausted as they were by the long night march, yet many men stepped out of the ranks to give a silent pat to the guns drawn up by the roadside."

A further withdrawal of the IInd Corps was now ordered, and by four o'clock the battered remnants of the 5th Division were moving towards St. Quentin. A retirement in the face of a numerically superior and victorious army is at all times a dangerous operation, even when the lines of communication are clear. But when, as now, the roads are packed with refugees and their belongings, vehicles of all kinds, and wounded, through which slowly moving medley the guns, cavalry, transport, and worn-out infantry have to thread their way, it becomes in the highest degree difficult and hazardous. Units necessarily became very much mixed. Then with the darkness came rain, further increasing the difficulties of movement. Here, therefore, was an army outnumbered and exhausted, forced to retire along roads blocked with traffic, and with the enemy at its heels. Such a desperate state of affairs might well have alarmed the most resolute commander. But the British Expeditionary Force had already left its brand on the enemy, and at Le Cateau the 5th and 3rd Divisions had broken the thin end of the German wedge. Otherwise the IInd Corps could never have reached the Aisne. Indeed, the failure of the German Army to enter Paris may partly be ascribed to the British stand at Le Cateau.

But though Smith-Dorrien's Corps was allowed to slip away unmolested the situation was critical in the extreme. No time was to be lost. During the first halt, which was at Bohain at 10 p.m., an attempt was made to sort out the scattered units. All through that pitch-dark night and the following day the men struggled on. At dawn on the 27th they arrived at St. Quentin, when a roll-call revealed the strength of the battalion—now under the command of Lieut. N. B. Oakes—to be as follows: "A" Company, 31; "B" Company, 19; "C" Company, 38; "D" Company, 16; attached, 7; total 111. At six that evening Ham was reached, where a few more stragglers and some transport rejoined. On August 28 Field-Marshal Sir John French addressed the men and congratulated them on the stand they had made at Le Cateau, which, he said, had saved the left wing of the army. That the Commander-in-Chief himself should utter such words must thrill and inspire the regiment for all time. Later on in the day General Smith-Dorrien, their corps commander, also personally congratulated them, proudly recalling the services of the 1st Battalion while under his command in the South African war.

On the evening of the 28th our men reached Pontoise, where they remained in bivouac till the following evening, enabling them to snatch a few hours' rest. Here the remnants of the battalion, now aggregating 229, were organised into one company, under Lieut. N. B. Oakes, and attached to the 1st East Surrey Regiment. On August 30, after a sultry march, they reached Attichy on the Aisne, where they bivouacked. The next morning, having crossed the river, they pushed on as far as Crepy-en-Valois. The enemy's cavalry hovered round the rearguard but made no serious attempt to delay the march.

The retirement was continued through Rouville and Nanteuil to Montge, and on September 3 the river Marne was crossed at Isles-les-Villenoy. On the morning of September 5, after a trying night march, the overwrought troops reached Favieres, where the 2nd Battalion, in conjunction with the

1st East Surrey Regiment, took up an outpost line facing north-east. The remainder of the 5th Division bivouacked round Tournan at a distance from Paris of only fifteen miles.

The following were mentioned in despatches for good work during the retreat from Mons : Lieut.-Colonel C. A. H. Brett, D.S.O. ; Sgt.-Major R. Burton ; C.Q.M.S. W. Curtis ; Drummer L. Jones.

CHAPTER IV

2nd Battalion

Tournant à Tournan—The advance to the Aisne—The battle of the Marne—Passages of the Petit Morin and the Marne—The battle of the Aisne—At La Bassée—Towards Ypres—H.M. The King and the Prince of Wales arrive in France—The 2nd Battalion spends Christmas of 1914 in Belgium

ON September 5 the tide of war turned. The German invasion had been brought to a standstill, and the Allies found themselves in a position to assume the offensive. The retirement, which had been continuous for nearly a fortnight, was suddenly stopped and a general advance ordered for the following day. The great news spread like wildfire, and on September 6 the British and French Armies, turning about, marched exultant through their own outposts.

The 2nd Battalion retraced its steps to Favieres and then, heading north-east, marched to Plessis St. Avoye and billeted for the night. The enemy was now reported to be retiring north and east in haste. During the march, while the battalion was halted in a paddock, the first reinforcement consisting of ninety men, under Captain A. Winn, joined. Captain Winn took over command of the battalion from Lieut. Oakes, organising it into two companies of two platoons each. On September 7 Major J. H. T. Cornish-Bowden, 1st D.C.L.I., arrived and assumed command of the battalion. That afternoon the battalion marched off eastwards, bivouacking for the night at Coulommiers, where Sgt. Rush and fourteen men rejoined. The next morning the pursuit was continued in a north-north-easterly direction, and at about ten o'clock an attack by the 14th Brigade, with the 2nd Suffolk and 2nd Manchester Regiments in support, was launched from Doue against St. Ouen. The enemy offered but feeble resistance, and the passage of the Petit Morin was effected without difficulty. The battalion then formed part of the advance guard as far as Champtortel, bivouacking for the night in a field near Rougeville, south of Saacy.

On September 9 the 5th Division recrossed the Marne by the bridge between Saacy and Méry, considerably to the eastward of the scene of its previous passage. At noon an attack was made by the 14th Brigade from La Limon across the valley towards Montreuil. As soon as the battalion reached the top of the hill the enemy poured in a heavy rifle fire from a wood on the right, shelling them at the same time from half-left. The cover in the wood was so thick that very few of the enemy could be seen, and a cleverly concealed German battery, firing from a hill to the south-east of Montreuil, did some damage before it was located. No further progress being possible, the brigade withdrew at sunset to a position about two hundred yards south of the wood. In the course of the day's fighting Captain A. Winn, who had joined the battalion only three days before, and Sgt. S. Clayton, were killed, Major Cornish-Bowden and C.Q.M.S. Williams being wounded.

During the night the enemy, after fighting this brilliant rearguard action, retired. The outposts were accordingly withdrawn and the brigade, forming a general reserve to the 5th Division, continued the advance on the 10th through Montreuil to St. Quentin (south of the Ourcq). Further reinforcements having joined on the march, the battalion was organised into four equalised companies. On September 11 they marched in heavy rain to Billy-sur-Ourcq, being billeted in the church, and on the following evening reached Chacrise after another drenching.

On September 13 a very early start was made. On arriving at Serches the brigade was ordered to make the passage of the Aisne at Moulin-des-Roches above Soissons. About 4 p.m. the battalion, in reserve, crossed the river under cover of the tall poplar trees and dense undergrowth fringing the north bank at that point. The actual passage was effected just above the damaged bridge at Venizel on rafts constructed by the sappers, the Germans all the while seeking to discover, from points of vantage, where the crossings were being made and where our troops would most likely break cover. As the men reached the further bank they moved stealthily towards the broken bridge where they were able to collect out of sight of the enemy.

Emerging from the river bank in a succession of very

open lines, and advancing towards the little village of Ste. Marguerite, the battalion was immediately subjected to shell-fire, which, though heavy, was rendered ineffective by the extended formation adopted. It soon became clear that the enemy's position was too strong to be stormed before dark; the engagement was therefore broken off and the night passed in position facing north-east near Missy, amid a good deal of fruitless firing. When the Chivres ridge was attacked the next morning the battalion was again in reserve. The ground was swampy and the undergrowth so dense that the brigade was not able to render a great deal of assistance. No rations were received until nearly midnight. For the next ten days the battalion remained on the right bank of the river. The weather was cold and wet, with occasional fine breaks. Their casualties during this period did not exceed a dozen.

On September 24 the battalion re-crossed the Aisne, this time by the pontoon bridge at Moulin-des-Roches, and marched to billets in Le Carrier, where a large reinforcement joined, bringing the strength up to nearly six hundred. After a few quiet days in the neighbourhood of Serches the battalion marched to G.H.Q. at Fere-en-Tardenois, taking over duties and billets from the Gordon Highlanders.

On October 5 the battalion furnished a guard of honour to the President of the French Republic on the occasion of his visit to the British Commander-in-Chief. On the following day Lieut.-Colonel H. F. H. Clifford arrived from Khartoum and assumed command of the battalion. On October 7 Captain C. H. Mowbray was wounded.

On October 8 the battalion entrained for Abbeville, which was reached the next day. On the 13th the battalion (less two companies) moved with G.H.Q. to St. Omer, the remainder joining from Braine on the 21st. On October 25 the whole battalion was transferred in thirty-four motor buses to the 8th Brigade (3rd Division) at Vieille Chapelle, meeting General Foch on the way at Cassel. Immediately on arrival they received orders to support the 9th Brigade which had been forced to yield some ground at Neuve Chapelle. During the night of the 24th–25th the 8th Brigade had also been heavily attacked.

Very early on October 27 the battalion relieved the 2nd Royal Scots, two companies going into the line between Neuve

Chapelle and Fauquissart. Although the enemy was quiet on this part of the 3rd Division front his snipers caused considerable annoyance, and at the request of the 2nd Battalion a battery was brought up to shell a building, known as the White House, where some of them had been located. Before the month was out there had been thirteen casualties from snipers, amongst them being 2nd Lieut. E. G. Fraser, who was shot through the lungs but recovered.

The month of November was passed in trench and billet, at first at Chapigny, Estaires, Vieille Chapelle, Givenchy, and Lacouture, and afterwards in Bailleul, Wulverghem, Neuve Eglise, Douve river, Westoutre, and the Scherpenberg. During the first week four men were killed, and 2nd Lieut. W. L. Llewellyn was wounded, by snipers. For gallantry on the 7th L/Cpl. J. Chinery was awarded the D.C.M. At Estaires the battalion was in support of the Lahore Division, marching on the 9th to Gorre to act in the same capacity to the 21st Indian Infantry Brigade and a French brigade under General Joubert.

On the 15th the 8th Brigade was ordered north to Bailleul, and on the following day the battalion relieved some French infantry in trenches to the east of Wulverghem. Here again the battalion was harassed by snipers, losing from this cause on the 18th 2nd Lieuts. R. C. P. Wilder and P. McDonagh (Royal West Kent Regiment, attached), and a week later at Douve river L/Sgt. R. B. Wombwell.

On the 30th the 8th Brigade marched to billets in Scherpenberg and Locre, where on the following day General Sir Horace Smith-Dorrien inspected and addressed the 2nd Battalion, the company commanders being Captains C. V. Champion de Crespigny, A. H. W. Temple, E. F. Hausburg, and H. L. Cautley.

On December 3 a detachment of fifty men under Captain W. B. Squirl-Dawson was sent to the scene of the presentation of medals by H.M. King George V, the remainder of the battalion being drawn up on the Locre–Scherpenberg road. His Majesty, attended by General Sir Horace Smith-Dorrien and Brig.-General W. H. Bowes (8th Brigade), passed slowly along the line in his car, and after addressing some remarks to Lieut.-Colonel Clifford proceeded to Scherpenberg hill to view the British trenches and watch the artillery shelling those of the enemy. His Majesty had landed in France at the end, and the Prince of Wales in the middle, of November. This was the first occasion since the battle of Dettingen, in 1743, that a king of England had been on active service, and the first occasion since the days of the Black Prince that the heir-apparent to the throne had taken the field in war.

On December 4 there occurred two of those accidents which are part of the normal daily risk of stationary warfare. First, owing to weather conditions, a portion of a trench collapsed, killing two men; then a bomb, while being examined, exploded, killing A/Sgt. E. W. Dunn and severely wounding C.Q.M.S. Sawyer, Sgt. Place, and Pte. H. Chinney. On the 6th the battalion came out of the line, marching to billets in Westoutre.

On December 14 the battalion, in the very early hours of the morning, took up a position in reserve on the main Kemmel–Ypres road, and at 7 o'clock a heavy bombardment was carried out by massed British and French batteries. An hour later the 8th Brigade, with the Gordons on the right and the Royal Scots on the left, attacked the trenches on the high ground south of Petit Bois and Petit Bois itself. On the left the attack was partially successful, but failed elsewhere, in spite of the gallantry displayed.

That afternoon the battalion, whose casualties had been very slight, moved up to take over the ground secured by the Royal Scots, "A" Company, under Captain A. H. W. Temple, relieving a company of the Royal Scots in a trench which they had captured. Twenty minutes later he was shot through the head, falling into the arms of Pte. R. G. Girbow, who was shot dead the next day in the same place. Captain Temple had only recently rejoined the regiment from the reserve of officers, and had served with the 1st Battalion throughout the South African war. Pte. R. Fuller was awarded the D.C.M. for gallantry and devotion to duty in leaving his trench voluntarily and assisting in the rescue of a wounded officer, he himself being wounded in doing so.

On December 15 a party of about eighty men came out during the afternoon and began digging casually in front of "A" Company. Clad in khaki, they were at first believed to be some of our own engineers, but were quickly recognised and fired on, when they at once made signals of surrender.

The battalion then sent out two parties—one on each flank—to take them over, whereupon the Germans opened fire on them. Our men, however, fully prepared for such an eventuality, retaliated instantly with a withering burst of rapid fire, the enemy being thus caught in his own sorry snare. Pte. R. C. Francis, who had volunteered to take a message across the meadow to the machine-gun officer, was shot dead after running the gauntlet for eighty yards, for which act of gallantry he was posthumously awarded the D.C.M.

Christmas was spent in billets in Westoutre. For many a long month the battalion remained in that neighbourhood, taking their regular turn of duty in the line. The circumstance of the 2nd Battalion spending the first Christmas of the great war in the little Flemish town of Westoutre, where their historic meeting with the 1st Battalion was presently to take place, is of twofold interest and constitutes one of those romantic coincidences which the hazard of war seems to provide. As long ago as 1692 the 12th Foot went to Flanders, and since that time the regiment has been there upon half a dozen different occasions, passing altogether several years in that country. History was therefore only repeating itself when in 1914 the 2nd Battalion found themselves spending Christmas there.

4TH BATTALION

The Territorial Army enters the line of battle—The 4th Battalion training in England—Lands in France—Joins the Jullundur Brigade at Vieille Chapelle—The defence of Givenchy, 1914—Christmas behind Bethune

The heavy casualties at the beginning of the war soon exhausted the supply of regular troops available in the Empire. The new armies were only in the early stages of formation and not yet ready to take the field. Still, the fighting line had to be reinforced somehow or other. The country had, therefore, to turn to the Territorial Force, asking them to waive the terms of their engagement and volunteer for service overseas. The result of this appeal was that before the end of 1914 twenty-three battalions of Territorial infantry, besides two or three cavalry and artillery units, went to France. The then British Commander-in-Chief subsequently declared that "without the assistance which the Territorials afforded between October, 1914, and June, 1915, it would have been impossible to have held the line in France and Belgium, or to have prevented the enemy from reaching his goal, the Channel seaboard."

One of these twenty-three Territorial battalions was the 4th Suffolk Regiment; but before attempting to follow its fortunes in France we must hark back to the eve of the great war.

On July 31 the 4th Battalion had assembled at Great Yarmouth for their annual training. Popular excitement as to the outcome of the declaration of war between Austria and Serbia was just then at its height, and on the following day orders were received that owing to the European situation the annual training had been cancelled, and that the battalion should return forthwith to their local headquarters for disbandment. In accordance with these instructions they left Great Yarmouth the same afternoon. It was, however, agreed after discussion that, as general mobilisation was assuredly imminent, the various companies on reaching their local headquarters should not actually be disbanded, but that arrangements should be made to house and feed the men locally, so that if and when mobilisation orders came they would be ready to move at the shortest notice. These orders reached Ipswich at midnight on August 4–5, the battalion assembled the next day and, on the afternoon of the 6th, moved to its war station at Felixstowe. The previous day the commanding officer had sent a telegram to the War Office offering the services of the 4th Battalion in any theatre of war. On arrival at Old Felixstowe the battalion set to work constructing a system of earthworks to be used in the improbable eventuality of an invasion.

Later in the month the battalion entrained at Felixstowe for Shenfield, where they were quartered in the industrial schools. After a short spell of training they were moved in rapid succession to Braxted, Peldon, and finally Severalls, where, together with other units of the Norfolk and Suffolk Infantry Brigade, they were quartered in some large new buildings. The battalion at once settled down to hard work, such rapid progress being made that when inspected by staff officers from the War Office shortly afterwards it earned a very good report. In mid-October word was received that the battalion had been selected for active service and would proceed to France, provided sufficient numbers consented to serve abroad, for it must be remembered that a Territorial soldier was not liable to foreign service without his consent. The offer was therefore put to the men, and to their everlasting credit the great majority elected for overseas, vacancies being easily filled.

All was now bustle and excitement. Early in the morning of November 5 the battalion, under Lieut.-Colonel F. Garrett, marched away from Severalls to the envy of the rest of the brigade, entraining at St. Botolph's for Southampton and the unknown across the Channel.

On arrival at the docks, instead of embarking as was anticipated, they were sent off to a rest camp, which was in a deplorable state owing to the wet weather, to be re-armed with the new rifles recently received. After two days, however, but before the new rifles had been issued, the battalion was ordered to embark. Leaving Southampton just before midnight in the s.s. *Rossetti*, they reached Havre the next day—November 9—and went into another dismal rest camp.

The officers landing in France with the 4th Battalion were as follows: Lieut.-Colonel F. Garrett, T.D., in command; Majors F. W. Turner, T.D., second-in-command, and F. Pretty; Captains M. F. Mason, S. Garrett, E. P. Clarke, E. L. Brown, F. S. Cubitt, F. J. Rodwell, H. D. Mitchell, and R. A. Parry; Lieuts. B. St. J. Glanfield, C. Catchpole, H. Pretty, H. F. Ling, H. K. Turner, M. A. Turner, and J. W. Pain; 2nd Lieuts. D. M. Ffrench, G. W. Stebbings, H. A. Row, L. J. Richards (Transport Officer), J. G. Frere, L. E. Milburn, R. S. Barnes, D. Pretty, H. M. Brown, F. J. C. Ganzoni; Captain R. Cockburn, Adjutant; Captain J. D. Wells, R.A.M.C.; Major W. Dooley, Quartermaster.

On the evening of November 13 the battalion left by train and twenty-four hours later reached St. Omer, at that time G.H.Q. of the British Expeditionary Force. Here they detrained, marching to billets in Blendecques, nearly three miles away.

The battalion immediately set to work training for mobile warfare and making themselves thoroughly familiar with their new rifles. The problem of exercising the men in musketry was solved by the adjutant (Captain R. Cockburn), who converted a neighbouring gravel-pit into a shooting gallery, snowballs placed in pockets scooped out of the face of the cutting serving for targets. On this novel range the whole battalion was put through a course of musketry.

On arrival at St. Omer the battalion had heard that Lord Roberts, while on a visit to the Indian Corps at the front, had contracted pneumonia and was seriously ill. A few days later they learned with deep regret that the great soldier had passed away. A most impressive memorial service was held at St. Omer on November 17, being attended by the Prince of Wales and representatives of the Allied forces. Lieut.-Colonel Garrett, Captain Cockburn, and twenty non-commissioned officers and men represented the battalion.

On the last day of November the battalion marched in rain and wind and over bad roads to Lambres. On December 1, as they were assembling to move off, His Majesty the King, attended by H.R.H. the Prince of Wales, passed through. On December 4 the battalion marched in a high wind to Vieille Chapelle, joining the Jullundur Brigade (Major-General Carnegy) of the Lahore Division (Lieut.-General Watkis), Indian Army Corps. The other units in the brigade were the 1st Manchester Regiment, 15th and 47th Sikhs, and the 59th Scinde Rifles. The battalion, displaying the keenest interest in their Indian comrades, were temporarily attached for instruction to the 1st Manchester Regiment, being reorganised on the double-company system and worked as four companies. On December 6 the battalion was inspected by the Corps Commander, Lieut.-General Sir James Willcocks.

On December 11 they marched to Bethune, billeting in a tobacco factory, and the following day went on to Beuvry. On the 14th " D " Company (formerly " E " and " H ") went into the trenches with the 1st Manchester Regiment. Two days later the remainder of the battalion moved up to Annequin before dawn, to act as reserve in an attack on the " Triangle," between Bethune and La Bassée, but the attack not developing, they returned to Beuvry about noon. Thus by mid-December the 4th Battalion had entered the battle-line. On December 17 " D " Company came out of the trenches, having had one man killed and two wounded—the first casualties sustained by the battalion in action.

On December 20 they moved out along the road towards La Bassée, turning off at Cuinchy, where they halted. "B" Company was then ordered across the canal and into the line with the 1st Manchester Regiment at Givenchy; "C" Company into support trenches half-way up the rise from the canal to Givenchy; and "D" Company into other support trenches at the brewery on the further bank of the canal. "A" Company remained in reserve in Cuinchy. During the forenoon the enemy succeeded in capturing a considerable part of Givenchy, but about five o'clock the 1st Manchester Regiment and "B" Company of the 4th Suffolk Regiment regained the village, together with the trenches to the north-east of it, an achievement referred to in Sir John French's despatches. Throughout the night and the following morning the enemy made repeated attacks. On the afternoon of the 21st the Jullundur Brigade was relieved by a brigade of Guards, who came up from Bethune and over the Pont Fixe, where they suffered heavily.

The defence of Givenchy was the first real engagement in which the 4th Battalion took part. It also marked the beginning of their association with that distinguished soldier, Lieut.-Colonel (afterwards Lieut.-General Sir E. P.) Strickland, who became their honorary colonel. It was under his command that the battalion helped to hold Givenchy during a critical period, and, by a strange coincidence, that the 1st Division repeated the performance in 1918.

On December 22 the battalion, whose casualties had been light, returned to billets in Beuvry, one man being wounded on the march. The next day they went on to Allouagne, near Lillers, where they spent Christmas and the opening days of the New Year. At the time of their arrival in Allouagne the weather was very wet and in places there were acres of standing water. On December 28 the battalion was again inspected by the Corps Commander, who on this occasion was attended by the general officers commanding the Sirhind and Jullundur Brigades.

CHAPTER V

1st Battalion

The 1st Battalion ordered home from Khartoum—Mobilising in England—Joins the 28th Division—Lands in France—In the Ypres Salient—Fighting near St. Eloi, severe though unacclaimed

LET us now revert to the 1st Battalion in Khartoum. Shortly after the declaration of war, Lieut. Wood and fifty men were sent to Port Sudan for duty, Captain Thomas and 2nd Lieut. Hunt, with a similar number of men, following to the same destination about a fortnight later. Early in September Major Clifford received orders by cable to proceed to France at once and take over command of the 2nd Battalion. Vague rumours regarding the German invasion of Belgium and France began to filter through to Khartoum, and before long the 1st Battalion, suddenly ordered home, left Port Sudan for England.

Disembarking from H.M.T. *Grantully Castle* at Liverpool on October 23, they proceeded in two trains to Lichfield, in Staffordshire, where they were accommodated in huts. All ranks were granted three days' leave, and then the task of mobilisation was undertaken. While at Lichfield the undermentioned received commissions: C.S.M.'s Biggs and Harrison, and Sgts. Eighteen, Garvey, and Mumford. The two first-named were posted to their own battalion, the others to the Oxford and Bucks L.I., the Norfolk and Wiltshire Regiments respectively. On November 17 the battalion was sent to Felixstowe, where Captain C. S. Wilson (3rd Battalion) and 2nd Lieut. J. S. D. Lloyd were posted to it, a large draft arriving from the 3rd Battalion. The 1st Battalion, allotted to the 28th Division (Major-General E. S. Bulfin), soon received further movement orders, and within three weeks proceeded to the divisional concentration area at Winchester, being placed under canvas in Hursley Park. Only one other battalion of the division having arrived, the

1st Suffolk Regiment was employed in pitching and preparing camps in a sea of mud for the remainder of its own (84th) Brigade, and also for the 85th Brigade. The bad weather continuing, the troops were sent early in January, 1915, into billets in Winchester, where another draft joined and the task of mobilisation was completed.

On January 11 Captain Campbell was sent over to Havre for disembarkation duty, and on the 15th 2nd Lieuts. Rushbrooke and Parsons arrived from the 3rd Battalion to take over details. On the same day an advance billeting party, under Lieut. O. I. Wood, left Winchester for France.

On January 16 the battalion, nearly a thousand strong, left Winchester and proceeded by route march in brigade to Southampton, reached without incident or casualty. The establishment of officers proceeding overseas with the 28th Division was fixed at twenty-six to a battalion, with one medical officer in addition. Except as already stated, the officers who left England with the 1st Battalion were as follows:

Lieut.-Colonel W. B. Wallace	Commanding.
Major F. A. White, D.S.O.	Second-in-command.
Captain D. V. M. Balders	Adjutant.
Captain H. E. Thomas	Commanding "A" Co.
Lieut. O. I. Wood	
,, S. Bradley	
,, E. D. C. Hunt	
,, H. P. Selby	
Captain F. W. Wood-Martin	Commanding "B" Co.
,, C. S. Wilson	
Lieut. D. K. Forbes	
,, C. F. B. Smith	
2nd Lieut. H. W. Harrison	
Captain E. N. Jourdain	Commanding "C" Co.
,, J. A. Campbell	
Lieut. F. Moysey	
,, L. G. S. Payne	
2nd Lieut. H. Biggs	

Captain F. S. Cooper	Commanding " D " Co.
,, P. S. Walker	
Lieut. P. C. Harris	
,, E. C. May	
2nd Lieut. J. S. D. Lloyd	
Lieut. J. H. McNicol, R.A.M.C.	Medical Officer.
,, B. Godbolt	Quartermaster.
,, N. Leith-Hay-Clark	Transport Officer.
,, R. W. Leach	M.G. Officer.

Captain Arnold was detached for duty as M.G. Officer, 84th Brigade, and Lieut. Bolton with the 28th Division Cyclists.

The same evening the battalion sailed in the s.s. *Mount Temple*, with the headquarters of the 84th Infantry Brigade and the 103rd Battery, R.F.A., anchoring for the night off St. Helens, Isle of Wight. Twenty-four hours later the vessel, escorted by destroyers, continued her journey to Havre, reaching that port about midnight. On January 18 the troops disembarked, and early the next morning the battalion (less two platoons which followed three hours later) left Havre in one train.

Before dawn on the 20th the battalion detrained at Hazebrouck, being rejoined by Lieut. Bradley's party. They then proceeded by route march to Merris, where the advance party, under Lieut. Wood, directed them to their billets. The 22nd and 23rd were occupied in route marches, heavy firing being heard throughout each day. The weather was damp and raw, and on the last day of January there was a fall of snow. The time was taken up with route marching, bombing exercise, digging, and practising the relief of trenches. Some anxiety was felt as regards boots, as those recently issued to the battalion were already showing signs of disintegration.

On January 28 Field-Marshal Sir John French inspected the 28th Division, the 84th Brigade being drawn up in a field outside the village of Strazeele. After the inspection some of the sergeants belonging to the 2nd Battalion arrived from La Clytte on a visit. The 1st Battalion was now ordered to form two grenadier platoons, specially intended for bombing work, to be attached to the right company of the battalion.

On February 2 the battalion proceeded from Merris to Vlamertinghe in a convoy consisting of thirty-eight buses, marching on to Ypres in bitter cold to the infantry barracks, which were reached about an hour before midnight. The latter stage of the journey was carried out over *pavé* roads—the last word in discomfort for marching. On arrival in Ypres it was found that the billets were receiving too much attention from the enemy's artillery and aircraft to be really restful. However, after barely three hours' halt the battalion was detailed to carry up supplies. Throughout the night the carrying parties came in for the usual shelling, the first experienced by the battalion in the great war. Here, too, they sustained their first casualty, Pte. Cook, "D" Company, being hit between the shoulders by a bullet while carrying up rations to the trenches in the early morning of February 3.

The 1st Battalion was now in the Ypres salient, where it was destined to spend the next few months. They were months of mud and blood, glamourless yet never-to-be-forgotten. By the end of January Lieut. Leach had been sent back sick, and on February 3 Major White went down with pleurisy, both being invalided to England. The battalion had therefore to go into the trenches short of officers, and for that reason no officer was withdrawn from the companies to take over the duties of second-in-command. From now till May 8 there were only two officers—the C.O. and the Adjutant—at battalion headquarters.

On the night of February 4–5 the battalion was to relieve the 2nd Cheshire Regiment in the trenches between the Ypres–Comines canal and Hill 60 inclusive. A report, however, having been received that part of the 83rd Brigade had been driven out of their front-line trenches, "C" and "D" Companies, under Captain F. S. Cooper, were moved as soon as darkness permitted to Blauwe Poort Farm with orders to clear up the situation. No action being required of them, the two companies eventually moved up in relief of the 2nd Cheshire Regiment, the remainder of the battalion arriving from Ypres and carrying out the original order. The relief was completed before daybreak, battalion headquarters being situated at Verbrandenmolen. During the night Pte. Palfrey was wounded; but the first man in the 1st Battalion to give his life in the great war was Pte. W. Nunn, who was shot through the head while cooking breakfast early in the morning of February 5. The next day Lieut. Biggs had his cheek grazed by a bullet.

Throughout February 9 the enemy shelled unremittingly one part or another of the Verbrandenmolen sector. The trenches held by the battalion were in a shocking state, those on the right being two feet deep in water. Battalion headquarters, despite the attention it had received from the enemy's artillery during the afternoon, remained intact. The next evening the battalion returned to Ypres, and during the night of the 11th–12th went into billets near Ouderdom.

On the afternoon of February 15 the Germans attacked and, at one point, succeeded in piercing the divisional front line. Two battalions of the 85th Brigade at once delivered a counter-attack, but it was only partially successful; the 1st Suffolk Regiment was therefore ordered up towards evening to take over some temporary trenches, to the south of Ypres and west of the canal, which those two battalions had occupied. These so-called trenches consisted of banks scarcely affording cover from view, and ditches mostly waist-deep in water. Furthermore, they were seriously overlooked and enfiladed, and in fact untenable. "B" Company, wrongly led by its guide, was taken almost up to the German wire. Captain Wood-Martin, however, managed to extricate his company and bring it back with only two casualties, namely, Lieut. D. K. Forbes and C.S.M. Noonan, both wounded. Shortly afterwards Lieut. C. F. B. Smith was killed while gallantly attending to Lieut. Forbes, who died of his wounds a few hours later.

Before the battalion arrived one of the trenches known as "O" Trench had been captured by the enemy, but was now reported to have been retaken by the Buffs that evening. "C" Company, under Captain Jourdain, and led by two guides of the 3rd Middlesex Regiment, was ordered to relieve the Buffs in this trench and to endeavour to hold it till morning, when they were to fall back to a new trench, about a hundred yards in rear, to be dug during the night. On the way up Lieut. L. G. S. Payne was wounded. When they arrived, however, they learned from the Buffs that the major portion of this trench, divided into two unequal parts by a large traverse, was in the hands of the enemy. The front platoon of "C" Company therefore immediately began bombing up the trench, but at the traverse were definitely stopped by grenade and machine-gun fire. All attempts to get beyond this point failed, the company sustaining many casualties, including Captain J. A. Campbell, twice wounded. This officer, on reaching the first-aid post, sent for Captain Balders and informed him as to the situation. Soon afterwards Sgt. J. Allen arrived at battalion headquarters with a similar report. Unable to expel the enemy from the trench, and seriously overcrowded in the small portion they had taken over from the Buffs, "C" Company suffered heavy casualties during the rest of the night, including Captain Jourdain killed. By dawn the survivors had all been taken prisoners.

Lieut. Wood, East Surrey Regiment, who had been in the attack which had partially recaptured "O" Trench, came to our battalion headquarters and reported that the enemy were now sweeping the ground in rear of the trench with machine-gun fire. Sgt. Allen was sent up to try and get further news of his company, but was shot dead. In the early morning, however, Sgt. H. Quantrill came back from "C" Company. He had been badly wounded through the thighs, but managed to crawl to battalion headquarters and give information at a time when so much was uncertain. He was subsequently awarded the D.C.M., the first gained by the battalion in the great war.

Two platoons, under Captain C. S. Wilson, in support near the wood on the canal, were ordered up to make an attack on "O" Trench, but as day was now on the point of breaking the order was countermanded. On February 18 the battalion, having been relieved, marched to billets in Kruisstraat.

After standing knee-deep in icy cold water for forty-eight hours the men's feet were so numbed that when relieved few could get out of the trench without assistance, and the march back to Kruisstraat was both slow and painful. The casualties during this severe tour of duty were as follows—*Killed :* Captains F. W. Wood-Martin and P. C. Harris ; Lieuts. D. K. Forbes and C. F. B. Smith; and nineteen other ranks. *Wounded*: Captains F. S. Cooper and J. A. Campbell ; Lieuts. E. C. May and L. G. S. Payne ; and fifty-five other ranks. *Missing :* Captain E. N. Jourdain ; Lieut. F. Moysey ; and 2nd Lieut. H. Biggs ; and 171 other ranks. Captain Jourdain and many of the missing were afterwards ascertained to have been killed.

Captains Wood-Martin and Jourdain were gazetted to the regiment in 1899, and both served with the 1st Battalion during the South African war. Captain Harris was the youngest son of Colonel J. E. Harris, who commanded the 2nd Battalion 1888–1892. When the great war broke out Captain Harris was about to proceed to Japan on language leave. Lieut. Forbes had performed a great deal of valuable service in the 1st Battalion. Lieut. Smith was killed in a noble attempt to save Lieut. Forbes. The loss of all these officers and men was naturally a heavy blow to the regiment.

The remainder of the 18th was spent in billets, but during the night of the 18th–19th the battalion returned to the line. Owing to the shocking condition of the trenches it was now decided that whenever possible men should be relieved every twenty-four hours. During the night of February 21–22 the battalion returned to Ypres. It is a significant fact that the fighting of the previous fortnight, though costing the battalion eleven officers and three hundred other ranks, was not of sufficient importance to be included—even among the miscellaneous incidents—in the official list of the battles and engagements in the great war. For gallantry during these operations Pte. F. Riddlestone was awarded the D.C.M.

On February 23 the 84th Brigade set out for Bailleul, where they were to come under the orders of the 5th Division. The battalion, leaving behind about a hundred men who were unable to march, reached their billets at noon. The sick men rejoined the next day by bus. Brig.-General L. J. Bols now took over the command of the 84th Brigade from Brig.-General F. Wintour. On February 27 the battalion proceeded to Bus Farm, relieving the 1st Dorset Regiment in reserve trenches near Wulverghem. On March 3 they moved up into the front line, remaining there without incident till the 8th, when they returned to Bailleul.

After two days in the line at Ploegsteert they took over trenches in front of Kemmel on March 21, using the German Consul's house, which was in Kemmel itself, as battalion headquarters. On the 24th Lieut. H. P. Selby and four other ranks were wounded. The enemy snipers in this area were both watchful and wary. The road to the trenches was sunken and sodden, and continually swept by fire—a troublesome state of affairs. On the 28th battalion headquarters and the dressing-station were shelled, but fortunately escaped damage. That night the battalion, having been relieved, went back to Dranoutre. After a spell in the line at Lindenhoek they returned to hutments in Dranoutre. The relief on this occasion took several hours to complete owing to the machine-gun sections of the in-coming battalion losing their way in the dark.

On April 7 the battalion, together with the remainder of the 84th Brigade, was inspected by General Sir Horace Smith-Dorrien, and a few days later by Lieut.-General Sir Herbert Plumer, commanding the Vth Corps.

2nd Battalion

With the 3rd Division in the Vierstraat area—Trench warfare—The Flanders front—Trench foot

As far as the 2nd Battalion was concerned the year 1915 opened uneventfully. The British Expeditionary Force had settled down in front of Crown Prince Rupprecht's Army and was holding the sector of the Allied line between Ypres and La Bassée, with French troops on both flanks. During the early months of the year the battalion did not participate in any classified operations. They were merely helping to hold the line.

At that time the attitude of the enemy in the Vierstraat and Wytschaete areas was not violently hostile. There was not much shelling, most of our casualties being caused by rifle grenades and snipers' bullets. The type of rifle grenade used by the Germans possessed a longer range than ours, and therefore retaliation in kind was of no avail.

After the tide of the German invasion had been stemmed at the Marne the struggle, still swaying to and fro, gradually steadied down into stabilised warfare. Manœuvre became stricken with trench paralysis. Men were changed into moles. The war turned to one of attrition, not as the last resource of outwitted strategists as some aver, but as an inevitable stage in its development. This period continued until the beginning of the Somme offensive, and even that was designed as a wearing-out battle.

In Flanders, be it remembered, the word trench was often merely a euphemism for a mud bath. Life there almost reached the limit of human endurance. The stationary character of the war precluded all forms of regular exercise. Men had to undergo periods of prolonged crouching in water sometimes waist-deep, with the inevitable consequences of swollen feet, impeded circulation, and inability to walk, a condition subsequently known as " trench foot." Although our troops suffered severely from the same complaint during the Crimean war—now so many years ago—yet to this day, despite the advance of medical science, no absolute preventive measures, but palliatives only, seem to have been discovered. Apparently very young men are more readily affected by this scourge than older ones ; and, unfortunately, those who have been subject to one attack are more liable to a recurrence than the average man to a first attack.

But in addition to the physical hardships which the continual use of trenches involved, the cover they provided was totally inadequate owing to the unstable character of the parapets, which, almost as fast as they were built, slid back again into the slush at the bottom of the trench. Nor were there any dugouts or shelters worthy of the name.

Those who did not actually experience the first winter in the trenches can scarcely realise the appalling conditions under which the troops fought. The weather was vile, turning the low, swampy country into a bog ; and on every side was mud —relentless, ineffable mud. Indeed, the expression " Flanders mud " has become a technicality, a by-word in our language. The discomfort and drudgery of it all baffles description : while the spells of duty in the line were divided into hours of monotony and torturing suspense, and moments of frenzied, bewildering excitement such as few men experience in a lifetime.

Occasionally the wet weather and waterlogged ground rendered digging impracticable, an excavation instantly becoming a quagmire, and in such cases the troops constructed breastworks, ensuring at all events less mud underfoot, though offering a better target to the enemy. At that time the British line was not continuous, but broken into lengths of trench and breastwork, forming a series of isolated posts. However, as spring approached and the countryside dried up these strong points were gradually linked together. At first the firing and support lines were converted into continuous systems; then these were inter-connected by a series of communication trenches; and, finally, main communication trenches, running a mile or so to the rear, were constructed, completing a network of vast design.

Prior to the linking up of the trenches, troops holding the various isolated posts could only communicate with one another by night, when a sea of mud, with cavernous shell-holes in its bed, had to be crossed. Casualties occurring during the day had necessarily to wait till dark before being brought back to safety. Even with the construction of main communication trenches it was some time before adequate drainage could be secured, and troops moving to or from the firing line often preferred to risk a dash across bullet-swept, open country rather than face the prospect of crawling for half the night along a muddy ditch.

Reverting to the 2nd Battalion, we find them still nibbling at the enemy in the Vierstraat area. On January 26 Lieut.-Colonel Clifford, with his adjutant, Captain Williams, rode over to Merris to visit the 1st Battalion. There he found everyone on the tiptoe of expectation and ready to act at a moment's notice as the next day was the Kaiser's birthday, and it was considered probable that the occasion would be marked by general activity all along the line. However, as far as the 1st Battalion was concerned, the day passed quietly. As regards the 2nd Battalion at La Clytte, this festival happened to coincide with a parade held in the neighbouring field for the purpose of presenting D.C.M.'s to individuals of the 2nd Suffolk and 4th Middlesex Regiments. Major-General Haldane, commanding the 3rd Division, attended by Brig.-General Bowes, commanding the 8th Brigade, presented the medal ribbons and delivered an address. The awards in the battalion were to A/C.Q.M.S. A. McGough and Ptes. Francis, Fuller, and J. Chinery, but only the first-named was present, the others being killed, wounded, and sick respectively. About this time the battalion received the sad news of the death of R.S.M. R. Burton, which had occurred on January 24 in England. The deceased warrant officer, invalided at the end of 1914, had just been awarded the M.C. for valuable services rendered during the operations of that year, and was amongst the first recipients of this newly instituted decoration. Sgt.-Major Burton was buried in Tottenham.

Information having been received that large German reinforcements had arrived in the Menin area, the strength of the garrisons of the trenches in front of Vierstraat was increased accordingly. On February 8 H.M. The King of the Belgians witnessed some British artillery shelling Hollandscheschur Farm. The bombardment of this prominent landmark would have constituted one of the daily set-pieces but for the shortage of shells. On February 27 General Sir Horace Smith-Dorrien, with the divisional and brigade commanders, visited the headquarters of the 2nd Battalion in La Clytte to inspect Pte. Death's "Suffolk Death Trap," a new form of wire entanglement of which they all expressed their approval. About this time the following awards were announced—*D.S.O.*: Lieut.-Colonel H. F. H. Clifford; Major W. O. Cautley. *M.C.*: 2nd Lieut. H. P. Sparks; C.S.M. A. Stannard; Captain E. C. T. B. Williams; Sgt.-Major O. W. Parkinson. *D.C.M.*: L/Cpl J. Dempsey; C.S.M.'s C. A. Gates and W. Webb; Ptes. J. G. L. Burrell and J. Bailey; Pte. L. Jones; Cpl. F. Lynn; Pte. H. J. Scoggings; Cpl. H. G. Double.

March was, on the whole, a quiet month in the Vierstraat area. During this period the battalion, though in a state of constant readiness to act, was not once sent over the top nor called upon to repel any serious attacks. Yet such was the daily attrition and wastage in the course of ordinary trench routine that one hundred and forty casualties were sustained. On March 3 2nd Lieut. J. R. T. Roberts was killed while sniping, and on the 23rd Lieut. F. T. Schroder was killed by a rifle grenade.

On the 14th the battalion was inspected at La Clytte by General Sir Horace Smith-Dorrien, commanding the IInd Army. He was attended by Lieut.-General Sir Charles Fergusson, commanding the IInd Corps, and Brig.-General Bowes. The Army Commander's speech was both encouraging and complimentary. The next day Captain Sparks was shot through the coat-tail! On the 19th Lieut.-Colonel Hon. L. Butler, brigade major, left the 8th Brigade on promotion, his departure being very much regretted by all ranks. March closed, as April opened, with ordinary trench routine, and on April 11 the 2nd Battalion found itself back again in billets in Westoutre.

4th Battalion

Neuve Chapelle

In mid-January, 1915, the 4th Battalion, who had been resting at Allouagne, moved forward with the remainder of their brigade by way of Chocques, Hinges, and Locon to Vieille Chapelle, and on the 17th paraded in very cold weather for inspection by Major-General H. D'U. Keary, the new divisional commander, who was accompanied by Brig.-General E. P. Strickland, recently appointed to the command of the Jullundur Brigade. The next day there was a fall of snow.

During the night of the 19th–20th the battalion moved up through Lacouture and Richebourg St. Vaast and took up a position in front of Richebourg l'Avoué, a line they occupied on two or three subsequent occasions. The trenches were too waterlogged to be manned as a whole, and consequently a chain of posts was established. Lieuts. Frere and Ganzoni, sent up to take charge of two of these posts, found them about fifty yards apart and so full of water that there was nothing to prevent anyone from missing them altogether and wandering on into the German lines. The bulk of the battalion was distributed among the houses in Richebourg l'Avoué.

On January 23 they were relieved in the trenches, returning through Vieille Chapelle and Vendin to Allouagne, where they remained until the end of the month, having been transferred temporarily to the Bareilly Brigade of the Meerut Division. On January 31 they moved to Hingette and the next day to Le Touret, where they did duty with the 58th Rifles and the 41st Dogras at Rue du Bois, Rue de l'Epinette, and Dead Cow Farm. These trenches were of the grouse-butt type, a great improvement on those previously occupied. During neither of these spells of duty in the trenches did the enemy show much enterprise. On February 9 the battalion marched to Lacouture, and on the following day through Calonne to billets in St. Floris. The machine-gun section was now under the command of Lieut. J. G. Frere.

Photo by] [*Adolphus Tear*

THE 4TH SUFFOLKS AT NEUVE CHAPELLE
FROM THE PAINTING BY FRED ROE, R.I., R.B.C.

On February 23 Lieut.-Colonel H. W. Cruddas, 41st Dogras, arrived and took over command of the battalion from Lieut.-Colonel Garrett, ordered to hospital. On March 4 Captain E. P. Clarke was wounded near Rue du Bois. A few days later the battalion, having rejoined the Jullundur Brigade, went into billets at Lestrem.

On March 10 the brigade marched to Vieille Chapelle in readiness to take part in the battle of Neuve Chapelle, preparations for which had been in progress for some time. About noon they moved forward to a farm on King George's road, passing on the way a large batch of German prisoners who had just been captured. On the 11th, while moving towards the southern end of Neuve Chapelle with a view to attacking the Bois du Biez, a conference of officers was held in a shell-hole by the roadside. The illustration of this incident on the opposite page is reproduced from a painting now in possession of the 4th Battalion at Ipswich and displayed to public view in Christchurch Mansion.

The attack began at noon, but owing to the stubborn resistance offered by the enemy little if any progress could be made, and towards evening it became evident that the attack had failed. The battalion was holding a line of trenches in front of the Bois du Biez when, at about 8 p.m., a message was received ordering it to withdraw from the line and move into some ruinous billets along the Rue des Berceaux. As the battalion was in a strong position at the time, and holding its own without difficulty, it was conceived that this message was possibly a *ruse de guerre*, emanating from the enemy. The adjutant therefore went back to brigade headquarters to make enquiries and found the message was genuine. With much difficulty, owing to the darkness and shelling, the battalion was assembled and marched back through Neuve Chapelle to its former position along the Rue des Berceaux, some casualties being incurred during the operation. Very soon after its arrival the enemy began to shell the Rue des Berceaux, compelling the battalion to vacate its so-called billets and take to some trenches near Windy Corner. The buildings were set on fire almost as soon as the battalion had left them, an act supposed to have been that of a spy.

Shortly before dawn on the 12th the battalion was ordered to return to the position vacated the previous evening. As it moved off at the head of the brigade the enemy put down an intensive barrage on the column, inflicting many casualties and throwing the brigade temporarily into disorder. It was on this occasion that Lieut.-Colonel Cruddas, by his personality, leadership, and disregard of danger, first won that place in the hearts of all ranks which he held until his death. The character and bearing too of Brig.-General Strickland produced a further marked effect, and reawakened the spirit of the battalion. The brigade, rallying quickly, was now ordered to take part in another attack on the Bois du Biez. Severe fighting followed, lasting all the afternoon, the battalion remaining in position for the night.

In referring to the part played in the battle of Neuve Chapelle by the Jullundur Brigade the Corps Commander (General Sir James Willcocks) said: "This brigade underwent a two days' fiery ordeal, both in support and in moving up to Neuve Chapelle. They had been very exposed and subjected to a ceaseless fire from big and light guns, in addition to machine-guns and rifles, and nearly six hundred casualties resulted."

The battle of Neuve Chapelle was the first occasion on which British troops had driven the Germans from well-established positions in a trench-to-trench attack on a large scale, and the Jullundur Brigade was naturally proud of its share in that achievement. The losses sustained by the 4th Battalion amounted to 217, including the following officers—*Killed:* Captain Stephen Garrett; 2nd Lieut. H. A. Row. *Wounded:* Captain and Adjutant R. Cockburn; Captains M. F. Mason, F. J. Rodwell, and H. D. Mitchell; Lieut. H. K. Turner; 2nd Lieut. H. Hoyland.

The following were awarded the D.C.M. for gallantry in the field at Neuve Chapelle: Sgts. W. Pettitt and A. E. Pendle; L/Sgt. W. Smith; Pte. P. E. Sones. The last named, attached to the Lahore Signal Company, carried messages for forty-eight consecutive hours, under very heavy rifle and machine-gun fire. Corporal S. C. Balaam was promoted a King's Sergeant on the battlefield, and subsequently awarded the D.C.M.

On March 13 the remnants of the battalion were withdrawn to Richebourg St. Vaast, and on the following day to Croix Barbée. On the 15th they went into billets at Lacouture, and thence into some trenches (recently captured from the Germans in front of Neuve Chapelle), which they were destined to know well, occupying them on several occasions during the ensuing summer. At that time the German trenches were about four hundred yards from our line, with the Layes stream in between. On the 16th 2nd Lieut. R. S. Barnes was appointed acting adjutant in place of Captain Cockburn, whose successor, Captain A. G. Taylor, 1st Battalion, did not arrive from England till ten days later. On April 1 the battalion moved to Vieille Chapelle, and on the 13th to Croix Marmuse.

On April 17th the 4th Battalion was inspected by Field-Marshal Sir John French in a field near Lestrem. The Commander-in-Chief, specially welcoming them as a Territorial battalion, congratulated them heartily on their bearing at Neuve Chapelle.

CHAPTER VI

1st Battalion

The meeting of the 1st and 2nd Battalions at Westoutre—The battles of Ypres, 1915—Fortuin and Gravenstafel—St. Julien

ON April 12 the 1st Battalion marched from Dranoutre to Poperinghe, passing through Westoutre, where the 2nd Battalion were in billets. In this little Flemish village was added a memorable page to the history of the Suffolk Regiment, as here for the first time in the long, long annals of the regiment the 1st and 2nd Battalions met on active service. Lieut.-Colonel Clifford, commanding the 2nd Battalion, rode out with his adjutant, Captain Williams, and met the 1st Battalion when they had arrived within about a mile of Westoutre, leading them in. A halt was made near the village church, the battalion was dismissed, and Suffolk man received a welcome from Suffolk man. It was a memorable occasion. History was repeating itself, because the organisation of the people of England into Folk and Sex, such as Suffolk and Sussex, sprang originally from war; and here was a great mustering of South Folk, such as their own county must have witnessed in the days of old, with many others of their kinsmen hurrying to the fray. Men who had trained together met for the first time since they were drafted from the depot, and many a hearty handshake was given. The officers were entertained in the little makeshift mess, and afterwards a regimental group photograph was taken near the church. The 1st Battalion then fell in and, amidst tumultuous cheering, marched away to Poperinghe. The officers present at this meeting were—*1st Battalion:* Lieut.-Colonel Wallace; Captain Balders (Adjutant); Captain Arnold; Lieuts. Wood and Bradley; 2nd Lieuts. Harrison, Lloyd, and Chandler; Lieut. Godbolt (Q.M.); and Lieut. McNicol, R.A.M.C. *2nd Battalion:* Lieut.-Colonel Clifford; Captain Williams (Adjutant); Lieuts. Oakes and Sparks; and 2nd Lieuts. Trollope, Bunbury, Lowther, Vesey, and Pickard-Cambridge. The following attached officers were also present—*3rd Battalion:* 2nd Lieuts. Hoggan, Grose-Hodge, d'Albani, Hornby, Hume, Jolly, Kincaid-Smith, Neely, Prichard, White, Pargiter, Houlton, de Castro, and Jackson. *Other regiments:* 2nd Lieuts. Hooper, Bargh, Stovell, Charrington, and Hughes.

On April 15 the battalion marched to Vlamertinghe, moving forward to Zonnebeke two days later. On the way up to the trenches they were halted so that if required to support the action then in progress at Hill 60 they would be immediately available. That feature, now so famous, was in reality merely a spoil bank, made of the *remblai* from a cutting on the Ypres–Comines railway. However, as their services were not required at this point, they went on to their destination, reaching the trenches soon after midnight and relieving the 2nd Cheshire Regiment.

Two companies were now in the line; another, with battalion headquarters, was about a thousand yards in rear of them; and the remaining company, in dugouts in the railway embankment, about two miles away. On April 18 the enemy opened a fierce bombardment on a wide front, Major G. H. Walford, Suffolk Regiment, a most promising officer, who was Brigade-Major 84th Brigade, being killed while engaged in making a reconnaissance in the sector held by the 1st Welch Regiment. On the 19th the battalion had a tolerably quiet day in the line. Towards noon Ypres was heavily shelled, involving here and there amongst the occupants hurried, if temporary, changes of habitat. On the 20th the town was again heavily shelled, but on this occasion the battalion was not so fortunate, losing amongst others A/C.S.M. E. Howman. On April 21 the battalion supported the 1st Welch Regiment for about three hours with bursts of rapid fire which, though effective, were somewhat costly as the German trenches were very close and possessed loopholes, which those of the British did not. At one point the opposing trenches were within seven or eight yards of one another. It was indeed a lively time for the 1st Battalion, the Germans being well supplied with bombs, grenades, and trench mortars.

The northern edge of the Salient, as far east as the St. Julien–Poelcappelle road, was held by a French division, and from there to the Passchendaele–Becelaere road by Canadian troops. On the evening of April 22 the whole of the French division was suddenly put out of action by asphyxiating gas. For some time no one realised what had happened. Reinforcements were hurried to the north of Ypres, but throughout the 23rd the enemy continued to attack fiercely. On the night of the 23rd–24th the battalion, having been relieved in the trenches, went back into brigade reserve between Frezenberg and Verlorenhoek. There were no billets, the companies bivouacking under hedges and in hastily constructed shelters. Battalion headquarters was in an *estaminet* also used as a dressing-station.

The C.O. and Adjutant were late getting away from Zonnebeke as battalion headquarters—in a farm-house just in rear of the trenches—was being heavily shelled. They reached Frezenberg at dawn on the 24th, and shortly afterwards Lieut.-Colonel Wallace received orders that he was to command a mixed brigade consisting of the 1st Suffolk, 12th London, and 1st Monmouth Regiments. The two first-named battalions were already in the vicinity of Frezenberg, the other was to come up later. Lieut.-Colonel Wallace was told to take up a defensive position facing north-east on the Frezenberg Ridge. He therefore handed over command of the battalion to Captain Balders and, having issued instructions as to the position to be occupied, went back to Verlorenhoek, where he had arranged to have his headquarters.

Captain Balders at once set the battalion to work digging themselves in on the ridge astride the Ypres–Zonnebeke road. No sooner had the digging begun than a staff officer from the 28th Division came up to Captain Balders and told him to take the 1st Suffolk and 12th London Regiments and advance northwards, attacking any bodies of the enemy he might meet. The staff officer added that the Germans had broken through on the northern side of the Salient, and that only these two battalions stood between the enemy and the town. Actually the situation thus described was one of the most critical in the war.

Naturally, Captain Balders did not wish to act without orders from his brigadier, but it was clear that there was no time to be lost as the Germans were already shelling the two battalions. On looking round he noticed a gun limber which had been hit by a shell and, as one of the horses was unhurt, he cut the animal free and galloped over to brigade headquarters for orders. Here Lieut.-Colonel Wallace gave him authority to advance and instructions to try and establish himself in the hamlet of Fortuin. He thereupon hurried back to the battalion, made the men dump their tools, and gave the order to advance.

As soon as the troops began to move, the shelling, which had been steadily increasing, became extremely heavy. It was, in fact, coming from every direction except the west. On the way towards Fortuin a farm was passed in which a Canadian formation had established its headquarters. Captain Balders was called in and asked to take the 1st Suffolk and 12th London Regiments up to the Canadians, who were being very hard pressed. He explained, however, that his orders were to establish himself in Fortuin and that he must abide by them. Two Canadian staff officers accompanied him, maintaining that the reinforcement of this particular part of the line was a matter of supreme importance. Both these officers were hit while conversing with Captain Balders, who now decided to send help to the Canadians. By this time the shelling had become intense, the battalion being also subjected to heavy rifle and machine-gun fire from the left. Captain Balders soon became aware that St. Julien, which he had been informed was held by our troops, was already in the hands of the Germans.

The C.O. of the 12th London Regiment having become a casualty, Captain Balders took over command of the two battalions which he now halted to give himself an opportunity of appreciating the situation. A wounded Canadian officer then came up and told him that the two battalions were being anxiously awaited, and that if they did not come up soon it might be too late, as there was already a wide gap on the left of the Canadians. Captain Balders thereupon ordered Lieut. Bradley, with " A " and " B " Companies (about 150 bayonets) to reinforce the Canadian left flank, at the same time withdrawing the remainder of his two battalions about 500 yards and taking up a position covering Fortuin with his left flank thrown back, the 12th London Regiment being on the right.

The Suffolk companies, who were out in the open, dug all night, and by the morning had constructed a fire trench 4½ feet deep and complete with traverses—a remarkable achievement with only the small entrenching implement. This was gradually deepened to 6 feet and a fire-step added. Amongst the casualties on the 25th was Lieut. W. G. Chandler, wounded. When day broke on the 26th the situation looked so desperate that all maps and documents were destroyed. During the afternoon, however, the German shelling was lifted on to ground behind, from which it was inferred that Allied reinforcements were approaching. This assumption proved to be correct, for shortly afterwards troops came up on the left and right. During the night of the 26th–27th the battalion, having been relieved by the Northumbrian Brigade Territorials, returned to the Frezenberg Ridge.

Throughout the trying period of April 24–27 R.S.M. Chase was conspicuous for his splendid work in bringing up ammunition, water, and supplies under heavy fire. Lieut. McNicol and his stretcher-bearers displayed great gallantry in attending and collecting the wounded. Lieut. Godbolt also rendered valuable assistance in getting rations up through Ypres, which was being subjected to a heavy bombardment and was burning fiercely. During the 27th the battalion remained on the western slopes of Frezenberg Ridge in dugouts which they had constructed. Here Lieut. Bradley rejoined with the remnants of his two companies, Lieut. R. G. Prichard having been killed while they were supporting the Canadians. Lieut. Bradley said that from the Canadian front line he could see Germans detraining at Langemarck, and an officer haranguing them from the train before they started to attack. Lieut. Bradley referred in glowing terms to the work done in the Canadian line by Major E. M. Moulton-Barrett, 2nd Northumberland Fusiliers, in organising for the defence small parties of various battalions belonging to the 28th Division.

On April 28 battalion headquarters was shelled and set on fire, great difficulty being experienced in getting the wounded out of the dressing-station, which was in the same building. Lieut. McNicol again behaved with great gallantry, as did Lieut. O. I. Wood, whose arm was shattered while assisting with the stretchers. On the same day the battalion, shelled out of their dugouts, sought cover in the hamlet aptly named Verlorenhoek, but being heavily shelled again, were forced to return. At Verlorenhoek Lieut. McNicol once again displayed notable disregard of danger in clearing his newly established dressing-station, which he accomplished practically single-handed, carrying out the wounded on his back under heavy shell-fire.

It was on April 21, during the opening phase of the battle of St. Julien, that the battalion had its first experience of gas. The use of poisonous gas as a weapon of war was regarded by the British as a violation of the Hague Convention. The German gas attack on April 22 therefore came upon them as a complete surprise, and the troops had no means of countering its horrible effects. The value of gas used in this way for offensive purposes was soon found to have definite limitations, the control of the cloud being obviously a matter of great difficulty. Nevertheless the first cloud gas attacks were terribly effective, and if the Germans had had sufficient reserves at hand to throw into the enormous breach made in the Allied line on April 22 there is no saying what might have resulted. Certainly Ypres would have fallen, and the whole course of the fighting on the western front might have been changed.

In dealing out praise to the battalion for its share in the battles of Ypres of 1915 we must not overlook the achievements of the transport, who worked splendidly throughout that trying period. The Suffolk transport, under Captain Hoggan, were never off the road. They were required to take ammunition up to advanced brigade headquarters and to do a hundred other jobs: they did them all well. By carefully observing the shell-fire at threatened places and rushing the carts through, perhaps one at a time, they managed to continue functioning without casualty to man or beast, though one of the carts was hit and had the bottom knocked out of it.

The casualties sustained by the battalion during the ten days ending April 28 amounted to about four hundred, including the following officers—*Killed, or died of wounds:* Captain K. F. F. W. Arnold; 2nd Lieuts. D. E. Grose-Hodge, R. G. Prichard, H. B. Neely. *Wounded:* Captain and Adjutant D. V. M. Balders; 2nd Lieuts. T. Hume, H. W. Harrison, J. S. D. Lloyd, W. G. Chandler, and L. A. H. Stovell.

On April 28 a German aeroplane, flying very low, was brought down by rifle fire, landing in the battalion's lines. On the 29th the battalion were heavily shelled while digging new trenches, which they occupied on May 2. The intervening days were miserably spent, as the dugouts were half full of water and the hostile aircraft and artillery continually busy. On May 2 " A " Company, parading to occupy the new trenches, sustained thirteen casualties. On the 4th the battalion was bombarded with trench mortars, 2nd Lieut. F. E. Stantial being killed, and Captain R. W. Leach and 2nd Lieuts. H. J. F. White and L. M. Charrington wounded. The next day the battalion was heavily shelled and its headquarters hit.

Casualties had seriously depleted the ranks of the battalion, the men were on the verge of exhaustion, and the rain, almost incessant since the middle of April, had converted the trenches into streams of mud. On May 6 the situation suddenly quietened down, but the peaceful stillness which hung over the line during the night of the 7th–8th seemed to forebode a great disturbance. Just before dawn on May 8 Captain Balders went round the trenches and warned all ranks that an attack was to be expected at any moment, adding that the C.O. relied on the battalion to yield no ground, but to stand to the last.

4th Battalion

In the Salient with the Lahore Division—The battle of St. Julien—The battalion returns to the Neuve Chapelle area

On April 24 the 4th Battalion, who were in the Neuve Chapelle sector, were suddenly despatched northwards with the Lahore Division. Their destination was guessed to be Ypres, as news of the gas attack and of desperate fighting round the Salient had already begun to reach the troops. Late that night the battalion arrived at Boeschepe, after a trying march of eighteen miles over bad roads. The next day they pushed on in drenching rain to Ouderdom, passing Rosenhill huts, where the 2nd Battalion were in billets. Here Captain Fison was appointed orderly officer to the brigade commander in the place of an officer *degommé*, if rumour may be believed, for overboiling the general's egg.

On the 26th the Jullundur Brigade marched to Ypres. Its arrival, heralded by the usual shelling, contributed another battalion of the Suffolk Regiment to the garrison of the Salient, a third being at Reninghelst, barely six miles from the Cloth Hall. The battalion, under heavy shell-fire, moved round by the edge of the moat on the south side of the town. The brigade, opening out, then marched along the Zonnebeke road as far as Potijze, halting by the side of the road leading off to St. Jean. "Overhead the monster shells of the German 42 cm. guns could be heard hurtling through the air on their way to spread further devastation in Ypres, now a city of the dead, deserted by all else. The sound of these enormous projectiles resembled nothing so much as that of an express train tearing through the air, a resemblance which was, in fact, embodied in the name by which they were known, that of the 'Wipers Express.' To illustrate the destructive power of these shells it is sufficient to mention that a hole made by one of them in the ground near Ypres measured 72 feet across by 48 feet deep."[1]

At 2 p.m. the Lahore Division advanced to the attack. The Jullundur Brigade was disposed as follows: Front line, right to left, 1st Manchester Regiment, 40th Pathans, and 47th Sikhs. Second line (400 yards in rear), 59th Rifles, supporting the Manchester Regiment, and the 4th Suffolk Regiment supporting the 47th Sikhs. Before the battalion had even crossed the road Major F. W. Turner and several men were hit.

Shortly afterwards clouds of gas from the German trenches began drifting across the British front from right to left, quickly enveloping the Allied troops, and especially the French, who were hurled back. Rallying again, they strove to counter-attack, but were overpowered by the poisonous fumes. The discharge of gas in such volumes amongst troops unprovided with means of countering its effects, coupled with a certain loss of direction and consequent overlapping amongst the brigades in the first instance, naturally led to confusion, French, British, and Indians becoming considerably intermingled. The attack was now broken off, and the battalion, still being heavily shelled, began to dig itself in. During the early hours of the following morning the Jullundur Brigade was relieved, the battalion withdrawing to its former position near Potijze.

On April 28 the battalion returned to the north of the Salient, entrenching themselves in a field between La Brique

[1] *The Indian Corps in France.* (Murray.)

and St. Jean and a quarter of a mile to the west of the latter. German aircraft quickly reported their arrival, and before long they were being shelled by those irrepressible guns from which the defenders of Ypres could find no respite. The next day the hostile artillery turned their attention on St. Jean, setting fire to the village church, which burned throughout the night. That evening the battalion returned to hutments in Ouderdom, and twenty-four hours later was on its way back to the Neuve Chapelle sector, where it was destined to spend the next six months. In getting through the battle of St. Julien with a total of only fifty casualties the 4th Battalion rightly considered themselves fortunate. The wounded included Majors F. W. Turner and F. Pretty ; Captains R. A. Parry and A. D. Whatman ; Lieut. J. W. Pain ; 2nd Lieut. R. D. Hume ; and C.S.M. A. Webber. Captain Parry was awarded the D.S.O. for gallantry on the 25th April in bringing to cover several wounded men. He persisted in this until severely wounded himself.

Early on May 2 the battalion reached Fletre after a very trying night march, and on the following day continued its journey to its old billets in Croix Marmuse.

2nd Battalion

From Vierstraat to the Salient

The capture of Hill 60, which took place a few days after the 1st and 2nd Battalions had met at Westoutre, may be regarded as the curtain-raiser to the battles of Ypres of that year. These battles, though not directly affecting the 2nd Battalion, tended to draw it into the heart of the Salient. The great drama opened on April 22 with the now celebrated gas attack : by the 23rd the situation had become sufficiently serious to warrant the issue of a warning by the higher command that the British force might be compelled to fall back behind Ypres, an eventuality happily averted.

The 2nd Battalion, who were still in the Vierstraat area, spent the latter half of April either in the trenches there or at Rosenhill huts in constant readiness to move. The remainder of the 8th Brigade were then sent to reinforce the line near

Hill 60, leaving the 2nd Battalion to hold a brigade front opposite Wytschaete Ridge, on the edge of the storm raging round Ypres. This they continued to do, with only inter-company relief, until they returned to La Clytte towards the end of May. Amongst their casualties during April was 2nd Lieut. A. J. B. Lowther—dangerously wounded in the head—a son of the famous Speaker of the House of Commons, who was subsequently created Viscount Ullswater.

On May 5 2nd Lieut. H. G. D. Winton was shot through the head and instantly killed behind one of the trenches. On the same day Lieut.-Colonel Clifford was wounded in the arm, but remained at duty. On May 11 C.S.M. C. A. Gates, D.C.M. and Cross of St. George, was killed by a shell outside the brigade dugout. C.S.M. Gates was one of the heroes of Mons and Le Cateau, and as cool and gallant a soldier as ever served the King.

In the line itself opposite the 2nd Battalion the enemy was so remarkably inactive that it was commonly alleged he had left behind only a caretaker instructed to fire off star-shells by night and occasional shots by day. To the back areas, however, he was more attentive, and the route to the trenches by way of the Vierstraat cross-roads was often distinctly unhealthy. On May 26 the 2nd Battalion, relieved at last, was sent to Gordon huts at La Clytte. But rest in peaceful billets was the will-o'-the-wisp of the Flanders marshes, and during the next two days the battalion carried several hundred " knife-rests " into the Salient, two companies leaving each day and travelling by Dickebusch, Kruisstraat, and along the Roulers railway to the Menin road at Shrapnel Corner, where the knife-rests were dumped. Two of the companies, not knowing the evil reputation borne by this spot, remained there while they formed close column of platoons. Having executed this movement, they marched leisurely back to Brielen, their new halting-place. The next time they passed that way they took the corner by platoon rushes in flying leaps.

From Brielen the battalion made several expeditions by night through Ypres to construct a communication trench leading from Shrapnel Corner to Cambridge Road and Railway Wood. On June 4 they made their acquaintance with Brandhoek camp, then a virgin field, from which they made further night excursions, digging trenches near Hooge and leaving in time to get clear before daylight.

On June 7 they left Brandhoek and returned to the Salient, companies inter-relieving one another between reserve trenches near Moat Farm, and support trenches and redoubts overlooking Zouave Wood and Hooge, the nights being spent in improving existing earthworks and sending up digging parties into the firing line. During the night of June 10–11 2nd Lieut. L. St. L. Windsor was killed in front of a new trench in process of construction near the Menin road. A few casualties occurred daily, those on the 15th including Sgt. A. Cobb, wounded.

CHAPTER VII

The nature of war—The battles of Frezenberg Ridge and Bellewaarde Ridge—The 1st Battalion sustains over a thousand casualties in six weeks—The 28th Division withdraws to Bailleul and Borre

NO one who has not had actual personal experience of war can have the very slightest idea of what it means, the unutterable demands it makes, the unutterable sacrifices it entails. To try and represent war on paper or canvas is futile ; on the stage merely grotesque. It cannot be copied ; it exists only in the original. Hence the remarkable prevalence of amateur strategists. Before the great world crisis there were many who regarded soldiers as mercenaries and a campaign as a kind of picnic at which men cracked jokes and won medals and decorations. When, in 1914, an opportunity was afforded to these scoffers of finding out what war really means, some of them restraining their curiosity remained at home ; others answering the call had the shock of their lives. They discovered that the theatre of war was not a comedy playhouse at all, and that the battlefield was a stage from which many a player made a ragged and bloody exit. They went forth to the great adventure to find it the most serious thing in life. They learned to their dismay that capturing a German trench was a far more difficult matter than finding the equations of curves or conjuring up verse from some dead language or other ; and they would gladly have exchanged these refinements for the richer gifts of personality and the courage to endure.

Lord Wolseley always used to protest vigorously against war being dismissed as merely horrible, declaring that it brought out all the noblest qualities in a man. That is true, for often in the midst of a battle some individual, perhaps hitherto held in light esteem, will suddenly rise superior to his fellow-men, to the admiration of all. Death the leveller, war the appraiser. But it is a question whether in modern war, with its poison gas, liquid fire, and its thousand engines, and waged as it is in the air, under the ground, and even under the sea, we are not approaching the limit of human endurance. Chivalry has given way to devilry, and science appears to be driving " grim-visaged war " along the high road to suicide.

The world crisis of the twentieth century marked a complete change in the character of war. Formerly confined to the fighting classes of the belligerent nations, it is now levied against all and sundry. Even women and children of neutral powers are no longer immune. And as the character of war has changed, so has that of the battlefield also. Indeed, to the lay mind, accustomed to the splendour and romance of former wars, and to " battle's magnificently stern array," it is difficult to convey any accurate picture of the bloody dowdiness of modern fighting. Instead of galloping horses, the flash of sabres, the sheen of lances, and the clash of steel against steel; instead of serried ranks of men in brilliant uniforms, moving with great precision and ceremony, with colours and standards flying, endowing the scene with beauty and enchantment, the modern battlefield merely presents a vast mutilated area, a confused and ghastly monochrome of machines and men, with the ground scarred and pitted, the trees lying torn and twisted by the roadside, and the buildings wrecked as if by earthquake.

The adjutant's warning to the 1st Battalion was not delivered in vain, for at dawn on May 8, the storm returning burst over ravaged Ypres, and violent shelling began all along the line. At about ten o'clock a determined attack was launched against the point of the Salient, and soon the battle of Frezenberg Ridge was raging in all its fury. As for the 1st Battalion, they had a galling time. The din was terrific. The enemy were sending over projectiles of every calibre and description. High-explosive shells crashed in all directions, scattering bricks and timber like chaff before the wind. Huge guns and howitzers roared incessantly, shaking the earth; and the crackle of machine-guns and musketry, mingling with the boom of mortars and bombs, made a noise that sounded like an army of riveters at work during some titanic thunderstorm. Amid the roar of battle vile yellow-green poison gas floated like a spectre through the British lines, and before it men reeled back, livid, choking, and blinded.

Every engine of war, every invention of the devil, every device and wile of hell seemed to be in action against the Allies. All communication by wire was completely cut off for a distance of two miles behind the line, and getting into touch with anyone was almost an impossibility. The only roads up to the Immortal Salient ran through the town of Ypres itself, which was now in flames, presenting a wonderful spectacle. Who in those early days would have dared to foretell that such intensity of bombardment would ever be surpassed?

The difficulties experienced by the transport in endeavouring to get up to their various units were inconceivably great. The roads, torn up by shells, choked with fallen and falling debris, and running here and there between raging fires, were at times quite impassable. Other routes had therefore to be followed and ways forced through. Frequently touch with battalions could not be maintained at all, in which case the transport units, after exhausting every means in their power, had to dump their supplies as near the support trenches as possible and hope for the best.

For days the 1st Battalion had been struggling in the bloody havoc of war. It seemed, indeed, as if hell itself had been let loose. The colonel, the adjutant, most of the officers, and the regimental sergeant-major had become casualties, battalion headquarters had been destroyed, but still our men held on, clinging to their ground with desperate tenacity. Verily the full flood of the attack had swept over them; the enemy had succeeded in making a big breach on our right, and before noon the battalion had been completely overwhelmed. The casualties on May 8 amounted to over four hundred, including the following officers and R.S.M. M. S. Chase, who was severely wounded—*Killed, or died of wounds:* Captains F. W. W. T. Attree and R. Chalmers[1]; 2nd Lieuts. G. P. Hornby, R. A. Pargiter, D. W. Cox, and S. Wrinch. *Wounded:* Captain and Adjutant D. V. M. Balders. *Wounded and missing:* Lieut. C. Ainsley; 2nd Lieuts. G. Bargh and K. H. E. Cayley. *Missing:* Lieut.-Colonel W. B. Wallace and 2nd Lieut. L. B. Jolly.

On May 9 the remnants of the 1st Battalion were collected in Balloon Wood. The same day a draft, under Captain B. D. Rushbrooke, arrived from Felixstowe and camped outside

[1] Captain Chalmers had been slightly wounded a few days previously but had refused to leave the battalion.

Poperinghe. This draft was met by Lieuts. Venning and Hoggan, Lieut. and Quartermaster Godbolt, and twenty-seven survivors from the trenches. This mere handful of men, temporarily reorganised under the command of Captain Rushbrooke, was sent on May 10 to some huts on the north-west side of Ypres, reaching their destination about midnight after a trying march. The following evening they returned, with the remnants of the 84th Brigade, to their camp near Poperinghe. Throughout the 11th the artillery of both sides was very active, the Germans bombarding Ypres with incendiary shells, which started a fresh fire in the town on the south side. Here Captain F. M. Roxby joined and assumed command of the battalion.

On May 12 the remnants of the 84th Brigade were formed into a composite battalion, and billeted in some farm buildings near Poperinghe. By this time the strength of the 1st Suffolk Regiment had risen to eleven officers, including Lieut. McNicol, and 286 other ranks. On May 13 Major Maycock arrived and took over command of the battalion, which moved on the following day into billets in the peaceful and pretty village of Herzeele. A week later, in the little village square, the Field-Marshal Commanding-in-Chief inspected the 84th Brigade and congratulated them on the part they had played in the battles of Ypres.

A gas attack, and heavy shelling gradually extending to the reserve area, ushered in May 24. The 84th Brigade was soon called upon to recover some trenches which had been lost, and accordingly the battalion, less than four hundred strong, fell in and moved towards Ypres. During the forenoon valuable information was obtained by Lieut. S. Bradley and 2nd Lieut. A. F. Kemble by means of a reconnaissance carried out with great gallantry under fire. As the main bridge over the canal into Ypres was being heavily shelled, 2nd Lieut. Kemble, making use of the information he had just gained, guided the battalion to a small pontoon bridge which he knew to be intact. After negotiating the bridge successfully the battalion set off across country at a smart pace and, skirting the pond at Zillebeke, reached Witte Poort Farm at about five o'clock in the evening, having sustained a few casualties on the way from artillery fire directed from an observation balloon.

In front of the farm ran a sunken road, with a deep ditch bordered by a hedge on the far side ; beyond lay a field with a fringe of wood at its lower end in which the Germans were entrenched, their position being only about a hundred yards away. The two companies, under Captain Rushbrooke and Lieut. Venning, forming the firing line, followed by those under Captain Roxby and 2nd Lieut. Inskip in support, trickled across the road, the Germans holding their fire as they did so. The battalion, crouching in the ditch with bayonets fixed, now received from Major Maycock the order to charge. Captain Rushbrooke on the right began pushing his way through the hedge, all the others following suit. Instantly the Germans poured in a most deadly fire, which so thinned the line that the objective was never reached. The order was therefore given to retire and reform.

Shortly afterwards Brig.-General Bols ordered the remnants of the brigade to launch another attack. Bellewaarde Farm was to be taken at all costs ; so at midnight the battalion again moved up to the west side of Witte Poort Farm, but not in touch with either of its flank units. The attack was to be launched on a front of about four hundred yards. Two companies were put into the firing line on the extreme right, the other two, under Lieut. Venning, being in support. Again the order was given to charge, and the battalion led by Major Maycock began to advance, but immediately came under a withering fire as on the previous occasion. Men fell in heaps everywhere, and within a few minutes the advance was definitely held up. The attack, as a whole, failed ; but 2nd Lieut. T. Packard and C.S.M. F. Pye, with a corporal and half a dozen men, managed to dig themselves in on the sunken road, where they were joined by men from other units until their numbers rose to nearly a hundred. This position was held throughout the day and until the brigade was relieved, constituting one of the many gallant episodes in the great war, for a record of which the official despatches may be searched in vain. Heavy shelling took place on the 25th, and during the day 2nd Lieuts. Inskip and Locket, with some stragglers, returned to battalion headquarters in G.H.Q. trenches. The same night the battalion, now reduced to 3 officers and 181 other ranks, was relieved, marching back through Ypres to Balloon Wood, west of Vlamertinghe. On

May 26 Captain Needham arrived and assumed command of the battalion. The casualties in the battle of Bellewaarde exceeded 140, including the following officers—*Killed :* Lieut. S. Bradley. *Wounded :* Lieut. A. T. C. Taylor ; 2nd Lieuts. G. K. Lightbody and J. W. Houlton. *Missing : (killed) :* Major F. W. C. Maycock, D.S.O. ; Captain B. D. Rushbrooke. *Missing (wounded and taken prisoner) :* 2nd Lieut. A. F. Kemble.

Major Maycock had joined the Suffolk Regiment in 1897, and was awarded the D.S.O. in 1906 while serving with the King's African Rifles. The names of several officers and other ranks were brought to notice for gallantry and distinguished service during the battles of St. Julien, Frezenberg, and Bellewaarde. The subsequent honours list was not large, but contained the name of Lieut. J. H. McNicol, R.A.M.C., awarded a popular M.C., and A/Cpl. H. J. Daniels, the D.C.M.

On May 26 the battalion returned to its old billets in Herzeele, where Major Sinclair Thompson assumed command, and a fortnight later marched to Rosenhill. On June 12 they took over trenches near St. Eloi, where the activities of both sides were mainly directed towards mining, counter-mining, and sniping. After a few days in bivouac near Dickebusch, where 2nd Lieut. T. Packard was severely injured at bombing practice, the battalion returned to the line, and on June 28 2nd Lieut. G. E. Locket, who had done so much excellent work, was killed while tracing telephone wires. He was buried the same evening in the brigade cemetery near Ridge Wood.

Major F. A. White, D.S.O., now rejoined and assumed command of the battalion, which shortly afterwards moved to Ridge Wood. On July 4 an exceptionally good draft, composed of cavalrymen trained as infantry, joined under 2nd Lieut. J. V. FitzG. Prestidge. Minden Day was spent in Arcadia dugouts, and enough blooms of one kind and another were found to enable the time-honoured regimental custom of wearing commemorative roses to be kept up. On August 6 Captain E. G. Venning, while observing from a point immediately in rear of one of our trenches, was shot through the neck and killed instantly. All ranks of the battalion deplored the loss of a valuable, gallant, and popular officer. His body was conveyed to Locre the same evening and buried in the village churchyard.

On August 18 the battalion marched to Scherpenberg, where they were inspected by Lord Kitchener and the French War Minister, and the same evening went into the line. The next day, just after the sector had been visited by the Corps Commander (Lieut.-General Sir Charles Fergusson), the enemy posted up a notice in their trenches to the effect that the Germans had taken Kovno.

The snipers in the battalion were now very busy, and accounting regularly for their opposite numbers. As for the enemy, they were sending over a good many rifle grenades, but showed little enterprise. On one occasion a bundle of German newspapers was flung into the trenches. On August 24 a patrol from "D" Company went out before dawn and secured a flag which the enemy had carefully fixed in position on their parapet. The next day another was put up in its place, but this was also acquired by a patrol under Lieut. West. On August 31 2nd Lieut. O. P. Pulverman and three other ranks were wounded by a rifle grenade.

September opened with a spell of very wet weather, during which the battalion moved backwards and forwards several times between Kemmel and Locre. On the 1st news was received that 2nd Lieut. Pulverman had died of his wounds. He was buried the same evening in Dranoutre cemetery. Just before noon the enemy opened fire on the trenches with heavy artillery; one shell burst amongst the officers' dugouts, instantly killing 2nd Lieut. E. H. Nowell. On September 21 the battalion rejoined the 84th Brigade at Locre. The 28th Division was now withdrawn from the IInd Army and billeted round Bailleul and Borre, whence they could be summoned to meet any unexpected eventualities in the impending offensive at Loos. The call soon came, and on the 26th they marched to Le Cornet Malo.

2nd Battalion

The first attack on Bellewaarde—The Suffolk man, a rare fighter and digger—Sanctuary Wood—The Ypres ramparts—Hooge

At dawn on June 16 the Vth Corps assaulted Bellewaarde Ridge, the 3rd Division attacking Railway Wood, Bellewaarde Farm, Y Wood, and the trench system in between. The leading troops got into Y Wood, and through it, quicker than was anticipated, with the unfortunate result that they were shelled by their own artillery. Pressing forward, they reached the edge of Bellewaarde lake, but were unable to maintain themselves in that advanced position. The success achieved did not fulfil expectations; however, the whole of Y Wood fell into British hands. The 2nd Battalion, in reserve, came in for the aftermath of the battle. At nightfall "B" Company was told off to dig a trench linking up Y Wood with the adjacent culvert on the Menin road. During the operations they were considerably harassed by tear-shells, the first they had experienced; nevertheless the task was completed before daylight. The battalion was next required to hold this trench, together with part of the old German line in Y Wood, spending four tiresome days in consolidating the new line under persistent shell-fire, and in the gruesome and horrible task of clearing up a battlefield. On the 16th Sgt. W. Mills was killed; on the 17th C.S.M. J. Barker was killed, 2nd Lieut. Trollope and a score of others being wounded. On the 18th 2nd Lieut. E. F. Llarena was killed in Y Wood by a shell. That night 2nd Lieut. J. R. Prentice was shot dead while putting out wire near Hooge, C.S.M. A. McGough, D.C.M., being also killed. On the 19th the battalion was relieved in a cloud of tear-gas, returning to Brandhoek after a tour of trench duty which, though brief, had not left them unscathed. On June 28 Lieut.-Colonel Clifford, much to the regret of all ranks, relinquished command of the 2nd Battalion on appointment to that of the 149th Brigade. He was succeeded for the time being by Captain H. L. Cautley.

In order to cope with the vast amount of pioneering work which stationary warfare demands, the system of earmarking a battalion for this special duty was introduced in some brigades. All the Suffolk battalions bore a good reputation for digging as well as fighting, and it befell the 2nd Battalion to act in this capacity on and off from July to September. The lot of a pioneer battalion in front of Ypres was surely no light one. It was usually in the trench area for longer periods at a time than a battalion holding the line, and when an attack was in progress it was held in reserve, as often as not to be swept into the trail of the storm.

An important trench constructed in the Salient by the 2nd Battalion was that known as Oxford Street, running from a point south-east of Ypres, near the Roulers railway, over towards Moat Farm. Work thereon was started by the battalion on July 10, when the whole trench was marked out and roughly dug, to be completed the following week by "A" and "B" Companies while they were billeted in the ramparts. During the day a German balloon would ascend behind Sanctuary Wood just high enough to enable the occupants to see whether the party was at work or not. The interval between the appearance of the balloon and the arrival of shrapnel and whizz-bangs was often inconveniently short. These German shells, however, caused more annoyance than damage, the deep borrow-pits which had been made for sandbag filling serving a double purpose and providing excellent cover. The trench ran through a field of flax, then in full bloom, permitting the parapets to be picturesquely camouflaged.

Early in July the battalion made its first acquaintance with Sanctuary Wood—"Sanitary" Wood as the men used to call it. The northern end, known as Zouave Wood, was on account of its proximity to Hooge little better than a shambles. The whole wood—for it really had some right to the title in those days—was a place to be avoided if possible, as warning notices of the lurking danger, such as "Beware of Snipers," amply testified. Every inch of the ground was closely watched by German marksmen: not a leaf stirred unobserved by their keen eyes; not a man showed himself but instantly provoked the answering crack of a rifle. Gradually, however, the trees were all torn away by shell-fire, leaving only their stumps, and the place became an abomination of desolation.

From Sanctuary Wood working parties were sent out nightly to dig trenches till, on July 9, the battalion returned to Brandhoek camp, where Major C. H. Turner joined and assumed command. The next day the battalion went into the South Lancashire dugouts, about a mile to the west of Ypres. Two companies, with battalion headquarters, then moved to the ramparts in Ypres, the other two returning to Sanctuary Wood. The ramparts were by far the most comfortable billets in Ypres at that time. Large trees were growing on the top of the earthworks, giving to all within a rare feeling of security. The officers messed together in a spacious casemate, the men being berthed in quite elaborate dugouts alongside. Here everyone rested, listening to the strains of music from a piano which a year before had no doubt charmed other ears.

On July 19 the 8th Brigade, having exploded a mine just north-west of Hooge, advanced to the attack. "C" and "D" Companies furnished bombing and carrying parties, the remainder of the battalion moving into the reserve line near Moat Farm. Some first-rate work was done by Lieut. de Castro and 2nd Lieut. Greig. The battalion bombers were well to the fore, and distinguished themselves by holding the mine crater throughout that night and the following day. 2nd Lieut. T. D. Pickard-Cambridge, in charge, was specially mentioned by the O.C. 1st Gordon Highlanders for good service on this occasion and was awarded the M.C. On July 22 the battalion left Hooge and once more returned to Brandhoek.

They were not, however, allowed to ruminate in camp for long, and on the 24th were put into trenches on the south bank of the Ypres–Comines canal. Battalion headquarters were at Spoilbank, at that time—save for one or two violent interruptions—a peaceful garden settlement. Throughout a strenuous month the men, when not actually in the line, worked at Spoilbank and in Bellyache Wood. The latter, a portion of a wood lying between the railway and the canal, earned its homely name from the water supplied by a neighbouring well. The company on duty there used to spend part of its time at the trysting-places known as Fir Lane and Pear Tree Walk—two communication trenches leading towards the Bluff—a neighbourhood with which the 2nd Battalion became especially familiar during the following winter.

In Bellyache Wood, which abutted on the German lines, life was of a varied character. The dugouts, built of timber

SANCTUARY WOOD
From the Water-colour Sketch by G. C. Danvers

from the surrounding pines, though boasting certain architectural pretensions, provided more comfort than security, neither condition being constant. At times the men enjoyed spells of restful ease, with meals and baths in the open ; at others, the whole *mise en scène* was swept by a hurricane of shells, and each dugout seemed to be the bottle on the wall that everyone was striving to hit. The company in reserve at Spoilbank was chiefly employed in constructing a communication trench from battalion headquarters to the support line near the small redoubt known as Norfolk Lodge. Thus a trench built by Suffolk men received the name of Norfolk Trench. On July 30, in the German liquid fire attack at Hooge, the battalion was not involved, but stood to arms. Thereafter it was constantly engaged in making demonstrations and feint attacks with the object of relieving the pressure in that sector until August 9, when the 6th Division made their successful counter-attack and the situation became easier. On August 7 2nd Lieut. J. L. H. Smith and Sergeant-Master-Cook Pooley were wounded ; and on the 20th Captain Phelan, M.C., R.A.M.C., who had come out from home with the battalion, was transferred to a field ambulance, being succeeded by Lieut. J. E. Cox. The battalion then returned to camp near Ouderdom, on September 2 marched to Vlamertinghe and, the day following, on to Kruisstraat dugouts to be employed in pioneer work between Moat Farm and Hooge. At Ouderdom 2nd Lieut. D M. Greig was accidentally wounded by a bomb. On September 23 the battalion moved to Maple Copse.

4TH BATTALION

The battle of Aubers Ridge—The attack at Rue du Bois—In the Neuve Chapelle area—A peaceful September

By the first week in May preparations were in full swing for an attack on Aubers ridge by three British Corps, in support of the French offensive between the right of our line and Arras. The Indian Corps, with the Ist and IVth Corps on its right and left respectively, was to make the thrust at Rue du Bois, its immediate objectives being Biez Farm, the village of La Tourelle, and the distillery. The Meerut Division was detailed for the attack, the Lahore Division—which had only just returned from Ypres—holding the line. During the night of May 5–6 the 4th Battalion took over trenches opposite the Bois du Biez and close to Port Arthur, where they came in for a great deal of shelling. On May 9 the attack was delivered. The Germans fought with remarkable bravery and determination, and in spite of great efforts little was gained. Lieut. D. Pretty was mortally wounded by a shell and died two days later. On the 19th the battalion came out of the line, returning to billets near Pont du Hem. Their casualties on May 9 and subsequent days exceeded a hundred, the wounded including 2nd Lieuts. G. W. Stebbings, L. E. Milburn, E. I. L. Pym, and A. R. Boeree.

After the battle of Aubers ridge, the 4th Battalion remained in the Neuve Chapelle area for a long and monotonous period, during which little occurred outside the ordinary round of trench duty. This consisted of trudging along muddy roads through devastated country to fetid trenches, remaining there for an uncertain spell of sniping, digging, and shell-fire, and then marching back to billets again. Periodical visits to the baths afforded welcome and necessary relief to the men, wearied by the endless and circumscribed routine which made up their lives. On these occasions the whole battalion betook themselves by companies—gregarious bathers migrating for a day or so, like flights of wild duck—to some familiar haunt, such as Pont Riquel or La Gorgue.

On June 21 the Germans bombarded the 4th Battalion's trenches with 5·9 howitzers, 2nd Lieut. K. R. Mason and three men being killed and three others wounded. A troublesome anti-aircraft gun, the destruction of which was supposed to be the object of this bombardment, was removed during the night to another position. On July 10 the divisional commander, Major-General Keary, held a parade at Estaires for the presentation of medals, Sgts. W. Pettitt and A. E. Pendle, L/Sgt. W. Smith, and Pte. P. E. Sones, receiving the D.C.M.

On one occasion during August, when the bomb catapult was put into operation, the enemy seemed to have received the impression that a general action was afoot and immediately began hurling bombs out of their trenches entirely at random. On August 18 Captain E. L. Brown, M.C., was killed while out on patrol duty. From then onwards until the last week in September there was relative quiet, not only in this sector, but practically along the whole British line. The 4th Battalion furnished endless working parties, being in fact kept so busy in this respect that they were allowed little time to look after themselves. Otherwise the normal conditions of existence comprised desultory shelling, mine and bomb warfare, continual sniping, and shooting at aeroplanes, in which forms of encounter all ranks showed both enterprise and courage, generally maintaining the upper hand.

CHAPTER VIII

The Service Battalions of the Suffolk Regiment

AT the outbreak of war the British regular army, including Army Reserves, together with the Special Reserves (the old Militia) and the Territorial Force, on mobilisation amounted to about 700,000 men. The Territorials, being a home-defence force, were not liable, except as volunteers, for foreign service. It was clear, therefore, from the very outset, that many new divisions would have to be added to the army, and as early as August 8, 1914, Lord Kitchener asked for 100,000 more men. To meet such demands, Service battalions were raised. The early history of the Suffolk Service Battalions forms the subject-matter of this chapter.

Well within the first year of the war, over two million men had been enlisted for the land forces of the Crown by purely voluntary methods. Conscription did not come into force in this country until January, 1916. The expansion of the British Expeditionary Force from 160,000 men to considerably over 3,000,000 was described by the Prime Minister in the House of Commons as " probably the greatest feat of military organisation in the history of the world."

In all, five Service battalions were added to the Suffolk Regiment, namely, the 7th, 8th, 9th, 11th, and 12th. The 10th, though raised as a Service battalion, was soon converted into a Reserve battalion and is therefore not included in the total. The calling into being from nothing of five fighting battalions, all destined to make for themselves wonderful and glorious histories, constitutes the most remarkable episode recorded in these pages.

7th Battalion

Raised in Bury St. Edmunds—Lands in France—Arrives in the Loos area.

The 7th Battalion was raised in Bury St. Edmunds on August 20, 1914, by Major C. D. Parry Crooke, being shortly afterwards transferred to Shorncliffe and allotted to the 35th

Infantry Brigade with which it remained, with one or two brief intervals, throughout the war. At that time the 35th Brigade was commanded by Brig.-General C. H. C. Van Straubenzee, who earlier in the year had given up the command of the 2nd Battalion. The brigade was originally composed of the 7th Norfolk, 7th Suffolk, 9th Essex, and 5th Royal Berkshire Regiments, and belonged to the 12th Division, commanded at first by Major-General J. Spens, and then by Major-General F. D. V. Wing, who took the division to France.

Under the direction of the battalion staff—including R.S.M. J. Martin—the new unit quickly began to take shape and to acquire some knowledge of soldiering. On February 24 they set out for Aldershot and, at the end of a week of strenuous marching in cold weather, reached their destination, being quartered in the Blenheim barracks with the 9th Essex Regiment. The battalion soon revealed an aptitude for shooting, taking first place in the brigade in their musketry course.

On May 30 they entrained for Folkestone, and crossing the Channel by half-battalions in the two ships *Invicta* and *Queen* reached Boulogne the same night. The officers landing in France with the battalion were as follows: Lieut.-Colonel C. D. Parry Crooke, in command; Majors S. B. Stotherd, second-in-command; V. F. Currey, and W. J. Terry; Captains C. H. Turner, A. C. Hall, H. R. Gadd (Adjutant), C. A. Cobbold, and C. R. Logan; Lieuts. T. M. Chitty Thomas, T. H. Kinder, C. H. Sorley, V. A. R. Isham, G. W. Deighton, V. A. Davoren, and G. D. Wood; 2nd Lieuts. F. R. Althaus, P. Gedge (M.G.), P. B. B. Nichols, G. J. Frost (Bombing), A. A. de Jongh, A. L. James, H. G. W. Todd (Transport), H. P. Bamkin, L. L. Bright, C. Heigham, G. C. Eagle, and C. F. W. Morbey; Captain B. J. Hackett (M.O.); Lieut. J. Hearn (Quartermaster).

The battalion at once proceeded by rail and road to Acquin, halting there for four days. On June 5 the division marched to Campagne, and on the 6th to Pradelles—a long, unforgettable march rendered tiresome and exhausting by *pavé* roads, thoughtless staff work, and great heat—an average of nearly two hundred men falling out in every battalion. On the following day they reached the 12th Divisional concentration area at Nieppe.

Charles Sorley, writing from Acquin, describes how his battalion arrived at a little hamlet " smelling pleasantly of manure," with " white dawn stealing through the plane trees and across the fields of rye, and placid weariness in all the bearing earth." He tells us of the peacefulness of the inhabitants, and the abundance of their cider, " unfathomably gold." He speaks of the immense casualness, the organised disorderliness, which seemed existent everywhere within the war area ; and the war itself, with its periods of stabilisation between one attack and another, he likens to a game of chess, with " the chess-players waiting a long time between the moves."

On June 16 " B " Company was detailed for a tour of duty in the trenches, one man being wounded on the way up to the line, the 7th Battalion thereby sustaining its first casualty in the war. On the 22nd, Sgt. G. Robins was mortally wounded, the first fatal battle casualty in the battalion ; shortly afterwards, Lieut. C. Heigham was wounded. Changing places with the 9th Essex Regiment every six days, the battalion next took over trenches in Ploegsteert, in which area they remained for the next six weeks. When in support, they were called upon to furnish working parties, or employed in handling bricks, filling sandbags, or digging in wires. On the night of July 18, 2nd Lieut. H. P. Bamkin and Pte. H. Armsby were killed on patrol duty. Their bodies were recovered and brought back to the trenches by Ptes. J. A. Orbell, H. Searle, and F. Davies, of the patrol, all three being subsequently awarded the D.C.M. for their gallantry on this occasion.

On August 1 a bombing party under Lieut. Sorley went out and did some very good work, in the course of which a bomb, exploding prematurely, killed one man and wounded two others of the party, Lieut. Sorley himself escaping miraculously. On September 9 2nd Lieut. G. J. Frost died in hospital in Bailleul from injuries received while giving a demonstration in bombing a few days previously. A bomb had been thrown short and 2nd Lieut. Frost, rushing forward to fling it into a trench and thus avert an accident, sacrificed his life.

On September 26 the battalion left Ploegsteert and proceeded to Merris, arriving at three o'clock in the morning after a tiring march. On the 28th they went by bus to Gonnehem ;

the next day they marched to Labourse, and on the 30th to Loos—just then one of the storm-centres of the western front—where shortly before midnight they took over trenches in front of the Chalk Pit from a brigade of Guards. The march up to the line was a difficult one, because owing to the main road to Loos being heavily shelled, a route had to be taken over the old British trenches, the advance in the dark being rendered difficult by the slippery chalk soil, and continually checked by wire, shell-holes, and the debris of the battlefield.

8th Battalion

Raised at Shorncliffe—Lands in France—In the front line between Becourt and Fricourt

The 8th Battalion was raised at Shorncliffe in the early part of September, 1914, being sent a month later to Colchester to join the 53rd Brigade of the 18th Division, then in process of formation under the command of Major-General F. I. Maxse. After months of strenuous training in open-order warfare at Colchester, Salisbury Plain, and Codford, the 18th Division was ordered to France, and on July 25, 1915, the 8th Battalion, over a thousand strong, landed at Boulogne to join the ever-growing armies in the field. The following officers left England with the battalion: Lieut.-Colonel (Brevet-Colonel) F. Graham, in command; Majors E. A. Iremonger, second-in-command, and G. H. S. Crofton; Captains A. H. Catchpole, J. C. G. Matthews, A. Wood, P. C. Bull, S. W. Card, and C. V. Booth; Lieuts. J. W. Lack, J. A. Head, G. L. M. Fache, R. U. E. Knox, C. J. H. Nicholson, and O. S. I. Northcote; 2nd Lieuts. H. J. P. Creagh, J. R. Keats, F. T. Keats, W. T. Sanctuary, H. B. Stutfield, R. H. Cooper, H. A. Angier, A. F. Pullinger, J. C. Dominick, T. Usher, R. S. Chibnall, and W. J. Bell; Captain S. W. H. Silver (Adjutant); Lieut. R. M. Ridley (Quartermaster); Captain E. K. Martin, R.A.M.C. (Medical Officer); Rev. Donald Fraser (Chaplain); Lieut. W. L. C. Silver (M.G.O.); Captain S. W. Ford (T.O.); 2nd Lieut. C. L. Sanctuary (S.O.).

The 53rd Brigade (Brig.-General W. B. Hickie) consisted of the 8th Norfolk, 8th Suffolk, 10th Essex, and 6th Royal

Berkshire Regiments. After resting for a week at Pierregot, just north of Amiens, where the division joined the Xth Corps, IIIrd Army, the brigade moved up to the Albert sector, receiving from the 51st Highland Division, in the line between La Boisselle and Becourt Château, practical instruction in stationary warfare. During the first night of this period a mine was exploded in the Ilot sector in front of one of the Suffolk companies, who were called on to assist in consolidating the crater.

On August 20 the 53rd Brigade was inspected at Daours by the army and corps commanders, who were accompanied by M. Pichon and M. Barthou, of the French Ministry. Two days later the 18th Division began taking over that part of the line lying between the Carnoy–Mametz road and a point east of Becourt, the 53rd Brigade being in front of Mametz. On the 23rd the battalion moved up to Bronfay farm, and while holding the line in that sector sustained its first casualties, Drummer E. Patterson being killed and a dozen other ranks wounded.

On September 13 Captain S. W. Card succeeded Captain S. W. H. Silver as adjutant. On the 16th the battalion marched to billets in Albert where Colonel Graham relinquished command.

9th Battalion

Raised at Shoreham—Joins 24th Division—Lands in France—Towards Loos

The 9th Battalion was raised at Shoreham, Sussex, in September, 1914, from contingents from all parts of Suffolk. It could boast many faces already known to the regiment. The new unit, daily growing in numbers, was now allotted to the 71st Brigade, 24th Division. The first commanding officer was Lieut.-Colonel C. E. De L. Solbe, who owing to ill-health was succeeded three months later by Lieut.-Colonel E. C. M. Lushington. Both these C.O.'s came from the Indian Army. Major W. F. Coleman, an officer well known in the regiment and formerly adjutant of the 2nd Battalion in India, was appointed second-in-command. Other figures equally familiar were Majors Arbuthnot and Davies, Lieut. Starling, and R.S.M. Hurrell.

The battalion spent the first three months of its existence under canvas; then—owing to continuous bad weather—it was transferred to billets in Brighton, its stay there coinciding with a visit from H.M. The King, who came to see the wounded Indian soldiers in the Pavilion. On March 10 the battalion returned to Shoreham, abandoning their blue uniform for the ubiquitous khaki. Soldiering in earnest now began, and field-days were frequently held, Cissbury Ring being the scene of many a mock encounter. In April they were sent to Reigate, and in mid-June to Blackdown. There the battalion, now up to full strength, was inspected by H.M. The King, with Lord Kitchener in attendance, and congratulated on its smartness and physique. Major E. H. D. Stracey, 9th Norfolk Regiment, was now appointed to the command. The battalion adopted as its field badge a triangular patch of Cambridge blue, worn below the collar on the back of the jacket.

The 9th Battalion were already in despair lest the yearling war should end before their services were required, when in mid-August their anxiety was relieved by the receipt of orders to proceed to France. On the 30th of that month they were railed to Folkestone and after an uneventful crossing disembarked at Boulogne about midnight. The machine-gun section and transport went by Southampton and Havre. The officers landing in France with the battalion were: Lieut.-Colonel E. H. D. Stracey, in command; Majors F. G. Davies and L. C. Arbuthnot; Captains C. T. Packard, M. F. Heigham, G. B. Steward, L. Ensor, F. R. Hedges (Adjutant), P. L. Scudamore, and H. F. Law; Lieuts. T. T. Stevens, S. W. Church, H. C. Stanford, F. R. C. Cobbold, S. H. Byrne, J. T. C. Fallowes, C. F. Beyts, R. England (M.G.O.), and W. L. Brookes (Sig. Off.); 2nd Lieuts. C. Allerton, A. H. Guinness, L. Wilmot-Johnson, C. Wayman, O. A. E. Allen, H. G. Frost, J. C. Rowbotham (T.O.), and A. Williamson; Lieut. N. R. Rawson, R.A.M.C. (M.O.); Lieut. R. Starling (Quartermaster) and R.S.M. C. H. Hurrell. On the journey down to the port, Captain A. P. Mack unfortunately broke a small bone in his foot and was unable to embark, but rejoined the battalion a few weeks later.

On August 31 the battalion proceeded by rail to Montreuil and thence by road—a dusty march of five miles—to Alette, where they remained billeted in " barns " for about three weeks. The 71st Brigade (Brig.-General M. T. Shewen), to which the 9th Battalion had been allotted, belonged to the 24th Division (Major-General Sir J. G. Ramsay) of the XIth Corps (Lieut.-General Sir R. C. B. Haking).

On September 21 Major R. V. G. Brettell, formerly of the East Surrey Regiment, was appointed to the command of the battalion in the place of Lieut.-Colonel Stracey, transferred in a similar capacity to a battalion of the Norfolk Regiment.

During the night of the 21st–22nd the battalion set out for Matringhem. Continuing their journey on the following night, they reached Ham-en-Artois at three in the morning, where one of the companies found that its billets consisted of a tumbledown barn and a pigstye. However, at seven o'clock the battalion moved over to Le Cornet Bourdois, where they secured billets in the brigade concentration area. The next night the march was resumed. Another dawn found them all tired out, with " only a mile to go." Without orders, the whole battalion fell out and sat down by the roadside. One of their officers, a gallant but fiery major, told them they were " a d——d rotten mob," and that he was ashamed of them. The major's forcible style being well known, his outburst was taken in good part, and after each man had been served with a mug of tea, the journey was continued without a murmur to Bethune, where they were comfortably quartered in barracks.

The march from the coast had been an exceptionally trying one. The battalion had been on the move in drenching rain for four nights in succession, covering a distance of nearly seventy miles, and now within a few hours of their arrival in Bethune they were ordered to move again. But great occasions demand great efforts, and, in the presence of Field-Marshal Sir John French, the division set out from the market-square in the highest spirits for the front.

11th Battalion

Raised at Cambridge—Arrives in France

At the outbreak of war, men of Cambridgeshire and the Isle of Ely who enlisted for infantry were generally sent to the depot of the Suffolk Regiment at Bury St. Edmunds. By the end of August, however, it was found impracticable to accommodate any more recruits at Bury, whereupon the War Office instructed the Territorial Force Association at Cambridge to form a relief camp, a sort of temporary reservoir for the overflow of enlisted men, which Colonel C. T. Heycock, V.D., was asked to command and organise, with Captain G. L. J. Tuck as adjutant.

From September 5 recruits instead of going to Bury were accordingly retained in Cambridge, being billeted in the Corn Exchange and fed under local arrangements. Within a few days the numbers had swollen to three hundred, the men being consequently transferred to the boys' county school. Many cadets from the University O.T.C., who were awaiting commissions, offered their services, and an experienced second-in-command was found in Major A. S. W. Stanley. Encouraged by these results the permission of the War Office was sought for the formation of a Cambridgeshire Service Battalion, as it was felt that the large number of recruits coming forward entitled Cambridgeshire and the Isle of Ely to a unit which should be strictly their own. Its precise title was not, however, seriously discussed until after the battalion had been formally recognised. On September 25 the Cambridgeshire Service Battalion, without regiment or number, was an accomplished fact, and three months later became the 11th Suffolk Regiment. On September 30 the battalion moved to the Melbourne Place Schools, and on the same day Lieut.-Colonel C. W. Somerset, M.V.O., formerly of the Indian Army, arrived and took over command, Colonel Heycock being appointed to that of the 2/1st Cambridgeshire Regiment (T.F.). The battalion was organised as four companies, grouped territorially.

The 11th Battalion remained in Cambridge until May 19, when it was sent up to Yorkshire, a large crowd assembling at the station to give parting cheers. The total strength was then 47 officers and 1404 other ranks, of whom 17 officers and 320 other ranks were left behind and transformed into the 13th Suffolk Regiment. At Studley Royal, Ripon, the 11th Battalion joined the 101st Brigade (Brig.-General H. G. Fitton) of the 34th Division, a typical New Army division which came into being in June, and was first commanded by Major-General E. C. Ingouville-Williams, C.B., D.S.O.

Training on the Yorkshire moors was their introduction to

manœuvring in hilly country, and months later in France, whenever a steep incline had to be negotiated, it was greeted with cries of " Ripon ! " in mocking disapproval. The battalion next went to Whitburn to fire a musketry course, and at the end of August the 34th Division was concentrated on Salisbury Plain, at first under canvas at Perham Down, Tidworth, and then in huts near Warminster, east of Sutton Veny.

Inspections by general officers now became epidemic, one of these being carried out by a Russian and another by three Japanese generals. The first-named—the only Russian soldier seen by the battalion throughout the war—was a handsome man of gigantic stature and, as he stood on a mound to take the salute, completely dwarfed everyone. On December 13 the 34th Division was ordered to mobilise for service in Egypt, and a consignment of sun helmets arrived. The weather at that time was particularly wet and gloomy, and the prospect of campaigning under a strong eastern sun was welcomed by all. However, the evacuation of Gallipoli having been decided on, the orders for Egypt were cancelled, the sun helmets returned, and the destination of the battalion was changed to France.

The battalion left Sutton Veny on January 7 and 8. The secret of its destination was so well kept that even at the railway station the only clue as to direction was the position of the engine. Headquarters and two companies crossed to Boulogne the same afternoon ; the remainder, following in a second train, were delayed by a breakdown near Reading, and spent the night in Folkestone. The first half-battalion crossed the Channel in stormy weather, one man being so ill that he neglected to disembark and was taken back to England and across again before he rectified his error. The second half was rewarded for delay by a smooth passage.

The following officers embarked with the battalion for France : Colonel C. W. Somerset, M.V.O., in command ; Major P. F. Morton ; Captains G. L. J. Tuck (Adjutant), C. L. Morgan, O. H. Brown, J. W. Wootton, H. W. Stace, C. E. Townley, A. E. Seddon, and A. K. Bird ; Lieuts. J. C. Platts, G. N. Seddon, J. H. Brett, F. L. Tempest, I. D. Claughton, N. B. Bagenal, R. V. Burrowes, and P. V. Emrys-Evans ; 2nd Lieuts. R. Q. Gilson, I. A. Mack, H. A. Shaw,

A. B. Wright, W. H. Parker, W. M. Fiddian, C. O. F. Jenkin, J. C. Foster, A. C. Telfer, and A. W. McGain; Lieut. D. W. Harper (Quartermaster).

12TH BATTALION

Raised at Bury St. Edmunds as a Bantam Battalion—Goes to France

The 12th (East Anglian) Service Battalion was originally formed as a Bantam Battalion, in accordance with the decision of the War Office to reduce the minimum height to five feet. Enlistment began on June 21, 1915, men being accepted to a height of five feet two inches, that of the officers and non-commissioned officers being normal.

The formation of the battalion dated from July 7, 1915, recruits being drawn mainly from Suffolk, Cambridgeshire, The Isle of Ely, and Essex. The battalion was quartered in the barracks at Bury St. Edmunds, its administration being in the hands of Colonel V. W. H. Graham, commanding the depot. Major James was the recruiting officer, R.Q.M.S. F. C. Williams being the first N.C.O. posted; a little later Lieut. and Quartermaster R. Blunden was gazetted, and R.S.M. Game appointed. Lieut.-Colonel R. E. P. Pigott, C.I.E., V.D., of the Indian Auxiliary Force and 12th Essex Regiment, assumed command of the battalion from July 29, at which time the battalion consisted of three other officers (Lieut. and Adjutant L. Lloyd, and 2nd Lieuts. V. W. Barrett and C. A. Nisbet) and sixty-two other ranks. The training of this nucleus was carried out by non-commissioned officers who had taken their discharge from the Suffolk Regiment. In placing on record his appreciation of the great services rendered to the country by these old soldiers, Colonel Pigott said that whatever measure of efficiency the battalion attained was due in no small degree to their labours in turning raw material into trained soldiers in the shortest possible time.

Recruits were now coming in fast, and a draft of two hundred Bantams arrived from the depot of the Middlesex Regiment. On November 25 the battalion, eight hundred strong with sixteen officers, left for Bordon, joining the 121st Brigade (Brig.-General J. C. Campbell), 40th Division

(Major-General H. G. Ruggles-Brise). The G.S.O.2 of the division was Major F. D. Finlay, an officer who had served for many years in the 2nd Battalion.

On arrival at Bordon 2nd Lieut. A. H. M. Jackson was transferred from the 22nd Middlesex Regiment, and appointed captain and adjutant. All available time was now devoted to battalion and brigade training. One of the main difficulties experienced was that many of the Bantams were under the regulation age, and parents were continually claiming them. When, at the beginning of December, the brigade marched to Pirbright, a clean sweep was made of these youths, 133 being discharged from the battalion.

On arrival at Pirbright, divisional training began. At that time the 121st Brigade consisted of the 12th Suffolk, 22nd Middlesex, 13th Yorkshire, and 18th Notts and Derby Regiments. In April it was decided to disband two of these, and to form two strong battalions from the material thus set free. The 12th Suffolk Regiment, with Colonel Pigott retaining the command, was chosen as one of the battalions to remain, absorbing half the 22nd Middlesex. The 13th Yorkshire was the other selected battalion, the 20th and 21st Middlesex joining the 121st Brigade in place of the disbanded battalions. Major T. Eardley-Wilmot, York and Lancaster Regiment, was appointed second-in-command.

The 12th Battalion was now considered fit for service overseas, and ordered to France. On June 4 they entrained at Brookwood for Southampton, and on the 6th disembarked at Havre.

CHAPTER IX

The 5th Battalion—Its origin and early history—Sails for Egypt—Lands in Gallipoli—Suvla Bay—Death of Lieut.-Colonel Armes—Have you heard them tamping ?—An international tug-of-war—Goose shooting—The Blizzard—The evacuation—The battalion sails for Egypt

THE West Suffolk Volunteers, which sprang into existence in 1859 when the formation of Volunteer Rifle Corps was sanctioned by the War Office, originally consisted of ten out of the twenty-one companies raised in Suffolk at that period. These ten companies were soon amalgamated as the 1st Administrative Battalion Suffolk Volunteers, the direct ancestor of the 1/5th Battalion Suffolk Regiment (T.F.).

Wearing the old grey uniform and shako, they made their first appearance as a battalion at Bury St. Edmunds on June 14, 1861, the distribution being as follows : [1] The 6th Suffolk Volunteer Rifle Corps at Stowmarket, the 10th at Eye (two companies), 11th Sudbury, 13th Bury St. Edmunds (two companies), 16th Hadleigh, 18th Wickhambrook, 19th Brandon, and the 20th, first at Mildenhall, but after 1870 at Newmarket—a total of ten companies. The assembling of the Suffolk Volunteers was commemorated by verses from which these lines are extracted :

> The riflemen are coming
> From Hadleigh and from Eye,
> From Sudbury and Mildenhall,
> From places far and nigh,
> Stowmarket, Brandon, Wickhambrook,
> Brave hearts and true draw near,
> Ring out, ring out, blithe Bury bells
> And greet each volunteer.

In 1880 a re-organisation took place under which the 1st Administrative Battalion became the 6th (West Suffolk) Rifle Volunteer Battalion. Six years later its title was changed to that of the 2nd Volunteer Battalion, when it became an

[1] *The History of the 1/5th Battalion the Suffolk Regiment,* by Captain A. Fair, M.C., and Captain E. D. Wolton (Eyre and Spottiswoode).

integral unit of the county regiment. Among the early commanding officers were Lieut.-Colonel J. H. F. Anstruther (a Peninsula veteran), Lieut.-Colonel Schreiber, Lieut.-Colonel G. L. Andrewes, and Lieut.-Colonel C. Marriott, under whom the battalion steadily advanced until its reward came in 1900–1 during the Boer war, when the Suffolk Volunteers were called upon to furnish two companies, towards both of which the 2nd Volunteer Battalion contributed strong contingents. These two Volunteer Service Companies, mobilised and trained at Bury, sailed in February, 1900, and March, 1901, respectively. While in South Africa they were attached to the 1st Battalion Suffolk Regiment, the old regimental history recording that " throughout their tour of active service they had taken their full share of all military duties and had borne all privations cheerfully."

The officers of these service companies were Captain G. F. Whitmore, in command; Lieuts. P. Hudson, G. H. Mason, H. S. Marriott, and C. L. Read, drawn from the four Suffolk Volunteer Battalions. For services rendered in the Boer war the 4th and 5th Battalions were granted the right to bear " South Africa " on their colours as a war honour.

Under the Territorial scheme of 1908 the 2nd Volunteer Battalion became the 5th Battalion (T.F.) Suffolk Regiment, and with the 4th Battalion Suffolk Regiment (formerly the 1st Volunteer Battalion) and the 4th and 5th Norfolk Regiment, formed the Norfolk and Suffolk Infantry Brigade of the East Anglian Division which, as the 54th Division, won high honours in the great war.

During the summer of 1914 the 5th Battalion carried out its annual training at Holkham Park, the numbers present being 27 officers and 912 other ranks, made up as follows— *" A " Company:* Stowmarket 104, Eye 42; total 146. *" B " Company:* Beccles 107, Bungay 23; total 130. *" C " Company:* Hadleigh and Bildeston 73. *" D " Company:* Sudbury 71, Long Melford 36, Bures 27; total 134. *" E " Company:* Bury St. Edmunds 82, Barrow 24; total 106. *" F " Company:* Bury St. Edmunds 76, Lavenham 43; total 119. *" G " Company:* Haverhill 56, Clare 39; total 95. *" H " Company:* Newmarket 83, Mildenhall 26; total 109. Camp was struck on July 26, and upon the declaration of war a few days later each detachment commander received orders to mobilise.

The mobilisation scheme, issued in 1913, had been prepared with such forethought and thoroughness that the concentration and equipment of the battalion in Bury St. Edmunds were completed by noon on August 5, and at eight o'clock that evening the battalion arrived at its war station—the heights on the Walton side of Felixstowe overlooking Harwich harbour and the intervening marshes. The battalion soon set to work digging trenches and constructing defences, and on August 12 suffered a loss by the death of Pte. F. Unwin—possibly the first Territorial soldier to die in the great war.

The brigade, having been railed from Felixstowe to Brentwood, started on a march through Essex which lasted several weeks, halting for a few days at a time in various small towns and villages, and finally settling down at Mile End, near Colchester, where some large buildings sheltered the bulk of the brigade for the next eight months.

Shortly after their arrival at Mile End the men were asked to volunteer for service overseas. This came as a surprise to some who had not realised the national character of the war and that the fighting would not be confined to regular armies, nor even to belligerents. However, about three-quarters of the battalion agreed, those unable to respond to the call forming the nucleus of a new battalion, the 2/5th. The 1/5th, by means of recruitment, were soon able to complete their establishment, a vigorous training programme being meanwhile put into operation.

The rôle of the East Anglian Division was coast defence, and in addition to its ordinary duties the battalion was employed in constructing a new line of defence at Elmstead Market, patrolling the coast and picqueting the roads. As the training progressed inspections became more frequent, culminating in November in a review of the brigade by His Majesty the King on the Braiswick golf links. In January, 1915, the battalion was reorganised on the four-company system, and two months later marched from Colchester to West Stow for field-firing. The route lay through districts from which the battalion was recruited, the majority of the men being thus able to billet themselves either in their own homes or those of their friends. The following month found the battalion back in these parts again, this time on their way to Thetford, where the open country afforded excellent facilities for brigade and divisional training—a dull and unintelligible business for the rank and file, but edifying for others. While here the Norfolk and Suffolk Infantry Brigade became the 163rd Brigade, and the East Anglian Division the 54th Division. The 1/8th Hampshire Regiment joined the brigade in place of the 1/4th Suffolk Regiment—already distinguishing itself in France.

The battalion remained at Thetford for six weeks, entraining on May 18 for Watford, Hertfordshire. In July the 54th Division was ordered to hold itself in readiness for service overseas; the battalion was therefore re-equipped, the serge uniforms being replaced by khaki drill. When the time for departure drew near the battalion was inspected, in Cassiobury Park, by a distinguished Suffolk man—Colonel the Earl of Stradbroke, President of the Suffolk Territorial Association.

On July 29, 1915, the battalion entrained for Liverpool in two parties, being accorded a splendid send-off by the hospitable people of Watford. On arrival at Liverpool the battalion, over a thousand strong all told, embarked in H.M.T. *Aquitania*. At 11 p.m. on July 30 the huge liner, carrying about 7000 infantry of the 54th Division, cast off and sheered out from the quay. With mingled feelings of sorrow and pride they watched the lights of England slowly fade away. The following sailed for Gallipoli with the battalion: Lieut.-Colonel W. M. Armes, T.D., in command; Major H. J. Hargrave; Captain and Adjutant H. M. Lawrence. *"A" Company:* Major R. H. Kendle, T.D.; Captains J. R. Rowley, A. Dennis; Lieuts. G. G. Warnes, P. Wilson (M.G. Section); 2nd Lieuts. G. K. Alston, B. A. Keen; C.S.M. Wright; and C.Q.M.S. Double. *"B" Company:* Captains B. E. Oliver, W. I. Tait; Lieuts. A. S. Parker, E. M. Ashton; 2nd Lieuts. G. Kilner (M.G. Section), E. J. Kendle; C.S.M. Hunt; and C.Q.M.S. Meen. *"C" Company:* Captains G. Lacy Scott, G. W. Ledward; 2nd Lieuts. B. W. Cockell, T. S. Hinnell, O. B. Wolton; C.S.M. Bell; and C.Q.M.S. Sills. *"D" Company:* Captains C. M. Oliver, R. M. Jackson; Lieuts. H. C. Wolton, N. Rooke, E. D. Wolton; 2nd Lieut. C. W. Cory; C.S.M. Nixon; and C.Q.M.S. Moody. Lieut. and Quartermaster A. J. Wills; Lieut. H. F. Everett, R.A.M.C. (T.F.), Medical Officer; Rev. C. Pierrepont Edwards, Chaplain; R.S.M. Beer; R.Q.M.S. Spall.

On August 6 the *Aquitania* arrived in the spacious harbour of Mudros; three days later the battalion, having been transferred to a small vessel called the *Fauvette,* crossed over to Imbros, where it remained for the night. On the afternoon of the 10th the transports carrying the 54th Division (Major-General F. S. Inglefield), consisting of the 161st, 162nd, and 163rd Brigades—the last-named under Brig.-General C. M. Brunker—steamed into Suvla Bay, the troops disembarking from lighters at " A " Beach. The battalion then marched to a point about two miles inland.

That evening Lieut.-Colonel Armes received orders to move forward and prolong to the right the position the Lancashire Fusiliers were holding on the south face of Karakol Dagh, thus filling the gap between that feature and the Salt Lake. The night was spent in digging trenches, and early the next morning the battalion took up a position slightly more advanced. This was occupied until the afternoon of the 12th, when verbal instructions were received that an advance of 1200 yards in the direction of due east should begin at four o'clock.

Sir Ian Hamilton had issued orders that a division, marching by night, should attack the heights known as Kavak Tepe and Teke Tepe at dawn on the 13th. As the country from Kuchik Anafarta Ova eastward was held by the enemy the Corps Commander decided to send forward the 163rd Brigade in the afternoon for the purpose of occupying Kuchik Anafarta Ova "and securing an unopposed night march for the remainder of the division."

Accordingly, at 4 p.m. on August 12 the 163rd Brigade advanced, the 1/5th Norfolk Regiment being on the right, the 1/8th Hampshire Regiment in the centre, and the 1/5th Suffolk Regiment on the left and directing the attack. The 1/4th Norfolk Regiment was in support on the left. There was no artillery co-operation other than that afforded by naval guns. The brigade immediately came under a most destructive fire from artillery, machine-guns, and infantry, and units became much intermingled; nevertheless they succeeded in reaching a position about 1500 yards from the starting-point. Here the battalion was checked, detached parties still endeavouring to push on. An hour later, however, the brigade was ordered to withdraw about 200 yards to a fenced ditch, affording better cover as well as a definite line of defence. Strangely enough this position, taken up so soon after the battalion landed, remained its front line right up to the evacuation. It was during this attack, "creditable in all respects to the 163rd Brigade," to quote the words of General Sir Ian Hamilton, that 16 officers and 250 men of the 1/5th Norfolk Regiment, under Colonel Sir Horace Proctor-Beauchamp, charged into the forest and were killed to a man.

The plain stretching inland from Suvla Bay is covered with long grass and trees, and the hills with tough prickly bushes, breaking up an attack and forcing troops to wind in and out in single file. The fighting at Suvla was not static warfare, but hill warfare, requiring long practice and a high standard of training to prevent loss of cohesion, co-operation, and direction, and to avoid confusion. Some of the troops engaged had not had sufficient training to carry out in its entirety so ambitious a programme.

For the next three days the battalion was subjected to persistent sniping and desultory artillery fire. But that was not all, for the great shortage of water and the lack of shelter from the powerful rays of the sun caused further trouble. Sleep by day was rendered almost impossible by the swarms of flies, while at night little could be obtained, every available man being employed. On August 15 the battalion having been relieved returned to the reserve trenches where its casualties were ascertained to have been 186 killed and wounded and three missing. In addition, 6 officers and about 150 other ranks were sick, mostly suffering from dysentery.

The casualties amongst the officers were as follows—*Killed:* Lieut.-Colonel W. M. Armes (T.D.); Major R. H. Kendle (T.D.); Captain G. W. Ledward; 2nd Lieuts. C. W. Cory, T. S. Hinnell, G. K. Alston, and O. B. Wolton. *Wounded:* Lieuts. N. Rooke, G. G. Warnes, E. M. Ashton, A. S. Parker and H. F. Everett (R.A.M.C.). The great majority of these casualties occurred on August 12, after which action the Rev. C. Pierrepont Edwards, Brigade Chaplain, greatly distinguished himself while in charge of a volunteer stretcher-party, being shortly afterwards awarded a Military Cross. Colonel Armes, an energetic and popular officer with many years of volunteer and territorial service to his credit, had been in

Lieutenant-Colonel W. M. ARMES, T.D.

command of the 1/5th Suffolk Regiment since June, 1911, and his death was deeply deplored.

On the afternoon and evening of the 16th the battalion, under Captain Lacy Scott (now in temporary command), acted as support to another brigade. At noon on the 17th, while the 10th Irish Division were attacking along the Kiretch Tepe Sirt, the 1/5th Suffolk Regiment (together with the 1/8th Hampshire Regiment) were again ordered out in support. This involved a very arduous climb of 600 feet—under shrapnel fire and a scorching sun—to the top of a rough and broken ridge. Here the battalion took over the front-line defences for a short period, relieving an Irish battalion which had been reduced to a strength of eighty-seven effectives, showing the severe nature of the fighting in this area.

From the 18th to the 27th the battalion remained in local reserve trenches, and though harassed by shrapnel and rifle fire and kept hard at work, enjoyed a welcome relief from continual movement. Moreover, the men were able to bathe. For three days the supply of water for all purposes had been half a pint a day, and thereafter one pint, and as the men could have drunk treble that quantity and still remained thirsty, little indeed could be spared for washing.

On August 27 the 163rd Brigade was relieved by the 32nd Brigade and ordered to Karakol Dagh, where more shelter trenches were constructed. On the night of the 28th–29th the battalion marched in single file to Lala Baba, a distance of five miles. The men had to climb up and down the precipitous sides of the *dagh*, through deep gullies, and across the dry bed of the Salt Lake, now an expanse of soft yielding sand. There was no transport; everything had to be carried. Besides being in full marching order, with 250 rounds of ammunition, the men were laden with picks, shovels, camp kettles, tins for water, rations, blankets, and a score of other encumbrances. To men struggling against disease this five-mile march was a heavy task.

At Lala Baba the battalion remained in dugouts in the cliffs, furnishing working parties by day and occasional outposts by night. There was not much shell-fire, and on the whole this camp was the most agreeable they met with during their stay in the peninsula. Here hostile aircraft paid them their first visit and two bombs were dropped, one bringing down a large slice of the cliff and the other falling close to divisional headquarters. Late at night on September 1, after a false alarm, the battalion paraded to move to Kaiajik Aghala, bivouacking the next morning in South Wales Borderers' Gully. Two companies were then sent to the 3rd Brigade Australian Light Horse at Rhododendron Spur, and the remainder to Hill 60 with the New Zealand Mounted Rifle Brigade.

From September 5th to the 13th the battalion garrisoned Hill 60, which had been captured on August 27th by Anzacs and the 5th Connaught Rangers after a series of desperate engagements. This hill was a very important tactical feature, its crest commanding a view of both British and Turkish communications. Hence it became a constant bone of contention between the two armies. At that time parties were working there day and night in feverish haste to convert the hill into a redoubt, the most exacting precautions being taken against surprise. Only the crest of the hill had been captured, the Turks being within easy bombing range. The stench and flies were almost unbearable. Drinking water was very precious and difficult to obtain, having to be man-handled in tins for three miles, and that under shell-fire if attempted by day. Dysentery was playing havoc amongst the already depleted ranks. On September 15 the battalion took over Norfolk Trench, with a spring a few yards from the front line. The water from this priceless possession had been adjudged unfit for drinking, but the order was not rigidly enforced. On the 18th–19th Norfolk Trench was heavily attacked, a Turkish patrol making a fierce but unavailing attempt to bomb out a listening-post. During this tour of duty C.S.M. W. S. Hunt was killed and 2nd Lieut. E. J. Kendle wounded. The battalion then moved to Australia Gully West. On September 21 the following officers joined: Captain H. T. Copinger Hill; Lieuts. A. A. Maris, P. W. B. Ashton; and 2nd Lieuts. H. J. Temple, F. E. Haynes, and D. C. W. Smith. During the eight weeks since landing the battalion had lost in killed, wounded, and sick nearly four hundred of all ranks. Serge clothing was now issued in place of khaki drill.

At the end of September the battalion returned to Norfolk Trench. Mainly through the enterprise of Major Lawrence

(Adjutant), Captain Dennis, and 2nd Lieut. Kilner they collected 140 rifles, both British and Turkish, behind this trench. On October 1 Major Lacy Scott was invalided, Major W. J. Bowker, D.S.O., Somerset L.I., assuming temporary command until the arrival of Lieut.-Colonel H. J. Miers, 2nd Monmouthshire Regiment, a few days later. Early in October Captain O. E. Wormald and 2nd Lieuts. S. H. C. Waller, G. C. Fitzherbert, C. J. Norton, G. G. Oliver, and S. P. Leigh, with fifty-seven other ranks, reported their arrival; this was the only draft received in Gallipoli. October 11 was quite a red-letter day for the battalion, the Brigadier having ordered that "all ranks should be spared all fatigues for twenty-four hours in recognition of the satisfactory way the battalion had carried out its arduous duties whilst garrisoning Norfolk Trench with such a decreased strength." For gallantry while in charge of a digging party in Norfolk Trench Cpl. F. Harvey was awarded the D.C.M.

A few days later the battalion returned to Hill 60, in the defences of which great improvements had now been effected. The fighting in this noisy centre of activity consisted mainly of bombing encounters, the type of missile used by the battalion being of the primitive jam-tin variety, with occasional cricket-ball and tape bombs. It was only just before the evacuation that the first small consignment of Mills grenades was received.

From one part of the line the Turkish trenches were out of hand-bombing range, a catapult gun being installed at that point. These weapons occasionally blew themselves up, but were otherwise ineffective. By this time Hill 60 had become a perfect warren of underground saps, both British and Turkish, all destined shortly to be blown up. On October 15 two letters tied to stones were flung into the trenches by the Turks, both being invitations to spend a happy Christmas in Constantinople as prisoners of war. During the third week of October the following officers joined: Captain H. J. W. Oxlade; Lieuts. W. T. Haddock and L. B. Fox; 2nd Lieuts. J. H. Chapman, C. A. E. Horton, and T. F. Tomlinson. On October 22 2nd Lieut. S. P. Leigh, who had been attached for one night to the Norfolk Yeomanry, was wounded by a Turkish bomb, his right hand being blown off and right leg injured. On October 30 Lieut. E. D. Wolton was wounded on Hill 60.

A few days later the battalion moved to Dixon's Gully, where 2nd Lieut. G. G. Oliver had a lucky escape, his nose being grazed and several teeth knocked out by a bullet which had killed Pte. W. Hume.

Orders were now received that no unnecessary risks were to be incurred, the reason for this precaution—though not given out at the time—being that the evacuation of the peninsula was already under very secret consideration. On the other hand the enemy, exultant over being joined by Bulgaria, were now using men and munitions unstintedly. Early in the morning of November 14 the battalion took over Hill 60; the following evening mines were exploded, the Turks being subjected at the same time to heavy artillery and machine-gun fire. An immense fountain of earth shot up into the air in front of the battalion, working parties immediately sapping forward and establishing bombing posts near the edge of the crater which, however, they had been ordered not to occupy. An exciting night of bombing and sniping followed, at the end of which the battalion was relieved, but on the 17th they took over the hill again. Our men could hear the Turks mining beneath them, but the gallant Welsh Horse were hard at work counter-mining, and "Have you heard them tamping?" became the popular phrase of the moment.

In addition to the adventures, coincidences, and the chaff and humour which followed the soldier over all fronts and lightened toil and danger in each, two comic interludes came into special relief in Gallipoli. One owed its origin to the knife-rests which the Turks had placed in front of the crater referred to above, with a resultant tug-of-war in its most literal sense. The battalion was ordered to remove these knife-rests, but owing to the shell shortage a novel method of procedure had to be devised. Accordingly a bomb, fastened to a long rope, was fired at the knife-rest from a catapult gun. The rope, however, instead of becoming entwined in the knife-rests, fell into the enemy's trench. Before it could be hauled back again, the Turks seized it, and a tug-of-war ensued. From both sides could be heard hearty laughter and shouts of encouragement. The number of pullers grew so large that the rope broke, and both teams fell sprawling in the bottom of their respective trenches. The knife-rests remained unretrieved. Early on the 20th the battalion was relieved; at 2.45 p.m. the Turks exploded a mine under Turkey Trot trench, the relieving battalion and the Welsh Horse sustaining several casualties.

The second interlude was concerned with geese, which, as events turned out, only afforded food for thought. Since October, large flocks of these birds migrating south had been passing over the peninsula. Occasionally men in the trenches would fire at them, machine-guns even being used for the purpose. The sport proved infectious; the Turks joined in, and often their rifles could be seen pointing straight up into the air. Not infrequently a burst of firing merely meant that the geese were passing over, but the only goose known to have been brought down fell into No Man's Land, and so no one had it. Such is the glorious uncertainty of war.

On November 21 the weather changed, becoming bitterly cold, and soon the battalion was engaged in helping to carry down men of other units suffering from frost-bitten feet. On the 26th news was received that the 54th Division would embark for Mudros the next night for a period of rest. All the carefully constructed bivouacs were dismantled, and that evening in rain, sleet, and wind, the battalion baggage, including officers' kits, valises, and mess boxes, was taken down to the beach. On the 27th the weather culminated in a blizzard which continued for three days, preventing the 54th Division from embarking. The battalion was thus caught absolutely unprepared, without shelter from the elements. The trenches and dugouts were soon full of water; everyone was drenched to the skin. It would scarcely be possible to conceive conditions more miserable. As the wind rose to a gale, the temperature fell below freezing-point. The whole peninsula, especially the low-lying area of the IXth Corps, was gripped by frost and swept by a blinding snowstorm. The streams, now rushing down the gullies, carried with them the half-frozen bodies of both friend and foe. Over two hundred officers and men of the British force, and a greater number of the enemy, so Kiazim Pasha, Chief of the Staff of the Gallipoli Army, informed the author in Constantinople immediately after the armistice, actually died from exposure. One account[1] says: "Since the days of the Crimea no British Army has been exexposed to more suffering from the elements." Dysentery stopped as if by magic, but jaundice became correspondingly prevalent in its place.

[1] *The Times History of the War.*

At last the great storm abated, and after many cancellations the battalion, consisting of 19 officers and 249 other ranks—all emaciated and exhausted—embarked in H.M.T. *Osmanieh* during the night of December 6–7, and at 2 p.m. on the latter date arrived at Mudros. Here the freedom from the booming of the guns, the bursting of bombs, the crack of rifles, and the ravages of tempest and disease, were enjoyed to the full, and three days of unbroken rest and quietness turned a jaded battalion into the cheeriest of troops.

On December 9 a draft under 2nd Lieuts. F. Oakley and A. R. Alston joined. Two days later a medical inspection was held, revealing the fact that out of the whole battalion only forty-three fit men remained. During four months in Gallipoli the 5th Suffolk Regiment had lost over eight hundred officers and men in killed, wounded, missing, and sick. From these figures an idea can be gained of the conditions under which that campaign was conducted. Never before had anyone in the battalion realised what a precious thing is water.

On December 19 the 5th Suffolk Regiment disembarked at Alexandria from H.M.T. *Victorian*, and after marching to Ramleh tram station were conveyed by tram to Sidi Bishr, where they encamped. They had reached a land of peace and plenty at last.

CHAPTER X

The Suffolk Yeomanry

ON January 1, 1917, the old county Yeomanry Regiment, the Loyal Suffolk Hussars, were reorganised as infantry and as such became the 15th (Yeomanry) Battalion of the Suffolk Regiment. Before, however, attempting to follow its fortunes as an infantry battalion, it will be both appropriate and interesting to give a brief outline of the early history of that distinguished corps.

As far back as the year 1599 we read of the existence of " fencible cavalry " and " horse militia," the forbears of the yeomanry ; and it is recorded that in 1667 the Suffolk Horse took part in the repulse of the Dutch at Landguard. During the first year of the reign of George III the yeomanry force proper was first instituted, troops being raised independently in several counties. But in 1792, Mr. Arthur Young, a Suffolk man of Bradfield Combust, realising that such efforts were intermittent and necessarily purely local, put forward a considered scheme for arming the manhood of the country in a sort of horse militia, such service being likely to make an instant appeal to the horse-loving instincts of the British people. The suggestion found ready favour with the Government, and volunteer corps of cavalry, organised with the single view of home defence, soon multiplied throughout the country. In 1793 Mr. Young gave practical effect to his own recommendation by himself enlisting in the corps raised in the vicinity of Bury St. Edmunds and commanded by Marquess Cornwallis, then Lord Brome. Many gentlemen of fortune followed his example with happy results, for yeomen farmers and their sons, seeing their landlords and men of high consideration in the county enrolled in the ranks, responded eagerly to the call. The success of the scheme was assured.

From the files of the *Bury Post* we have been enabled to trace the formation of a troop of yeomanry in Bury in 1793—at the beginning of the Napoleonic wars with France which terminated with the battle of Waterloo. During the summer of 1794 numbers of volunteers were enrolled in Suffolk, and in August, "pursuant to adjournement" a general meeting of the "subscribers for strengthening the internal defences of the country" was held at Bury, under the presidency of Mr. Philip Bowes Broke. The amount contributed up to that time was nearly £7000: muster rolls were returned from several towns and hundreds, the men being requested to assemble at various centres, the list of which will be found interesting:—

Blything Hundred	Angel, Halesworth
Thedwastry and Thingoe	Angel, Bury
Bosmere and Claydon	Crown, Claydon
Hoxne and Hartismere	White Lion, Eye
Risbridge	Half Moon, Clare
Colneis, Carlford, Loes, Wilford, Plomesgate and Threadling	Shirehall, Woodbridge
Ipswich and Samford	Town Hall, Ipswich
Lackford	Bell, Mildenhall
Babergh	Black Lion, Melford
Blackbourn	Pickerel, Ixworth
Stow	White Hart, Stowmarket
Wangford	King's Head, Beccles
Cosford	White Lion, Hadleigh
Mutford and Lothingland	Crown, Lowestoft

At the head of this widespread patriotic movement were most of the leading men of the county, as the following list of officers, published in 1795, and containing many names which are still familiar, will show:—

Captains: John Rous, baronet; Charles Maitland Barclay, Horace Churchill, Philip Bowes Broke, Thomas Maynard, and Charles Lord Brome.

Lieuts.: Francis Brooke, George Doughty, Charles Berners, Edward Pryor, George Smith, William Fowke, and Robert Ride.

Cornets: John Clayton, John Meadows Theobald, Orbell Ray Oakes, Mileson Edgar, Francis G. Y. Lake, and George Brown Bohun.

In August, 1793, a regiment of Yeomanry Cavalry, consisting of six troops and described as "Fencible Light Dragoons," was quartered in Bury. They were inspected by General Johnson, who expressed his highest approbation of both men and horses. The first official return made to Parliament in connection with the Suffolk Yeomanry is as follows :—

Suffolk Yeomanry

Acceptances of the services of, by His Majesty.

	Date.	*No. of Troops.*	*Estbnt.*
County	May, 1794	4	50
,,	Jan., 1795	2	50
Ipswich	May, 1798	1	60
Bottesdale	,, ,,	1	40
Ickworth	,, ,,	1	40
Fornham	,, ,,	1	40

Effective strength : 206.

The early history of the regiment, especially that of individual troops, is somewhat obscure ; but it is believed that the first troop was raised in Bury St. Edmunds, though regimentally the Eye Troop bore the number one. On two or three occasions the Suffolk Yeomanry have been called out in aid of the civil power and have always maintained their reputation for efficiency. The regiment remained in existence throughout the wars of the great Napoleon, and was not released from its engagements until 1827, when a general reduction in the fencible corps took place. It is generally held that the Suffolk Yeomanry, though considerably reduced, was not actually disbanded, and that at least one troop remained. This troop was reconstituted in 1831 as the "Bury St. Edmunds Troop of Horse," or the 1st Loyal Suffolk Yeomanry Cavalry, under the command of Mr. Philip Bennet, of Rougham Hall, who for many years represented West Suffolk in Parliament. There was still no lack of enthusiasm, other troops being raised at Melford, Eye, and Saxmundham, though the two latter were soon disbanded. Each of the senior troops numbered about fifty men, with a trumpeter, a band not being added till after the two troops had ceased to exist.

The uniform of that period is described as having consisted of a rifle green coatee with brass epaulets, a black patent leather waistbelt, the trousers of pepper-and-salt with red stripe, the dress headgear a very black-haired shako with broad top and black horsehair plume, with a brass plate in front inscribed " The Loyal Suffolk Yeomanry." The mounts were Suffolk punches.

In the year 1860 a change in the uniform was made, when a tunic and cloth helmet with brass edgings and strap were adopted, a plume being afterwards added. The busby was introduced a little later, and from 1868 to 1872 the headgear consisted of a heavy brass helmet with white horsehair plume. The tunic became a little more elaborate as regards its facings and trimmings, and since 1872 the Hussar uniform of dark green tunic with yellow braid and busby with cockade has been worn. The Bury St. Edmunds Troop was amalgamated in 1869 with the Melford Troops, the Loyal Suffolk Yeomanry training that year at Sudbury. In 1872 the strength of the regiment was 145 all told, the average number on parade being 133. The commanding officer at that time was Colonel J. T. Ord, with Majors Bennet and Lord Rendlesham.

A few years later the Melford Troops were disbanded, some of the men going to the Lowestoft Troop and a few to the Essex Troop. Other troops were formed in Suffolk, with headquarters at Bury, Lowestoft, Stowmarket, and Ipswich, the two last-named being afterwards merged together.

Many changes have passed over the Loyal Suffolk Yeomanry since its formation in 1793, the regiment successively assuming the character of light cavalry, lancers, dragoons, and hussars. The corps was recruited from Suffolk, Essex, and part of Norfolk, and for some time the headquarters of its troops were at Bury, Chelmsford, Ipswich, and Lowestoft. Owing very largely to the exertions of Colonel A. G. Lucas the centenary of the regiment was celebrated during its training in 1893 by a military tournament and a complimentary ball, the regiment being honoured by a visit from its honorary colonel, H.R.H. The Duke of York, now H.M. King George V.

To hark back to the year 1875, a committee was appointed by the Secretary of State for War to consider various questions that had arisen with respect to the Yeomanry Cavalry, and submitted a report from which the following are extracts :—

" It has been represented by many witnesses that through the agency of the Yeomanry, a class of persons is made available for the defence of the country who would not enter any other branch of Her Majesty's service."

" We recommend that the organisation should continue to be by regiments, and that the training of the Yeomanry should be mainly directed to the duties of Light Cavalry. We think that the equipment of the Yeomanry should be that of Light Cavalry ; that every man should be armed with a breech-loading rifle, carrying a cartridge containing its own ignition, and should be required to go through the course of musketry prescribed for the cavalry."

In May, 1892, another committee was appointed by the Secretary of State for War to consider further the position of the yeomanry with a view to making recommendations as to the amalgamation of corps, and other reforms. The reason for this step was that for some years past the yeomanry force had been gradually dwindling in numbers. For example, the Suffolk Yeomanry, during the years 1890–1–2 had only been able to show an average of 129 efficients. This committee reported as follows :

" We have taken evidence and find that the Yeomanry is at present organised in 39 regiments with an establishment of 13,067 Yeomen. The total enrolled strength last year was 9,869 ; the efficient strength was 8,471 men. The average efficient strength per regiment was therefore about 217 men."

In accordance with the policy indicated by these two committees, the Suffolk and Herts Yeomanry were brigaded together, one regular adjutant being appointed to the two regiments. The squadron system was also introduced, one sergeant from the regular cavalry being appointed to each squadron, instead of to each troop as hitherto.

The annual training was usually carried out either at Yarmouth, Colchester, or Norwich. The following is a list of the officers of the Duke of York's Own Loyal Suffolk Hussars, Yeomanry Cavalry, in 1899 :—

Honorary Colonel

H.R.H. George F. E. A. Duke of York, K.G., K.T., K.P., G.C.V.O.

Lieut.-Colonels

A. G. Lucas (in command)
F. H. G. Cruickshank

Majors

R. B. Colvin
E. W. D. Baird
H. P. Levita

Captains

W. R. Greene
Hon. J. Petre
Hon. D. A. Tollemache
Prince F. V. Duleep Singh

Lieutenants

R. O. Kerrison
F. W. Jarvis
H. E. Crawley
G. C. Buxton

Medical Officers

A. Cooper
F. Treves

Honorary Chaplain

Rev. L. D. Kenyon-Stow

Uniform green ; facings and busby-bag, scarlet ; plume white.

At the beginning of the South African war the chance of the yeomanry came. It was soon made obvious that without a large mounted force it would be impossible to round up so mobile an enemy as the Boers in a country made for horsemen. Assent was therefore given to the proposals of several distinguished yeomanry officers for the formation of a corps to be styled the Imperial Yeomanry, which the following committee was appointed to administer :—

Colonel A. G. Lucas, Loyal Suffolk Hussars.
Colonel E. W. Beckett, Yorkshire Hussars.
Colonel Viscount Valentia, Oxfordshire Hussars.
Colonel The Earl of Lonsdale, Westmorland and Cumberland Hussars.
Captain Hon. W. L. Bagot, Reserve of Officers.
Colonel Rt. Hon. Lord Harris, East Kent Yeomanry.

The corps was organised in units of squadrons, four squadrons being assigned to a battalion. Each yeoman had to enlist for a year, or the duration of the war, and to be between the ages of 20 and 35 years ; he had also to satisfy the officer commanding a yeomanry regiment that he was a good rider and a good shot.

Of the first contingent, which sailed early in 1900, the Loyal Suffolk Hussars were called upon to find two squadrons of 5 officers and 120 men each ; these were numbered the 43rd and 44th Squadrons of the Imperial Yeomanry. The 43rd Squadron was composed of the following officers of the Suffolk Yeomanry :—

Captain J. R. Harvey ; Lieuts. W. R. Greene, R. O. Kerrison, E. Crawley, and G. C. Buxton. The 44th Squadron : Lieuts. Hon. W. E. Guinness and A. R. Buxton.

The following officers of the Loyal Suffolk Hussars also volunteered for service and proceeded to South Africa :—

Colonel A. G. Lucas, Deputy Adjutant-General.
Lieut.-Colonel R. B. Colvin, commanding 20th Battalion.
Major E. W. D. Baird, A.A.G.
Captain Sir S. H. L. Stuart, commanding Advanced Base Depot.
Captain Hon. J. Petre, Thorneycroft's Mounted Infantry. Killed at Spionkop.
Lieut. F. W. Jarvis, attached 13th Hussars.

The 43rd Squadron reached Capetown on February 25, and the 44th on March 28, 1900, and after going into camp at

Maitland proceeded by train to De Aar, where Lord Kitchener was organising a column of about 3000 men and 2500 horses to operate against the rebels who had seized the towns of Prieska and Kenhart. Space will not permit the full record of the doings of these two squadrons during the ensuing sixteen months. Serving at first under Lieut.-General Rundle, and afterwards with a brigade of yeomanry, under Brig.-General Brabazon, operating in the neighbourhood of Dewetsdorp and Wepener, they eventually joined a brigade under Lord Chesham belonging to Lord Methuen's Division, with which they traversed the greater part of the Western Transvaal. After taking part in the pursuit of De Wet they reached Mafeking in August, 1900, remaining there to refit.

The 43rd Squadron had now begun to feel the hardships of the campaign. After forming part of the Provisional Regiment, under Colonel Hon. W. Lawson, they were sent to Zeerust under Lieut. Buxton, the squadron having by this time been reduced to some 50 men and 30 horses. At Zeerust they remained with the garrison, practically in a state of siege, until ordered home with the first contingent in May, 1901. Leaving Capetown in the s.s. *Manchester Merchant* on June 27, under Captain G. C. Buxton, they landed at Southampton on July 18, and proceeded to Bury St. Edmunds.

Soon after the return of the Suffolk Squadrons from South Africa, numbers of officers and men belonging to the Loyal Suffolk Hussars, but residing in Norfolk and Essex, were transferred to the yeomanry regiment of their own counties. In consequence the Loyal Suffolk Hussars became much reduced in numbers; but under the command of Lieut.-Colonel Baird, a very successful recruiting campaign was inaugurated, with the result that three squadrons were maintained in Suffolk, with headquarters at Bury St. Edmunds, Ipswich, and Lowestoft, a fourth being recruited in Cambridgeshire, with headquarters at Cambridge. This organisation continued until August 4, 1914.

The experience gained during the South African war led to many reforms in the training of the yeomanry throughout the country. No longer were officers and men billeted in the local town selected for the training, but each regiment as a whole went out for a fortnight's training under canvas, the horses being picketed in lines. The training, similar to that of the regular cavalry, was most thorough, each regiment being inspected by the Inspector of Cavalry and by the G.O.C.-in-C. the Eastern Command. When, in 1908, the Territorial and Reserve Forces Act was passed, the Yeomanry and Volunteers underwent a complete reorganisation, the former becoming the reserve cavalry of the second line of our national defence, which in time of emergency was to replace the regular cavalry.

Little did the general public dream how soon the new system was to be put to the test. But during the few years that intervened between the passing of this act and the outbreak of the greatest war in history it is wonderful what was accomplished in the way of training and efficiency. Those officers and men who were serving throughout that period always looked back with satisfaction on those happy days, and felt that at any rate they had done their best to fit themselves for what was to come.

CHAPTER XI

The 9th Battalion at Loos—Sergeant Saunders wins the V.C.—The battalion in the Ypres Salient—Lieut.-Colonel de la Pryme appointed to the command —Is severely wounded—The battalion goes to the Albert sector

IN the summer of 1915 the French high command decided to assume the offensive in Champagne, and suggested that the British should assist by making an attack in Artois. Sir John French, fully realising the necessity for offensive action on the part of the Allies, acquiesced in the scheme without being unduly optimistic as regards its chances of success. The battle of Loos was therefore in a sense a concession to expediency.

It was decided that an attack should be made by the British First Army (Haig) on a six-mile front between the La Bassée canal and the village of Grenay, where it linked up with the French Tenth Army. At the same time, holding attacks were to be delivered at various other points in our line. The IVth and Ist Corps were to carry out the main attack, the newly-formed XIth Corps (Guards, 21st and 24th Divisions) being held in reserve under the orders of Sir John French. During the night of September 24–25, in drenching rain, the assaulting brigades moved into position.

Only one battalion of the Suffolk Regiment, namely, the 9th, was actually engaged in the main battle of Loos, the 1st Battalion not entering the battle zone till September 27, and the 7th Battalion not until the 29th. It will therefore be appropriate to deal with the 9th Battalion first.

The 71st Brigade reached Bethune about one o'clock in the morning of the 25th. The 9th Battalion, thoroughly tired after a succession of night marches and drenchings which they had stood well, went into barracks buoyed up with the promise of forty-eight hours' rest if circumstances permitted. At 4 a.m., however, Lieut.-Colonel Brettell was summoned to the Brigadier and ordered to assemble his battalion at a certain point in Bethune in readiness to march off at 7 a.m. The hour of starting was subsequently changed, and it was

11.30 a.m. before they set out along the Rue d'Aire into "the far-flung battle line." On the way up to Vermelles they passed a continuous stream of German prisoners and British wounded. After a short halt, the battalion formed up near Fosse 9, where they received a corps order to the effect that the 24th Division (less the 73rd Brigade) was to act as support to the 9th Division, the 21st Division advancing on its right, its own objective being Vendin-le-Vieil. The 11th Essex and 9th Suffolk Regiments were ordered to form the first line, and the 9th Norfolk and 8th Bedford Regiments the second line.

It was not, however, until 8 p.m. on that memorable September 25 that the 9th Battalion moved off and began to wend its way, in a double line of platoons, across the battle-field of Loos. A steady advance—not towards the 9th Division as originally intended, but in the direction of Vendin-le-Vieil—was maintained, the battalion passing in turn over its own support line, its own front line, the German front line, and the German support line. About midnight the advance was held up, the battalion digging themselves in between that hour and dawn, with the German support line still behind them. At 5 a.m. they were ordered back to that line.

During the forenoon of the 26th an order was received for the 21st and 24th Divisions to attack again at 11 a.m., the latter division being on the left. The 72nd Brigade was to carry out the attack on the front allotted to the division, with the 11th Essex Regiment (left) and the 9th Suffolk Regiment (right) in support of the brigade six hundred yards in rear. Unfortunately, however, this order was not received until 11.25 a.m., whereupon Lieut.-Colonel Brettell, passing a message down the line, ordered the battalion to advance immediately. Without hesitation each section mounted the parapet and began pushing forward under heavy artillery fire towards the objective of the previous evening.

The advance continued until the leading line had reached a point about two hundred yards or so beyond the Hulluch–Lens road where it was definitely checked. At 5 p.m. the right flank began to give way. For three hours the centre held on to the road, and during that time the flanks advanced and retired twice. Then the left flank, coming under a heavy machine-gun fire from the direction of Hulluch, was forced back. Here most of the 9th Battalion's casualties occurred.

At seven o'clock that evening a party consisting of three officers and about a hundred men, under Captain Packard, was ordered to hold the old German second line against counter-attack, remaining there until relieved. During the night no attacks were made, and at 2 a.m.—the party having been relieved by a company of the Coldstream Guards—Captain Packard withdrew his men towards Vermelles. Just before leaving, he got into touch with another party of the 9th Battalion, under Lieut. Church, both these detachments rejoining the battalion at Sailly-Labourse. The casualties in the battalion amounted to 135, including the following officers—*Killed :* Lieut. T. T. Stevens. *Wounded :* Lieut.-Colonel R. V. G. Brettell ; Major L. C. Arbuthnot ; Captain and Adjutant F. R. Hedges ; Captain H. F. Law ; and Lieuts. R. England and F. R. C. Cobbold.

For gallantry at Loos, Sgt. Saunders was awarded the V.C. under circumstances set forth in the *London Gazette* of March 30, 1916, as follows :—

" His Majesty the King has been graciously pleased to award the Victoria Cross to the undermentioned non-commissioned officer.

No. 3/10133 Sergeant Arthur Frederick Saunders, 9th (Service) Battalion, the Suffolk Regiment.

For most conspicuous bravery. When his officer had been wounded in the attack he took charge of two machine-guns and a few men and, although severely wounded in the thigh, closely followed the last four charges of another battalion and rendered every possible support. Later when the remains of the battalion which he had been supporting had been forced to retire, he stuck to one of his guns, continued to give clear orders, and by his continuous firing did his best to cover the retirement."

Sgt. Saunders was the first Suffolk man to win this coveted distinction in the great war while serving with the county regiment.

Out of a total of 112 battalions engaged in the main attack at Loos, 69 were Service Battalions. Some of these had only recently arrived at the front. The 9th Battalion, for example, twenty-five days after landing in France were flung into a pitched battle, to be swallowed up in the colossal. Such a conflict would have tried to the utmost the best-trained infantry in the world : as a first experience of fighting, it was indeed a staggering ordeal. The official history of the war says : " These partially trained units were being put to a test far too severe for their first experience under fire."

At Loos the British used gas for the first time. Though entirely strange and new to them, the men seem to have done the work well ; but the weather conditions were capricious, and at the critical moment the wind failed. Such is the uncertainty of war.

Lieut.-Colonel Brettell having been wounded, the command of the battalion devolved upon Major F. G. Davies. While the 9th Battalion were in the neighbourhood of Sailly-Labourse the 1st Battalion, under the command of Major F. A. White, D.S.O., marching up to the battle line, passed the 9th Battalion resting by the roadside, mutual recognitions, cheering, and good wishes resulting from this happy and unexpected meeting.

Having done its share in the battle of Loos, the 9th Battalion was sent to Ham-en-Artois, and then on to Proven, to rest and reorganise, being inspected at the latter town by Major-General J. E. Capper, who announced that he had taken over command of the 24th Division. On October 5 the battalion left Proven with the 71st Brigade and marched to Brandhoek, making its first acquaintance with the Immortal Salient a day or so later. On the 16th the battalion was inspected by Lieut.-General Sir John Keir, commanding the VIth Corps. On the 18th, while in trenches at St. Jean, a party of Germans boldly rushed the listening-post of " B " Company, wounding C.S.M. Thompson and one other rank before being ejected. At the end of October the 71st Brigade was transferred to the 6th Division, commanded by Major-General Sir Walter Congreve, V.C.

On November 1 Major W. H. A. de la Pryme, D.S.O., West Yorkshire Regiment, was appointed to the command of the battalion. The remainder of the year was spent in the Salient, the battalion occupying the line at Forward Cottage trenches, or at St. Jean. The weather was atrocious, and the period as a whole indescribably wretched and trying for everyone. When not actually in the line the battalion was at or near Poperinghe, furnishing everlasting working parties at night, which had to grope their way up to the front in rain, mud, and darkness, and under persistent shell-fire. All ranks were constantly exercised in the rapid manipulation of gas-masks in anticipation of gas attacks.

On November 25 the battalion was inspected by General Sir Herbert Plumer, the band playing for the first time since Loos. On December 4 2nd Lieut. A. H. Guinness was wounded. Some days later a telegram was received announcing the following awards for gallantry at Loos—*M.C.:* Captains C. T. Packard and G. B. Steward, and Lieut. C. F. Beyts. *D.C.M.:* Sgt. R. C. Bolingbroke and Ptes. J. W. Mann and C. Hales.

On December 19, while the battalion was in trenches in front of St. Jean, the enemy again became active. Gas was sent over early in the morning, followed by a very heavy bombardment lasting twenty-four hours. During this gas attack "D" Company, in reserve on the canal bank, rendered prompt assistance, marching up into the line in their gas-masks through intense fire. The casualties in the battalion amounted to over eighty, including 2nd Lieut. B. H. Collis, who died on the 20th from the effects of his wounds. The battalion received a congratulatory telegram from the Army Commander for having held its trenches so successfully on December 19–20, during the gas attack and bombardment. The 9th Battalion was the first unit of the new armies to experience and withstand a gas attack, demonstrating the fact that the gas-masks then in use, though primitive, afforded adequate protection if properly used. The battalion spent its first Christmas at the front resting in Poperinghe, moving back into camp behind Ypres on the 30th after a spell in the trenches at St. Jean.

Their first casualty in the New Year was C.S.M. O. T. Putley, who was killed in the trenches by a shell on January 4, having recently been recommended for a commission. On the last day of that month 2nd Lieut. A. Williamson was killed and 2nd Lieut. S. Kelsey wounded. On February 7 Captain N. R. Rawson, R.A.M.C., medical officer to the battalion, was wounded, and a fortnight later Lieut. V. W. Ory was also wounded. About this time the battalion made a welcome change of equipment from leather to web.

Early in March L/Sgt. G. E. White was awarded the

Sergeant A. F. SAUNDERS, V.C.

D.C.M. for going out on his own initiative and bombing single-handed a German patrol, who were cutting the wire in front of a listening-post at St. Jean. On the 21st the battalion was inspected by General Sir Douglas Haig, who, three months earlier, had taken over supreme command of the British Army in France and Flanders. On April 1 2nd Lieut. H. G. Frost, who had been attached to the Royal Flying Corps since the previous February, was reported missing. It was afterwards ascertained that he had been wounded and taken prisoner in an air-fight. On April 4 2nd Lieut. V. I. Hardy was wounded; on the following day the battalion proceeded to Calais, where they remained in camp for ten days, resting and thoroughly enjoying themselves. By the 18th they were back again in their old camp near Poperinghe, having completed the journey in four marches. Towards the end of the month the British Commander-in-Chief inspected two of the companies in camp. R.S.M. C. H. Hurrell and R.Q.M.S. G. E. Hammond—both of whom had been with the 9th Battalion since its formation, and had done splendid work—were appointed quartermasters of the 12th and 2nd (Home Service) Garrison Battalions respectively, dated May 2 and April 7, 1916.

On May 14 Lieut.-Colonel W. H. A. de la Pryme, D.S.O., was wounded by shrapnel at about two o'clock in the morning while going round the front-line trenches at Forward Cottage, his injuries unfortunately necessitating the amputation of his right leg. The 9th Battalion was thus deprived of the services of an able and gallant leader who, during the six months of his command, had won the confidence of all ranks. L/Cpl. W. Rose was with him at the time and, having helped to dress his wounds, carried him back to the dressing-station; for this act—and previous good work—Rose was awarded the D.C.M.

The battalion, now under the command of Major A. P. Mack, came out of the line on the 18th, this harassing spell of duty having cost them numerous casualties, including Lieut. L. Wilmot-Johnson, Lieut. F. R. C. Cobbold, and 2nd Lieut. C. H. Box, wounded. Soon after the battalion had reached their billets the Germans fired a single shell into the camp, wounding Captain M. F. Heigham, 2nd Lieut. F. H. Bright, and five men, the last-named officer being hit through the jaw while asleep. Round about Ypres, however, the bombing and shelling of camps were the daily and nightly experiences of battalions " at rest."

Early in June the battalion returned to the trenches at Forward Cottage and neighbouring posts, the whole Salient being shortly afterwards disturbed by the sounding of gongs, gas alarms, and klaxon horns, which told of the attack on the Canadians at Hooge and Sanctuary Wood. A day or two later the following awards for gallantry during the gas attack of December 19 were announced—*M.C.:* Lieut. R. England. *M.M.:* L/Sgt. G. H. Norton, L/Cpl. W. Facer, and Pte. T. Easy. The remainder of June was spent in camp near Poperinghe, the battalion being inspected on the 22nd by Lieut.-General the Earl of Cavan. On July 3 they marched to Bollezeele, moving a few days later to Houtkerque for purposes of recuperation and training in open warfare, and on the 22nd took over billets in Ypres.

1st Battalion

The 1st Battalion at Loos—The Hohenzollern Redoubt—Curly Crescent trenches—The battalion returns to Bethune—Sails for Egypt with the 28th Division

When the 1st Battalion arrived in the Loos battle area at Noyelles-les-Vermelles on September 27 the main attack was of course over. On the following day there was a lull, the battalion marching to Sailly-Labourse; but from September 29 to October 3 fighting was practically continuous, especially round about the Hohenzollern Redoubt and neighbouring trenches, where the Germans, having gained some ground, were now defending themselves vigorously. This redoubt was a formidable work, thrust out nearly five hundred yards in front of the German lines and close to those of the British; it was connected with their front line by three communication trenches abutting into the defences of Fosse 8, a coal mine with a high and strongly defended slag-heap, and scarcely less renowned. The two trenches forming the western face of the work were known to the troops as " Big Willie " and " Little Willie." The name Hohenzollern Redoubt was itself loosely applied, being sometimes incorrectly extended to the rambling network of trenches enmeshing the redoubt proper. An attack on one portion or another of the Hohenzollern Redoubt was carried out by each unit in turn, and became the set-piece of the 28th Division.

These operations were of a most difficult, even disheartening, character, carried out as they were in rain, mud, and mostly in darkness. The objective could be approached by communication trenches; but the continuous blocking of these trenches by everlasting working-parties moving backwards and forwards, and often indeed diverted *en route* by fresh orders, caused such congestion and confusion that units sometimes abandoned the comparative security of the trench and took to the open, an uncertain and hazardous alternative in the prevailing conditions and in the darkness. Hence the continual delay when assembling for an attack, and hence, too, the fact that units were often prevented from carrying out the task for which they had been originally detailed. In circumstances of such difficulty order and counter-order are notoriously dogged by disorder.

On September 29 the battalion, now lent to the 7th Division, was sent into reserve trenches near Cambrin. Then, after spending a night at Vermelles, it was ordered into Curly Crescent trenches, taking no less than eight hours to move up the communication trench, but only sustaining three casualties in the process, namely 2nd Lieut. E. C. Foulsham and two men wounded. That evening they were replaced under the orders of the 84th Brigade and sent down the Hulluch road to Vermelles to occupy the Lancashire reserve trenches.

On October 1 the battalion was ordered to move up to the support trenches to cover an attack by the 1st Welch and 2nd Cheshire Regiments on Little Willie. By daylight the next morning the battalion, under Lieut.-Colonel F. A. White—less "D" Company and seventy men of "B," under Lieuts. Parsons and Owen, who had been diverted to Big Willie for duty with a battalion of the Northumberland Fusiliers—reached the support trenches. During the night 2nd Lieut. D. L. Gates, commanding "D" Company, was killed. In the morning battalion headquarters and "A" Company moved up to the Central Keep; "B" Company occupied a trench near brigade headquarters; while "C" Company remained in the support trenches. "D" Company had not arrived.

Orders were now received for another attack on the Hohenzollern Redoubt. This particular effort—to be directed against Little Willie at 8.30 p.m.—was, if successful, to carry on beyond Fosse 8, where the troops were to dig themselves in on a new line facing half-right. Lieut.-Colonel White, accompanied by Major Sinclair Thomson, went out and made a personal reconnaissance of the position, and at 7 p.m. the battalion began winding up the Central Bergeau. Unable to make sufficient progress owing to the crowded state of the communication trench, they endeavoured to find their way in the dark across the open. However, the battalion not having arrived, zero hour was postponed till 10.30, and then till midnight.

Actually the attack did not take place till nearly 2 a.m. The original orders as regards direction were half-right by the moon, with the right set towards a red lamp outside the German trench; but by that time the position of the moon had of course changed considerably and the enemy, who were fully prepared, had omitted to display the usual red lamp. "B" and "C" Companies formed the front line, with "A" in support. Still "D" had not arrived. The three companies began groping their way towards the objective, but in the darkness—with no points to march on—direction was completely lost. There was no artillery support, and the attack went awry and failed. The casualties amounted to about 160, including the following officers—*Killed:* Captain and Adjutant O. I. Wood; 2nd Lieuts. D. L. Gates and M. L. Wortley. *Wounded:* Captain E. D. C. Hunt; 2nd Lieuts. H. P. Allanson, C. F. Wright, M. H. Keen, C. J. Saunders, E. C. Foulsham, and J. C. Hollinrake. By the death of Captain Wood the battalion lost an exceptionally good officer, who on this and many previous occasions had displayed remarkable courage, coolness, and energy. Cpl. N. A. Bott and Pte. B. H. Brill were awarded the D.C.M. for conspicuous gallantry throughout this attack.

"D" Company, which could not be found at the critical moment, had been detailed as a carrying party on the evening of the 1st. It afterwards transpired that this company had been appropriated *en route* and kept for the night in the front line. Endeavouring the next morning to get back to battalion headquarters, it was stopped on the way and sent off to another part of the front line. From here a party was sent back for tools and sandbags, but this was also diverted and did not return to the front line till the evening.

The order to repeat the attack was cancelled and the battalion, having been relieved, was sent back to the Lancashire reserve trenches and then to Annequin, where Major Sinclair Thomson assumed command in place of Lieut.-Colonel White, seriously ill. On October 6 the battalion proceeded to Perriere, and by the 18th were back in Bethune, being quartered in the barracks.

They had not been in Bethune very long, however, when they received movement orders of a totally unexpected nature, and on October 21 were sent to Fouquereuil to entrain. Here Major Hon. H. E. Joicey, 14th Hussars, joined and took over command of the battalion from Major Sinclair Thomson, invalided. On the 24th they arrived in Marseilles and embarked in H.M.T. *Ivernia*, when they learned that, together with the remainder of the 28th Division, they were destined for Egypt.

7th Battalion

The battle of Loos—The attack on the Hairpin—In front of Festubert and Bethune—Mud, mines, and grenades—The battalion goes down to the Somme.

The position taken over by the 7th Battalion, under Lieut.-Colonel C. Parry Crooke, on September 30 from the 1st Coldstream Guards was on ground gained in the main attack. The right sector ran along the edge of the Chalk Pit, and in front of the wood to the right of it, the German trenches being from one to two hundred yards away; but on the left the British line dropped back at a sharp angle, the opposing lines being from 1500 to 2000 yards apart. The hasty excavations which the Guards, working under great difficulties, had made with their entrenching tools were improved during the night, several casualties being sustained while linking up two lengths of trench in front of the Chalk Pit.

On October 1—a bright sunny day—at about eight o'clock in the morning, the enemy opened a very heavy artillery fire on a wide front, which continued all day and reached a pitch of great intensity in the middle of the afternoon, numbers of men belonging to " A " Company in front of the wood being completely buried. Early in the day Major Terry went over to the Norfolk Regiment to telephone (his own telephone being out of action) for the medical officer, and on the way back was killed by a shell. His message resulted in Captain B. J. Hackett, M.O. to the 7th Battalion, coming across the open to the Chalk Pit and rendering the necessary aid, for which he was awarded the M.C. Major Walter Terry joined the Suffolk Regiment in 1901, having seen service in the South African war. Always cheery and kind-hearted, and setting a fine example, he was extremely popular with all ranks.

The 7th Battalion had its headquarters in the Chalk Pit, the centre of the heaviest shelling. The enemy were so busy entrenching that there was an entire absence of rifle fire. On October 2 Major-General F. D. V. Wing, commanding the 12th Division, was killed—the third general of division killed during these operations. All ranks appreciated his frequent and informal visits to the trenches and his unfailing cheerfulness. Captain Charles Sorley,[1] referring to him in one of his letters, says, " Our Major-General never sleepeth." On that day the enemy showed less artillery activity, but the following morning their heavy guns and howitzers were again very busy. On the night of the 3rd the battalion moved in support trenches, and on the 7th to billets at Noyelles-les-Vermelles. On the 12th they took over trenches from the 1st Guards Brigade in front of the Quarries.

At 2 p.m. on October 13, after an intensive bombardment maintained by the British artillery for two hours, an attack on a front of about a mile was launched against the Quarries. The objectives allotted to the 7th Battalion were two trenches, known as the Hairpin, running from the British (the old German) front line to that of the enemy, a distance of about 250 yards. At the British end—where they were separated from the front line by bombing saps with stops—they were fifty yards apart, and at the other, fifteen. " B " Company, led by Major Currey, advanced across the open under cover of a smoke screen, but the smoke lifting, they came under a

[1] The distinguished author of *Marlborough and other Poems* (Cambridge University Press). The *Letters of Charles Sorley* (C.U.P.) have also been widely read.

very heavy fire from machine-guns. Though the objective was not reached, this part of the attack contributed materially towards the progress made at other points. This company sustained about seventy-five casualties, including Major V. F. Currey and 2nd Lieuts. C. W. L. Hartopp and R. Lee, killed; and Lieut. V. A. Davoren, wounded. Major Currey, a gallant officer with a gentle, unassuming disposition, joined the Suffolk Regiment in 1900.

Simultaneously an assault was made on the Hairpin trenches. "A" Company, under Captain C. A. Cobbold, headed by a bombing party from the 7th Suffolk and 7th Norfolk Regiments, attacked up the left arm, and "D" Company, under Captain Henty, the right arm. Violent opposition was encountered, Captain Cobbold being killed and 2nd Lieut. D. C. Smith mortally wounded, almost at the outset. The machine-guns were ordered to follow "A" Company, the command of which had now devolved on Captain Chitty Thomas, and while getting them into position Lieut. P. Gedge was killed.

Meanwhile "D" Company, attacking up the right arm, were held up by German bombers at the barrier. Here Captain G. H. Henty was wounded, but for a time strove pluckily to remain at duty. No sooner had Captain C. H. Sorley taken over command of the company than he himself was killed bravely leading a charge against this barrier; and Lieut. G. D. Wood, while helping some of his men to fill sandbags, also fell near the same spot. Lieut. G. W. Deighton, however, the only officer now remaining in "D" Company, continued bombing down the trench and eventually succeeded in clearing it of the enemy.

Thus gradually "A" and "D" Companies, now cut off from battalion headquarters, forced their way up to the edge of the Quarries, but the gathering opposition of the enemy, aided by the formation of the ground, prevented any advance beyond that point. Captain Chitty Thomas, who was in command, set to work consolidating the position, and ordered a trench to be dug connecting the two arms, thus completing the "Hairpin." After dark a German mortar caused a good deal of trouble, but by this time Lieut. Deighton had managed to get into communication by telephone with battalion headquarters and the mortar was silenced by one of the heavy batteries. Later the consolidated position was handed over to the 9th Essex Regiment.

Captain Chitty Thomas and Lieut. Deighton were both awarded the M.C. for their gallantry on this occasion, the latter also receiving the Croix de Chevalier of the Legion of Honour. The casualties in the battalion were as follows—Officers: killed, eight; wounded, three. Other ranks: killed and wounded, one hundred and fifty. Major S. B. Stotherd, wounded by a shell on October 15, died in Bethune four days later. He joined the regiment in 1884. On October 19 the enemy counter-attacked from the Quarries but was repulsed, C.S.M. C. Sharpe being killed, after which the battalion went back to Noyelles and then to Bethune. In November Brig.-General A. Solly-Flood took over command of the 35th Brigade.

The 7th Battalion, continuing to take their regular turn of duty in front-line trenches, passed the remainder of the year in the Hulluch-Givenchy sector amid a good deal of activity in the shape of mining, bombing, trench-mortar fire and gas. Towards the end of November they proceeded by rail and road to Boesenghem and Pecqueur. Mid-December found headquarters and one company in Givenchy, the remainder being at Le Quesnoy. Christmas was spent in billets at Les Choquaux, and when the year 1916 opened the battalion was in the line in front of Festubert.

On January 4 the 35th Brigade went into billets in the Bethune area, and a fortnight later—after two more spells in the line—the battalion entrained for Lillers, marching thence into corps reserve at Norrent Fontes. By the middle of February they had returned to Sailly-Labourse and taken over support trenches at Curly Crescent. During that month the enemy made two or three abortive attacks on the Hairpin. German bombers and snipers became rather aggressive, while their rifle grenades caused some loss and considerable annoyance. On the 27th, after several days of frost, a thaw set in, speedily reducing the trenches to a deplorable state. The next day Lieut. P. B. B. Nichols was wounded while wiring. Notable mining activity—one of the chief features of static warfare—characterised the months of March and April.

On April 24 the battalion proceeded to Lillers by train, marching to corps reserve at Floringhem and into the Ist Army manœuvre area at Estrée Blanche a fortnight later. At the beginning of June the battalion moved to Mazingarbe, being attached to the 16th Division for training. They were then transferred from the Ist Army Corps area to the Albert sector to take part in the forthcoming battles of the Somme. Journeying by rail from Fouquereuil to Vignacourt and thence by road through Franvillers, they reached Henincourt on July 1, moving up into support trenches the following morning.

2ND BATTALION

The second attack on Bellewaarde—The counter-attack on September 30—Sanctuary Wood—Divisional rest at Eecke—Back to the Salient—The Bluff, and its capture—St. Eloi—Vierstraat and Kemmel—In the G.H.Q. area

On September 25, the opening day of the battle of Loos, the 3rd Division delivered an attack from Railway Wood to Sanctuary Wood. This action by the Vth Corps became known as the second attack on Bellewaarde, and was part of the subsidiary operation designed by Sir John French to distract the attention of the enemy and hold him to his ground. When the action was over half the battalion went into front-line trenches in Sanctuary Wood, the remainder being in support.

On September 26—a day spent in clearing up the battle-field and repairing defences—Lieut.-Colonel d'Arch Smith arrived. The night of the 27th–28th was one of false alarms, and during the next the enemy fired a big mine under the trenches of the 4th Middlesex Regiment, causing further "alarums and excursions." Immediately the mine went up Captain Wynn with a party of men endeavoured to seize the crater, but, the supply of bombs failing, the attempt was frustrated. In the course of this fighting 2nd Lieut. R. F. Deck was killed, and Captain T. S. Wynn and 2nd Lieuts. R. L. Hartopp, N. R. Mossop, and J. S. Spong were wounded.

A fresh supply of bombs having been received on September 30, a counter-attack was ordered for that afternoon. The artillery bombardment of the mine crater, which was not very effective, ceased about 3.15 p.m., whereupon three companies of the 4th Middlesex Regiment, the 2nd Royal Scots and the 2nd Suffolk Regiment, in that order from right to left, began to advance. Unfortunately, at the very outset, Captain E. C. Smith, commanding " A " Company, was killed. The attack, gallantly carried on by Captain de Castro in the face of heavy fire from machine-guns and rifles, besides much bombing, succeeded in reaching the edge of the crater, where it was checked by barbed wire which Captain de Castro proceeded to cut. At this juncture Major C. H. Turner (in command), Lieut. J. J. Thill, and 2nd Lieut. C. L. Q. Law were killed, and Captain C. M. E. Dealtry wounded. The attackers, now forced to retire, formed a line which was subsequently strengthened and consolidated by the H.A.C. In addition to the officers already mentioned, the casualties—amounting to about 120—included Sgts. B. Barber, W. E. Seal, and F. Hester, killed. Major C. H. Turner, an able and gallant leader, joined the Suffolk Regiment in 1889, retiring some years before the great war.

On October 1 Captain J. V. R. de Castro was killed, and the regiment thereby deprived of the services of a most intrepid officer. That night the battalion returned to camp near Vlamertinghe. Between the 8th and the 21st they lived in Maple Copse, companies paying nightly visits to Sanctuary Wood and filling in trenches in No Man's Land, a labour rendered necessary by the readjustment of the line after the recent attack. In order that the enemy should neither use nor reconstruct the trenches connecting his new front line with that of the British, they were filled in with earth mixed with barbed wire, a further entanglement of wire being erected on the top. It was a nerve-racking task for the men, especially on a bright night, creeping along a trench which led straight to the enemy's parapet, and then destroying their only cover by pulling in the sandbags and earth on either side, and further hampering themselves with coils of barbed wire which had to be worked into the mixture. On October 21 the battalion was relieved, and having concluded its third sojourn in Sanctuary Wood, turned its back upon that god-forsaken locality for ever.

The battalion was now despatched by motor-bus to Eecke, near Hazebrouck, for divisional rest. This was the first real respite outside the danger zone the division had known for twelve months, and it was thoroughly enjoyed. It was during this period that the 2nd Battalion was transferred from the 8th to the 76th Brigade, thus parting company with its old comrades the 2nd Royal Scots and the 4th Middlesex Regiment. On November 16 2nd Lieut. R. H. Andrew left the battalion to take up the appointment of A.D.C. to the G.O.C. IIIrd Army.

The spell of divisional rest at Eecke having come to an end, the 2nd Battalion found themselves on November 21 back again in the Salient, and under canvas in a muddy field near Canada huts, whither they repaired during their periods of rest from the trenches all through the winter of 1915–16.

On November 28 the battalion took over the Bluff trenches on both sides of the Ypres–Comines canal. The banks of the latter were about sixty feet high, descending in steep stepped slopes to the water's edge; but where the British line crossed the northern bank ended abruptly in a massive mound known as the Bluff. Until a tunnel was made through this feature the only means of communication between the canal and the trenches to the north was the Gaby Glide—a straight, shallow trench down the steep canal bank. The top of the Bluff was used for sniping and observation.

The year wore on uneventfully, the time being spent in improving the trenches and barbed-wire defences. In mid-December a quantity of corkscrew iron standards was received, saving wiring parties a vast amount of labour. The supply of shells had now greatly increased, rendering effective retaliation possible for the artillery. In support of the battalion was a Belgian battery of "seventy-fives," staffed by a keen and enterprising set of officers, always ready to oblige the enemy with a few rounds of high explosive at the shortest notice.

Christmas Day was spent in the line; the ambitious artillery programme drawn up for the occasion was postponed till the 26th, each side indulging in its own meagre celebrations unmolested. On December 31 Major G. R. Crosfield, 4th Battalion Prince of Wales's Volunteers, temporarily assumed command of the battalion in place of Lieut.-Colonel d'Arch Smith, admitted to field ambulance. During the year the following awards—in addition to those already mentioned—were gained—*M.C.:* Captain C. M. E. Dealtry; Lieut. T. S. Wynn. *D.C.M.:* Coy. Sgt.-Major M. G. W. Theobald. In November, 1916, C.S.M. Theobald was the victim of a tragic accident at Sudbury station. He was buried with military honours at Waldingfield.

The battalion's first tour of duty in the trenches in 1916 began inauspicuously. 2nd Lieut. R. N. Mawer, the machine-gun officer, was sniped in the leg while looking for gun positions near the Bluff, 2nd Lieut. W. F. Burman in going to his assistance being also wounded. The next night, when out wiring, 2nd Lieut. D. M. Greig was wounded—the third time in five months.

During the third week in January, the miners, who were tunnelling in front of the Bluff, became aware that the enemy were counter-mining. On the night of the 21st–22nd, just after the battalion had returned to the line, a terrific explosion occurred. The ground shook violently, and an immense column of earth shot up in front of the Bluff, carrying away the south-eastern face of it. The explosion was not followed by any bombardment or attack, and for the moment no one realised what had happened. Men in the trenches next to the canal were buried several feet deep; ammunition boxes were hurled hundreds of yards; and all the surrounding trenches upon which the battalion had spent so much labour, as well as the system of tunnels within the Bluff, collapsed completely. The behaviour of the 2nd Battalion on this occasion was referred to by Major-General Haldane, commanding the 3rd Division, in the following terms: "About 2 a.m. on the 22nd January, 1916, the Germans exploded a mine under the trenches held by this battalion in front of the Bluff, close to the Ypres–Comines canal, causing fresh damage and a considerable number of casualties. The charge in the mine is estimated to have been between six and seven tons of gunpowder, which formed a crater measuring roughly sixty by forty yards, and forty feet in depth. Nearly a hundred men were killed, buried alive or injured by the explosion, the damage from which extended to several hundred yards in all directions. In spite of the unexpected nature of the occurrence, and the hour at which the mine was exploded, the troops maintained their coolness, quickly occupied the crater and prepared to meet an attack which, however, the enemy did not think fit to make.

Major Crosfield, commanding the battalion, quickly appreciated the situation and organised the defences while the enemy kept up rifle fire which caused several casualties.

Several officers, non-commissioned officers, and men were conspicuous by their coolness, and many behaved with gallantry, rescuing their comrades. The conduct of the battalion under these trying circumstances was excellent, all ranks behaving in a soldier-like manner, so that here the position, which might easily have become serious, was never in danger." For conspicuous gallantry on this occasion Sgt. H. Bragg was awarded the D.C.M.

January 27, being the Kaiser's birthday, was celebrated with a British bombardment to which the enemy replied vigorously, causing many casualties. The same night, a party of bombers, under Lieuts. Munday and Needham, attempted a raid on an enemy post near the canal with the object of securing samples—living or dead—of the units opposing them. All went well until Lieut. Munday, lying across the parapet, aimed a blow with a sandbag at the head of a passing sentry, but missing his mark only hit the sentry's shoulder. The alarm was at once raised, and all hopes of success wrecked for that night. The raiders were fortunate in getting back with only one casualty—Lieut. Needham wounded. Captain William Congreve, brigade-major to the 76th Brigade, was the leading spirit in these raids.

On January 28, some members of the Royal Navy, who were sight-seeing in France, paid a visit to the battalion. The weather was very wet and the sailors, looking at the state of the trenches, remarked they would rather serve on the water than in it. On February 7 this sector was taken over by the 17th Division, the battalion returning to camp near Poperinghe. On the 9th Brig.-General Clifford visited the battalion in camp just as they were parading to entrain at Poperinghe, and addressed a few words to the men. This was the last occasion on which he saw the battalion together.

On the 10th the battalion reached Houle, being billeted in and round a large brewery. In this agreeable environment, so full of promise and possibility, they were to remain for two months: but in consequence of the loss of the Bluff, the 76th Brigade was hastily recalled to Poperinghe. On February 16 the battalion travelled by bus to Ypres, marching into their old support trenches—now in our front line—where they remained for a week.

Towards the end of February the new pattern steel helmets were issued to some of the bombers of the 76th Brigade, the Royal Welch Fusiliers receiving theirs first. On the evening of issue a Suffolk man, working by himself in a communication trench a little way behind the front line, saw a Fusilier coming up the trench in the dusk wearing this strange headgear, and promptly hit him over the head with a shovel thinking he was a German. The Fusilier vigorously resented this familiarity; and in the end the two men, very much the worse for wear, were removed on stretchers to the field ambulance.

Since the loss of the Bluff, the 17th Division had made several vigorous counter-attacks to try and regain it, but without success, the Germans having massed a large number of guns against them, battering their trenches flat, besides inflicting heavy casualties. During this stay in the line the battalion was engaged in repairing the trenches and burying the dead.

It had now been decided that the 76th Brigade, reinforced by two battalions from the 17th Division, should attempt the recovery of the lost ground, the 2nd Suffolk Regiment, 8th King's Own, and 1st Gordon Highlanders carrying out the attack with the 10th R.W.F., 7th Lincoln Regiment, and 10th Sherwood Foresters in support. Accordingly, on February 23, the battalion withdrew to Reninghelst to prepare for the second action of the Bluff, practising the attack over dummy trenches representing those they were about to assault. During one of these practices a German plane flew over Reninghelst bombing the village. For the edification of German intelligence agents it was given out that the attack would take place at 4.30 p.m. on March 2.

On the night of March 1 the battalion moved into its assembly trenches, halting near Bedford House on the Ypres–St. Eloi road, to draw bombs. Had the enemy but known of the mass of troops blocking the road there for half an hour, he could have prevented—with a few shells—the 76th Brigade from being of much account in the attack. The assembly trenches were reached just after midnight, "A" Company, on the north side of the Bluff, finding theirs in a shocking state as a result of the bombardment of the previous days. That known as the Boche trench—an experimental one, dug very deep, revetted, and strutted overhead with timber—was in places impassable. "B," "D," and "C" Companies, in that order, were on the south side of the Bluff. The 8th King's Own and the 1st Gordon Highlanders were on the left, the 10th R.W.F. supporting the 2nd Battalion. It was now announced that the attack would take place at 4.30 a.m.

As our men rose from their trenches, a tremendous roar of rifle and machine-gun fire burst forth from the brigade on the right of the 76th. The Germans immediately sent up a shower of Very lights, and for a few seconds it was as light as day. At this warning signal, the enemy artillery opened upon the attackers, our batteries immediately putting down a heavy barrage on the German second line. Our leading troops, however, who had assembled within a few yards of the German front line, were already through, having taken the enemy completely by surprise. On the left the attack was not so fortunate, "A" Company being caught by the counter-barrage before they had time to debouch from King Street. By 7 a.m. the lost trenches had been recaptured.

Our front trenches, which had been entirely destroyed, were now partially re-dug, but the ground, churned up by shells, was in a chaotic state. The line was therefore but lightly occupied, all men who could be spared being sent back to the assembly trenches. At about eight o'clock the enemy began a bombardment which lasted all day and all night, with a few intervals to allow the guns to cool. Our artillery countered very effectively. At dusk, a bombing party, under Major Crosfield and 2nd Lieut. H. P. Gardham, entered the craters and captured forty-nine Germans who had been hiding in the saps all day.

The attack had been a conspicuous success, the enemy being driven from all the trenches he had wrested from the 17th Division, and by the evening the brigade was holding an even better line—battered though it was—than they did formerly. The usual aftermath of counter-attacks and bombardments followed.

The casualties sustained by the battalion during this operation amounted to over 250, out of a total of 500 taken into action, and included the following officers—*Killed:* 2nd Lieut. R. D. Locke. *Died of wounds:* 2nd Lieut. T. G.

Elkington. *Wounded:* Captain E. F. Ledward; Lieuts. R. Barber and S. P. Inskip; 2nd Lieuts. G. C. Munday and L. J. Baker. For gallantry at the taking of the Bluff, Lieuts. Barber and Trollope, and 2nd Lieuts. J. Bradley and Munday were awarded the M.C.

Distinctive badges were adopted by units in this attack, the 2nd Battalion wearing a two-inch black square on a six-inch yellow square in the middle of the back. This was the first occasion on which steel helmets were worn by the whole battalion. The rank and file did not take to them at all kindly at first; but "how use doth breed a habit in a man."

Heavy shelling continued throughout March 3, the assembly trenches on the canal being almost obliterated. The weather now broke and snow fell, adding to the hardships of the situation, but on the 4th the battalion went back to billets in Poperinghe. In addition to messages of congratulation from the army, divisional, and brigade commanders, the following was received from the Commander-in-Chief, and deserves permanent record:—

"To the Officer Commanding 2nd Suffolk Regiment.

"I have heard with great pleasure the good news of the capture of the Bluff and trenches north of the canal. I have been informed from day to day of the careful and methodical preparation which has been devoted to this enterprise. Please convey to all ranks concerned my hearty congratulations and thanks."

After a week in Poperinghe the battalion returned to the Bluff, but for two or three days only. On March 19 Lieut. and Quartermaster J. Roberts was wounded, being succeeded by 2nd Lieut. W. M. Lummis, who continued to officiate for two years.

On March 27, a violent explosion, felt in towns several miles behind the line, proclaimed that our mines at St. Eloi had done their work. Early the next morning, the battalion, resting at Ouderdom, was despatched by bus to Dickebusch, where they passed the remainder of the day in a hail storm, moving forward that night up the long communication trench to the St. Eloi craters under heavy shell-fire. On the 28th Lieut.-Colonel d'Arch Smith was injured, and Major

Thomas being sick, Captain G. C. Stubbs (attd. to the staff of the 3rd Division) assumed command of the battalion.

On reaching the trenches the situation was found to be obscure and complicated. Some of the craters had not yet been occupied by our troops, and the dawn of the 29th revealed the unhealthy fact that part of a trench on the right edge of the battalion sector was still held by Germans. Early the next afternoon our bombers, under 2nd Lieut. H. P. Gardham, endeavoured to clear this portion of the trench, but after making about twenty yards of ground came up against a barricade which the enemy had erected. Heavy machine-gun fire foiled all attempts to get beyond this point. The leading bayonet man, Pte. H. A. Southgate, recently decorated with the D.C.M. for gallantry at the Bluff, was killed trying to cross the barricade; 2nd Lieut. C. C. Field, in making a daring effort to mount his machine-guns in the open to cover the advance, also fell.

This operation afforded a good example of the costly underground warfare of the period. The bulk of our casualties during these three days in the line, which included Captain C. M. E. Dealtry and Lieut. F. W. Rix[1] wounded, were caused by the intense shell-fire to which the battalion was subjected.

On the 30th a shell crashed through a shelter occupied by two of our signallers, killing one of them; the other—a brave, cheerful man named Fuller—survived, but with the loss of both legs. On the last evening of the month the battalion, having been relieved, went back to Reninghelst.

One night during this spell of duty, a clergyman wearily made his way to Captain Carpenter's dugout. This was the Rev. E. Noel Mellish, who had been out in No Man's Land three nights in succession bringing in wounded men of his brigade, in which work he had been voluntarily assisted by Ptes. W. Sterry, W. Thompson, A. Corville, G. Reed, M. Titch, and S. Parmenter, all stretcher-bearers belonging to the 2nd Battalion. The gallant padre[2] was awarded the V.C.

On April 2 the battalion moved to the Vth Corps' rest area at Pinceboom, being transferred on the 5th to Caestre, and

[1] This officer died in 1927 from the effects of this wound.

[2] The Rev. E. N. Mellish, V.C., M.C., is now (1928) Vicar of Great Dunmow, Essex.

later to La Clytte for work on the Vierstraat switch. At Caestre Major F. A. White, D.S.O., rejoined. Towards the end of the month the battalion moved into the Kemmel trenches and shelters. On the 30th 2nd Lieut. H. Lonsdale was gassed, and slightly wounded, and on May 8, at Lindenhoek, 2nd Lieut. H. W. Wright was also slightly wounded. On May 28 the battalion marched to Caestre, occupying their billets of the previous month. On June 12 the battalion moved to Bailleul and on by rail to St. Omer for divisional training in open warfare. Here the fife and drum band was restarted. The latter half of the month was spent at Nortbecourt.

4th Battalion

At Neuve Chapelle—The Jullundur Brigade supports an attack on Mauquissart—The 4th Battalion joins the 15th Division at Verquin—Christmas at Raimbert—The death of Lieut.-Colonel Cruddas—The battalion transferred to the 33rd Division—Raids—Major Copeman assumes command—The battalion is hurried down to the Somme

On September 25, in conjunction with the main operations at Loos, the Indian Corps offered battle in the neighbourhood of Neuve Chapelle, the Jullundur Brigade supporting an attack by the Meerut Division in the direction of Mauquissart. The 4th Battalion, however, scarcely engaged at all, spent most of the day at Mogg's Hole, 2nd Lieut. C. H. Peart being slightly wounded.

At the end of October the Meerut and Lahore Divisions of the Indian Corps were ordered back to India. On November 14 the 4th Battalion came out of their trenches between the Sunken Road and New Cut Alley, and returned to Croix Barbée. On the following day they marched to Fosse and, travelling by bus to Verquin, joined the 46th Brigade of the 15th Division. After a spell in the line in front of Hohenzollern Redoubt, with the enemy about fifty yards away at the nearest point, the battalion marched to Raimbert and joined the corps reserve. Some excitement was caused one morning early in December, by the Germans suddenly standing up on their parapet and holding up their hands. They had previously sent over a message to the battalion on the left to say that the British would find more comfort as prisoners than as fighters.

This vain display of welcome provided our snipers with a number of excellent targets.

After a month at Raimbert, where Christmas was spent, the 15th Division moved up into the line, the battalion proceeding to Vermelles and occupying trenches between Devon Lane and Wingsway. Early in the morning of January 19 the enemy exploded a mine on our front between Newport and Brecon saps. Two of our men were killed; also six sappers who were buried in the mine shaft. The trench was completely blocked for the space of fifty yards. At nightfall the lip of the crater was manned by bombers.

At 3 a.m. on the 20th Lieut.-Colonel Cruddas went out to view the crater and was shot in the stomach; he was taken to the field ambulance with the utmost despatch, but died three hours later. That evening the battalion marched to Noeux-les-Mines, where he was buried in the presence of a large gathering. Lieut.-Colonel H. W. Cruddas joined the Royal Irish Rifles in 1889, afterwards transferring to the Indian Army. While serving in France with the 41st Dogras he was appointed to the 4th Battalion, by whom he will long be remembered as a most gallant and able commanding officer.

Upon the death of Lieut.-Colonel Cruddas, Captain E. P. Clarke temporarily assumed command of the battalion, which shortly afterwards moved from Noeux-les-Mines into the reserve trenches. On January 27 the enemy delivered an unsuccessful attack, the battalion holding the forward reserve trenches and lending a number of men as stretcher-bearers. Sent up to Loos on the 30th, they found the versatile enemy particularly active with rifle grenades, and adopting the following method of attack. Having prepared a mine under a selected point in our line, the Germans would bombard with rifle grenades, not the selected point, but the trenches on both sides of it. Our men would naturally edge in towards the undisturbed portion, when the Germans would fire the mine. These grenade storms became a great source of annoyance, causing numbers of casualties daily. It was therefore decided to send back ten grenades for every one received. In addition to this, two special "strafes" were organised, four hundred grenades being dropped into the enemy's trenches on each occasion. These reprisals put an end to the trouble.

Heavy and prolonged shelling ushered in the month of

February, the village of Loos and the trenches occupied by the 4th Battalion being subjected to an intense bombardment on the 3rd, shells coming over at the rate of between forty and fifty a minute for no less than seven hours, and rendering the communication trenches absolutely impassable. This was the worst day's shelling the battalion ever experienced. Lieut. K. W. Turner showed both gallantry and coolness in leading his company up into the support line, from cellars in the village, through this tornado of projectiles. Cpl. O. G. Aviss, without waiting for orders, brought his platoon up as well, being subsequently awarded the D.C.M. for acting promptly and upon his own initiative in a difficult situation. During the bombardment the enemy fired a number of incendiary shells, producing a wonderful spectacular effect. Early the next morning the battalion came out of the line, having sustained fifteen casualties only. On February 10 Major A. G. Taylor returned to the battalion and assumed command. On the 18th 2nd Lieut A. G. B. Patten was wounded whilst wiring ; the next day one of our companies made a spirited attack on an enemy sap in an attempt to capture a new trench-digger being used by the Germans.

On February 27 the battalion was transferred from the 15th to the 33rd Division, commanded by Major-General H. J. S. Landon. After inspection in the church square at Noeux-les-Mines by Major-General F. W. N. McCracken (15th Division), they marched to Bethune and joined the 98th Brigade under Brig.-General E. P. Strickland, an officer already well known to them.

On March 17 the battalion proceeded to Annequin, all ranks wearing the new steel shrapnel helmets for the first time. On the following day Major F. W. Turner returned from England and took over command. That evening, during the heavy bombardment of Cambrin, the battalion felt the effects of the tear-shells which fell on the La Bassée road. A week later, while the battalion was in the line in the Cuinchy sector, the enemy sprung a mine in front of " A " Company and close up to their wire. L/Cpl. Pizzey, with Ptes. J. Nunn and D. Cragg, at once occupied the near lip, where they remained the whole day entirely cut off from the front-line trenches, all three being subsequently awarded the M.M.

April passed in ordinary trench routine. During the night

Photo by] [*Adolphus Tear*

LIEUTENANT-COLONEL H. W. CRUDDAS, D.S.O.

of May 13–14, a raid was made by a party from the battalion into the German trenches. The party was drawn from "C" Company, and consisted of thirty-one N.C.O.'s and men, with Captain R. Brunger in charge and Lieut. R. D. Hume as second-in-command. The artillery assisted with a barraging fire to isolate the portion of trench attacked, but the enemy were on the alert and bombed the party before they were able to get into the trench. A hand-to-hand fight ensued on the parapet, the raiding party making good use of their supply of bombs. They were then called off by Captain Brunger and retired in good order, having lost three killed and seven wounded. The raid was so well carried out and under such difficult conditions that the following honours were awarded to those mainly concerned—*D.S.O.:* Captain R. Brunger. *M.C.:* Lieut. R. D. Hume. *M.M.:* L/Sgt. W. Beaden and L/Cpl. G. Webb. About 6.30 p.m. on May 14 the enemy blew another mine in front of the battalion's right fire-trench, "A" Company being again involved. Lieut. H. F. Bond was in command, assisted by Lieut. J. F. L. Fison, who was acting as intelligence officer. The crater, which the Germans had quickly occupied, was effectually cleared, the near lip being consolidated as a sap-head. A wounded German officer was captured, this being the first prisoner to the credit of the battalion. In connection with this raid Lieuts. H. F. Bond and J. F. L. Fison were awarded the M.C., and Sgts. A. Everard and J. Woodward the M.M. The crater was officially named the Ipswich Crater.

In view of an expected push in June, the brigade commander decided to recommend Lieut.-Colonel F. W. Turner—who owing to his wound had had little actual war experience —for the command of a training battalion at home, and on May 22 Major H. C. Copeman, D.S.O., 9th Essex Regiment, arrived and assumed command of the battalion. The next day our artillery carried out several bombardments, doing considerable damage to the enemy's defences and enabling our snipers to inflict a number of casualties through the gaps thus made.

On June 10 Brig.-General Strickland, promoted from the command of the 98th Brigade to that of the 1st Division, bade farewell to the battalion, being succeeded ten days later by Brig.-General F. M. Carleton. The following were mentioned in Sir Douglas Haig's despatches of the King's Birthday, 1916—Lieuts. H. Pretty, F. G. C. Fison, and J. G. Frere; C.S.M. W. Roach.

During this period the 4th Battalion met the 7th Battalion, then at Mazingarbe. On June 18 the former took over trenches in the Givenchy sector. The next day our engineers blew a mine, and two hours later the enemy retaliated with a heavy bombardment, completely burying some of our men. However, after two hours' digging, they were extricated alive without serious injury.

On the morning of June 21 the enemy heavily bombarded the right half of the Suffolk sector, but that night the battalion was relieved by the 1st Royal Welch Fusiliers. Within two hours of the completion of the relief, the enemy blew a series of mines. One of these was sprung near the Duck's Bill, and as a result of the explosion and of the fighting which followed, the Fusiliers lost the greater part of two companies, but succeeded nevertheless in driving out the enemy who had entered their trenches. The 4th Battalion then moved back to Gorre, where their chaplain, the Rev. F. Stone, bade them farewell, being succeeded on the 25th by the Rev. C. F. Gendall. On July 2 they took over some peaceful trenches on the Cuinchy village line, remaining there till the 7th, when the 98th Brigade was relieved and hurried down to the Somme, the 4th Battalion reaching Fricourt on July 14 and bivouacking in a position east of that village.

8th Battalion

At Buire and Albert—Moves up to La Boisselle—Aerial torpedoes and oil-drums—The defence of the mine-shafts—Winkling—Remarkable night-work—Major Hill assumes command—Alongside the French on the Somme—Death of Lieut. F. T. Keats—Working parties and raids

Towards the end of September the 8th Battalion went into divisional reserve at Buire, on the Ancre, where Lieut.-Colonel J. E. F. Dyer, 7th Dragoon Guards, took over command. On October 6th, the battalion was inspected by General Sir Charles Monro, commanding the newly-formed IIIrd Army. On the 7th and 11th respectively 2nd Lieut. J. R. Keats and Lieut. O. S. I. Northcote were slightly wounded.

On November 25 2nd Lieut. F. C. Walker was killed whilst out on day patrol to one of the craters at La Boisselle, having only joined the battalion three days previously.

About this time the command of the 53rd Brigade was taken over by Brig.-General H. J. M. Macandrew. At the beginning of December the battalion again went into divisional reserve at Buire, on the Ancre, and after spending Christmas at Daours returned to the line at La Boisselle. On December 31, just before midnight, the enemy opened fire with artillery, machine-guns, and rifles, apparently for no other purpose than to speed the dying year.

The sector held by the 8th Battalion at La Boisselle straddled the main Albert–Bapaume road, the front line running through the cemetery of La Boisselle village. Situated thus on a *route nationale,* offering a direct line of advance to either of the combatants, the sector possessed considerable tactical and strategic importance. The conformation of the ground in front of Albert led to a curious siting of the trenches in that neighbourhood. On the left of the battalion front the British and German lines were nearly a thousand yards apart, a tour of duty on that flank being regarded almost as a rest cure. But on the right, the repeated efforts of the French to gain possession of the fortified stronghold of La Boisselle village had resulted in drawing the opposing lines nearer and nearer together until they were only a few feet apart. Indeed, when the battalion first arrived there, it was actually possible for British and German sentries to cross bayonets.

Such remarkable proximity led naturally to much mining and bombing activity. When the battalion took over these trenches the ground was already a mere confusion of craters and heaps of broken chalk, and every other day a fresh mine or camouflet was blown, making matters worse. The Germans were also busy with their mortars, lobbing into our trenches every kind of projectile, from the terrifying "oil-drum" to the more deadly aerial torpedo. The latter, larger than a 12-inch shell, was capable of being projected a considerable distance with accuracy. For a hundred of these various missiles to be thrown into the battalion's short length of trench in one day was no unusual experience. As all our available ammunition was being accumulated at other points in the line our reply merely consisted of a few rifle grenades or, as an extreme measure, half a dozen rounds from a 4·5 howitzer firing American ammunition, some of which, remaining strictly neutral, refused to explode.

The mine shafts, constructed by the French in the spring of 1915, added very considerably to the difficulties of this sector. These mines, sunk too far forward, with their defence a matter of vital importance owing to the number of miners working below, necessitated the construction of strong posts at the shaft-heads for their protection. All these, being well-known to the enemy, offered permanent targets for his trench mortars. Moreover, the troops were expected to dispose of the spoil from these mining excavations in such a way as to give no indication to the enemy, though movement of any kind was difficult and dangerous. It may therefore be readily imagined that, even in parts of the line officially reported as quiet, life was often harassing enough.

It was about this time that the type of raid familiarly known as a " winkle " came into vogue. These raids were carried out on a narrow front, the plan being to isolate a small section of the line by means of a box barrage from every available gun. The garrison, taking refuge in their dugouts from the barrage, were quickly surrounded and extracted ignominiously at the point of the bayonet, like winkles on a pin, almost before they had time to realise that a raid was in progress. The 8th Battalion never actually shared this fate, though on one occasion when holding the line in Maricourt wood they were only saved by the foresight of our artillery, who put down an intense protective barrage with such promptness that the raiders were beaten back.

Towards the end of January the battalion took part in a remarkable night operation, carried out between Ovillers-la-Boisselle and the Redan—called Keats' Redan in honour of 2nd Lieut. F. T. Keats, whose platoon held it and organised its defences. On that occasion nearly two whole brigades sallied forth into No Man's Land under cover of darkness and, unobserved by the enemy, constructed before daylight a new trench system six hundred yards in advance of our front line, 1500 yards long and complete with communication trenches and wire, all at a cost of two casualties, one of which was caused by a pickaxe in the process of digging.

On February 7 Lieut.-Colonel J. E. F. Dyer, the popular and able commanding officer, left the battalion, the command being taken over by the former brigade-major of the 53rd Brigade, Lieut.-Colonel G. V. W. Hill, Royal Irish Fusiliers, who continued to lead the battalion until its disbandment in 1918. The only other event worthy of notice during the month occurred on the 20th, when battalion headquarters were shelled continuously for over two hours, to the amusement of the battalion, who might almost be said to have " stood to " to watch the performance. It is a remarkable but well-known psychological fact that soldiers, so often themselves subjected to the appalling conditions of bombardment, would joke when they saw their neighbours in a similar predicament, while the shelling of a superior headquarters was often greeted with hearty laughter.

The early part of March was spent in Franvillers, where some useful training, general smartening up, and recreation afforded the new commanding officer a welcome opportunity of getting to know the officers and men more intimately. Here Major L. C. Arbuthnot, who had been wounded at Loos with the 9th Battalion, joined. On the 14th the battalion marched to Grovetown camp ; a new portion of front was then taken over in Maricourt, and though the trenches were in a shocking state, and even untenable in places, it was a welcome change. The 18th Division was then on the right of the British line and in touch with the French on the Somme. It was in this sector that the battalion earned its first special mention from the brigadier for all-round good work in the line. They had also constructed a bath-house in the brewery, where the whole battalion could bathe in thirty-six hours, though actually in the line.

On March 27 2nd Lieuts. H. J. P. Creagh and A. F. Pullinger were wounded, and Lieut. G. L. M. Fache was slightly wounded, remaining at duty. On the same day the battalion went into divisional reserve at Etinehem. Early in April they returned to Maricourt, remaining there till the 25th, when the whole brigade went out to St. Sauveur for four weeks' training. On May 24 they took over another part of the line in front of Carnoy, where a vast amount of work was done and from which the brigade made a successful attack some weeks later. On May 25 Lieut. F. T. Keats, a gallant and promising officer, was killed by a sniper while reconnoitring some craters in front of our line. For a fortnight in the middle of June the battalion furnished working parties in preparation for the impending Somme offensive, which was to mark the transition from trench fighting to battles of movement. The great increase in our heavy artillery was now becoming apparent everywhere.

From June 23 to 27 the battalion was again in the line and carried out two raids, its first offensive operations. Though neither was a very marked success, some useful information was obtained and several casualties were inflicted on the enemy. In the raid on the 25th 2nd Lieuts. L. H. Kenny and H. W. Whatling were killed. During this tour of duty smoke-screens were used on several occasions. On June 28, while in bed in his billet, 2nd Lieut. E. H. Dixey was wounded by a shell, from the effects of which he died on July 3. The casualties in the battalion during this brief spell amounted to eight officers and seventy-two other ranks killed and wounded. On June 30 the battalion moved from Bray up to Carnoy to act as reserve—practically to two brigades—in the great wearing-out battle that was to open the next morning.

11th Battalion

Making friends with the French people—The death of Brigadier-General Fitton—In the line at Bois Grenier—A trench idyll—Fleurbaix—Nortbecourt—Arrives in the Albert sector.

The 11th Battalion remained one night in camp on St. Martin's hill, overlooking Boulogne, and on January 10 reached Renescure, a village between St. Omer and Hazebrouck, possessing a fourteenth-century château of graceful design destroyed during the war. In their leisure hours the men gave voluntary assistance to the farmers, driving pigs, filling dung-carts, and laughing at the strangeness of the implements employed. " The men are as happy as sandboys," wrote an officer. " They spend a deal of their time in inspecting and passing professional judgments on cattle, poultry, and the like. One stalwart got up two hours before réveillé to-day to admire the way the French women milk. The country is exactly like the fens near Cambridge. It is a queer fact that the war seems further off here than in England. Native life about Renescure appears quite normal, the farms busy and prosperous, the people quite undisturbed and taking everything for granted. The men got their first pay yesterday and were very glad thereof. There was much merriment in neighbouring *estaminets*. Foreign liquor proved too strong for one or two of them, but on the whole they are amazingly virtuous."

Soon after its arrival in France Lieut.-General Sir Rowland Maxwell visited the battalion. His brother, Major A. C. Maxwell, had been second-in-command after the battalion left Cambridge, but was prevented from embarking by serious illness, his place being taken by Major P. F. Morton until the appointment in mid-January of Major W. A. Farquhar, Royal Scots Fusiliers. On January 19 Brig.-General Fitton was wounded while visiting the trenches and died in hospital shortly afterwards. Thus the first casualty in the 101st Brigade was its distinguished commander. On the following day the infantry of the 34th Division were inspected by General Joffre, who was accompanied by Sir Douglas Haig.

The 34th Division now joined the IIIrd Corps, the battalion moving to Morbecque, where on January 24 the 101st Brigade was inspected by its corps commander. In a high-pitched voice, clearly audible to the four thousand men assembled, he told the brigade what was expected of it, concluding with an unforgettable metaphor. "Discipline," said he, "is the root of all training. You should therefore stick to it and thereby climb to the top of the tree."

On the last day of January the battalion moved forward to Vieux Berquin, marching the next day to Erquinghem under a blue sky which happened at the time to be the arena of an air-fight immediately above. The battalion was attached to the 68th Brigade for billets, but on February 2 moved into the trenches, being attached for instruction to the 69th Brigade, who were holding the line about a mile to the south-east of Bois Grenier. Here they remained for five days and sustained their first casualties.

The battalion reached the trenches early in the night, before the bustle of ration parties had subsided. The darkness was continually illuminated, for a thousand Very lights hung from the black velvet sky. Rifle shots and the traversing fire from machine-guns startled the air : monstrous rats came to life from behind the sandbags, scampering boldly along the trenches and splashing through the mud. A door opened, or a sackcloth curtain swung aside, revealing a dugout candle-lit. A patrol was crouching on the parapet, or feeling a way through the wire ; presently it was lost to sight along a line of pollarded willows. A working party was filling sandbags and beating them into position with the flat of their spades. A gust of wind carried the taint of burning coke. Gradually, imperceptibly, the black-and-white pictures of the night were coloured by the sun. A dark phantasmal mass became a hooded farm wagon, derelict. For a space the war slept. By day there was stillness, broken now and then by a sniper firing suddenly through a loophole, or by a bombardment scattering men and things. Day was appallingly prosaic, but night was beautiful and romantic. When the lights shot up into the sky the trenches became like fairyland.

On February 9 the battalion rejoined the 101st Brigade at Morbecque, being billeted on the outskirts of the village not far from Hazebrouck, a centre of amusement. On the 21st they returned to the line at Bois Grenier, where a good many casualties occurred, including Lieut. I. D. Claughton, killed on March 2. After three such tours, with intervals of rest and work, the battalion was relieved and sent back to divisional reserve at Fort Rompu, moving a week later into the brigade reserve at Fleurbaix. On March 13 they were congratulated by the brigade commander, Brig.-General R. C. Gore, on their work in the line, especially that of their snipers, for whose excellent achievements the intelligence officer, 2nd Lieut. W. H. Parker, was mainly responsible.

On the 27th the battalion took over front-line trenches south-east of Fleurbaix village. There had been much snow and cold weather of late, but now a hot sun came out to herald the arrival of an Anzac division from Gallipoli. Handing over to an Australian unit on the 7th, the battalion marched to billets near Sailly, and a few days later, having been allotted to G.H.Q. reserve, reached Nortbecourt forty miles behind the line. From the surrounding hills they could see the sands of Gravelines, and beyond Calais the ships in the Channel.

The relief of the battalion from the Armentières sector,

and the special nature of their subsequent training, pointed to hard times ahead. Life at Nortbecourt was too pleasant to be without omen. It roused their suspicions. Fattening up, some said: true words spoken in jest. The direction of the coming move was soon an open secret. Engineers and pioneers of the 34th Division were already down on the Somme, learning the ground from their opposite numbers. A passing reference in a letter to a statue of the Virgin and Child, leaning down from a cathedral tower, supplied an easy clue; and what censor could say how many soldiers rightfully vaunted the name of Albert?

The long rest came to an end on May 5. A train carried the battalion to Calais and then bore them away into Picardy. On arrival at Amiens they set out in drizzling rain along the straight road to Albert, passing at midnight the IVth Army headquarters at Querrieu, and reaching their destination—La Houssoye—at two o'clock in the morning. Thenceforward, until the hour of attack on July 1, was one long moment of suspense. Every movement of preparation seemed, in some way or other, to foretell the vague immensity of coming events. Rumour and speculative fancy ran wild, supplying the spice of adventure to what was in fact a stern and ugly business. Men spoke always of the great push, which would end when and how none could tell.

On May 9 the battalion moved forward to Bresle, where their brigade was in reserve, the other brigades of the 34th Division being respectively in the line, and in support at Becourt and Dernancourt. On the 19th the battalion went into the support brigade area at the last-named, with two companies under Major Farquhar in Becourt wood. Two days later the battalion took over the right sector of the divisional front, its right resting on the northern end of the Fricourt ridge and the left facing the ruins of La Boisselle. They held this sector for two periods of six days each, with a break of four days of comparative rest. During the first of these periods "A" Company (Captain H. W. Stace) suffered severely, a section of Lieut. P. V. Emrys-Evans' platoon being all but exterminated by a night-time bombardment of canisters, the most pernicious missiles used by the enemy in this part of the line. During the second period the German activity continued unabated, the casualties including 2nd Lieut. A. H.

Wrixon, killed. On one occasion a number of men were so deeply buried by the explosion of a shell that it took two hours to set them free. To these bombardments we were denied the satisfaction of adequate reply, at least in kind, for our batteries, loth to disclose their emplacements, rarely fired through the seventeen hours of daylight.

These twelve days in the line constituted the battalion's first real experience of the tremendous strain of war. After a few days in Bresle they assembled, on June 16, in Becourt wood, where Captain A. K. Bird and Lieut. R. V. Burrowes were both severely wounded. On the 23rd the battalion marched back to a camp behind Albert ; but on the 27th, in readiness for the assault on the 29th, two companies moved up into Becourt wood and the remainder to dugouts on the Usna-Tara ridge. On the 28th the attack was postponed owing to the continued bad weather. On the 30th the whole battalion concentrated in Becourt wood near the château, part of which was used as its headquarters. Though only a thousand yards from the German trenches, this spot seemed far away from the war. The undergrowth round the château was a riot of wild and garden flowers. Dogs barked at the guns, the vagrant cuckoo called to its mate, and nightingales sang through the hours of darkness.

CHAPTER XII

The 1st Battalion in Egypt—The 28th Division goes to Macedonia—Arrives in Salonika, the City of Spies—The retreat from Serbia on Salonika—The advance to the Struma—Ravages of malaria—Operations in the Struma valley—The action of the Karajakoi villages—The capture of Yenikoi—The affair of Barakli Dzuma—The storm-centre travels to lake Doiran

THE 1st Battalion, having disembarked at Alexandria on October 30, found life under canvas in Egypt wonderfully restful after the strain and turmoil of France. The climate was perfect, and the sea bathing greatly appreciated by all. This empyrean spell of peace and quiet on the shores of the blue Mediterranean was, however, destined to be of short duration.

On November 10 camp was moved to a site about a mile to the east of Abu Qir. On the 21st the regimental transport and eight of our officers sailed from Alexandria in H.M.T. *Manitou*, and the following day the battalion left camp in two trains for the same port, embarking in H.M.T. *Anchises*. The latter ship got away in fine weather on the 23rd with over nineteen hundred souls on board, the 1st Suffolk Regiment supplying the ship's staff for the troops as follows—*O.C. Troops:* Lieut.-Colonel Hon. H. E. Joicey. *Adjutant:* Captain J. A. Campbell. *Quartermaster:* Lieut. B. Godbolt. *Sergeant-Major:* A/R.S.M. Nunn. On account of the presence of hostile submarines the vessel steered a very zigzag course; alarm parades were held frequently, and everyone had to drag his life-belt about with him wherever he went. The climate soon began to change; on the 26th rain was encountered, and on the following day the *Anchises* anchored off Salonika in a blizzard. Disembarkation, however, did not take place until the 29th.

Before following further the fortunes of the battalion it will be convenient to review briefly the situation as it stood at the end of November, 1915, when the 28th Division (Major-General C. J. Briggs) landed at Salonika.

In the autumn of 1915 Bulgaria decided to throw in her

lot with the Central Powers, which meant that unless timely assistance could be sent Serbia would be overwhelmed. By treaty this was the duty of Greece, but her ruler, King Constantine, who was secretly under the influence of Germany, did not fulfil the treaty obligations. At the end of September the Allies decided to send help to Serbia, and in October three French divisions and the 10th (Irish) Division from Gallipoli, landed at Salonika, the intention being that this force should advance up the valley of the river Vardar and establish communication with the Serbs. But help had come too late, for the Serbian army had already been practically destroyed, the remnants making for the Adriatic. The force, however, advanced and took up a position from the north of lake Doiran to the Vardar to cover the further landing of troops at Salonika.

During November and December French and British reinforcements continued to arrive, and by the middle of the latter month the force ashore amounted to eight French and five British divisions. Meanwhile the situation at Salonika was full of difficulties and in many respects remarkable. Troops had been landed in neutral territory, and it was impossible to divine what attitude the Greeks themselves would assume. Their army was mobilised and concentrated about twenty miles north of Salonika. The German and Austrian consuls remained, and the town abounded with enemy agents. A train ran daily to Constantinople, an enemy capital.

Such was the state of affairs when the 1st Battalion landed. The blizzard had ended, but the country lay wrapped in snow and the cold was intense. The battalion marched through Salonika—their numbers being carefully checked by enemy agents—to the village of Lembet, where they were crowded into such tents as were available. A day or so later the regimental transport arrived, the animals being dug into the hill-side to afford them some protection from the cold.

On December 6 the Bulgarians attacked the covering force in the positions between lake Doiran and the Vardar. Heavily outnumbered, the three French divisions and the 10th (Irish) Division were driven, after three days' fighting, across the frontier into Greece. It being confidently expected that the enemy would follow up his success by an immediate advance on Salonika, a defensive position to protect the town was hurriedly taken up by the main force, upon which the covering troops withdrew. This position, extending from the gulf of Orfano on the east and describing a semicircle round the north of Salonika on the west, became known as the Birdcage line.

The battalion, still in camp at Lembet, dug feverishly for the next few days. The siting of the line was rendered difficult at the outset by very thick mists, bad maps, and ignorance of the country. No definite information as to the course of events on the frontier was issued. For aught the battalion knew they might have been liable to attack by Bulgarians, Germans, Austrians, or Greeks. As regards the last-named, the battalion was ordered to post picquets by night to give timely warning of any doubtful behaviour on their part, but by day to treat all Greeks as brothers. Their transport, dead animals, and stragglers littered the main road, while their unconventional habits made it difficult to extend to them that welcome which the higher command inculcated.

On December 14 the 84th Brigade (Brig.-General G. A. Weir) struck camp and after following the main Seres road for five or six miles marched across country in a westerly direction, making for a high rocky ridge rising abruptly from the plain beyond the village of Gnoina. On this ridge, which bore a certain resemblance to the rock of Gibraltar, the brigade bivouacked for the night in cold, wet weather. Orders were, however, received for the brigade to return to the Birdcage line the next morning, and soon after midday the battalion halted on the forward slopes of the ridge near the village of Aivatli.

In the event of any attack on the Birdcage position the Gnoina ridge would have proved valuable to the enemy for purposes of observation; hence at first sight it appeared desirable to deny to them such a point of vantage by our own occupation of it. But it was situated so far in front of the Birdcage that troops holding it would have been isolated, besides being exposed in all probability to a heavy concentration of artillery fire. The decision therefore to evacuate it was, no doubt, sound.

The battalion pitched camp on a spur above the village of Aivatli, a position which it was destined to occupy till the following May. Work was immediately started on a new line to the Birdcage. Sited on the forward slopes the front-line trenches were located just high enough up the slope to give an uninterrupted field of fire over the plain. The position was necessarily rather exposed, and entrenching slow on account of the large amount of rock encountered; but as regards artillery observation and infantry field of fire it was excellent, and with a little improvement the numerous ravines provided good communication from front to rear. The battalion spent January, 1916, in daily work on the position, and by the end of that month it was clear that any attack on Salonika could be stubbornly resisted. Early in the year Major R. M. B. Needham, second-in-command, left the battalion to take up the appointment of D.A.A.G., 26th Division, Captain J. A. Campbell, the adjutant, becoming second-in-command in his stead.

Work went on, but no attack came. The enemy having driven back the covering force into Greece, did not exploit his success, but putting the frontier into a state of defence, was content to sit down along it, our mounted troops thrown out well to the front keeping a watchful eye on him. As the Birdcage position neared completion whole days were devoted to battalion training, followed in March and April by brigade exercises. During these months nothing was seen of the enemy beyond an occasional visit from his bombing aeroplanes.

Early in May the 84th Brigade advanced, the battalion camping at Likovan on the Seres road, some five-and-twenty miles from Salonika. Here, when not employed in road-making, they indulged in further training, including one divisional exercise. This training, coupled with hard work, soon bore fruit in the shape of improved efficiency, moral and physical fitness, the last-named unfortunately soon to be undermined by the advance into the malarial valley of the Struma.

On May 22 Major-General H. L. Croker took over the command of the 28th Division from Major-General C. J. Briggs, who had been appointed to that of the XVIth Corps.

Trouble being feared in Salonika, the battalion left Likovan with the 84th Brigade on June 6 and marched to Guvezne, but on the 9th it returned to Likovan, taking part in the advance to the Struma the next day.

As already stated, the Bulgarians had prepared a position along the frontier, constantly watched by us and the Greeks. But in May the Greeks suddenly withdrew from the frontier and, without a word of warning, handed over Fort Rupel and several others with all their warlike stores to the enemy, one Greek army corps actually taking active service with the Central Powers. The Allies therefore issued an ultimatum to Greece insisting on the demobilisation of the Greek army.

The advance to the Struma was carried out on a broad front and under trying conditions. Brigade groups moved across hilly country, the roads for the transport being constructed day by day. The weather had now become very hot, with the usual accompaniment of flies and mosquitoes. The men had no protection from the sun beyond that afforded by their bivouacs, and mosquito nets had not yet been provided.

On July 7 the battalion relieved the 1st Welch Regiment in the right sector of the brigade outpost line. This sector, seven and a half miles long, was held by the battalion without incident beyond occasional sniping until the end of the month.

It was during this period that the ravages of malaria began. In many cases whole battalions were reduced in a few days to a strength of perhaps fifty effectives. Medical units, themselves stricken, were at first unable to cope with the influx of sick. The battalion, thanks to the excellent work of its medical officer, Captain McNicol, and its own preventive measures, fared considerably better than other units, its strength never falling below four hundred ; it was thus able to render valuable help by providing hospital orderlies for the field ambulances, as well as a proportion of drivers for the small arms section of the ammunition column.

On July 31 the battalion left the Struma valley for the hills, arriving on August 2 at the 64th kilometre stone on the Salonika–Seres road, near which it remained for more than a fortnight. About August 10 rumours of a proposed offensive reached the battalion, but while the preparations were being made the enemy, anticipating us, suddenly took the offensive himself. The principal blow was directed against the Serbs on the left of the Allies, but on the right he advanced through Demirhissar to the Struma. On August 19 the battalion was rushed down to the Struma valley to support the 2nd East Yorkshire Regiment of the 83rd Brigade which was holding the bridge-head at Orljak, and two days later took over the bridge-head defences of that place.

The battalion was now in close touch with the enemy, but although mutual shelling and patrol encounters took place daily there was no actual engagement until September 10. At about 5 p.m. on that day the 2nd Northumberland Fusiliers attacked the village of Nevoljen, two platoons of "C" Company, 1st Suffolk Regiment, under Lieut. J. C. Parsons, acting as right flank guard. The Fusiliers captured the village without much difficulty, but an hour later, being driven out by a most vigorous and determined counter-attack, withdrew to their original line, our two platoons conforming.

The remainder of September was spent in minor engagements, generally arranged to draw the enemy under the fire of our artillery. Our position conferred upon us the advantage of perfect observation: it was, in fact, a gunner's paradise. The plain of the Struma valley is here from six to eight miles wide, the river running close in to the foothills on our side. The infantry were holding approximately the line of the river. Our artillery, cleverly sited along the higher ground, enjoyed a magnificent field of view and fire, whereas the enemy, having advanced to positions near the river line, had all his artillery out on the plain.

In October the battalion took part in larger operations in the Struma valley. At this time the French and Serbs were launching an offensive with the object of taking Monastir, the three British divisions on the Struma (10th, 27th, and 28th) assisting by threatening the Rupel Pass, thus pinning down the enemy's reserves and preventing their transference to meet the advance of the French and Serbs.

In accordance with the general plan our advance began with the 27th Division on the right taking the villages of Karajakoi Zir and Karajakoi Bala, followed up early on the morning of October 3 by an attack by the 30th Brigade (10th Division) on the larger village of Yenikoi, situated on the left of the other two. The 1st Suffolk Regiment—the right battalion of the 28th Division—was ordered to co-operate in this attack by capturing some enemy trenches a little to the north of the Salonika–Seres road between the 78th and 79th kilo stones, and afterwards to link up with the 30th Brigade at Yenikoi.

The attack of the 30th Brigade, assisted by armoured cars in action on the road, began at 5.30 a.m. An hour later "A" Company (Captain I. G. Owen), supported by "B" Company (Captain T. Stubbings), advanced, and before eight o'clock these two companies had established themselves in a position on the line of the road about the 79th kilo stone, in touch with the 30th Brigade. "C" and "D" Companies occupied Mazirko, a village about half a mile in front of our main trench line.

During the forenoon the enemy launched a strong counter-attack against Yenikoi and the two forward Suffolk companies. As this attack threatened to envelope our left flank two companies of the 23rd Welch Pioneers who were busy wiring were employed to prolong the line to the left. The Suffolk and Welch battalions were now holding the line of the road from the 79th kilo stone to Mazirko, with their left flank refused. The counter-attack was repulsed with very heavy loss to the enemy, a large proportion of their casualties being due to the accuracy of our artillery fire. Shortly afterwards the enemy, who had been shelling heavily since the attack began, succeeded in breaking Orljak bridge, thereby interrupting temporarily our communication with the right bank of the Struma.

At 4 p.m. the enemy subjected Yenikoi to a sudden intense bombardment, forcing the 30th Brigade to evacuate the village and withdraw to its original line. In accordance with orders issued in anticipation of this eventuality "A" and "B" Companies conformed, retiring in good order on Mazirko. The 30th Brigade having been ordered to retake Yenikoi, two Suffolk companies—"C" (2nd Lieut. E. Clemson) and "D" (Captain D. R. A. Eley)—advanced at 7.30 p.m. according to the original plan. It was now dark, and the Bulgarians, finding we had retired, were apparently closing in on Yenikoi, for "C" Company encountered a body of them before reaching the 79th kilo stone. This company, gallantly led by 2nd Lieut. Clemson, immediately charged with the bayonet, drove them off, and took up a position at the 79th kilo stone. "C" Company sustained several casualties, including 2nd Lieut. J. D. Wiles killed, but they inflicted heavier losses on the enemy, and their determined advance secured the flank of the 30th Brigade. For this action 2nd Lieuts. Clemson and Sturdy received the Military Cross.

During the night of October 3–4 " C " and " D " Companies were again ordered to retire on Mazirko, this being accomplished without interference from the enemy. Before dawn " B " and " D " Companies moved out yet again to the 79th kilo stone, but the enemy having learned a lesson had now withdrawn some four or five miles towards the foothills on his side of the plain. Unfortunately we were not strong enough to follow up our success.

Thus ended what must have been one of the most spectacular battles of the war. Those who had the good fortune to be spectators on the hills in rear of our position had the whole battle-plain spread out like a panorama in front of them. The enemy sustained about five thousand casualties; those of the battalion amounted to no more than eighty, including some half-dozen officers. Of these 2nd Lieut. J. D. Wiles was killed as already stated; 2nd Lieuts. N. de H. Hall and C. U. Kilner died of their wounds on the 7th and 8th respectively.

On the night of October 4–5 the battalion, having been relieved by the 2nd Buffs, marched to Orljak ravine, remaining there until the 10th, when it proceeded to Idris Mah (Mahalesi) and took over a sector of the defences from the 2nd Northumberland Fusiliers. On the 12th the battalion marched to Orljak bridge, where with other troops it was inspected by H.R.H. The Crown Prince of Serbia. The next day, on a parade held at the same place, the following awards were made for gallantry during the operations of October 1–5—*M.C.:* 2nd Lieuts. E. Clemson and J. R. Sturdy. *M.M.:* Sgt. H. Long; A/Cpls. J. Barratt and G. Davey; Pte. G. Harrington.

At the end of October the battalion left Idris Mah and relieved the 2nd King's Own (83rd Brigade) at Elisan, a village in the Struma plain and now forming part of our front line. The 83rd Brigade on our left was preparing for an attack on a large village to their front, named Barakli Dzuma, which the Bulgarians were holding strongly. The objects of this attack were much the same as those of the recent operations in the Struma valley; and in order to make the advance appear to be on as wide a front as possible the 1st Suffolk Regiment was ordered to co-operate on the right of the 83rd Brigade by seizing the village of Kumli, occupying it lightly, and retiring on Elisan if seriously attacked.

Early on the morning of October 31 the advance commenced. Two companies of the 1st Battalion, under Major J. A. Campbell, attacked Kumli and drove the enemy out of it with the loss of only one man killed. About twenty prisoners were taken, the remainder of the garrison escaping. Lieut. Palmer's platoon was then posted in the village, the remainder of the two companies returning to Elisan. A section of R.F.A. was placed between Elisan and Kumli to assist in creating the impression that we had really occupied the latter village.

Meanwhile the 83rd Brigade had captured Barakli Dzuma with over three hundred prisoners, and though counter-attacks were eagerly awaited, none came. In a Chinese *Book of War,* dating from about 500 B.C., it is written: "If a victory be gained by a certain stratagem, do not repeat it: vary the stratagem." The truth of this still holds, and the Bulgar realised it. However, during the afternoon, though suspicious of the situation at Kumli, he advanced warily on that village. As he approached, 2nd Lieut. Palmer withdrew his platoon on Elisan, the two field-guns conforming according to plan. The teams had to go out from Elisan to fetch the guns, and both the section and the platoon were shelled briskly during the withdrawal.

On November 4 Major J. A. Campbell left the battalion to take up the appointment of brigade-major to the 66th Brigade, XIIth Corps, Captain D. R. A. Eley becoming second-in-command.

During November minor operations arranged in conjunction with the attack on Monastir by the French and Serbs were carried out by troops of the 28th and 10th Divisions, and on the 16th the battalion was detailed to storm the village of Barakli. Leaving Elisan at three o'clock in the morning the battalion, covered by a screen of scouts under 2nd Lieut. Durrands, marched to a point 1200 yards south of Barakli. At 6.30 a.m. the attack began, the front line (Captain Eley) consisting of "A" Company (Captain Owen) and "D" Company (2nd Lieut. Lee); and the second line (Captain Stubbings) consisting of "B" Company (2nd Lieut. Palmer) and

"C" Company (Captain Clemson). Detachments of other regiments delivered covering fire, at a range of about a thousand yards, from positions in the direction of Barakli Dzuma. After some resistance the enemy decamped hurriedly, leaving the village in the hands of the battalion, with twelve dead, three wounded and a machine-gun. The casualties were very slight, but included 2nd Lieuts. H. Bradon killed and H. V. Lee mortally wounded. 2nd Lieut. Bradon had only received his commission overnight.

As the Bulgars showed no inclination to counter-attack, and our reserves were inadequate to enable us to tackle their stronger positions near the foothills, operations practically ceased. Even if the enemy were at first deceived into thinking that our advance in early October was a determined stroke at the Rupel Pass, they must by this time have realised that we were not in a position to do more than threaten. However, the troops in this part of the line were not called upon for further offensive action, for the main stroke on the left flank was progressing well, and on November 19 Monastir fell into the hands of the French and Serbs, thus bringing these operations to a successful conclusion. No fighting of any importance took place in the Struma valley during the remainder of the campaign, the scene of activity being transferred to the XIIth Corps front between lake Doiran and the river Vardar, where trench warfare conditions had already settled in.

CHAPTER XIII

Six Suffolk Battalions on the Somme and another in the Lens area—The 8th Battalion at Albert—Bazentin—Delville Wood—Distinguishes itself at Thiepval—The Ancre Heights—Schwaben Redoubt—Miraumont, or the battle of Boom Ravine—Gallantry of L/Cpl. Savage—Resurrection Trench —Arras

IN the battles of the Somme, which it will be remembered began on July 1, 1916, and lasted till November 18, the main opening attack was delivered by the British on a front of between fifteen and sixteen miles, employing thirteen divisions, with another six in close reserve, two of which came into action the same day. The principal effort was made by Rawlinson's IVth Army on a front of about ten miles between the river Somme and its tributary the Ancre. In the battles of the Somme, 1916, the British sustained approximately 405,000 casualties.

Although six battalions of the county regiment earned this great battle honour only two were engaged in the first day's fighting, namely, the 8th Battalion, belonging to the 18th Division (Major-General F. I. Maxse), XIIIth Corps (Lieut.-General W. N. Congreve); and the 11th Battalion of the 34th Division (Major-General E. C. Ingouville-Williams), IIIrd Corps (Lieut.-General Sir W. P. Pulteney). At that time the 7th Battalion were moving up towards Ovillers, the other three battalions, namely, the 2nd, 4th, and 9th, being about St. Omer, La Bassée, and Poperinghe respectively. It will be appropriate to deal with these Suffolk battalions in the order of their arrival in the battle zone, which is that given above. Our attention is therefore primarily directed towards the 18th and 34th Divisions.

The 8th Battalion, not being one of the battalions ear-marked for the attack on July 1, held front-line trenches immediately prior to that date during the preliminary bom-bardment, by far the heaviest the troops had yet witnessed. In particular, trench-mortar shells—of the football type used for cutting the enemy's wire—were now to be seen in the air by the dozen at a time, a most exhilarating sight.

On July 1, at 7.30 a.m., after a final hour of exceptionally heavy bombardment—to quote Sir Douglas Haig—our infantry attack was launched. Mines were exploded and smoke discharged, and the infantry began moving forward through the hostile barrage. Before noon Montauban had been carried by the division on the extreme right of the British line, and shortly afterwards the high ground surrounding the village, as well as the Briqueterie, had fallen to the 18th Division. The 8th Battalion, being in brigade reserve, did not take a very active part in the attack, since they were not called upon to support it ; nevertheless they did much excellent work in the way of carrying up material, ammunition, and water on their two-brigade frontage, in recognition of which they received a congratulatory message from the G.O.C. 55th Brigade. Their casualties for the day, hardly exceeding a score, included 2nd Lieut. D. R. Williams, wounded. The next morning the battalion took over almost the whole of the 53rd Brigade front, and were afforded the rare opportunity of witnessing a desperate battle (for Contalmaison and Mametz wood), on a majestic scale, taking place less than a mile away in their immediate front without being involved themselves, or even disturbed by fire. On the 5th the battalion brought in the first of its war trophies—a 77 mm. field-gun. Two days later, as they were passing Bronfay Farm, they met the 2nd Battalion going up. The drums of the latter played the regimental march as each company went by, an act of comradeship and chivalry which was stirringly appreciated by all ranks of the 8th Battalion.

On the 14th the battalion was again in the line, along the eastern edge of Bernafay wood, the 53rd Brigade having been lent to another division with the object of attacking Guillemont and Ginchy. This attack, three times postponed, was finally abandoned owing to the loss of the village of Longueval and the greater part of Delville wood, the forming-up points for the proposed assault. On July 16 Major S. W. Ford and Captain R. U. E. Knox, D.S.O., were wounded.

At midnight on July 18–19 the 53rd Brigade was unexpectedly launched, at very short notice and without reconnaissance, in a most unenviable counter-attack designed with the object of clearing the village and wood. The jumping-off line was to be Princes Street, in the village of Longueval. By the time the brigade had assembled and the necessary orders had been issued it was already dawn. The two miles of open country which stretched between it and the objectives had therefore to be traversed in broad daylight, with every available German gun trained on the assaulting troops. This was the battalion's first experience of open warfare. Deploying as soon as they came under machine-gun fire, they moved forward with fine courage. Princes Street was already in the hands of the enemy. The leading companies, under Major A. H. Catchpole and Captain A. Wood respectively, advancing with determination, encountered strong resistance near the church in Longueval village. Both company commanders were wounded and heavy casualties sustained. After a day of fierce fighting the remnants of these two companies, under 2nd Lieut. G. L. Crandon, consolidated their position. Major P. C. Bull, getting his company into a part of the line where the enemy looked like breaking through, managed to dig in and hold on. During this action Captain S. W. Card was wounded, Captain G. L. M. Fache succeeding him as adjutant. The Rev. J. B. Fraser rendered yeoman service to the wounded and was awarded the D.S.O. Captain Pratt, the medical officer, worked unceasingly under fire, receiving the M.C. The battalion runners acquitted themselves admirably. The sunken road at the entrance to the village was an absolute shambles. Here Major J. C. Markes, the brigade major, was killed while with the battalion.

Though this counter-attack was unsuccessful, the line in the village was advanced about three hundred yards, and the dangerous bottle-neck entrance to Delville wood considerably widened—an important gain, having regard to the fact that the wood was garrisoned by more than three battalions whose only line of entrance and egress lay through this bottle-neck. At the end of this costly engagement units were naturally very much mixed up; different, indeed, was the scene now compared with three days before when officers of the battalion were reconnoitring there.

On the evening of the 19th orders were received to consolidate those portions of the village and wood which we had succeeded in regaining. The next day a fresh attack, described later on, was delivered by the 76th Brigade. Early in the morning of the 21st the 53rd Brigade was relieved and glad to be quit of a most unpleasant locality. One incident only is worthy of recall. Before dawn on the 21st two parties of the enemy were seen approaching one of our forward trenches, one showing signs of surrender and the other hostility. No risks were taken ; both parties were fired on and none seen to return. The casualties in the battalion were considerable, amounting to 8 officers and 230 other ranks. Captain J. W. Lack died of wounds, and 2nd Lieut. A. H. Page was killed, the wounded including Major A. H. Catchpole, Captain S. W. Card (Adjutant), Captain A. Wood, and 2nd Lieuts. C. S. Foulsham, H. C. Crosher, and V. N. Rawes. The following decorations were awarded—*D.S.O.:* Major P. C. Bull. *D.C.M.:* L/Cpl. A. J. Knights. *M.M.:* Sgts. C. E. Catchpole and J. Mason ; Cpl. G. Swan ; Ptes. Thurlow and Leader ; Drummers Himpson and Hines.

On relief, the battalion proceeded to a camp on the Bray–Albert road, and thence by rail and road to Godewaersvelde, where it remained for a week. The whole of August and the early part of September were spent in training at various places, such as Estaires, Bailleul, Bouzincourt, and Forceville, practising at the last-named for a forthcoming attack on Thiepval and the Schwaben redoubt, in readiness for which the battalion took over—on September 24—a portion of the line just south of Thiepval. This attack, now fixed for September 26, had been very carefully rehearsed by the whole battalion over specially prepared trenches, the actual ground being reconnoitred by as many of them as possible. In fact, no stone had been left unturned, from the division to the battalion, to make the operation a success.

The IInd Corps attack was carried out by the 11th Division (right) and the 18th Division (left) ; that of the 18th Division by the 53rd Brigade (right) and the 54th Brigade (left) ; and that of the 53rd Brigade by the 8th Suffolk Regiment (right) and the 10th Essex Regiment (left). The 8th Battalion were therefore in the forefront of the battle. Zero hour was fixed for 12.35 p.m. Their objectives were firstly, Schwaben trench ; secondly, Zollern trench ; and thirdly, Medway trench and part of Schwaben redoubt. "A" Company (Captain Angier) and "D" Company (Captain Keats) were the assaulting companies, "B" Company (Captain Usher) and "C" Company (Captain Sanctuary) being in support and reserve respectively.

Throughout the morning the enemy's position was shelled continuously. As soon as the barrage started the whole battalion moved forward, the two companies in rear striving to get north of the Hindenburg trench at the earliest possible moment, that being the line on which the hostile barrage generally fell. This plan worked admirably, "C" Company gaining the original British front line without a single casualty. Within six minutes Joseph trench, together with a large number of prisoners, had been captured, and after another similar period the first objective had been carried. Well within an hour the leading companies, following the barrage closely, had captured the second objective, where they were halted until the assault of the final objective began—the only hitch in the plan from the point of view of the 8th Battalion. At 2.14 p.m. the advance was resumed. Desperate fighting ensued, and after the leading companies had pushed on another 250 yards the advance was definitely held up by heavy machine-gun fire from both flanks. "A small party, under 2nd Lieut. S. H. Mason, even reached a point well in advance of the battalion and started to dig themselves in under heavy fire from Medway and Bulgar trenches. They hung on till 6.30 p.m., though Mason was killed and several of his men were killed and wounded."[1] However, before midnight the consolidation of Zollern trench had been completed, and several strong points established at places previously selected.

At 1 p.m. on the 28th the attack was renewed; "B" and "C" Companies participated, the other two being left behind to hold Zollern trench. Their objectives were, firstly, Bulgar trench, and secondly, part of Schwaben redoubt. The first was quickly carried, but the fighting then became very stubborn, and it was not until half-past two that all the objectives had been gained and touch on both flanks established. The next evening the battalion went by bus to billets in Forceville. In these operations they captured some trench mortars, machine-guns, and automatic rifles; their casualties amounted to over two hundred, including the following officers—*Killed:* 2nd Lieuts. H. Grimble, G. S. Long, and S. H. Mason. *Died of wounds:* Captain C. L. Sanctuary. *Wounded:* 2nd Lieuts. W. P. Ballantine and J. Hannaford; Captain O. G. Parry-Jones, R.A.M.C.

[1] *The 18th Division in the Great War* (Blackwood).

The 8th Battalion may well be proud of their share in the desperate battle of Thiepval, perhaps their greatest achievement. The Commander-in-Chief personally visited the divisional commander to express his appreciation, and congratulatory messages were received from the Reserve Army, Second Army, and IInd Corps commanders, that from the last-named running as follows :

From Lieut.-General C. W. Jacob, commanding IInd A.C., to the 18th Division.

"The Corps Commander wishes to thank you and all ranks of your division for their admirable work to-day. Thiepval has withstood all attacks on it for exactly two years, and it is a great honour to your division to have captured the whole of this strongly fortified village at their first attempt. Hearty congratulations to you all."

The battalion remained out of the line at Forceville, Candas, Heuzecourt, and Albert till October 14, when they took over trenches near Courcelette. An attack on Regina trench, arranged for the 16th, was postponed owing to bad weather until the 21st, when the battalion was relieved.

On November 3, after a short spell in the line, they returned to Albert. That morning one of the battalion's patrols captured four prisoners under circumstances which called forth special praise from the corps and the division. On November 19 the 53rd Brigade began marching back to a rest area near Abbeville, the battalion proceeding to Hautvillers, reached on the 27th, where they stayed for the remainder of the year training. On the way to the rest area from the line the 8th Suffolk Regiment was inspected by the Army Commander, who remarked that he had not seen a battalion in France with better march discipline.

After Christmas the battalion marched to Neuilly l'Hôpital, returning to the Albert sector at Aveluy on January 15 and taking over trenches between Miraumont and Sixteen Roads on the 27th. The weather was frosty and the ground covered with snow, rendering digging most difficult. On January 10 2nd Lieut. H. H. Willson died from the effects of a bombing accident.

The frontage held by the battalion was about three-quarters of a mile in length, and consisted of a chain of posts, there being no trenches. From dusk till dawn the whole length of front was patrolled by two trained parties of scouts. Excellent work was done by the battalion snipers, a forward post having been found from which fire could be brought on to an exposed portion of enemy trench, resulting in sixteen known casualties in four days. This provoked the Germans to make a determined raid, and on February 1 a strong party sallied forth from their trenches, but owing to the gallantry and prompt action of 2nd Lieut. R. C. Bolingbroke they were driven off and balked of their purpose, one of the raiders being wounded and captured. In this affair Pte. C. Cornwell of the battalion scouts greatly distinguished himself. Two days later the battalion went into brigade support at Warwick huts, furnishing working parties. Then, after a few days at Varennes, they took over front-line trenches at Boom ravine, opposite Grandcourt, on the 15th.

On February 17 the advance towards Miraumont began, the 18th Division (Major-General R. P. Lee) with two others delivering the attack at 5.45 a.m. The operations of this and the following day, known officially as the actions of Miraumont, but to the 8th Battalion as the battle of Boom ravine, were carried out under very trying weather conditions, the severe frost which had lasted for a month suddenly breaking on the eve of the battle and a rapid thaw converting the ground into a morass of the worst description. Very few duck-board tracks existed there at the time, and the nearest huts being over two miles from the front line, the carrying parties had a most difficult task. The process of forming up for the attack had to be carried out at night in a thick mist and under a hostile barrage as well—zero hour having become known (treacherously it was alleged) to the enemy.

The battalion gained its objectives quickly in spite of stubborn fighting in front of the uncut wire, and the leading waves succeeded in establishing themselves within a few hundred yards of Petit Miraumont. The work of consolidation was rendered less difficult by the mist, which prevented enemy observation and permitted freer movement across the open than was normally possible.

In this action, which reflected the greatest credit on all ranks of the 8th Battalion, one incident stands out conspicuously. Seeing his company held up by wire, L/Cpl. W.

Savage with seven men having discovered a small gap therein, rushed fearlessly through into the enemy's trench, killing with his own hand the first four Germans he met and effecting the surrender of the rest of the party, which consisted of fourteen men with a machine-gun. L/Cpl. Savage was decorated with a D.C.M. The casualties in the battalion amounted to 130, including the following officers—*Killed:* 2nd Lieuts. A. Hubbard, C. E. Bird, and L. H. Walters. *Wounded:* Captains J. R. Keats and T. H. Whitehead; Lieut. A. S. Jeffery. This victory marked the beginning of the retreat to the Hindenburg line.

After spending a few days at Wellington Huts, Aveluy, the battalion returned to trenches between Petit Miraumont and Pys on March 3. On the 6th, as a preliminary to the storming of the village of Irles, the battalion attacked and captured Resurrection trench. Their casualties, which were remarkably slight, included 2nd Lieut. V. N. Rawes, wounded. The battalion then went into brigade reserve, with headquarters at Zollern redoubt, remaining there till after the capture of Irles on the 10th, when they went off on one of those well-known circular tours, designed as a relief from the strain, tedium, and immobility of trench warfare. This tour included a stay of three weeks in Ham-en-Artois, after which the battalion began moving south, returning to Arras at the end of April.

11TH BATTALION

Albert—The 11th Battalion sustains the heaviest casualties in the 34th Division—Captain Brown repeatedly distinguishes himself—Pozières—The Intermediate line—Bois Grenier—Death of Captain Brown—Roclincourt

The only other Suffolk battalion engaged in the bloody fighting of July 1 was the 11th, belonging to the 34th Division, whose position in the front of attack was opposite the village of La Boisselle, with the 8th Division on its left and the 21st on its right. The 34th and 8th Divisions, the latter of which lost the appalling total of 5500 men on the Somme, formed the IIIrd Corps (Lieut.-General Sir W. P. Pulteney).

Most of the divisions in Rawlinson's Army had had much experience of former fighting. The 34th was yet untried, and for them July 1 was a grand and terrible occasion. At five o'clock that morning the 11th Battalion began issuing from Becourt wood and moving towards its jumping-off places. At 7.28 a.m. a mine, containing 80,000 lbs. of ammonal, was fired opposite the left of the 101st Brigade, and two minutes later the assault was launched.

The 11th Battalion, following the 10th Lincoln Regiment, was in the left rear of the brigade, its line of advance running through the centre of Bailiff Wood. It soon became evident that the enemy in La Boiselle were in great strength, for they were able not only to resist the onslaught of the 102nd Brigade on both flanks of the village, but also to maintain a tremendous machine-gun fire on the 101st Brigade on the right of the 102nd from the very moment of leaving its assembly trenches. Before the leading wave had advanced a hundred yards, before the men had time to shake out to their correct intervals and gain their proper formation, casualties began. Soon men were being spun round and were dropping everywhere. A company commander, who was wounded, wrote : " My very last memory of the attack is the sight of Gilson in front of me, and C.S.M. Brooks on my right, both moving as if on parade, and both a minute or two later to be mortally hit."

In spite of casualties, the advance continued until the lines of men had been reduced to bands of three and four. These, joining themselves together without regard to company or battalion, pushed on into the thick of the fight. What more was possible ?

By eight o'clock in the morning the issue of the battle, as far as the battalion was concerned, was practically decided, and to the wounded who lay out that day on the battlefield all that can have seemed to remain of their effort was the great mass of prostrate figures which formed as it were a diagram of forward movement, thinning gradually towards the enemy and tapering here and there where some two or three had contrived to reach the edge of the German wire.

Throughout the day little rushes were attempted by survivors, many of whom must have been already wounded. Occasionally a man was seen running singly till he fell. One particularly fine effort was directed by a dozen men against a part of the German trenches known as the Heligoland redoubt. They sprang suddenly, as it seemed, to life, and dashed forward at a sharp pace, only to be burnt to death by a discharge of flame-throwers as they breasted the parapet. The sight of their crumpled figures, staggering back from the tongues of flame and smoke, tearing hopelessly at their burning clothes, and then falling one by one was terrible to behold.

During the night of the 1st–2nd a message was received from Captain O. H. Brown of the 11th Battalion that he was in Wood alley with a score of Suffolks and a couple of hundred men of other units in the brigade. Owing to their own gallantry, and to the magnificent example set by Captain Brown, assisted by Lieut. Robson, 15th Royal Scots, these troops were able to establish and consolidate themselves in Wood alley, covering the left flank of the 21st Division. It was not until 1 a.m. on the 3rd that a reinforcement of about four hundred of the brigade was collected at Bellevue farm and sent to Colonel Sir George McCrae, commanding the 16th Royal Scots, who had taken charge of all 34th Division troops in the neighbourhood of Wood alley and Scots redoubt. This reinforcement included about 140 Suffolks, under 2nd Lieut. W. M. Fiddian, all of whom did splendid work. At 2 a.m. on July 4 the 101st Brigade was relieved by the 69th Brigade, marching back to Becourt wood and thence to Long valley. Major Wright thus describes the return of Captain Brown : " By 8 a.m. on the 4th Brown had brought his men back to Becourt wood. When they had rested a little he marched them on to a camp in Long valley, in the hills a mile west of Albert. Covered with the grime of the past three days, his torn sleeve revealing the same bandage that had been roughly fixed in No Man's Land, he rode at their head mounted on Eliza, a half-blind mare, the most obstinate and ungainly of the officers' chargers. Whenever he turned back to inspect the fours of his column they cheered him loudly." What finer tribute could be paid to any man ?

The casualties sustained by the 11th Battalion in the battle of Albert were the largest of any single battalion in the division, and amounted to 691 of all ranks, including the following eighteen officers—*Killed :* Lieut. R. Q. Gilson ; 2nd Lieuts. A. W. McGain, A. A. McLean, S. Thomas. Also Captain I. A. Mack, 11th Suffolk Regiment, commanding 101st T.M.B. (not included in total). *Wounded :* Major P. F. Morton ; Captains C. L. Morgan, J. W. Wootton, and O. H. Brown (at duty) ; Lieuts. G. N. Seddon, G. R. Hattersley,

N. B. Bagenal, and P. V. Emrys-Evans; 2nd Lieuts. H. A. Shaw, C. O. F. Jenkin, J. C. Durham, and F. C. Shaw. *Missing (killed)*: 2nd Lieuts. D. J. Darley and J. D. Weston.

The Germans, who had long expected this attack, had made very thorough preparations to meet it. Villages, such as La Boisselle, had been fortified above and below ground. The trenches were connected by underground passages, with roomy dugouts of a depth and strength to shelter men and machine-guns from the heaviest bombardment. Pulleys and slides had been installed in the dugout shafts to enable the machine gunners to bring their guns instantly into action. Indeed, the quickness with which the Germans manned their battle stations on July 1 had all the semblance of black magic.

On July 5 the battalion marched to Henencourt wood, where they remained with the rest of the 101st Brigade for some days. On the 6th Major W. A. Farquhar left the battalion on appointment to the command of the 20th Northumberland Fusiliers, Captain Tuck succeeding him as second-in-command, and handing over the adjutancy to 2nd Lieut. W. H. Parker. Large drafts arrived from various units about this time, and once more the battalion was complete in numbers, but in numbers only: the work of reconstitution remained.

While making a reconnaissance near Mametz wood on July 22 Major-General E. C. Ingouville-Williams, C.B., D.S.O., the brave and chivalrous commander of the 34th Division, was caught in a bombardment and killed. The loss was widely mourned, and all who attended his funeral at Warloy cemetery experienced those sensations of respect and attachment which did not die at Quebec or Corunna. Three days later he was succeeded by Major-General C. L. Nicholson (now Major-General Sir Lothian Nicholson, K.C.B.), who remained in command of the 34th Division until March, 1919.

On July 30 the battalion marched to Becourt wood, and on the last day of the month into the line a little north of Bazentin-le-Petit. On August 3 the line taken up by the 101st Brigade faced north, with a frontage of about eight hundred yards, the left resting on the Bazentin-le-Petit–Martinpuich road, two hundred yards north of the former village. The enemy line, known as the Intermediate trench, lay about two hundred yards north of the British line. The Germans held the western half of the trench and the British the eastern. On the same day 2nd Lieut. V. K. Mason was killed in the trenches. On the 4th, at 1 a.m., the 101st Brigade attacked the Intermediate trench but without success. Only four companies, two from the 11th Suffolk Regiment and two from the 16th Royal Scots, were detailed for the assault and only one company, "B" of the 11th Suffolk Regiment, actually carried it out. Gallantly led and skilfully handled by Captain O. H. Brown, "B" Company captured their objective at the scheduled hour and consolidated and held on to it until ordered to withdraw at the approach of daylight when it was certain that support would not be forthcoming. The withdrawal was successfully conducted under the adroit supervision of Captain Brown, who was among the last to leave the captured position. The casualties, numbering nearly a hundred, included 2nd Lieut. M. Tallon, missing (believed killed), and 2nd Lieuts. A. C. Mason and J. D. Maxwell, wounded. In the evening the battalion was relieved, two companies going into trenches south of Bazentin-le-Petit wood and the remainder into trenches in Mametz wood.

On the evening of August 5 Lieut. F. L. Tempest, with ten volunteer bombers from each company, proceeded to the line held by the 15th Royal Scots due north of Bazentin-le-Grand. An attack, carried out by the bombers of these two battalions, was successfully launched and three or four bays were gained without serious opposition. Then hostile artillery fire, together with pineapple bombs from automatic *grenatenwerfer*, came down on the attackers, putting the leading section out of action. These "pineapples," accurately discharged as usual, blew up a large part of our supply of bombs and drove our party back. A critical situation was saved by Sgt. Negus, L/Cpl. Cave, Ptes. Taylor and Cockerton, and one or two others—all highly skilled bombers who knew how to play a losing game. Pte. Cockerton was wounded early in the fight, but carried on until wounded again. The second wound cost him both his legs. Early next morning the party returned having lost in killed and wounded more than half their number. Thus ended the third out of the six separate attempts made by units of the 34th Division to clear the Intermediate trench.

On the 12th 2nd Lieuts. W. Curtis and R. J. Coles were killed, and the next day Captain A. E. Seddon was wounded. The fighting in which the battalion had been involved since the end of July became known officially as the battle of Pozières. It was the last of the Somme battles of 1916 at which they were present, for in mid-August they moved out of the Albert sector, reaching Erquinghem on the 20th, and going thence into the Bois Grenier line, where they remained for the rest of the year.

On September 3 Major Tuck assumed temporary command of the battalion in the place of Colonel Somerset, invalided. When the latter officer left for England Major E. H. Kendrick, D.S.O., Royal Dublin Fusiliers, was appointed to the command of the battalion with effect from October 4. On October 12 a remarkably successful raid was carried out by 2nd Lieuts. F. M. Myers, K. Scott-Walker, and H. S. Grand, with thirty-six other ranks.

On November 1 the battalion sustained a heavy loss by the death of Captain O. H. Brown, D.S.O., M.C., who was killed by a stray bullet while visiting his trenches. A gallant and able soldier, and a brilliant scholar, he was buried in Bois Grenier cemetery the following evening, mourned by all who knew him.

The remainder of the year passed uneventfully. Christmas was spent in Erquinghem, and towards the end of January, 1917, the battalion left Bois Grenier after their prolonged stay in that neighbourhood, travelling in lorries at night to the Meteren area behind Bailleul. At the close of three weeks' training they set off towards Arras, and on February 24 moved up into the line south of Roclincourt, occupying the right sector of the front held by the 34th Division, XVIIth Corps (Lieut.-General Sir C. Fergusson). The time was spent in distributing stores, carrying up ammunition, and raiding and wire-cutting, all in preparation for the forthcoming Arras offensive. On April 5 Major Tuck rejoined from Aldershot and resumed his appointment as second-in-command.

7th Battalion

July 3—The first attack on Ovillers—Heavy casualties—Pozières—Ration trench on August 8—Transloy—The attack on Luisenhof farm, near Gueudecourt, October 12—Christmas at Ambrines—Marches to Arras

At daylight on July 2 the 7th Battalion moved nearer towards the battle-line, passing on the way up convoys of wounded coming back from the first day's fighting, and taking over support trenches while it was still early morning. During the day the battalion was able to watch from these trenches the struggle for the possession of Contalmaison.

On July 3 the battalion, under the command of Major G. H. Henty, took part in the frontal attack on Ovillers. In this operation the 12th Division attacked on a two-brigade front, the 35th on the right, with the 5th Royal Berkshire (right) and the 7th Suffolk (left) Regiments in the front line. The 37th Brigade was on the left, the 36th being in divisional reserve. The battalion assaulted in eight successive waves, the leading ones starting ten minutes before zero hour, which had been fixed for 3.15 a.m. The first four waves penetrated as far as the enemy's third line, portions of them getting into the village itself; but owing to the darkness the succeeding waves lost touch, enabling the Germans to surge in and cut them off. At the third line of resistance, after very severe fighting, the attack was brought to a standstill, the battalion losing heavily. All the company commanders were killed, Major Henty and Lieuts. Bowen, Taylor, and Hood being the only officers who came through untouched. The casualties amounted to 470 of all ranks, including the following—*Killed:* Captains G. D. Brooke, G. W. Deighton, M.C., T. H. Kinder, and C. R. Logan; 2nd Lieuts. T. W. Chalk, E. H. Dixey, J. L. Fish, R. W. Frost, A. C. Shears, C. F. Sworder, W. J. P. Woods, and E. S. Wright; C.S.M. J. J. Dean. *Died of wounds:* Lieut. L. H. Gilson (July 29). *Wounded:* Lieut. D. W. A. Nicholls; 2nd Lieuts. W. P. Cooper, K. W. Hunn, E. F. Cox, and E. C. Kelly. *Missing:* Captain J. Logan, R.A.M.C. The last-named, medical officer to the battalion, went out during the night of July 3–4 to collect wounded and did not return. Lieut. D. W. A. Nicholls and Lieut. H. A. Short were awarded the M.C. for gallantry in this engagement.

Thus, at the battle of Albert, was this fine battalion almost destroyed. The remnants, however, stayed in the trenches till July 8, when they went into Albert for a night and thence into the ruins of La Boisselle village where, incidentally, they were heavily shelled. On the 10th they went back to the Bois de Warnimont to reorganise.

On July 12 Major A. H. Wilson, D.S.O., from the 7th East Surrey Regiment, arrived and assumed command. After a few days' rest the battalion did a short tour of duty in trenches near the White City, in front of Beaumont Hamel, where 2nd Lieuts. W. F. Burman and T. Hume, and C.Q.M.S.'s Knight and Clark, were wounded.

On August 3 the battalion took over trenches west of Pozières. Scarcely had the relief been completed when the enemy began shelling the communication trenches, the bombardment lasting several hours. At 2 a.m. on the 8th the Germans made an unsuccessful assault on Ration trench, but shortly afterwards they renewed the attack and captured about seventy yards of the trench. That evening at sundown, however, it was retaken, Captain Isham's company attacking with great dash and gaining an additional two hundred yards of it. The battalion's casualties during this phase of the long-drawn battle of Pozières included the following—*Killed :* Captain A. L. James ; Lieut. A. F. Taylor ; 2nd Lieuts. N. C. Collins and S. R. Trask. *Died of wounds :* 2nd Lieut. G. B. Ashworth. *Wounded :* Captain C. Heigham ; 2nd Lieuts. L. A. G. Bowen, R. T. Larkins, and A. C. French ; C.S.M. W. Watts. For this action Captain V. A. R. Isham was awarded the M.C. Lieuts. A. F. Taylor (killed) and H. E. Gainsford, and Cpl. Everitt, M.M., also distinguished themselves, the last-named receiving a bar to his military medal.

From midnight of August 15–16 the 12th Division was placed temporarily under the orders of the VIth Corps (Lieut.-General J. A. L. Haldane, IIIrd Army (General Sir E. H. H. Allenby). At the end of the month the battalion went into brigade reserve in the Arras sector, where some successful raids were carried out against the German lines at Beaurains. The 7th Battalion furnished a guard of honour to the Army Commander on September 15, remaining in this sector in comparative quiet until the 27th, when they proceeded by bus to Brevillers and Becordel. About this time Captain P. B. B. Nichols, M.C., left the battalion for staff employ.

At the beginning of October the 12th Division moved up to Gueudecourt. The 35th Brigade, in reserve, went to Bernafay wood, the 7th Battalion being marooned in drenching rain in a shell-holed wilderness without shelters of any description. After spending a week in digging out quarters and building walls of sandbags and sleepers they were sent on October 10 into the front line at Bull's Run, near Flers, the men grimly jesting that the war might end any year now.

On October 11 the battalion, having been allotted its task in the battle of Transloy—already in progress—received orders to take part in an attack on Bayonet trench and Luisenhof farm, which had been fixed for the 12th. Going in overnight, they were heavily shelled until they had occupied their assembly trenches just before dawn. All the company headquarters were in a large dugout in the sunken road leading to Gueudecourt wood. After passing a reasonably quiet forenoon the battalion set out across the open at 2 p.m., coming immediately under a very heavy cross-fire of every description, but mainly from machine-guns and automatic rifles. Close to the German trenches the attack was held up by machine-gun nests and wire, and the waves, unable to get any further, lay down. At this juncture remarkable bravery was displayed by several officers, non-commissioned officers, and men. Lieut. Eagle is reported to have died fighting in the German first line, into which he had forced an entrance alone. 2nd Lieut. Marshall, in a shell-hole with his servant and a sergeant, was bombed and sniped all the afternoon, and later killed; they were close up against the German wire, but refused to go back. Captain Isham, badly wounded during the afternoon, spent the night in a shell-hole, being visited by Lieut. Bowen (himself wounded), who remained with him till dark.

The full story of this sad day, on which the battalion sustained over five hundred casualties, has never been described in print. Let it suffice to say that all ranks, especially the reinforcements which had recently arrived from the 6th (Cyclist) Battalion, acquitted themselves admirably. The failure of the attack was due in some measure to the facts that the enemy's wire had been only partially destroyed, and that our barrage during the launching of the attack was ineffective. Before zero hour Captain Leith-Hay-Clark had been twice buried by shells. Of the fourteen officers who went over the top on that occasion all became casualties as follows—*Killed*: Lieut. H. G. W. Todd; T/Lieut. W. L. C. Silver; 2nd Lieuts. C. E. Catchpole, F. N. Cowper, G. C. Eagle, J. S. Hearn, T. Hood, H. Sawyer, R. R. Rash, W. R.

Marshall, and L. d'A. Stapley. *Wounded:* Captains N. Leith-Hay-Clark and V. A. R. Isham, M.C.; Lieut. L. A. G. Bowen; 2nd Lieut. F. D. V. Thursby. For this action the Rev. A. E. Cousins, chaplain to the battalion—at all times courageous and helpful—was awarded the M.C., and Lieut. Bowen, wounded for the second time in three months, was similarly decorated.

On October 22 the battalion travelled by bus to Lattre St. Quentin, and then on to Arras, in which sector they remained in comparative quiet during a period of stabilisation. In November Brig.-General Solly-Flood, on being appointed B.G.G.S. in charge of training the British Armies in France, gave up the command of the 35th Brigade, which, in the cauldron of the Somme, he had led in four separate offensives, all of which had been crowned with success except the last one at Gueudecourt in October, where on the north of the village they came upon hidden masses of wire uncut. He was succeeded some weeks later by Brig.-General Berkeley Vincent.

On December 19 the battalion went into rest billets at Ambrines, spending Christmas there, and after five weeks' training was lent as a working battalion to the 36th Brigade, being employed on the new railway between Agnez and Acq. The last week of February was spent in the training area at Montenescourt, the battalion moving to Arras on March 2, and into the front line on the 9th. On March 15 the enemy carried out a raid which fell mainly against the unit on the left of the 7th Battalion, though the latter sustained a score of casualties during the preliminary bombardment. The following day they moved into billets in the cathedral crypt, whence they sent working parties into the line. On March 18 Lieut.-Colonel F. S. Cooper, D.S.O., joined and took over command of the battalion, which then repaired to Beaufort and Montenescourt for a few days' training. During the night of April 6–7 the battalion marched back to Arras, sleeping in the cathedral crypt. The next day 2nd Lieut. B. G. Snelson was wounded.

2nd Battalion

Arrives on the Somme at Les Celestins—The battles of Bazentin and Delville Wood—Death of Major Congreve—August 16–18—Gallantry of Pte. Waterson—A quiet front in the Loos sector—Death of Brig.-General Clifford while commanding the 149th Brigade—Back to the Somme—Ancre, or the battle of Serre—To Arras—The Wellington caves.

On July 1 the 2nd Battalion set out from St. Omer for the Somme. The following day Lieut.-Colonel d'Arch Smith was invalided, the command devolving upon Major G. C. Stubbs. The battalion reached the wood known as Les Celestins, on the Somme, on July 6, and within an hour of its arrival Major Stubbs was very slightly wounded, remaining at duty. Early in the month the 3rd Division was transferred to the XIIIth Corps (Lieut.-General W. N. Congreve, V.C.), to which the 8th Battalion already belonged. The XIIIth was one of the five corps comprising Rawlinson's (IVth) Army.

On July 8 the battalion bivouacked in Carnoy, one company going into the line, where its commander—Lieut. W. G. Chandler—was wounded almost immediately. The following night two patrols, under 2nd Lieuts. H. P. Gardham and R. A. Johnson respectively, went out and reconnoitred the enemy's wire under the direction of Major Congreve, the Brigade-Major, Sgt. F. Lynn, D.C.M., who was with Lieut. Gardham's patrol, being killed. On the 10th Lieut. E. A. Pickard-Cambridge was wounded.

July 14 witnessed the opening of the battle of Bazentin Ridge. The 76th Brigade was still in reserve, but the other two brigades of the 3rd Division played an important part in the centre of the main attack. During the day the battalion moved to the southern end of Caterpillar wood, at the western entrance of the valley of that name, which until then had been No Man's Land. Two incidents stand out prominently in connection with the attack on the 14th: one, the staggering intensity of the preliminary bombardment; the other, the advance of the cavalry, the moral effect of which was certainly remarkable.

On the afternoon of the 18th the Germans counter-attacked, forcing their way with fine courage but at great cost into Delville Wood and the northern end of Longueval, which troops of the 3rd Division had just cleared. In consequence, two companies were sent up to Longueval ridge to support the attack of the 1st Gordon Highlanders on Longueval, the remainder of the battalion moving from the wood into Caterpillar valley itself, where they were persistently shelled.

Early on the 19th Captain and Adjutant Trollope and Lieut. T. D. Pickard-Cambridge were wounded, 2nd Lieut. V. C. Russell taking over the duties of adjutant. Throughout this time of stress Captain J. D. Marshall, R.A.M.C., medical officer to the battalion, always proved himself equal to the occasion, being subsequently awarded the D.S.O. in recognition of his splendid services.

On July 20 the battalion, having assembled and deployed in Pont Street, took part in the renewed attacks on Longueval and Delville Wood. It was still dark when the artillery bombardment lifted and the advance began. The two Suffolk companies in the forward line moved in double lines of platoons with a front of 140 yards each. Much bitter fighting followed, which, though indecisive locally, enabled a footing to be gained in High Wood by a division (33rd) containing another Suffolk battalion—the 4th, and the British line to be linked up thence with Longueval. The casualties in the 2nd Battalion were heavy, and included the following officers—*Killed:* Captain A. L. Platts; Lieut. H. N. Kemble; 2nd Lieuts. S. Johnson and S. G. Bennett. *Wounded:* 2nd Lieuts. G. F. Igglesden and W. H. Hamlyn. *Missing:* Lieut. C. B. Bevan; 2nd Lieuts. A. L. Evans, H. P. Allanson, A. G. B. Patten, A. C. Taylor, and J. Bradley, M.C. With the exception of 2nd Lieut. Patten, who was wounded and taken prisoner, all these missing officers were subsequently reported killed. During this attack Brevet-Major W. La Touche Congreve, D.S.O., M.C., brigade-major to the 76th Brigade, was killed by a sniper while reconnoitring. On personal as well as public grounds the battalion deplored the loss of a man whose never-failing courage, zeal, and enterprise ranked him amongst the prodigies of the great war. Major Congreve was posthumously awarded the V.C. for repeated acts of most conspicuous bravery.

On July 21 the battalion returned to Breslau trench, and a few days later moved out of the battle zone to Bois des Tailles. Minden Day of 1916 was spent in Mericourt, whither a good many of the 4th Battalion repaired from Dernancourt, everyone bedecking himself as best he could with the roses of Picardy in honour of the regimental day. While at Mericourt a draft of " Bantams " arrived. Though good fighters, they could not march in the ranks with the taller men, always parading as a separate party.

After a fortnight's rest at Mericourt, on the Somme, the battalion moved up into the line south-west of Trones Wood, near Maltz Horn farm, taking over some newly-dug trenches from the 55th Division. For the first few days all was crush and confusion; the trenches were too narrow to move in or pass along, and the only communication trench to the rear was used by two brigades as well as the French 418th Regiment. On August 16 orders were received to carry out an attack in co-operation with the French. Zero was fixed for half-past five in the evening—an unusual hour. After a heavy bombardment the battalion moved forward upon the heels of the barrage, the objectives and dividing lines—difficult to recognise—having been pointed out on the ground to Major Stubbs and the company commanders by Brig.-General R. J. Kentish. On the right the attack was successful, some 250 yards of Cochrane alley, together with a party of men belonging to the German 124th Regiment, being captured; but on the left it was brought to a standstill by heavy machine-gun fire, and at night the battalion withdrew to its original line. The 17th was a day of clearing up, our snipers accounting for a number of Germans seen moving about. That evening one company was sent up to support an attack by the 10th R.W.F., which took place in the early hours of the 18th; but owing to the intense darkness, and to the fact that the assembly-tapes had been carried away by shell-fire, there was some confusion and the attack failed. During the afternoon the 1st Gordon Highlanders and other troops carried out another attack. To make room, two Suffolk companies moved out of the line, the other two in Cochrane alley supporting the attack by fire. This attempt was more successful than the previous ones, partly no doubt because the enemy had been hard pressed for several days and his resistance was weakening. During the fighting, the pluck and dash of one of our men attracted the notice of the French officer (418th Regiment) commanding the outposts, who sent in the following report to Major Stubbs :—

"No. 10265, Pte. W. Waterson, 2nd Suffolk Regiment.

Soldat très courageux et extrèmement adroit. S'est distingué au combat à la grenade et a tué 17 *Allemands à lui seul.*"

Waterson was promptly awarded the D.C.M.

The Suffolk companies had carried out their allotted tasks so successfully that in the evening the Germans turned a battery of five-nines on to Cochrane alley, creating great havoc for an hour or more. During the night these two companies were relieved, the battalion reassembling at Talus Bois and marching back to Happy Valley the next evening, having sustained 281 casualties, including the following twelve officers—*Killed :* Lieut. A. E. Walford ; 2nd Lieut. F. E. C. Hall. *Missing* (afterwards reported killed) : 2nd Lieut. W. F. Burgess. *Wounded :* T/Major G. C. Stubbs (at duty) ; T/Captain R. F. Barton ; Lieut. W. B. Higgins ; T/Captain H. P. Gardham ; Lieut. H. S. Collett ; 2nd Lieuts. F. W. Francis, W. G. Carrington, J. M. V. Percy, and V. C. Russell. On August 19 2nd Lieut. C. J. Moss died.

Lieut. A. E. Walford was a brother of Major George Walford, Suffolk Regiment, killed in the Salient in April, 1915. For these operations Lieuts. D. G. Steel and J. A. G. Chalmers were awarded the M.C.

The battalion then began its march back to the Loos sector, reaching Mazingarbe at the end of the month, and taking over a comparatively quiet part of the line.

Just before the battle of Flers-Courcelette, the regiment heard with profound regret of the death of Brig.-General Clifford, who was killed on September 11 near High Wood while commanding the 149th Brigade, 50th Division. Brig.-General H. F. H. Clifford, D.S.O., joined the 2nd Battalion on the 11th February, 1888. In the early part of October, 1914, he landed in France and took over command of his old battalion, relinquishing it during the following June on promotion to that of the 149th Brigade. In August, 1915, the 50th Division was moved down to the Somme to take part in the attack of the 15th September. Immediately upon their arrival the troops of the 149th Brigade were employed in the construction of assembly trenches from which the attack was to be launched.

The trenches under construction formed three sides of a

big parallelogram, the trenches on each flank being designed as means of access to the main assembly-trench. The last-named was nearly, but not quite, completed when Brig.-General Clifford, with his staff captain, went up to inspect the work, a space of some twenty-five or thirty yards still remaining to be excavated before a junction could be effected. When Brig.-General Clifford reached the point where the construction work on the main assembly trench ended, instead of retracing his steps and inspecting the trench from the other side, which he might have done in perfect safety, he attempted to reach it by walking across the open space through which the trench had not yet been driven. When he was about half-way across he was shot through the heart by a sniper in High Wood. He was buried with military honours in the British cemetery east of Albert.

A very valuable life was thus wasted ; but those who knew Brig.-General Clifford intimately believe that his action on this occasion was deliberate and in obedience to a rule which he had, of set purpose, imposed upon himself. He was deeply impressed by the feeling that there was something unfair about the comparative immunity from danger enjoyed by officers of high rank, by the notion that this sentiment must be shared by the men under his command, and by the conviction that it was his duty to set a high example by declining to take any very special precautions for the preservation of his personal safety. Once before, when in the Salient, he had done precisely the same thing as that which cost him his life, but on that occasion escaped with a sniper's bullet through his left arm ; and it was in the same spirit that when commanding at the front he never once omitted a daily visit to whatever unit was manning the foremost line. "He seemed to us to bear a charmed life," his divisional commander (Major-General Sir Percival Wilkinson) wrote to Sir Hugh Clifford,[1] alluding to the risks which for so long he had habitually taken. If Brig.-General Clifford had survived, he would have been the next brigadier to be given the command of a division.

On September 19 2nd Lieut. S. G. Cowper was wounded, remaining at duty ; and at the end of the month Brig.-General R. J. Kentish handed over command of the 76th Brigade to Brig.-General C. L. Porter. After a period of training at

[1] Brig.-General Clifford's elder brother ; afterwards Governor of Ceylon.

Photo by] [*Bassano*

BRIGADIER-GENERAL H. F. H. CLIFFORD, D.S.O.

Enquin-les-Mines, the battalion moved down to the area behind the Serre sector in the middle of October. An attack was known to be impending, but the bad weather threatened to preclude the possibility of operations on a large scale. However, preparations continued, and on November 6 the battalion was sent into the trenches. At the last moment attack orders were cancelled, the same thing happening again on the 10th, the postponement in both cases being due to the weather. Finally, on the 12th a beginning was made. The whole trench area was waterlogged and in such a deplorable state that the battalion, abandoning the communication trenches entirely, moved into its assembly positions across the open, luckily unmolested.

At 5 a.m. on November 13 the first wave floundered forward into No Man's Land—in reality, a sea of mud in which movement was barely possible. Three-quarters of an hour later the attack began. The mist which hung about the low ground thickened as the smoke of the barrage increased, making direction extremely difficult to maintain. Within a very short time all the officers in the leading companies had fallen, and owing to lack of leaders no real progress was made. In spite of the atrocious weather conditions prevailing, portions of the leading Suffolk companies actually reached the German second line. But all was in vain, and the battalion having been reorganised in its original front line, remained there for the rest of the day, marching back to Courcelles the next morning. Their casualties numbered 272, including the following eleven officers—*Killed:* A/Captain D. G. Steel, M.C.; 2nd Lieuts. J. D. Anderton and J. Farren. *Wounded:* 2nd Lieuts. E. V. Power, E. L. Grimwade, A. A. Johnson, and W. S. Hale. *Missing:* Lieut. B. W. Devas, 2nd Lieut. C. H. Allison (both afterwards ascertained to have been killed), 2nd Lieuts. H. W. Wright and K. M. Dingley.

The battle of Serre, as it was called in the battalion, or that of the Ancre, to give it its official title, was the last of the Somme battles of 1916, which had been attended by almost incredible casualties. It was ruefully remembered by those present as the least successful and most dispiriting engagement in the history of the 2nd Battalion in France. In fact, the whole period spent in the Serre sector was one of unhappy memory. The winter was exceptionally wet, the water in the trenches being often waist-deep. The battle casualties during those two trying months were not high, but much sickness prevailed, and on several occasions men on duty, dropping from exhaustion, were actually drowned at their posts. On December 19 2nd Lieut. W. A. Baillie was wounded, and on the following day 2nd Lieut. P. S. St. P. Bunbury killed. Christmas was spent in Bus-les-Artois.

The battalion remained in the Serre sector till January 7 when they marched to Bertrancourt, going on by bus to Puchevillers. On the 9th the brigade marched to the Halloy–Pernois district, where they remained training till the 27th, the frost and snow on the 9th and 10th being very severe. Leaving Pernois on the 28th they reached Arras on February 16, after six marches aggregating about sixty miles, passing through Chelers and Hauteville and halting for a week at each of those places.

During their stay in Arras they were detailed for work on dugouts and tunnels. This was followed by railway construction work at Grouches and Milly, near Doullens, and meant that for a whole month they were employed entirely as a labour battalion. The same thing was happening everywhere up and down the line, and pointed to the need of special formations for that purpose.

The battalion, still belonging to the 3rd Division (Major-General C. J. Deverell), and forming part of the VIth Corps (Haldane), IIIrd Army (Allenby), moved on March 16 to Denier in the corps area, lying east and south-east of Arras. They had been in that city in mid-February, and were destined to see much more of the district during 1917 and the year following. When they first knew Arras it was almost in the front line, but after the Allied offensive the battered city became quite a back area until 1918 when the German waves surged towards it again.

After an active period of attack practice at Denier, the battalion moved to Wanquetin, returning to Arras on April 6. From the cavalry barracks they entered a sewer, large enough for the tallest man to walk upright, proceeding thence along tunnels to Wellington caves. These underground barracks constituted a remarkable feature of Arras. Realising the difficulty and danger of assembling and housing large numbers of troops in the city itself, the authorities made use of a system of caves and cellars which had been there for many years. Special entrances were constructed, the various caves connected by subways, the whole place lit with electricity, and new subways made to exits near the front line, these being opened up at the last moment to allow units to reach their assembly positions. On April 7 2nd Lieut. W. Hamp and his orderly were wounded in Rue de Temple.

4th Battalion

Bazentin—Switch trench—The 4th Battalion supports an attack on High Wood —Pozières—The attack on August 18—The 33rd Division allowed a short rest—Christmas in the trenches near Rancourt—The advance to the Hindenburg line.

While the 4th Battalion was moving up through Becordel to the position between Fricourt and Mametz where they bivouacked during the night of July 14–15, the battle of Bazentin Ridge was raging in all its fury. They were not destined, however, to remain long thus upon the fringe of hostilities, and at dawn went out under the command of Major H. C. Copeman, D.S.O., to support the 1st Middlesex Regiment in an attack on Switch trench. After severe fighting, a line immediately in front of the village of Bazentin-le-Petit was taken up and held for the remainder of the day. The casualties in the battalion, exceeding two hundred, included the following—*Killed:* Captains Maurice A. Turner and Herbert K. Turner; 2nd Lieuts. W. H. Milburn and W. H. Packard. *Wounded:* Captain H. Pretty; 2nd Lieuts. D. H. Pilkington, H. Scrimgeour, N. H. Smith, E. H. T. Woods, H. F. Bond, M.C., W. J. Dooley, E. J. Harding, G. E. E. Burton, and A. E. Moorsom; C.S.M. W. Walker, D.C.M., was killed, and C.S.M.'s H. R. Scoggins, M.M., and S. Ives, M.M., were wounded. On July 16 2nd Lieut. Burton died of his wounds.

Early the following morning the battalion on relief went into reserve in Shell valley, digging itself into roadside trenches for the night. After a day of heavy shelling they returned to front-line trenches, an old German bomb-store in the north-east corner of Bazentin-le-Petit wood being subsequently used as battalion headquarters instead of a deep dugout taken over as such. Throughout the 19th the heavy shelling continued. Early on the 20th, the battalion returned to Shell valley, but was shortly ordered to move up to a position near the cemetery in support of the 19th Brigade in an attack on High Wood. Violent opposition was encountered, and little progress made, though portions of the 33rd Division succeeded in establishing a footing in the wood. Our casualties included 2nd Lieut. G. A. C. Goodall killed, and 2nd Lieuts. S. W. Turner and C. T. Eaton, and Lieut. W. H. M. Pattisson, wounded. Relieved early on July 21 the battalion went back to Mametz wood which was bombarded throughout the day and night with high-explosive, shrapnel, and tear-gas shells. At dawn on the 22nd the battalion reached billets in Dernancourt, where a large draft with several officers joined. Here also Major F. Pretty—wounded at Ypres—rejoined. On July 21 2nd Lieut. H. H. Boyne, attached to the Machine-Gun Corps, died of wounds.

On Minden Day a number of officers and men went over to Mericourt at the invitation of the 2nd Battalion, who were resting there. On the same day Major E. P. Clarke assumed the duties of Staff Captain, 98th Brigade. On August 6 the battalion took over trenches in Fricourt wood, and during the next few days furnished working parties for the construction of Thistle alley communication trench. These parties sustained a number of casualties, amongst them being 2nd Lieut. C. G. Sykes, wounded.

On August 13 the battalion moved from Fricourt wood into support trenches in Bazentin-le-Grand. In the afternoon Brig.-General F. M. Carleton (98th Brigade) came to the 4th Battalion headquarters, where the commanding officers met him, to explain the plan for attacking—on the 18th—Wood Lane trench, running across our front south-eastwards from High Wood. One battalion was to attack on the right and another on the left, when—according to the trite phrase—the centre would "fall automatically," or other troops would be detailed to attack it. Zero hour would be 2 p.m. After the other commanding officers had left the brigadier remarked to Lieut.-Colonel Copeman that his battalion would probably have to attack in the centre. Such indeed proved to be the case.

On August 14 the battalion went into the front line, their left resting on the corner of High Wood, and immediately set to work digging jumping-off trenches, an unpleasant task, as being in No Man's Land they came in for some of our own shells as well as those of the enemy. During the night of the 15th–16th Captain H. N. Duke and 2nd Lieut. K. C. Shuttleworth were wounded while thus employed. During the afternoon of the 17th, a tiresome day of persistent bombardment, a shell burst close to battalion headquarters, severely wounding the adjutant, Lieut. K. W. Turner, who lost his leg. He was succeeded by Captain J. F. L. Fison, employed at divisional headquarters.

On the 18th, not long before zero hour, Captain H. F. Ling was wounded, and still later, Lieut. R. D. Hume, M.C., entailing important changes in command at the last moment. Captain Ling remained in the trenches until the attack was over. Neither of the battalions on the right and left was able to make much progress. The 4th Battalion, in the centre, pushed forward. For a time two of our companies occupied Wood Lane trench, but being unsupported, and 2nd Lieut. Bedwell (the only officer to reach the trench) having been killed, it was impossible to hold on. However, considering that the battalion had attacked after four days in the front line, it was justly pleased with its work. A rough night followed, during which the battalion was relieved. Early next morning they moved to Fricourt wood, and at sundown proceeded to a camp north-east of Meaulte, near the Albert road. The casualties on August 18 were as follows—*Killed:* 2nd Lieuts. V. L. S. Bedwell, H. C. Pawsey, and E. Norton, and 33 other ranks. *Wounded:* Captain H. F. Ling; 2nd Lieut. N. E. Suttle, and 108 other ranks. *Missing:* 50 other ranks. Total, 196.

While the battalion was in camp between Becourt and Meaulte some German aeroplanes came over, dropping bombs but doing no damage. On August 24 the 33rd Division was able to make further progress to the north and east of Delville Wood, the battalion moving forward to a different set of trenches in Fricourt wood, with headquarters in a deep dug-out. At 3.45 a.m. on the 25th a bombardment opened for an attack two hours later; and that afternoon the battalion advanced first to Montauban alley and then to Carleton trench, and during the night to Savoy trench and George street.

When going round the trenches at daybreak on the 26th,

Lieut.-Colonel Copeman, finding his left in Bazentin-le-Grand, established his headquarters there. On the 28th the battalion moved up into the newly captured portion of Wood lane, the company in support in Orchard street being heavily shelled. On August 30 the Germans made a violent bombing attack on Wood lane, but this being repulsed with loss, they bombarded Orchard trench once more, causing a good many casualties, including Captain B. St. J. Glanfield, and 2nd Lieuts. C. W. Botton and C. M. Oliver, wounded. Shortly afterwards Captain Glanfield died of his wounds. The next day the battalion went back to a camp near Dernancourt. During the relief, Captain B. B. Noble, R.A.M.C., medical officer to the battalion, returned to Orchard trench to attend to the casualties and was himself wounded.

On September 1 the battalion proceeded by bus to Allonville, starting off the next day on a march through Candas, round Doullens, and up as far as the river Canche. On the 2nd Brig.-General J. D. Heriot-Maitland, C.M.G., D.S.O., took over the command of the 98th Brigade on the march. After a period of trekking and training the battalion returned to the Albert sector on the 26th, occupying trenches in front of Hebuterne. For one day in mid-September the battalion enjoyed the use of the divisional baths at Gaudiempre. On the 17th Lieut.-Colonel Copeman was awarded the order of St. Stanislaus, third class.

At the beginning of October they moved back to St. Amand and on to Sus-St. Leger, the time being spent in general instruction and in special training in a wood near Oppy, similar in shape to Bois Rosignol at Gommecourt, which at that time the brigade was believed to be destined to attack. On the 10th the battalion was inspected by Major-General R. J. Pinney, the new divisional commander, and some days later proceeded in French buses to Corbie, marching thence on a bitterly cold morning to Meaulte, and the brickfields near Bernafay Wood. On October 24 they moved in very wet weather into Trones Wood, occupying four days later some poor front line trenches on newly gained ground in front of Les Bœufs.

The next five days were spent in making minor attacks to gain ground, but these only met with partial success, though on the 28th Dewdrop trench fell to the 98th Brigade. On the

29th 2nd Lieut. E. Hignett was wounded, and two days later 2nd Lieut. E. G. Joyce was killed and 2nd Lieut. C. A. Harris mortally wounded. The last of these attacks was made on November 1, our casualties including 2nd Lieut. G. H. C. Adams killed. The battalion then moved back to the Flers line, Lieut.-Colonel Copeman receiving the congratulations of the Corps Commander, Lord Cavan, for the work done by the 4th Battalion since taking over the line. Throughout this tour of duty the enemy shelling had been persistently heavy.

On November 3 the battalion moved back to hutments on the Montauban–Carnoy road, being transferred two days later to a canvas camp near Meaulte. On the 9th they went by train still further back to Huchenneville and neighbourhood, remaining there till the end of the month. On November 26 Major-General Pinney presented M.M. ribbons to the following: Sgts. A. G. Everson, J. Rutter, J. Podd, and H. Simpson; L/Sgt. C. A. Pizzey; Cpls. A. Capon and L. Smith; L/Cpl. E. Shepherd; and Pte. C. Martin.

At the beginning of December the battalion went to Bray-sur-Somme, and on the 9th to Maurepas, relieving some French infantry in bad trenches north-east of Bouchavesnes the following day. Then, after a spell at Suzanne, where the divisional commander presented the D.C.M. ribbon to Pte. B. J. Simkin, the battalion took over trenches south-west of Rancourt on Christmas Day. These were extremely wet and muddy, and like front-line trenches in many other sectors were not approachable during daylight. On Christmas night a Russian prisoner, who had escaped from the Germans, made his way into our lines. Boxing Day witnessed great aerial activity, and the next day much heavy shelling. The battalion then marched back to Maurepas, going on to Bray-sur-Somme by lorry. Between Rancourt and Maurepas one company had to put on their masks owing to shell-gas. On December 29 they went by rail to Longpré, marching on to Villers-sous-Ailly.

After three weeks' training in that neighbourhood they marched through snow back to Longpré, proceeding by rail to Edgehill station and then by road to a dismal camp near Dernancourt, devoid of all comfort. On January 21 they relieved French troops in brigade reserve in Howitzer wood, taking over front-line trenches south of Bouchavesnes two days later. After a camp inspection by the G.O.C. XVth

Corps on the last day of the month they moved into trenches in front of Clery-sur-Somme, where on February 5 Lieut. J. Gordon Brown was killed.

On February 13 a party from the battalion, consisting of 2nd Lieuts. L. P. Bennett and A. W. Hare, and fifty-three other ranks, carried out a successful raid. Having got through the German wire, they captured all the occupants of a dugout; but as the prisoners were being sent back under escort a shell —believed to have been one of our own—fell among them, killing the whole party. Considerable casualties were inflicted on the enemy, those of the battalion only amounting to ten. 2nd Lieut. L. P. Bennett, who commanded the raiding party with great coolness, was severely wounded and died the next day. On March 19 Sgt. W. Jermynn was awarded the Italian bronze medal for gallantry; the following day 2nd Lieut. C. C. S. Gibbs was appointed adjutant as from January 1. Towards the end of March Captain Hon. M. G. Tollemache joined the battalion.

After some three weeks in camp in and near Sailly Laurette, well occupied in training, they left on April 1 and marched northwards. The start next morning was delayed by snow, and when near Molliens-aux-Bois a furious snowstorm was encountered. On the 5th they reached Beaurepaire farm, in the IIIrd Army area, joining the 18th Army Corps. One day on the march, to the surprise of the men, a wild boar was seen crossing a field. Eventually, after a circular tour round Doullens, they reached Berles-aux-Bois on the 8th, Lieut.-Colonel Copeman and the company commanders leaving the battalion on the march and riding forward to reconnoitre the Cojeul valley by Boisleux.

9th Battalion

Mailly-Maillet wood—In front of the Quadrilateral—The battle of Flers-Courcelette—Death of Lieut.-Colonel Mack—Gallantry of Captain Ensor—The battle of Morval—And of Transloy—Resting at Annezin—Christmas in army reserve at Nœux-les-Mines—A prolonged stay in the Loos-Hulluch sector

Early in August the 9th Battalion, taken out of the raging inferno of the Salient, was thrown into the simmering cauldron of the Somme. Reaching the Albert sector on the 4th of that month under the command of Lieut.-Colonel A. P. Mack, they took over trenches in front of Mailly-Maillet wood, remaining there till the 28th with the intermission of a week at Louvencourt. In that sector they were allotted the distressing task of clearing the battlefield of the fallen of the Ulster Division. On the 21st they sustained some casualties, including 2nd Lieut. S. T. Askham, missing (afterwards reported killed), and Lieut. A. H. Guinness, wounded. After a few days' rest at Beauval, Montonvillers, and Cardonette, the battalion moved to Mericourt l'Abbé on the Ancre, and thence into the Sandpit area at the south-eastern edge of Ginchy, where on September 11 they took over trenches from the 4th Battalion Grenadier Guards.

On September 13 the battalion took part in an attack by the 6th Division (Major-General C. Ross) on the Quadrilateral, the 71st Brigade being on the left and the 16th on the right. The 9th Battalion attacked with three companies in the front line and one in support, zero being at 6.20 a.m. The battalion got through the German outpost line quite easily, but on gaining the open ground, which stretched for about four hundred yards to the enemy's wire, came under a terrific machine-gun fire from the formidable strong point known as the Quadrilateral. Across this bare expanse the men struggled bravely forward, Lieut. Macdonald with others getting close enough to throw a bomb into the German stronghold before being wounded. No further progress could, however, be made. At 7.30 a.m. another attack, in which "A" Company participated, was launched; and in the evening a third. Still no entrance could be effected. The battalion therefore, in touch with the units on both flanks, dug itself in on a line about half a mile in front of the jumping-off trenches of the morning.

One incident in this fighting is worthy of mention. During the forenoon, Captain Ensor, knowing that Lieut. Macdonald had been hit, went out to try and find him. After running from shell-hole to shell-hole for about three hundred yards under fire and in full view of the Germans, and calling out Macdonald's name, he found him lying very seriously wounded. Then, having put iodine on his wounds and made him as comfortable as possible, he ran the gauntlet back to where his men were dug in. The next morning before it was light, Captain

Ensor with his orderly went out again and tried to bring in his wounded subaltern, but after carrying him for about two hundred yards the orderly was shot dead. Captain Ensor, however, had succeeded in getting Lieut. Macdonald within the zone of his own stretcher-bearers, who brought him in. Lieut. Macdonald eventually recovered, though in hospital for five and a half years.

The casualties were as follows—*Killed:* Captain S. H. Byrne; 2nd Lieut. G. D. Gardiner; and 15 other ranks. *Wounded:* Captains V. W. Barrett and N. R. Rawson (R.A.M.C.); and 2nd Lieuts. C. Wayman, A. G. Douglas, G. W. Collyer, D. K. Macdonald, H. E. Falkner, A. Fudge, F. Goatcher, and H. Almack; and 185 other ranks.

On September 15 the offensive was resumed, eleven British divisions forming the striking force, with the French co-operating to the southward. The 6th Division, to which the 9th Battalion belonged, was in the centre of the XIVth Corps (Earl of Cavan), the Guards' Division being on its left, and the 56th Division (the extreme right of the British line) on its right. After a bombardment lasting three days the assaulting lines, aided for the first time by tanks, moved forward as the sun rose up behind the German trenches. Thus opened the battle of Flers–Courcelette.

The final objective assigned to the 71st Brigade was the occupation of the ridge between Morval and Les Bœufs. But the task of the 6th Division on that day was an unenviable one, and the goal beyond their reach; for immediately in front of them lay the Quadrilateral, still intact, bristling with machine-guns, and absolutely barring the way.

Zero hour was again 6.20 a.m. The 9th Battalion, supporting the 9th Norfolk Regiment, were not, however, required to advance till an hour and a half later, by which time the barrage had become very heavy. The trying experiences of the 13th were repeated, and on leaving the trenches the troops came under a withering machine-gun fire from the Quadrilateral, against which it was impossible to make any headway whatever. At 8.30 a.m. Lieut.-Colonel Mack, who had moved his headquarters into the front-line trenches at zero hour, was killed by machine-gun fire while watching the battalion. All the senior officers having been killed or wounded, the command then devolved upon Lieut. and Adjutant C. Allerton.

Lieutenant-Colonel A. P. MACK

The battalion, unable to move forward, but still maintaining touch with the units on its flanks, gradually dug itself in, and although under heavy artillery fire, held this position until relieved just before midnight. During the evening Major M. F. Heigham arrived and assumed command of the battalion.

The casualties were as follows—*Killed:* Lieut.-Colonel A. P. Mack; Lieuts. J. T. C. Fallowes and L. A. Whillier; 2nd Lieut. F. Wilson, and 35 other ranks. *Wounded:* Captains L. Ensor and S. W. Church; Lieut. J. N. Harmer; 2nd Lieuts. W. H. Hoile, C. G. Gardner, G. Hopkins, R. T. Scott, and 99 other ranks. *Missing:* 2nd Lieuts. S. J. Price and R. G. P. Smith, and 93 other ranks. Both the missing officers and many of the other ranks were afterwards reported killed. Owing to the death of Lieut.-Colonel Mack, which was widely deplored, no recommendations in connection with February 13 were submitted as far as the 9th Battalion was concerned. Captain Ensor's wounds proving severe, this heroic officer was eventually invalided out of the army. In the spring of 1917 he was awarded the M.C.

On September 17 the battalion moved into trenches in support which they were holding when the 6th Division captured the Quadrilateral on the following day, " after what must be conceded as a magnificent defence, which had cost the division upwards of 3500 casualties."[1] On the 19th the battalion marched to Ville-sur-Ancre.

Sir Douglas Haig states that in spite of the secrecy maintained the enemy had obtained some information regarding the attack on September 15 and our intended use of tanks. After this battle of Flers–Courcelette there was a brief lull in the fighting owing to continued bad weather, no major operations taking place between the Somme and the Ancre till September 25, when the villages of Morval, Gueudecourt, and Les Bœufs were assaulted, the last-named being carried by the 6th and Guards' Divisions. On the 25th the 9th Battalion was in reserve, moving into the front line the next day and remaining there till the close of the month.

The fighting between the Combles valley and the Albert–Bapaume road on September 25 and three following days became known as the battle of Morval, from which the 9th Battalion—in reserve on the first day of the battle and scarcely

[1] *History of the 6th Division* (Hugh Rees, Ltd.).

involved at all on the last—emerged with slight casualties. On the 27th 2nd Lieuts. H. A. Jones and L. C. Rae were wounded; and on the 30th, 2nd Lieut. W. Wilson. On the 28th Major F. Latham, D.S.O., Leicestershire Regiment, arrived and assumed command of the battalion. During the first week in October, while in rest billets, news was received that Lieut. and Adjutant C. Allerton had been awarded the D.S.O., and 2nd Lieut. W. F. Fitch the M.C.

After two more spells in the trenches the battalion went back to Corbie where they were visited by Major L. C. Arbuthnot, Town Major at Albert, and Major L. S. Roberts, Indian Army, who was commissioned from the 2nd Battalion in 1895. On October 28 the battalion moved to Annezin, and after a month's rest marched to Le Preol. The remainder of the year was spent in the La Bassée and Loos sectors. On December 5 2nd Lieut. E. J. Seddon was wounded; a fortnight later the battalion moved from divisional reserve in Beuvry to army reserve at Nœux-les-Mines, south of Bethune, where Christmas was spent.

While the attention of the British high command and the public was directed towards the advance to the Hindenburg line, and to the Arras and Flanders offensives, the 9th Battalion was unobtrusively holding the line in the Loos–Hulluch sector, remaining there until the autumn of 1917. The atrocious weather conditions which had prevailed during the summer and autumn of 1916, and had robbed the Somme offensive of the strategic results to which it approached, were followed by a severe winter. Throughout that season trench duty was exceptionally arduous for the whole division. At times battalions relieved from the front line one night would be put in elsewhere the next. Beyond this, and an occasional raid or heavy bombardment, little occurred that can be chronicled.

The opening days of January found the battalion in the Quarries sector, Hulluch. In the line, in support, in reserve, now at Philosophe or Mazingarbe, now at Labourse, they remained in this strategic backwater till the summer had gone by and they were ordered south to prepare for the Cambrai operations. On February 4 2nd Lieut. J. R. Colthorpe was wounded. During the night of the 12th–13th the 71st Brigade carried out a raid in which 2nd

Lieut. G. King was killed. A few days later the battalion moved into rest billets in Bethune, Major M. F. Heigham being appointed Town Major of that place. On the 27th Major J. B. O. Trimble, M.C., assumed temporary command of the battalion in his stead. During March 2nd Lieut. H. C. S. Throssell was killed, Captain L. C. Scholefield wounded, and Captain L. G. Thomas gassed; and early in April 2nd Lieut. Colthorpe was wounded for the second time in two months.

12TH BATTALION

Death of Captain Nisbet—The battalion goes into the line at Calonne—The Maroc and Loos sectors—The occupation of Péronne

On June 7, 1916, the 12th Battalion, whose arrival in France had raised the number of Suffolk battalions serving overseas to the worthy total of nine, reached the town of Lillers, where they set about making themselves comfortable, being under the impression that they would remain some time. They were soon, however, to discover the vanity of seeking an even tenor of existence on a battle-front, and within thirty-six hours were ordered to march forthwith to Chocques and La Beuvrière, the first of a long series of rude awakenings.

At La Beuvrière four other ranks were injured at the bombing school; and on June 21, at Barlin, another bombing accident occurred, attended by heroic circumstances. One of the men dropped a bomb, the pin of which had been withdrawn. Captain C. A. Nisbet, seeing the danger, snatched up the bomb to throw it clear of the trench, but as he did so it exploded, killing him instantly.

On June 24 the battalion went into the line at Calonne, being attached for instruction to regular battalions. Here for the first time they came under fire, sustaining about fifteen casualties. Early in July the 40th Division moved into the right sector of the Ist Corps line in the Lens area, the battalion taking over trenches at Maroc, including the Double Crassier. Here L/Cpl. A. C. Handy, of the 12th Battalion, was awarded the M.M. for attacking single-handed, and on his own initiative, a German patrol, this being the first honour gained by the 40th Division. During the month 2nd Lieuts. R. J. C. Jewitt, H. W. Robinson, and D. G. Carr were wounded. For nearly four months the 121st Brigade held the Maroc and Loos sectors, the battalion being four days in the line and four in support with monotonous regularity. During this period they carried out several successful raids. In one of these, which took place on August 4 under Lieut. C. H. Rolph and 2nd Lieut. H. A. Redding, the latter gained a military cross. On August 12, Colonel Pigott having been invalided, Lieut.-Colonel T. Eardley-Wilmot, York and Lancaster Regiment, was appointed to the command of the battalion.

Towards the end of October the 40th Division was withdrawn from the line for a rest, which had been much talked of and looked forward to for some time. The "rest," however, turned out to consist of a series of tiresome marches, the villages of Les Brebis, Bruay, Chelers, La Breuviette, Barly, and Berneuil being visited in lightning succession. At the last-named, where fresh clothing was issued, the battalion certainly halted for ten days. Then after another rest at Mouflers they marched on to Sailly-le-Sec, which despite its name seemed to be the wettest place in France. Here in a hutment camp the 12th Battalion spent its first Christmas on active service. On December 27 they went on to Suzanne to another hutment camp, built and hitherto occupied by French troops. On December 31 the battalion moved up into the line, taking over a sector in a slough at Bouchavesnes. The trenches were indescribably bad, with no dugouts and no drainage, and remained literally thigh-deep in liquid mud throughout the tour of duty. The next front-line sector held by the battalion was at Rancourt, where they stayed for two months.

The 40th Division then moved further down towards the Somme into the Maurepas area, where they relieved the 33rd Division. Rumours were already rife of an intended German retirement. On March 18 Lieut.-Colonel Eardley-Wilmot and Captain F. Miskin went forward and entered Péronne, which they found deserted: the Germans had retreated to the Hindenburg line. This was quickly followed by a general advance along the whole front of the XVth and other corps, and for the next few days the 40th Division was employed mainly in road-making.

CHAPTER XIV

5TH BATTALION

Egypt—The Sinai Peninsula—The invasion of Palestine—The First and Second Battles of Gaza—The storming of El Arish redoubt—The Third Battle of Gaza—The battle of Nebi Samwil—The capture of Jerusalem.

THE history of the 5th Battalion in Egypt affords a very vivid contrast to that of the preceding four months in Gallipoli. A life of peace and comfort in an agreeable climate was a welcome change indeed. The land and its people were strange to them—the desert, the Pyramids, the Sphinx, the donkey-boys, all was new and diverting. In the towns every other man seemed to be a bootblack, and if you stopped heedlessly for a moment in the street you would have one boot polished before you knew it. The countryside was often reminiscent of the Bible. The methods of cultivation provided fascinating scenes; the water-wheels with the patient buffalo plodding on his endless round; the primitive wooden ploughs sometimes drawn by a camel and a donkey—ludicrous pair!

On January 25 a violent wind swept over the camp, leaving scarcely a tent standing. On the 30th Lieut. W. T. Haddock died in hospital, being buried on the following day in the military cemetery in Alexandria. On February 2 the battalion proceeded to Mena camp, Cairo, the 54th Division shortly after its arrival being inspected by Lieut.-General Sir J. G. Maxwell, commanding the forces in Egypt. Towards the end of the month Lieut.-Colonel H. J. Miers was obliged to relinquish the command owing to ill-health, being succeeded by Major and Adjutant H. M. Lawrence—a very popular appointment. At Mena the battalion had its first experience of the *khamsin*, a hot, sand-laden wind that springs up from the south.

After a stay of nearly two months at the foot of the Pyramids the battalion was transferred to the Suez Canal, reaching Geneife on the last day of March. At that time, about every ten miles or so a permanent pontoon bridge spanned the canal, from the bank of which a light railway, with a macadamised road parallel to it, ran eastward into the desert for about seven miles. The battalion post at Geneife, just south of the Little Bitter Lake, was a busy centre where all day long stone for the new road was being unloaded from dhows. Here H.R.H. the Prince of Wales embarked after visiting the Egyptian front towards the close of April.

At the beginning of May the battalion moved to the front line, about eight miles east of the canal, occupying the posts of Salford and Oldham, where they experienced their worst *khamsin.* The heat was very great and water short, but as the latter came by barge, train, and camel combined it was really surprising that the supply was so regular. Entrenching in that part of the world was no easy task. The sand was so fine and unstable that, in order to dig a trench six feet deep, it had to be thrown double that distance from the trench. Moreover, the sides had to be revetted with boards and matting, and each revetment well anchored or braced.

At the end of May the battalion moved to Serapeum rail-head—about twenty miles to the north—and thence into the front line, furnishing company posts at Peter's Peak and Habieta. On June 13 a hostile aeroplane bombed Serapeum. The front line consisted of a chain of posts about three-quarters of a mile apart, garrisoned till June by companies, but afterwards by half-companies or platoons. In summer the troops stood to at 3.30 a.m. In mid-July short leave to Egypt was opened. On Minden Day the battalion was ordered to march to rail-head, the arrangements to celebrate the great regimental day being therefore cancelled. At Serapeum Lieut.-Colonel F. H. A. Wollaston, D.S.O., Rifle Brigade, joined and assumed command of the battalion.

On August 5 the battalion entrained for Moascar, whence they marched through Ismailia to Ferry Post. After four months of desert and sand the march through Ismailia, with its beautiful avenue of trees and comfortable residences, was very agreeable. From bridge-head they proceeded by rail and lorry to rail-head, and thence across the desert to Sphinx, Round Hill, Plateau, and Katoomba posts. The cause of this hurried move was the unsuccessful attack on Romani then taking place. The battalion here suffered a great loss through the promotion of Major H. M. Lawrence to the command of the 1/5th Cheshire Regiment, 53rd Division. It was mainly due to his enthusiasm and popularity that the battalion was recruited practically to full strength before the war. He knew the majority of the men personally, and the non-commissioned officers were almost all men who had had the benefit of his training. A keen disciplinarian, he always tempered justice with kindliness, and his own example of good-humoured obedience never failed to evoke a similar spirit in all ranks. Even after he left the battalion he remained their staunch friend; indeed, it is not too much to say that whatever subsequent credit and distinction came their way was always regarded as being due to his abiding influence and example.

On September 12 the battalion took over the Serapeum bridge-head, one company going to Toussoum and another to Deversoir, the battalion once more rejoicing in the pleasures of bathing. Here was met the tell-tale device known as the drag-track, consisting of a broad strip of sand along the whole front, swept smooth at sundown and examined in the morning for footmarks. Invisible at night, it proved an invaluable record of every visitor. The company at Deversoir furnished a guard on the fishing-boats on the Little Bitter Lake, receiving the welcome toll of one-half the catch. Patrolling made heavy demands in the way of night work, and at Toussoum only one man was excused each night.

October 12 witnessed a move to rail-head, where for the first time since April the whole battalion was together in one camp. On the 25th the Commander-in-Chief inspected the defences and on the following day accorded the troops a holiday as a mark of satisfaction.

On November 14 the battalion marched across the desert to the front line, a distance of about fifteen miles, experiencing their first shower of rain since April and greeting it with cheers. On the 28th the line was readjusted, battalion headquarters moving from Round Hill to Gazelle Heights, where the Rev. E. D. Rennison, C.F., joined. Conditions were now reasonably comfortable, the desert air being wonderfully exhilarating. Christmas of 1916, spent at Gazelle Heights, Habieta, Mount Lofty, and the Sphinx, will always be remembered as one of the happiest in the war.

Early in January the battalion moved back to Moascar, near Ismailia, for divisional training. On February 1 the 163rd Brigade left Moascar for Palestine, crossing the canal by the Kantara bridge and following the ancient desert route trodden thousands of years before by the armies of the Egyptians and Assyrians. Leaving Kantara in gloriously fine weather, they proceeded by daily marches along the splendid wire-netting road, like velvet to walk on, the marches being very much alike and varying only in length, namely, from five to nine miles. At Gilban on the 3rd the battalion saw for the first time some of those new engines of war—tanks. Two days later, at Romani, a welcome draft joined. Near camp were some date-palm groves, the first seen since leaving Kantara. The water supply was ample ; in the distance was Katia oasis, and further away, in the opposite direction, the small post of Dueidar. A march over the sand to the sea at Muhammadiya will always be pleasantly recalled by all those who took part in it. After a few days' rest the battalion moved on through Rabah, Khirba, Bir-el-'Abd, Salmana, and Tillul (where heavy rain was experienced), reaching Mazar on the 16th.

On February 23 the battalion left Mazar, remarking on its way to Maadan patches of bright red poppies and yellow daisies. Leaving Maadan, from which the minaret of the mosque of El Arish was visible, the battalion marched across a depression with salt crust upon the soil, turned by mirage into a shimmering lake through which the leading battalions appeared to be wading. El Arish was reached on February 25, the battalion marching past Major-General S. W. Hare, commanding the 54th Division. Here the sea bathing was much appreciated. Early in March a Turkish aeroplane came over very high up. "Archies" flecked the sky with little white clouds, but without causing it any apparent uneasiness.

On March 7 the battalion crossed the Wadi-el-Arish, camping three miles to the east of it behind a crescent of sandhills which the Egyptian Labour Corps were converting into a chain of strong posts. The duties here consisted mainly of guarding wells, of which there were hundreds scattered about over miles of country.

Acting upon instructions received from home, General

Sir Archibald Murray, Commander-in-Chief of the Egyptian Expeditionary Force, now undertook the invasion of Palestine, though with forces, as he considered, totally inadequate for that purpose. The Turkish positions extended from the sea at Gaza to Beersheba, a distance of about thirty miles. General Murray decided to advance along the line of the coast, and by the middle of March the railway, which had been pushed on as rapidly as possible, had reached the Turkish frontier at Rafah. As regards the British forces, the Desert Column (Lieut.-General Sir P. Chetwode, Bt.) was covering the construction of the railway; the 52nd Division had established itself at Sheikh Zuwa'id, the 54th Division being between that place and El Arish.

On March 20 the advance was resumed, General Murray being anxious to force an issue with the Turks before they could withdraw from Gaza to a position nearer their own base, as they had done in the case of Weli Sheikh Nuran. As the troops moved eastward the country gradually improved, showing signs of cultivation, with thin patches of oats relieved by occasional banks of red poppies.

On the 25th—after having completed the stages of El Burj and Sheikh Zuwa'id—the 54th Division marched out of Rafah, the 5th Battalion treading upon Turkish soil for the first time since leaving Anzac Cove. Bivouacking during the day in some gardens at Khan Yunus, the division reached In Seirat at one o'clock on the morning of the 26th in readiness for the attack on Gaza. Three hours later, yawning, cold, and hungry, but filled with the same thoughts that must have fired the Crusaders of old, the battalion stood by while the mounted troops, delayed by a thick fog, crossed the Wadi Ghuzze. That accomplished, the infantry pressed on, the 5th Battalion acting as advance guard to the brigade. The attack on Gaza had been entrusted to the 53rd Division, assisted by the 161st (Essex) Brigade, 162nd and 163rd Brigades protecting the right flank. The mounted troops, working round the enemy's left, attacked Gaza from the rear. The day was gloriously fine, and the battalion's objective—the ridge of Sheikh Abbas—stood out clear and well-defined. The first part of the advance was through fields of corn, knee-high, and heavy with dew, the many-coloured spring flowers shining like gems amongst the golden barley. But beyond the Wadi Ghuzze the country changed completely, the line of advance being crossed by numbers of steep ravines, their descent and ascent making very hard going in the hot sun.

Sheikh Abbas was occupied without opposition, and the battalion, having taken over a sector of the outpost line, began digging trenches along the top of the cliff. During the day Gaza was entered by the attacking troops both in front and in rear, but not captured. In the evening the 163rd Brigade received orders to move to Mansura, about two miles away towards the sea. The broken nature of the country proved too much for the guides in the darkness, and the battalion spent the entire night in what seemed aimless wandering. It was about 7 a.m. before all the companies had assembled in the basin under the Mansura escarpment. Here during the morning the battalion was shelled by an enemy battery from the very ridge they had occupied the previous day, suffering some casualties from shrapnel. In the course of the day our artillery brilliantly combated the vigorous counter-attack launched by the Turks. The enemy guns concentrated on the limbers bringing up ammunition to the guns in the dip ; these limbers, coming up at a gallop, with shells bursting all round them, provided a magnificent spectacle.

The battalion, having drunk the last of its water, watched with anxious eyes for signs of the water camels, but owing to the enemy shelling these could not come up till evening. There had been no issue of water since 3.30 a.m. on the previous day, and the battalion had to exist for two broiling and strenuous days and one restless night on one bottle of water, suffering the extremes of heat and thirst. However, at 7 p.m. water and ration camels arrived, and everyone drank his fill and had a meal from his iron rations. A general retirement across the Wadi Ghuzze was then ordered. Slowly, in column of route, with the jackals howling all round, and the candle left burning at brigade headquarters, the battalion, with eyelids heavy with sleep, marched by devious ways back to In Seirat. It was an eerie and uncanny night, and the experience dramatic in the extreme. The battalion only sustained twenty-seven casualties, including 2nd Lieut. R. C. Fyson, wounded. They remained at In Seirat for about three weeks, engaged in road-making for the first week, with only brackish water to drink and this husbanded like gold. One day a British aeroplane, apparently in difficulties, flew over the battalion, followed by a Turkish plane. Two companies opened fire on the Turk and drove him off. The British plane returned safely, the pilot waving his thanks for the assistance given.

The second battle of Gaza was fought on April 17–19. The British forces had been reinforced by the arrival of the 74th Division, but the Turks had also been reinforced, and furthermore had had time to construct an elaborate system of defence works covering Gaza. The objective of the 163rd Brigade was a series of trenches afterwards named Tank redoubt, and situated about two thousand yards behind the Sheikh Abbas ridge. The brigade left In Seirat on the night of April 16, and secured the ridge with little opposition. The next two days were spent in consolidating this position under occasional shell-fire. The main attack was launched at 7.15 a.m. on the 19th, the 5th Battalion being in brigade reserve. Two tanks assisted the brigade, but one was very soon disabled, and the other, after having reached the redoubt and inflicted considerable casualties on its defenders, suffered a similar fate. The second attack on Gaza was repulsed along the line with heavy loss to both sides, the other three battalions of the 163rd Brigade, on ground devoid of cover, being decimated by machine-gun fire. At noon the battalion advanced in perfect order and dug themselves in on the slope of a slight rise on top of which the other battalions had suffered so heavily. The night was spent in collecting wounded. The position appeared to be completely isolated, and when the battalion had withdrawn behind the Sheikh Abbas ridge the Turks could be seen scouring the trenches, probably in search of loot. For gallantry in this battle Captain H. T. Copinger Hill was awarded the M.C. and R.S.M. J. French the D.C.M. The battalion's casualties were eighty-seven, including Captain H. J. W. Oxlade ; Lieut. L. B. Fox ; 2nd Lieuts. C. J. Norton, C. C. Reed, and G. Ditton, wounded.

From now onwards till November the line from the sea to Mendur (slightly west of Sheikh Abbas) was consolidated and held without any diversion, except occasional raids and bombardments. Till the end of May the battalion were on the right flank, and it was here that " C " Company captured an enemy patrol.

Early in June the battalion spent a delightful week in camp by the sea, after which they moved into brigade reserve three-quarters of a mile behind the sandhill sector of the Gaza line. For the next week they were busy providing working parties. The fineness of the sand caused much extra work, all sandbags having to be doubled to prevent the sand from running out. It is recorded that twenty thousand sandbags were required to revet both sides of a communication trench a hundred yards long.

During the month of June an artillery bombardment of the Turkish salient known as Umbrella Hill provided a grand spectacle. The 54th Division afterwards adopted the figure of an umbrella, blown inside out, as its distinctive badge. The battalion next moved to Samson's ridge, the most prominent feature in that sector, and offering an extensive view of the country beyond Gaza. Every afternoon the white houses of that town caught the sun, making them look like fairy dwellings to sand-weary eyes. Samson's ridge naturally received a good deal of attention from the Turkish artillery. On June 28 General Allenby assumed command of the Egyptian Expeditionary Force.

In the middle of July the Turkish line was heavily shelled without, however, extorting any reply. A party, furnished by two battalions of the Hampshire Regiment, raided Beach Post and, with the loss of two men, killed or captured the entire garrison of the post, numbering ninety-five. On two occasions during the latter half of July Umbrella Hill was successfully raided. After the second of these the Turks opened a violent bombardment, causing many casualties, including 2nd Lieut. W. F. S. Kell (acting brigade bombing officer), who was killed. Early in August the battalion indulged in another restful spell by the sea. Nights of unbroken sleep, no stand-to, and unlimited bathing made the break a thoroughly enjoyable one. The change in the appearance of the country since the previous March was, however, remarkable. The many-coloured flowers, the golden barley, the waving grass knee-high, all had vanished, leaving nothing but grey dust in their place.

The battalion next went into divisional reserve at Apsley

House, settling down to strenuous training. Towards the end of August they took over the Carnarvon redoubt. On September 29 the battalion, which a day or so before had received warning of coming operations, moved to its previous camp near the sea at North Belah and began training for the assault. A model of the objective—El 'Arish redoubt—copied from excellent aeroplane photographs, was made exactly to scale, and, every man having been allotted his place and task, the assault was carefully practised. Some days were spent in the trenches from which the attack was to be launched, and frequent reconnoitring parties went out, one being ambushed by a strong enemy patrol. On October 25 steel helmets were issued to all ranks, and the battalion, now at Marine View near Gaza, spent the rest of the month rehearsing the attack.

For the third battle of Gaza the British forces were much better equipped than for the first attacks on that stronghold. General Allenby had received considerable reinforcements, including much-needed heavy artillery and up-to-date aeroplanes. The Turks, with some accession of strength, were still holding the line from the sea at Gaza to Beersheba. The third British offensive was to open with a sudden dash at the latter town, and upon the result of that operation the date of the attack on Gaza depended. On the night of October 27 there was a high wind, followed by heavy rain and a thunderstorm; bivouacs were blown down, and everyone was drenched. On the last day of the month Beersheba was captured. The next evening at dusk the brigade moved forward to its jumping-off point, the trenches at Fusilier ridge. At 11 p.m. Umbrella Hill was stormed by the 52nd Division, after which the enemy bombarded the front-line trenches for two hours. The attack on Gaza was fixed to take place at three o'clock on the morning of November 2. The objectives of this attack were the enemy works from Umbrella Hill to Sheikh Hassan by the sea, the extent of front being about six thousand yards, and the furthest objective (Sheikh Hassan) three thousand yards from the British front line. At 1 o'clock the battalion advanced to a position—previously marked out—in No Man's Land, and two hours later began moving forward under cover of a perfect artillery barrage.

As soon as this barrage lifted the 5th Battalion waves

dashed into the first-line trenches of El 'Arish redoubt, " B " and " D " Companies leading, with " A " and " C " in support. Captain J. R. Rowley, a most popular officer and the first to enter the trench, was here mortally wounded, and died the same evening. Only small parties of the enemy held out, and the first line was soon cleared. The second line was captured in the same way; likewise the third; but with their flanks exposed, the troops were withdrawn to the second line, which they consolidated. On the night of the 4th the line was reorganised, the battalion taking over the whole of El 'Arish redoubt. On the 6th the enemy gave the battalion the heaviest and most concentrated bombardment it had experienced, but at daybreak on the 7th patrols reported that the Turks had gone. The operations had been successful all along the line, and Gaza was at last ours.

The Turkish trenches proved to be of excellent workmanship and design. Most of the wooden revetments consisted of doors, of many patterns and varieties of wood, from the houses in Gaza. The sandbags were of gay-coloured cloths, sewn, according to rumour, by fair hands in the harems of Stamboul. An order by General Kress von Kressenstein, found in El 'Arish redoubt, ran as follows: " I have inspected your trenches and am well satisfied with them. They are excellent, and if these trenches cannot be held, then it is no use digging any trenches."

The casualties sustained by the battalion in the third battle of Gaza amounted to over 150, including the following officers—*Killed* (*died of wounds*): Captains J. R. Rowley and T. J. Catchpole; Lieut. T. O. Taylor. *Wounded:* Lieuts. C. M. Fyson and H. C. Goldsmith; 2nd Lieut. S. A. Baylis. The undermentioned honours were gazetted in connection with these operations—*M.C.:* Captains H. C. Wolton and L. B. Fox; Lieut. H. C. Goldsmith. *D.C.M.:* Pte. W. Allum; L/Cpl. A. M. Rosling; Sgt. J. W. Pearson. Several military medals were also awarded. It is interesting to note that amongst the troops opposed to the 54th British Division on this occasion was the 54th Turkish Division.

The pursuit of the Turks northwards was now in progress, and on November 14 the brigade left Sheikh Hassan for Herbie, passing Beit Hanun, the Turkish rail-head, where thousands of shells were found abandoned. Halting for the night at Mejdel, Esdud, and Kubeibeh, the battalion reached Shushe on the 19th, bivouacking on very stony ground between the road and the railway. During the next few days heavy rain fell, especially at night. On the 21st a guard of honour was despatched under Captain E. D. Wolton to take part in the Commander-in-Chief's entry into Jerusalem. On reaching Half-way House, however, they found themselves in the midst of a brisk engagement, and on December 2 returned to the battalion. Jerusalem was not entered until December 9.

On November 24 the battalion marched to Ramleh, going into divisional reserve. The little town looked well from a distance, and boasted a crusaders' tower, with crypts, and a monastery in which Napoleon had slept. Welcome supplies, such as chickens and eggs, greeted the troops. The wine of the country seemed to them delicious, but perhaps what impressed them most of all was the church, with its clock and bell; they had almost forgotten that such things existed.

On November 26 four Turkish aeroplanes, having discovered the battalion's camp, bombed it, killing seven men and wounding seven others. The next day the battalion moved out in support of the 162nd Brigade, and assisted in repulsing an attack at Wilhelma. On December 1 the battalion returned to the 163rd Brigade and moved to a camp near the oil refinery and Jewish farm colony at Ludd. Four bullocks, killed by Turkish shell-fire, provided the first fresh meat since Gaza. On the 4th two companies, under Major Copinger Hill, M.C., moved to the bed of a ravine in rear of Beit Nabala, near Zeifizfiyeh—a post captured by the Turks, but retaken five minutes later by a prompt and vigorous counter-attack.

The Suffolk Yeomanry

War, and the mustering squadrons—The great renunciation—The regiment sails for Gallipoli as a dismounted unit—Lands at Anzac Cove—The evacuation—Egypt—On the Canal—The broken spur—The Second Battle of Gaza—The capture of Beersheba—The entry into Jerusalem

Immediately on the declaration of war the various squadrons of the Suffolk Yeomanry, four in number, received orders to mobilise at their respective headquarters by noon the following day, and such was the organisation of the squadron leaders and their permanent staffs that the whole regiment was able to assemble on the cricket ground at Ipswich by August 7.

The Suffolk, Norfolk, and Essex Yeomanry, and the Essex R.H.A. (battery and ammunition column), together with the usual complement of ancillary units, formed the Eastern Mounted Brigade, at that time commanded by Colonel H. W. Hodgson, C.V.O., with Captain W. Gibbs, 7th Hussars, as brigade-major. Consequent on the reduction of the establishment of a yeomanry regiment on a war footing from four squadrons to three, one squadron had to be merged into the others; and on August 12 the Suffolk Yeomanry, thus organised, left Ipswich and proceeded to its war station at Woodbridge, where the headquarters of the brigade were already established in the Bull Hotel.

The following officers joined the Suffolk Yeomanry on mobilisation: Lieut.-Colonel F. W. Jarvis, commanding; Majors Hon. W. E. Guinness, J. W. R. Tomkin, M. Barne. H. F. Courage, and F. Goldsmith; Captains C. E. Pym, J. S. Agnew, E. A. Greene, and T. De la G. Grissell; Lieuts. Hon. E. C. G. Cadogan, Hon. H. Lygon, E. W. Paterson, and G. P. Barker; 2nd Lieuts. P. K. Hodgson, V. C. W. Agnew, R. O. W. Pemberton, H. Musker, W. S. Hyde Parker, J. de B. Crossley, E. H. Buxton, and E. C. M. Flint. *Adjutant:* Captain E. Northen, 19th Hussars. *Quartermaster:* Captain T. Earle. *Medical Officer:* Lieut. E. S. Stork. The strength of the regiment on mobilisation was 408 N.C.O.'s and men.

The early days of the war were taken up with preliminary troop training, completing requirements as regards horses, and enlisting recruits, who kept flocking in until in a short time the regiment was 250 over establishment. In due course the surplus was drafted off to the second line, under Lieut.-Colonel B. E. Spragge, D.S.O., and sent to Ely. The regiment then settled down to intensive training, being fortunate in having an ideal drill ground for cavalry at Martlesham Heath; and, despite the shortage of qualified drill instructors, in three months could have given a good account of itself. Later on in the war, when the battalion was in the trenches, one Suffolk hero was heard to call out to his neighbour, "Dew you keep yar hid down Bor, dew you'll niver see Martlesham Lion agin!"

During November the brigade was inspected by His Majesty the King. In December the regiment moved out of its billets in the town and took over huts and stabling erected at Grove Farm. Thus the time passed until, in July, the brigade was moved nearer the coast, the Suffolk Yeomanry going to Leiston, where the men remained under canvas, the horses being picketed in lines. All yeomanry regiments were now asked to volunteer for service overseas as dismounted troops, and as a result of the appeal the Suffolk Yeomanry were soon instructed to hold themselves in readiness for active service. Only a regiment, compelled to change at short notice its equipment from that of a mounted to a dismounted unit, can realise the work thrown on the quartermaster by such a transformation. Fortunately the regiment had, in Major J. O'Donnell, an officer of wide experience, having previously served in two cavalry regiments as well as the South African Constabulary, and he made it his business to see the equipment complete to the last strap.

Orders to proceed to Gallipoli arrived at the beginning of September, and then came the parting with the horses, probably the saddest disappointment experienced by the regiment throughout the war. Early in the morning of September 23 the regiment entrained for Liverpool, where they embarked in the White Star liner *Olympic*. The strength of the regiment on embarkation was about five hundred, including the following officers: Lieut.-Colonel F. W. Jarvis, in command; Major Hon. W. E. Guinness, second-in-command; Majors J. W. R. Tomkin, F. Goldsmith, and C. E. Pym; Captains E. A. Greene, T. De la G. Grissell, and Hon. E. C. G. Cadogan; Lieuts. G. P. Barker, R. O. W. Pemberton, H. Musker, E. C. M. Flint, J. F. Crisp, and G. R. Arbuthnot-Leslie; 2nd Lieuts. C. B. A. Jackson, R. E. Eversden, A. C. McKelvie, D. B. Ginn, G. B. Horne, A. L. Martyn-Linnington, and R. P. Woodhouse. Captain Viscount Duncannon, adjutant; 2nd Lieut. E. W. Tuttle, quartermaster; Rev. J. W. Blencowe, chaplain; Captain Taylor, medical officer. The total number of troops on board amounted to nearly eight thousand, all Yeomanry.

After remaining at anchor in the Mersey for a whole day the *Olympic* sailed on September 25, the voyage being uneventful as far as the Mediterranean. Here, on October 1, two boats containing thirty-five sailors from a French ship, which had been sunk earlier in the day, were picked up ; and during the afternoon a submarine was sighted, possibly the one that had accounted for the Frenchmen. The *Olympic*, whose escort had left her at Gibraltar, opened fire on the submarine with her gun. The submarine dived, but the huge liner, being an easy target, changed her course and did not resume it till after dark. No other serious event happened during the voyage, which in some respects seemed all too short. Amongst the officers on board were twelve members of Parliament, who thought it a suitable opportunity to dine together ; but the sporting element soon discovered that there were others on board besides legislators, and not to be outdone arranged a dinner of past and present masters of hounds, who sat down twenty-four in number. A far more lively evening ensued, a hunting-horn being produced and passed round for each master to blow in turn.

After a record voyage of under eight days the *Olympic* arrived at Mudros, apparently to the surprise of the authorities, who seemed uncertain as to the disposal of the troops. However, after a delay of five days, they were transhipped by brigades into small transports and despatched to Gallipoli, the Eastern Mounted Brigade being destined for Anzac. The Suffolk and Norfolk Yeomanry were packed like sardines into the small Khedivial liner *Abbasia*. The distance was short, and all on board, hoping to reach their destination soon after dark, made light of their discomforts. But on nearing Anzac Cove a sudden squall came on and, after endeavouring for some hours to get the lighters alongside, the idea of landing that night was abandoned, the transports putting back to Imbros. It was not until October 10 that the jetty, partly destroyed by the gale, had been repaired, and during the night of the 10th–11th the Suffolk and Norfolk Yeomanry landed at Walker's Pier.

The first few days on Turkish soil were spent in constructing dugouts in New Bedford Road gully, the rest camp of the regiment when not in the line. All units, short of both officers and men, eagerly welcomed the newly arrived regiments, and soon the Suffolk Yeomanry were allotted a considerable sector of the line. During the daytime things were generally quiet except for sniping and shelling, the latter occurring with almost time-table regularity, so that the regiment soon came to know when to expect such displays of activity. During the night rifle fire was incessant.

On October 16 a demonstration was undertaken, involving most of the troops on the peninsula, and supported by gunfire from the navy, the object being to ascertain which particular Turkish trenches were occupied and in what strength, and how long the Turks would take to bring up their supports. At a given signal every available man fired one round, and then began to shout and wave his bayonet above the parapet as if about to charge. The Turks, however, ignoring this diversion, looked on stoically, and made no reply whatever.

It soon became evident that the ranks of the regiment would be seriously depleted, if not by enemy action at any rate by sickness, dysentery causing the numbers rapidly to dwindle. During the great blizzard of November 27–28, to which a reference has been made in a previous chapter, the Suffolk Yeomanry moved to Norfolk Street and Hill 60, and were more fortunate than their comrades holding the flats.

On December 8 the 54th Division, to which the Eastern Mounted Brigade had been attached since landing in the peninsula, was withdrawn, the brigade being allotted to the Australian and New Zealand Army Corps under Major-General Godley. They were the only English troops in the corps. The evacuation of the peninsula had, however, now become a settled policy, and on December 14 an advance party of the regiment left for Mudros, the remainder following within the succeeding week.

Many and ingenious were the devices prepared by the versatile soldier to cover up the tracks of the departing troops. Blankets, laid along the communication trenches, prevented the tramp of feet from being heard by the enemy ; and after the invaders had gone the sounds of war continued to rise from trenches already deserted and empty. Now and then a bomb thrown from a catapult, the india-rubber being released by a time fuse, fell among the Turks, while rifles, fired by means of water dripping from one tin into another attached to the trigger, went off at intervals.

On December 21 all that remained of the Suffolk Yeomanry, after having already embarked in two different ships, was finally transferred to the *Anchises*, which upon leaving harbour collided with another vessel and had to remain until the next morning to ascertain the extent of the damage. This turned out to be trifling, and the *Anchises* sailed for Alexandria. Thus fortunately ended the evacuation of the peninsula, the ships having been favoured by a full moon and a calm sea. On arrival at Mudros the wind began to rise, and the next day the weather became so stormy that it is doubtful whether the evacuation could have been carried out. The total casualties during these ten weeks were 11 officers and 282 other ranks, mostly caused by sickness.

On arrival at Alexandria the regiment went into camp at Sidi Bishr, where a few officers and men joined from hospital, bringing the total strength up to 16 officers and over 200 other ranks. During February the Eastern Mounted Brigade was amalgamated with the South-Eastern Mounted Brigade, with the title of the 3rd Dismounted Brigade, under Brig.-General H. W. Hodgson. For a time they were buoyed up with the hope of becoming cavalry once more, but in March the brigade moved to El Kubri, on the Suez Canal, where, employed as infantry, it began to take its share in the heart-breaking task of digging defences. The troops used to work from four o'clock in the morning till eight, resting through the heat of the day. On resuming work at four in the afternoon it was generally found that most of the sand had been blown back into the trenches dug in the morning. A similar time was spent at El Shatt and El Ferdan. In July the brigade moved by rail to Alexandria, and after another short stay at the old camp at Sidi Bishr the regiment was sent to Dabaa, the operations against the Senussi not having been concluded. In December orders were received converting the Suffolk Yeomanry into infantry, and immediately intensive training began in earnest. The regiment was particularly fortunate in having at the time as adjutant Captain W. E Clutterbuck, M.C., Royal Scots Fusiliers.

In the early days of 1917 the three dismounted brigades which had been formed from the yeomanry regiments after the evacuation of Gallipoli were converted into infantry brigades, the Suffolk Yeomanry—whose title had now been changed to that of the 15th (Yeomanry) Battalion of the Suffolk Regiment—being allotted to the 230th Brigade, 74th Division (Major-General E. S. Girdwood), whose divisional sign was a broken spur. During the first week of April the 230th Brigade assembled at Deir el Belah and soon received orders to prepare for the second battle of Gaza, in which the 74th Division were in reserve. On the 18th the battalion crossed the Wadi Ghuzze, taking up a position in the ravines and natural folds in the ground behind Sharta, where they dug themselves in and remained till the last week in May. The next three months were spent in training.

On June 28 General Allenby took over the command of the Egyptian Expeditionary Force, and after a protracted survey of the situation decided to attack the left flank of the Turkish position. In the interval which elapsed between the first and second offensives the strength of both British and Turkish armies in southern Palestine had been increased, the former considerably. During the last week of October troops began marching towards Beersheba, the capture of which was an essential preliminary to the main scheme. On October 30 the 74th Division concentrated south-west of Wadi Saba, moving only by night and remaining hidden by day. Meanwhile, in order to mislead the enemy, the camps in the area round Deir el Belah were left standing though almost untenanted. During the night of the 30th–31st an outpost line was put out, the 15th Battalion being in brigade reserve. At dawn the attacking battalions deployed. The Turks at once began shelling, and the 15th Battalion, while waiting in reserve, sustained some forty-eight casualties in a few minutes. By 1 p.m. all objectives had been secured, and in the evening the 15th Suffolk and 16th Royal Sussex Regiments advanced, capturing and consolidating the ground along the north of Wadi Saba.

On November 6 the battalion was again in action. The 230th and 229th Brigades attacked the system of trenches and redoubts covering Sheria, the battalion starting for the assault at 3 a.m. Before it was yet daylight 2nd Lieuts. W. A. Wood and H. J. Boocock had been killed, and Lieuts. A. L. Martyn-Linnington and K. H. C. Badger wounded. In the case of " B " Company, all the officers had become casualties. Under cover of a ridge the battalion reorganised; " D " Company, in reserve, was brought up into the line, " A " and " C " moving to the east of Wadi Union. Supported by a section of the Machine Gun Corps, the attack was quickly resumed and the enemy driven from all objectives, whereupon the battalion received orders not to advance further. A considerable number of prisoners was taken by the brigade, and a battery of guns captured intact. During the day the Turks endeavoured by a counter-attack to recover these guns but were beaten off. That evening the battalion was relieved, and twenty-four hours later took up an outpost line covering Wadi Sheria. This action had completely turned the Turkish flank, and the next morning the Anzac Mounted Division rode through on the right of the 74th Division. In order to supply the 53rd Division in the hills, the 74th and 10th Divisions had temporarily to give up their transport and were consequently withdrawn to rail-head. During the third week of November the battalion was engaged in salvage work on the Gaza battlefield.

The 74th Division began to march north again on November 23, reaching Latron on the 28th in preparation for the advance on Jerusalem. The attack was ordered for 5.15 a.m. on December 8. The night was very dark, it was raining in torrents, and the ground over which the troops had to advance was very difficult. By 11 a.m. the 230th Brigade had captured Beit Iksa, but further advance being held up by heavy shelling and enfilade machine-gun fire, the positions taken along the northern slopes of Nebi Samwil, facing the villages of Beit Nebala and El Jib, were consolidated. At 8.30 a.m. on the 9th Jerusalem surrendered, and the line was advanced to four miles north of the city.

CHAPTER XV

2ND BATTALION

The battles of Arras, 1917—The First Battle of the Scarpe—The unsuccessful attack on Guemappe—The Second Battle of the Scarpe—And that of Arleux—Infantry Hill—Gallantry of Captain Simpson—The battalion transferred to a quiet sector—Ypres once more—Polygon Wood—Farewell to the Salient—Back again to the Wancourt-Guemappe sector

ON Easter Sunday—the day before the battle of Arras—the Rev. G. C. Danvers, chaplain to the 2nd Battalion, and himself a Suffolk man, who had done so much good work in the Serre sector on the Somme in 1916, held a Communion service in the Chalk Caves at Arras. A sketch of this solemn and impressive scene, made on the spot at the time by Lieut. W. J. Allum, appeared in the *Illustrated London News*, and is here reproduced.

The 2nd Battalion emerged from the caves on April 9, and moved into its assembly trenches. The preliminary bombardment, which had been going on for several days, was then nearing its height. To men who had been so long underground, the noise sounded like that of " cannons overcharged with double cracks," and after the silence of the caves was almost deafening. Attached to the 9th Brigade for these operations, the battalion was ordered to support the 4th Royal Fusiliers, the objective being a strong position known as the Harp. When the Fusiliers reached a certain point the battalion was to pass through them and carry on to the north and east sides of the redoubt.

At zero the Fusiliers advanced. On the way to the Harp a valley had to be crossed along which the enemy put down a 5·9 barrage, but the 2nd Battalion, moving in artillery formation, managed to get through almost untouched.

From our original line the ground for some distance in front was clearly visible, and it was obvious from the steady forward movement of our men that the attack was going well. Prisoners began to trickle in, and soon the whole objective was in our hands. About noon battalion headquarters moved up into the Harp. No counter-attacks came, and in the early afternoon the 8th Brigade passed through and continued the advance. In the evening the battalion returned to the old Hindenburg line, where they were replaced under the orders of their own brigade. The day had been an unqualified success and, as is so often the case in similar circumstances, the casualties were comparatively light, scarcely exceeding a hundred all told, 2nd Lieut. K. J. W. Mowbray being killed, and 2nd Lieuts. D. O. Thorn and J. N. Taylor wounded.

April 10, a stormy, cheerless day, was spent in reorganising and waiting for orders, which did not arrive till nearly midnight. In the darkness movement over battered trenches and amongst masses of tangled wire was both difficult and slow, and it was not until five o'clock the following morning that the battalion reached the Brown line, a distance of only five miles.

On April 11, at very short notice and without preparation, the battalion was ordered to take part in an attack on the village of Guemappe. The objective, however, could not be seen until an intervening ridge had been crossed, and at first the front-line troops mistook the buildings on Les Fosses farm for the village. On account of the terrific enfilading machine-gun fire from the right everyone edged off a little towards the other flank, the troops advancing with their steel helmets tilted over to the right and their heads awry, as though they were marching along in a hailstorm. Certain progress was made, but our men—with totally inadequate artillery support—being unable to cross the long forward slope to cover, swept as it was by a tornado of bullets from front and flank, crept into shell-holes as best they could. While halted there they witnessed a gallant but fruitless mounted attack on Monchy-le-Preux by some of the 3rd Cavalry Division. Two or three attempts were made to gain more ground, but without success, and the battalion was forced to consolidate where it lay. An exceptionally trying day followed. Movement was almost impossible, preventing inter-communication and—still worse—the collection of casualties, in spite of the usual gallant service performed by the stretcher-bearers.

In the afternoon a fresh battalion attacked, but with no more success: so the long day wore on until darkness

THE CHALK CAVES AT ARRAS, EASTER SUNDAY, 1917
DRAWN BY A. FORESTIER FROM THE ORIGINAL SKETCH BY W. J. ALLUM
Reproduced by permission of the "Illustrated London News"

intervened, enabling something to be done. About midnight a relief, carried out in circumstances of extreme difficulty, was completed, the battalion moving back to trenches near Tilloy. On April 13 the 29th Division relieved the 3rd Division, the battalion returning to billets in Arras. The casualties, amounting to 124, included the following officers—*Killed:* 2nd Lieut. H. G. Walne. *Died of wounds:* 2nd Lieut. V. Francis. *Wounded:* A/Captain L. J. Baker; 2nd Lieuts. H. J. Lewin and S. G. Cowper. *Missing (killed):* 2nd Lieut. A. Pryke.

Thus the battalion's undisputed success in the opening phase of the first battle of the Scarpe on April 9 was followed two days later by a complete failure. In the first case, however, the attack was carefully organised, while in the second it had to be launched without preparation or effective artillery support, before the plan of operations could be properly explained, and then carried out by tired troops.

On April 23 the battalion, now in corps reserve, occupied trenches in the Harp, moving up on the following morning to Shrapnel and Pick trenches, which had been battered to pieces and rendered useless. Their casualties during these last trying days of April, including the battle of Arleux, in which, however, they were but lightly engaged, amounted to eighty-one, Captain J. D. Marshall, R.A.M.C. (at duty), 2nd Lieut. V. C. Russell, and C.S.M.'s Taylor and Harber being wounded, the two last-named severely.

On May 4 the battalion moved into the Monchy defences, eventually leaving the area on the 14th and going back through Duisans and Lattre St. Quentin to Denier, where on May 19 Major A. de L. Long, Gordon Highlanders, joined and assumed temporarily the duties of second-in-command. On May 21 the G.O.C. 3rd Division made presentations as follows in connection with the first and second battles of the Scarpe to those able to attend—*M.C.:* A/Captain L. J. Baker (absent, wounded); 2nd Lieut. A. Pryke (posthumous award). *M.M.:* Sgt. A. Jackson; Ptes. J. Ashworth, F. Anderson, W. Howes, and G. Tribe. The next day Sgt. A. Ablott was also awarded the M.M.

On June 1 the battalion moved from Denier to Arras, where two days later they bedecked themselves with roses in honour of the King's birthday. Here Major Long left the battalion on promotion. On June 12 after brigade attack practice, witnessed by the commanders of the IIIrd Army (General Hon. Sir Julian Byng), VIth Corps, and 3rd Division, the battalion took over trenches near Monchy-le-Preux, moving the following night into their assembly positions for an attack on Infantry Hill, a neighbouring feature, "green and of mild declivity," but of commanding position.

On June 14 at 7.30 a.m. the attack was launched. Within ten minutes Hook trench had been captured, and an hour later the remainder of the trench system on the hill fell into our hands. After a certain slackening in the situation the enemy counter-attacked at about five o'clock in the evening, the garrisons of Hook, Tool, and Long trenches being subjected to a violent bombardment. On June 18 at 2 a.m. the enemy north and south of Bois du Vert attacked in force, causing heavy casualties in Hook and Long trenches. The Germans succeeded in getting almost up to the parapet of the former before being finally checked. In helping to repel this counter-attack the 529th Company R.E. lost half its strength. Day now broke, enabling great losses to be inflicted on the Germans as they fled from one shell-hole to another. The casualties in the battalion between June 13 and 18 amounted to 250, including the following ten officers—*Killed :* Captains H. C. Nutter and E. E. C. Gomme ; Lieut. R. F. Barton ; 2nd Lieuts. W. T. Woodward, F. W. H. Speyer, and T. E. Lawes. *Wounded :* 2nd Lieuts. M. C. Ayton, A. J. Courtney, R. S. Read, and G. M. Wilson, the last-named remaining at duty. A/C.S.M. G. Smith died of wounds ; C.S.M. H. G. Double, D.C.M., and C.Q.M.S. G. W. Double, M.M., were wounded.

In the counter-attack on Infantry Hill A/Captain W. L. Simpson played a conspicuously gallant part and was considered by many to have deserved a V.C. He was, however, subsequently awarded a military cross. Lieut.-Colonel Stubbs, D.S.O., received a bar to the D.S.O. for the same action. Captain Gomme, killed on June 18, was wounded at Infantry Hill but remained at duty. These operations, in spite of the heavy casualties they occasioned, are not even mentioned in the official list of battles and other engagements fought by the military forces of the empire during the great war—a striking indication of the scale and intensity of the fighting on the western front.

After the fight at Infantry Hill the battalion returned to Arras, the remainder of the month being spent in Famechon. On June 29 Lieut.-General Haldane presented military medals to five-and-twenty men of the battalion. In the following day's orders Sgt. J. H. Jones was awarded a bar to his M.M. On July 1 the battalion marched through Doullens to Bihucourt, passing through the old line at Serre, and on the 3rd reached Fremicourt. In the Bapaume area, where they remained for the next two months, trench life was altogether abnormal, the opposing lines diverging to a mile or more. In spite of the usual patrolling in No Man's Land, contact with the enemy in this seemingly limitless void was never established.

On July 9 Lieut.-Colonel Stubbs, D.S.O., left France to take up the appointment as instructor at the Senior Officers' School, Aldershot, handing over command of the battalion to Major J. L. Likeman, General List. Previous to his departure the battalion was inspected by the G.O.C. IVth Corps (Lieut.-General Sir Charles Woollcombe). On Minden Day Lieut. and Adjutant V. C. Russell, who was wounded on April 28, rejoined at Beugny, Captain F. H. Vinden having officiated during his absence. On September 7 the battalion arrived at Barastre, remaining there till the 18th, when they entrained for Godewaersvelde. On arrival there they marched to a camp of tents and barns between Watou and Abeele. Two or three days later they moved to Brandhoek, then to Ypres, and into the line on the 25th, the time being spent in preparing themselves for the battle of Polygon Wood, scheduled to begin the next morning.

The 2nd Battalion had not been in the Salient since March, 1916. The few who knew it then found many changes. Our line had been carried forward some miles, and big guns were standing where our front trenches had been. The ground, churned up by nearly three years of shelling, was now scarcely traversable, except by tracks specially prepared by the engineers. All these were, of course, known to the enemy, and movement into and out of the line was always fraught with danger.

On September 26, according to plan, the IInd and Vth Armies attacked on a front of about six miles between St. Julien and Tower Hamlets, the 2nd Battalion participating in the advance of the Vth Corps towards Zonnebeke. The

3rd Division, starting from the Ypres–Roulers railway, assaulted with the 76th and 8th Brigade, the former being on the right of the railway—the brigade boundary. The attack was timed for 5.30 a.m., the battalion having moved into position four or five hours previously.

Punctually at zero hour the companies moved forward in a thick mist which precluded visual signalling and thereby added to the difficulties of inter-communication. The battalion occupied a frontage of four hundred yards, which, owing to the introduction of the pill-box system and other developments in the German method of defence, was greater than had been the practice. The battalion started off in support of the 8th King's Own, but with orders to pass through them at the first objective.

The assault was highly successful, all the objectives being secured and our line carried forward about a mile. To the 2nd Battalion fell the honour of capturing the village of Zonnebeke. In the evening a strong counter-attack against the left brigade forced the line back on that flank, leaving it somewhat in the air; nevertheless our position remained intact. The 27th, except for sniping activity, was a day of comparative quiet until the evening, when the enemy launched another counter-attack. The 28th passed in like manner, except that our troops were further harassed by hostile aircraft flying very low. On the last day of the month the battalion came out of the line. So ended a most successful operation. The casualties for these four days of fighting amounted to 258, including the following officers—*Killed*: 2nd Lieut. C. R. Bond. *Wounded*: Captain K. M. Walker; 2nd Lieuts. E. P. Newell, C. G. Davall, S. B. Smith, J. R. Leach, F. W. C. Thomas, L. J. Baker, M.C., and A. W. C. Major, the two last-named remaining at duty.

This was the last the battalion was to see of the dread Salient. They left, as they had come, amid the fury of war; and almost as long as they remained within range of his guns the enemy dropped gas-shells amongst them as if in mockery at their departure.

The 76th Brigade next took over trenches in the Bullecourt area. On October 22 Sgt. N. A. Bott, D.C.M., M.M., was granted a commission and posted to the battalion. Early in November the enemy sent over a number of gas-shells during the night; several men were gassed, but only one fatally. To every display of activity, either by our patrols in reconnaissance or our trench-mortars in wire-cutting, the enemy replied with a retaliatory barrage. The weather was now often wet and stormy, and on the 25th a gale swept over the line, causing great havoc. On December 19 Major C. B. Nichols assumed temporary command, Lieut.-Colonel Likeman proceeding on leave.

As Christmas Day was spent in the trenches, New Year's Day—at Blairville—was observed as a general holiday, the battalion having its Christmas dinners; but owing to the extreme cold and the frostbound state of the ground outdoor sport was impossible. The New Year's honours list contained awards of the M.C. to Major C. B. Nichols and C.S.M. Webb. On January 12 the G.O.C. VIth Corps inspected the battalion.

On January 25 the battalion moved into support positions in the Wancourt–Guemappe sector, taking over front-line trenches the next day. Early in February a valuable reinforcement of about a dozen officers and nearly two hundred men arrived from the 8th Battalion. The battalion next went into the line on both sides of the Cojeul river. Little occurred of any note in that neighbourhood during the next few weeks except that on March 8 one of those raids, the cumulative results of which were of such importance, was carried out by 2nd Lieuts. Bott and Cook, for which Sgts. E. Richmond and E. Burrows, L/Sgt. H. Smith, and Ptes. J. Lodge and F. Robinson were subsequently awarded the M.M.

4th Battalion

Arras, 1917—The Hindenburg tunnel—The Second Battle of the Scarpe—The great struggle for Guemappe—The battalion goes to Flanders—Four months in the Salient—The Third Battle of Ypres—The battle of Polygon Wood—The battalion leaves the 33rd Division and joins the 58th Division

On April 11, after a tiresome day of waiting, the battalion moved up through Blairville in deep snow to Madeleine redoubt, a system of trenches situated where the Albert–Arras railway crosses the Ficheux–Mercatel road.

On April 12 the battalion, whose division (33rd, Major-General R. J. Pinney) was now allotted to the VIIth Corps

(Lieut.-General Sir T. D'O. Snow), IIIrd Army (General E. H. H. Allenby), moved forward into two hollow roads in front of Neuville–Vitasse, its headquarters sharing with that of the 1st Middlesex Regiment an ample German dugout, large enough to hold at least a hundred men.

On April 16 the battalion began taking over trenches in the Hindenburg line, a slow, laborious relief not completed till the next day. Headquarters and two companies were established in the famous Hindenburg tunnel, which, having a section of nearly seven feet square, ran underground for miles. It was provided with ample recesses, numerous entrances consisting of stairways with thirty or forty steps and iron railings, sleeping-bunks with wire beds, and—at the Sensee valley end—even a water supply. The remaining two companies were in the former German front line, liberally provided with concrete machine-gun posts. Relieved on the 20th, the battalion returned to Neuville-Vitasse, but two days later began moving up into the line again for the second battle of the Scarpe.

Zero hour on April 23 was fixed for 4.45 a.m., the British troops attacking on a front of about nine miles. The 4th Battalion, with two companies in the front line and two in support, was to attack southwards down its trenches as far as the edge of the Sensee valley, and to link up with a brigade making a frontal attack on that portion of the Hindenburg line still in the hands of the enemy. This being a battle of two dimensions, certain troops were detailed to mop up in the tunnel, but it was an almost impossible task to drive back the Germans on the surface and under it as well.

At first all went smoothly. The barricades fell, the companies pushed forward gallantly almost to the edge of the Sensee valley, and 650 prisoners, with a *grenatenwerfer* and five machine-guns, were brought in, seventy prisoners having been rounded up in one tunnel entrance and marched back to the rear by a former Bantam.[1] Success seemed certain. "A" Company had pressed forward to within two hundred yards of the Sensee valley, "D" in the support line being about level with them. The enemy, however, now counter-attacked vigorously, and these two companies being

[1] When asked how he had managed to collect so many prisoners he replied that 'he had surrounded them.'

unsupported on their flanks were compelled to fall back. The tunnel proved to be a source of weakness, for in it, sheltering from the bombardment, was a large force which came up in the rear when the counter-attack began. Part of "D" Company, having been cut off, withdrew across country in rear of the support trench, where 2nd Lieut. H. W. Woods was killed. The maze of communication trenches between the front and support lines, which it was impossible to guard or even watch, afforded the enemy excellent cover during his advance. Two companies of the 5th Scottish Rifles came up to support "C" and "D" Companies; but it was all in vain, and by 3 p.m. the enemy were back at the barricades of the morning. Twice during the course of the day had battalion headquarters turned out and manned the parapet. Captain J. Gaston, the medical officer, passed through his aid-post men of eight different units.

Another barricade was hastily constructed in rear of the original one. At 6.30 p.m. a fresh attack was actually being launched when it was cancelled. It drew forth vigorous retaliation, but by ten o'clock the firing had once more subsided.

The battalion, having been relieved, moved out at 8.30 a.m. on the 24th. Their astonishment may be judged when, on getting out of the trench in order to pass the barricade built at brigade headquarters in the alarm of the day before, they looked back and saw British troops walking about on the hotly contested ground of the previous day. They then learned that the Germans, evidently hard hit, had withdrawn some distance during the night, and that a considerable length of the Hindenburg line had been gained. Their casualties in the struggle for Guemappe on April 23 amounted to 315, including the following officers—*Killed:* 2nd Lieut. H. W. Woods. *Wounded:* Captain J. C. Rash; 2nd Lieuts. A. W. Hare, W. R. Wolton, F. Dallimer, D. Glen, B. C. Rigby, B. S. Evans, and S. C. Williams.

The battalion next moved to Boyelles, where it was shown great hospitality by the 18th Middlesex Regiment, and on the following day marched to Grosville, near the larger village of Rivière, for a short rest. Here the battalion received congratulatory messages from the divisional and corps commanders, the latter having watched them as they marched into Blairville. After an enjoyable rest the battalion marched to Douchy-les-Ayette and on to Boyelles, just then a region of continual bombardment. In the middle of May it took over an unpleasant position in the Sensee valley, with battalion headquarters in a flimsy dugout immediately in front of some massed batteries from which premature shells caused a certain number of British casualties. On May 20 the 33rd Division carried out an attack, but the 4th Battalion was not called upon to leave its trenches. During the last week of June the battalion completed its farewell tour in the Hindenburg line; the enemy shelling on the 27th was particularly heavy, the casualties including 2nd Lieut. W. G. Haynes, killed. On July 6, footsore and weary after a series of long marches, the battalion reached Warlus, where it rested.

Leaving the Somme on the last day of July, the battalion travelled by train to Adinkerke, in Flanders, and on the following day marched in pouring rain to La Panne. One day Cpl. Whalley went down to the beach at La Panne, where he met and was recognised by a Belgian fisherman who before the war used to put into Southwold harbour, where Whalley was employed. Interspersed with tours in the line, the remainder of the month was spent in the Franco-Belgian frontier at various camps along the coast between Oost Dunkerke and Bray Dunes. One of these—Wellington camp—was heavily bombarded with 8-in. shells on the 19th, two companies being forced to bivouac in a neighbouring field. On August 21 a working party of four hundred strong was shelled returning to Queensland camp and sustained fifteen casualties, including 2nd Lieut. W. J. S. Cotton, who died of wounds on the 23rd.

On September 1 the battalion was railed from Bray Dunes to Watten, marching to billets scattered round the villages of Zudrove and Moulle. On the 7th, when going up to inspect trenches, Captain H. D. Mitchell was wounded. Marching through Cassel, Steenwoorde, and Meteren, the battalion reached Reninghelst on September 20, moving up to Bellegoed farm on the 23rd, and into support trenches the following morning, with B.H.Q. near Clapham Junction. The enemy shelling of the area, which had been going on all day, continued throughout the night, and at daylight on the 25th reached a pitch of great intensity, extending back to brigade headquarters at Stirling Castle. The headquarters of two companies were hit, one twice.

On the 25th the enemy attacked, gaining a foothold in the front-line trenches at several points. During the day these trenches changed hands more than once, and by nightfall the situation had not been restored. An attack, rehearsed at Reninghelst, had been ordered for the 26th, but as the troops detailed for it were already heavily engaged and would be unable to reach their starting-points by zero, a change of plans was found necessary at the eleventh hour. "B" Company, during the afternoon of the 25th, advanced under intense shell-fire to the support of the 2nd Argyll and Sutherland Highlanders, who were endeavouring to recapture the front-line trenches. Not being actually employed in the counter-attack, they took up a position, in support, in a very battered trench, where they experienced a terrific bombardment and sustained many casualties. On the evening of the 25th commanding officers were suddenly summoned to brigade headquarters to hear the details of the new scheme. The two days' shelling had wrought great disfigurement to the face of the countryside, and Colonel Copeman, who was accompanied by L/Cpl. G. Whiting, M.M., on returning at 9 p.m., found difficulty in keeping to the track.

Shortly after midnight the battalion took up a line running from Glencorse wood to FitzClarence farm, having picked up "B" Company on the way. No advance could, however, be made as some of the troops on the left were not ready. Gradually the situation grew worse. The moon had gone, the shelling became more persistent, and a thick mist rose. Colonel Copeman asked the brigade to allow the 4th Battalion to go forward alone. This was not sanctioned, but at 5.45 a.m. he arranged an advance of his and the other battalion, with the men linked hand in hand so as not to lose touch in the darkness. As they cleared the irregular line of shell-holes and ditches which they were holding, down came a tremendous barrage in the face of which a regular advance was impossible. Some of the platoons, however, made certain progress. Captains Lake and S. Scrimgeour, with a score of men, succeeded in reaching the Blue Line, later making a further advance and capturing two machine-guns and fifteen prisoners, who gave valuable information. About noon a battalion of another brigade passed through and on towards the objective. Shortly afterwards Captain Lake was wounded, and the following morning Captain Scrimgeour and his party, having been relieved, rejoined the battalion. By the evening of the 27th the division had succeeded in capturing all its objectives. The relief of the division commenced in the afternoon, the battalion finally arriving at Bellegoed farm about midnight, having sustained 265 casualties, including the following officers —*Killed:* Lieut. H. C. Hattam; 2nd Lieuts. L. C. Palmer and W. P. Westwood. *Wounded:* Captain E. L. D. Lake; A/Captains S. W. Turner, M.C., and G. G. B. Bannerman; 2nd Lieuts. R. Fisher, S. C. Roberts, and R. D. Hume, M.C.

The work of the 33rd Division (Major-General P. R. Wood, in temporary command) in helping to drive the enemy from the limited foothold he had gained in the heavy and confused fighting on the 25th, was referred to in despatches; with regard to that of the 26th Sir Douglas Haig records that English, Scottish, and Welsh battalions of the 33rd and 39th Divisions, that had borne the brunt of the enemy's attacks in this area on the previous day, gallantly fought their way forward. The Commander-in-Chief also showed his special approval of the work of the 33rd Division by inspecting its brigades separately.

After the battle of Polygon Wood the 4th Battalion went by train from Ouderdom to Ebblinghem, marching into billets at Lynde. On October 4 orders were received to move to Setques, near St. Omer, but these were cancelled about midnight and others received to go to the forward area. Arriving in Ypres on October 5, the battalion marched to dugouts in a railway embankment near Shrapnel Corner, whence, under the orders of the 7th Division, they furnished working parties for the next ten days in very bad weather. The battalion then moved to Kortepyp camp, near Neuve Eglise, where a batch of officers joined. On the 21st Ptes. C. Packard and C. Martin, and L/Cpl. G. Whiting were awarded bars to their military medals, nine others receiving the M.M.

Early in November the battalion returned to Ypres, furnishing working parties near Château wood and Westhoek, 2nd Lieut. S. Yates and some others being wounded. After a few days at Merris, Meteren, and Neuve Eglise the battalion moved up to Potijze, and on the 17th to Abraham heights, near Passchendaele, 2nd Lieut. G. W. Fisher being killed and 2nd Lieut. O. C. Mitchell wounded. Next day they went into Passchendaele itself, where they sustained a number of casualties, including 2nd Lieut. K. C. Shuttleworth, killed.

After a spell in the Passchendaele area lasting, with short breaks, till December 12, the battalion went by train to Godewaersvelde, marching to billets scattered round about Eecke, where the remainder of the year was spent. In the New Year's honours list Lieut.-Colonel H. C. Copeman was appointed a C.M.G., Captains H. Pretty and L. J. Richards receiving the M.C. Early in 1917 Captain N. Bolingbroke joined from the 8th Battalion.[1]

The battalion remained in the Salient till January 30, when they proceeded by rail and road to Noire Carme. While there the establishment of a brigade was reduced from four to three battalions, the spare battalion being taken either to help form a new brigade or to bring the other battalions up to strength, or to form a pioneer unit. The lot befalling the 4th Battalion was the last-named, a decision which disappointed them without bringing in its train any compensation in the way of honourable retirement into a quieter life. On February 11 they marched away from camp, headed by the band and drums of the 1st Middlesex and 4th King's (Liverpool) Regiments, and the pipers of the 2nd Argyll and Sutherland Highlanders, an act of courtesy very much appreciated by all ranks of the 4th Suffolk Regiment. Brig.-General Heriot-Maitland and his staff were at the starting-point to see them off. The battalion left the 98th Brigade and the 33rd Division, in which they had served for nearly two years, with every regret, and judging by the expressions of friendship displayed on all sides, the feeling was mutual.

On February 15 the battalion arrived at Appilly, marching to a camp in Rouez wood, where they came under the orders of the 58th Division (Major-General A. B. E. Cator, D.S.O.), IIIrd Corps, Vth Army. Ten days later the battalion moved to Chauny and Bichancourt. Here they enjoyed a peaceful time at work in the divisional area, being employed up to the eve of the great German offensive in road-making, improving billets, and in various defence works in and about Basse

[1] Captain N. Bolingbroke served with the 1st Battalion in the South African War, and with the 7th, 8th, and 4th Battalions during the Great War.

forest, chiefly wiring vistas through the wood to be swept by fire from machine-guns. Early in March, while still at Bichancourt, the battalion was reorganised on a three-company basis.

7TH BATTALION

The Arras offensive—The First Battle of the Scarpe—The battle of Arleux—The Monchy defences—A successful raid—The Cambrai operations—The tank attack—Hard fighting in the German counter-offensive on November 30—The battalion in the Lys valley

Shortly after dawn on the loud Easter Monday of 1917 the 7th Battalion, under Lieut.-Colonel F. S. Cooper, marched into the cellars in Arras, filing through the underground passages and sewers until they reached the caves and finally debouching into their trenches, where they awaited zero hour.

The 12th Division held the centre of the VIth Corps front, which lay almost due east of the city. The 3rd Division, to which the 2nd Battalion belonged, held the right of the corps front, the boundary-line between the 12th and 3rd Divisions being the Cambrai road. The movements of the 35th Brigade during the early stages of the battle are well described in the *History of the 12th Division,* which says: "Owing to the strong resistance met with, the Blue Line had not been completely captured in the scheduled time. Nevertheless, General Scott ordered the 35th Brigade to advance according to the plans laid down, considering its appearance on the battlefield would force the Germans still holding out to surrender. The brigade proceeded through the tunnel to the caves, and thence, as the enemy's fire on our trenches was negligible, it debouched, and moving over the top closed up to the leading troops of the 12th Division.

"At 12.15 p.m. the 7th Norfolk Regiment on the right, with the 5th Royal Berkshire Regiment on the left, followed by the 7th Suffolk and 9th Essex Regiments, passed through the 37th and 36th Brigades. At 1.5 p.m. the Blue Line was definitely in our possession. The real task of the 35th Brigade now commenced. There was no intervening system of trenches, but opposition was expected at Maison Rouge, and the enemy's batteries were known to be in the valley that had to be traversed. The plan was to capture Feuchy Chapel redoubt and its surroundings and to pierce the line just west of Orange hill.

"On the capture of the Blue Line the Germans, becoming disorganised, were caught on the run, and the 35th Brigade had the joy of seeing them retreating in disorder. The 7th Norfolk Regiment pushed forward to level with the Bois des Bœufs. The 7th Suffolk and 9th Essex Regiments now proceeded to the final objective. The Essex gained Feuchy Chapel redoubt, but the greater portion of this attack was stopped by Church Work, uncut wire, and machine-guns. All attempts to cut the wire by hand and proceed were frustrated, and a line was taken up along the Feuchy road."

The weather on the 9th—by no means good—gradually became worse, and during the night and the following day much sleet and snow fell, the conditions being deplorable. About midnight Lieut.-Colonel Cooper, having been informed that the wire was to be cut by our artillery at daybreak, withdrew the battalion; next morning the attack was continued, and by noon the 7th Battalion had captured the final objective. Patrols were then pushed forward and the position consolidated. On the night of April 12–13 the 12th Division was relieved by the 29th Division and returned to Arras. The casualties of the battalion in the first battle of the Scarpe included the following officers—*Killed:* Captain D. W. A. Nicholls, M.C.; 2nd Lieuts. C. L. Elvey and H. R. Isaacs. *Wounded:* Captain E. F. Ledward; Lieut. G. F. A. Lewin; 2nd Lieuts. H. H. Collis (died of wounds April 12), C. A. E. Horton, H. R. Howell, H. M. Bond, E. G. Hannant, W. W. Stallard, and S. B. Leader.

The battalion then went off on a circular tour, marching through Wanquetin, Halloy, Fosseux, and Gouy-en-Artois, and returning to Arras by bus on the 24th. The next morning they moved up to the railway triangle, and that evening took over trenches south of the Scarpe from the 17th Division in readiness for the forthcoming battle of Arleux.

On April 28 an attack on a front of about eight miles was delivered by British and Canadian troops, the 12th Division making their thrust between the Scarpe and Monchy. The battalion, going over the top at 4.45 a.m. to attack the new Blue Line, passed through the 5th Royal Berkshire Regiment, who had captured Bayonet trench and also some 150 yards of Rifle trench. They immediately came under a most devastating machine-gun fire from Rœux, which the troops operating on the north side of the river had not yet taken, and suffered very heavy losses. Portions of the various companies managed to reach the first objective but were unable to gain further ground. All the officers except the colonel and the adjutant having been killed or wounded, these small parties returned to the Black Line as soon as it grew dark, and at 1 a.m. the battalion (now reduced to 190 effectives) withdrew to the support line. On the 29th about a hundred men, under Major Henty, took over the left support trench. During the night of April 29–30 a handful of men returned to battalion headquarters from the first objective, which they had occupied and held since the early hours of the 28th. The casualties amongst the officers at the battle of Arleux were as follows—*Killed :* Lieut. J. P. C. Ashworth, M.C. ; 2nd Lieuts. H. C. Hewlett and E. W. Rush. *Died of wounds :* 2nd Lieut. W. Dingley. *Wounded :* Captains P. Gurrey and H. A. Short, M.C. ; 2nd Lieuts. G. C. Drummond and G. A. Ling.

2nd Lieut. Rush was formerly a company sergeant-major in the 2nd Battalion, and had only recently been given a commission.

The remnants of the battalion having been organised into two weak companies went into reserve at Railway triangle and Orange lane till the middle of May, when they returned to Arras, marching two days later to Simoncourt and Fosseux for a month's rest and training. Throughout the summer months they remained in the neighbourhood of Arras, mainly in the Monchy sector, where the chief activity was raiding. An important operation of this kind took place on August 9. This raid, rehearsed over dummy trenches designed from air photographs, was carried out by parties from three brigades acting simultaneously, that furnished by the 35th Brigade consisting of 350 men from the 7th Battalion. As soon as it was light the artillery began to bombard a belt of enemy trenches 2000 yards long by 300 yards deep, the bombardment being continued throughout the hours of daylight. While this was in progress the front line was very thinly held, the bulk of the battalion being in caves in its own headquarters line. During the evacuation of the front line Captain L. A. G.

Bowen, M.C., and 2nd Lieut. A. Green were gassed with phosgene shells. At 7.45 p.m. the strong patrols and raiders, accompanied by small demolition parties of Royal Engineers, began moving forward under a creeping barrage, the 7th Battalion heading towards Bois du Vert and the Mound. Within a short time prisoners began to trickle in. As soon as the German first line had been reached a box barrage was put down and his second line raided. The operation was a marked success, and though the casualties were heavy, valuable information was obtained and great damage inflicted. The battalion brought back sixty-nine prisoners and two machine-guns. Captain Morbey was killed on his own parapet, after the raid was over, by fire from a German aeroplane. The casualties included the following officers—*Killed :* Captain C. F. W. Morbey ; Lieut. H. Ranby ; 2nd Lieuts. C. Le Cheminant and S. N. Smith. *Wounded :* Captain J. C. G. Matthews ; 2nd Lieuts. C. W. B. Palmer, C. T. Postlethwaite, and J. R. Tamlyn. For this raid Captain J. C. G. Matthews and Lieut. D. S. Black were awarded the M.C. In August Captain R. K. Barton and 2nd Lieuts. E. E. Ladell and L. F. Coxwell were wounded.

The 7th Battalion saw a good deal of the 2nd Battalion while in the Arras sector in 1917. Having returned to Arras itself on October 21, they went back with the remainder of the 12th Division into the Le Cauroy area, north of Doullens, where they practised various methods of attack in conjunction with tanks. At the close of the month they were in Fontaine l'Etalon and two neighbouring villages, and a fortnight later entrained at Bouquemaison for Péronne. Marching by stages towards the front line principally under cover of darkness, and lying carefully concealed throughout the day, they reached successively Sorel-le-Grand and Peizière, whence on November 19 they moved into their position of assembly for the Cambrai operations.

The 12th Division, belonging to the IIIrd Corps, stood on the right of the line, just south of the road leading out of Gouzeaucourt towards Lateau wood, and attacked along the Bonavis ridge. The obstacles in front of the German line consisted of three belts of wire, each being about eighty yards wide. To have dealt effectively by means of bombardment alone with this triple mass of wire would have been a lengthy task. The tanks, however, overcame the difficulty very quickly, their tracks forming lanes through which the infantry could pass unhindered. The 35th Brigade attacked with two battalions in the front line, the 7th Battalion supporting the 5th Royal Berkshire Regiment, with orders to leapfrog as soon as the first objective had been gained. The battalion was in position ready for zero hour by 3 a.m. on the 20th, the tanks and artillery having moved up similarly unobserved.

The surprise was complete, the main Hindenburg system being rapidly overrun. Sir Douglas Haig says: "In this advance the 12th (Eastern) Division (Major-General A. B. Scott), moving along the Bonavis ridge on the right of our attack, encountered obstinate resistance at Lateau wood, which sheltered a number of German batteries. Fierce fighting, in which infantry and tank crews displayed the greatest gallantry, continued throughout the morning at this point, and ended in the capture of the position, together with the enemy's guns."

Operations were continued, and further progress was made during the two following days, when the whole of the enemy's defensive position was passed. The situation then gradually calmed down, the 12th Division constructing a new linc of trenches, running at right angles to their original front and overlooking the Scheldt canal. The few casualties sustained by the battalion included Captain A. J. A. Harris; 2nd Lieuts. W. C. M. Palmer, F. J. Doouss, G. R. Pocklington, S. R. Hill, P. A. Baker, and the Rev. E. Jones, C.F., wounded.

After three weeks of fighting and marching the men were worn out and badly needed a rest. On the night of November 29 the battalion was relieved and sent back into the brigade reserve, moving into a sunken road less than half a mile behind the front line. Headquarters were in the Cheshire quarry, the officers being accommodated in old dugouts some distance from their men. The position was only intended as a temporary one, and possessed no trench system.

That evening Lieut.-Colonel F. S. Cooper left the battalion seriously ill, Major Henty assuming command. Major Walker arrived after dark, and in ordinary circumstances would have taken over command the next day. But events were destined to turn out very differently. Early in the morning of November 30 the hostile artillery became very active, and almost before the battalion had had time to stand-to Germans in enormous masses swarmed round the flanks of the division, attacking from all sides. At the same time numbers of low-flying aeroplanes wheeled about overhead firing machine-guns and dropping bombs. Men banded themselves together, offering such resistance as lay in their power. The machine-gun posts were rushed in detail. Some time before the position was lost a fight ensued round Cheshire quarry, in which Major Henty and Captain and Adjutant Taylor were killed and Captain A. G. Bryce, medical officer to the battalion, was wounded. The casualties in the battalion amounted to 232, including the following officers—*Killed:* Major G. H. Henty; Captain G. H. R. Taylor (Adjutant). *Wounded and missing:* Captain A. G. Bryce, R.A.M.C.; 2nd Lieut. T. Hawkins. *Missing (prisoners):* Major P. S. Walker; Captains L. A. G. Bowen, M.C., J. W. Haughton; 2nd Lieuts. W. E. Teager, H. F. T. Hamilton, H. Thomson, J. C. Dabbs, C. G. Poulter, and H. W. Crook.

The German counter-offensive of November 30, quickly organised and resolutely delivered, was in retaliation of our surprise attack of the 20th. Their success, however, was not achieved without heavy casualties.

After this temporary reverse a new line had to be taken up, the next few days being spent in consolidating it amid considerable artillery and sniping activity. On December 3 twenty-eight men, who had been captured on the 30th but had contrived to escape, rejoined the battalion. The next day the battalion marched back to Heudicourt, where a roll-call showed the strength as 250; nearly 100 men from the right half battalion were waiting here, including 2nd Lieuts. Spurgeon and Hodgson. After marching back to Cartigny they went by road and rail to Bouzincourt and on to Berguette. At Calonne-sur-la-Lys Major J. H. Lindsay, D.S.O. (London Scottish), joined on December 18 and took over command of the battalion, which a few days later marched to Chapelle Duvelle, spending Christmas there.

Except for occasional periods in the line at Fleurbaix or Bois Grenier, the battalion remained in the Lys valley for over three months. Early in February a large draft of officers and men joined from the 8th Battalion, and towards the end of the month Lieut.-Colonel G. V. W. Hill, D.S.O., from the

8th Battalion, arrived. Major P. C. Bull, D.S.O., became second-in-command, the company commanders being Captains W. C. Hull, M.C., C. Knight, M.C., E. J. Greene, M.C., and G. L. Crandon, M.C. Captain C. B. B. Clee was appointed adjutant, Lieut. R. J. Lawler having officiated since the end of November.

8th Battalion

Arras—The Third Battle of the Scarpe—The battalion in front of Cherisy—Transferred to the Salient—The battles of Ypres, 1917—Pilckem—Resting at Rubrouck—The First Battle of Passchendaele—The 8th Battalion disbanded at Rousbrugge

At the close of April the 18th Division, having been transferred from G.H.Q. Reserve to the VIIth Corps, concentrated in the neighbourhood of Arras. The arrival of the 8th Battalion brought the number of Suffolk battalions in that area up to five, the 2nd, 4th, 7th, and 11th having already been engaged in the opening battles of the Arras offensive. Shortly after reaching Neuville Vitasse, the 18th Division received operation orders for the third battle of the Scarpe—a well-planned scheme of vast pretensions.

After the moon had set, and in the darkness before the dawn of May 3, the long lines of troops were set in motion. The 18th Division attacked with two brigades, one of which (55th) captured Cherisy and advanced to a depth of about three thousand yards. Along the front immediately to the north and south of that village matters had not gone so smoothly, and the 55th Brigade, with both flanks in the air, was forced to withdraw to its original position. While the 53rd Brigade (in support) was moving up in broad daylight and in full view of the enemy, it came under a heavy artillery fire, the battalion sustaining numerous casualties, including 2nd Lieut. E. R. R. Peck, M.C., killed, and Lieut.-Colonel Hill, slightly wounded. About noon the Germans counter-attacked vigorously, retaking Cherisy after much bitter fighting and remaining in possession. On the 5th 2nd Lieut. S. A. Trounce was killed during a bombardment of our front and support lines. A fortnight later the 33rd Division, on the right of the 8th Battalion, carried out an attack. The battalion, held in readiness to move forward, was not required to do so, and on the following day went into divisional reserve.

At the end of three weeks they returned to the line. On June 16 Captain P. R. Meautys, M.C., Brigade-Major to the 53rd Brigade, was killed by a stray shell. On the following day the battalion proceeded to Souastre. On the 26th the 2nd Battalion marched over from Famechon, the two battalions having dinners together; and when the 2nd Battalion started its return march, they were headed by the band of the 8th Battalion. On July 3 the 8th Battalion entrained at Mondicourt, arriving the next day in the neighbourhood of Steenvoorde, where the Archbishop of York delivered an address to the brigade. The battalion then commenced special training at Reninghelst and Dickebusch for the forthcoming Ypres offensive, leaving camp on the 30th for the forward area.

The battles of Ypres of 1917 began on the last day of July, the main blow being delivered by four army corps of the Vth Army, under General Sir Hubert Gough, attacking on a front of nearly eight miles. The front allotted to the IInd Corps (Lieut.-General Sir Claude Jacob), to which the 8th Battalion belonged, extended from the Menin road to the Zillebeke–Zandvoorde road. This difficult stretch of country, especially that part where the Menin road crosses the ridge, was perhaps on the whole the scene of the most desperate fighting in the opening battle, although the depth of the British advance was greatest in the direction of Langemarck.

The intention was that as soon as the 30th Division had gained the Black Line, the 18th Division who were in support should go through them and carry on. The 53rd Brigade (Brig.-General H. W. Higginson) were then to attack the Green Line, and, if the situation developed favourably, the Red Line also. The 8th Battalion reached its assembly positions about 2 a.m. on July 31, and by zero hour (3.50 a.m.) had established its headquarters at Wellington Crescent. During the latter stages of this move, enemy shells set fire to some dumps and a tank, lighting up the ground with remarkable effect. As "C" Company was passing through Zillebeke a shell burst amongst them, killing and wounding several of the men.

The troops of the attacking division, which the 53rd Brigade were to leapfrog when the first objective was taken, moved forward between the 8th and 24th Divisions. The 8th Suffolk and 6th Royal Berkshire Regiments, ready and expectant, waited for the front-line reports that would tell them the way was clear for their advance. "By a tragic mistake the 30th Divisional infantry wheeled to their left and assaulted Château wood instead of Glencorse wood. The misleading information that Glencorse wood was in our hands caused the 53rd Brigade to plunge into a fatal gap. One of the Suffolks' scouts met, near the Menin road, an officer of the 17th Manchesters, who reported that Glencorse wood had been captured. Contradiction came from Lieut. R. C. Bolingbroke who, before being wounded, penetrated as far as the line of the first objective. Bolingbroke reported that the enemy was still holding ground west of Glencorse wood."[1]

Early in the morning Lieut. Bolingbroke went forward with the battalion scouts to clear Sanctuary wood and place signposts to guide the companies. They came under fire from a corner of the wood, Cpl. Fletcher being twice wounded. This was the work of a daring sniper, who did much damage before he was killed. Soon after 6 a.m. Lieut. Bolingbroke sent back a message to say that the 30th Division were on the north side of the Menin road, and in Château wood.

As the troops advanced a barrage was encountered in the splintered remains of Sanctuary wood, on the further edge of which they came under a destructive machine-gun and rifle fire. A platoon of "B" Company, under Lieut. Chibnall, was the first to get up to Lieut. Bolingbroke. These two officers decided to attack the second line (Surbiton Villa) with such troops as they could collect, and without waiting for support. The line was taken, Lieut. Chibnall and Sgt. J. Mason, M.M., being killed, and Lieut. Bolingbroke wounded, at the head of the platoon. In the course of the severe fighting in the vicinity of Surbiton Villa, Pte. F. J. Read with a small party of "A" Company (Major H. A. Angier, M.C.) rushed a German machine-gun, killing the whole team.

The battalion got on to the Menin road near Clapham Junction and advanced several hundred yards beyond it, where they were checked and forced to take up a line of shell-holes. The attack practically finished here, as by this time the enemy were in great strength round Glencorse wood. While

[1] *History of the 18th Division* (Blackwood).

Major Fache was crawling up the Menin road with a runner, a cock pheasant alighted about fifty yards ahead of them, though shells were dropping everywhere. The runner shot the bird, carrying it out of action on the end of his rifle with great pride. It was possibly not the first time he had killed game without a licence.

By this time all our tanks had been put out of action. The battalion, having advanced altogether nearly a mile and made a hard but unavailing fight to get still further, now dug themselves in. Thus ended, as far as the 8th Battalion was concerned, the battle of Pilckem Ridge, in which they sustained 177 casualties including the following officers—*Killed :* Lieut. R. S. Chibnall ; 2nd Lieuts. J. D. Wheeler and A. C. Savage. *Wounded :* Captain G. L. Crandon, M.C. ; Lieut. R. C. Bolingbroke, M.C., D.C.M. ; and 2nd Lieuts. W. Brown and L. C. Rae, the last-named remaining at duty.

On August 6 the IInd Corps commander (Lieut.-General Sir Claude Jacob) addressed the 8th Suffolk and 6th Royal Berkshire Regiments in Dickebusch, complimenting them. On the 10th the battalion marched to the Château Segard area, but almost on arrival were ordered to Ritz street, concentrating there at three in the morning. At dawn on the 11th the enemy put down a very heavy barrage on that area, which slackened during the day but increased at dusk. An attack had been ordered for the early morning of the 12th, but owing to the barrage, the rain, and finally to the intense darkness, the companies, wallowing in shell-holes, found it impossible to reach their assembly positions in time, and the attack had to be cancelled. On August 16 a carrying party of six officers and two hundred men transported a large mass of wiring material to the front line. The following evening the whole battalion left the Café Belge in buses and proceeded to Rubrouck for rest and training. Their casualties for the period August 10–17 included 2nd Lieuts. K. J. Winkworth, killed on the 12th, and G. G. Hannan, who died on the 17th from wounds received the previous night.

At Rubrouck Major Fache on promotion handed over to Captain C. B. B. Clee the adjutancy he had held with great distinction through many a stormy month ; at the same time the following awards were announced—*Second bar to D.S.O. :* Lieut.-Colonel G. V. W. Hill. *M.C. :* Captain C. A. C. Argles ;

2nd Lieut. W. Brown; C.S.M. D. Wells, M.M. *D.C.M.*: Cpl. F. Bowers; L/Cpl. B. J. Platten; Pte. F. J. Read.

On September 23 the battalion moved to Road camp, St. Jan ter Biezen, marching a fortnight later to dugouts along the Yser canal bank, near Essex farm. At midnight on October 11–12 the battalion began moving up towards Rose trench, situated near Poelcappelle on the Langemarck side. The march was a long one, carried out in drenching rain, and on its way up the battalion was heavily gas-shelled. Rose trench was found to be a brimming ditch, and the surrounding ground a swamp, continually being churned up by shell-fire. For the remainder of the night the troops had to stand in icy water up to their waists. Battalion headquarters was in the debris of a small brick building called Pheasant farm, which could only be entered by crawling on all fours.

On October 12, at 5.25 a.m., a British attack was launched between the Ypres–Roulers railway and Houthulst forest. An hour later Lieut.-Colonel Hill moved the battalion forward in artillery formation in the wake of the 55th Brigade, the right company being directed towards the left corner of Poelcappelle. Between Rose trench and the Langemarck–Poelcappelle road a considerable enemy barrage was encountered, and after crossing the Langemarck–Dixmude road, companies had to deploy owing to machine-gun fire. The whole ground was pock-marked with shell-holes, often so full of water that men had to struggle to prevent themselves from drowning. The valleys of the streams were altogether impassable. Major Fache, C.S.M. H. E. Backhouse, and a runner, tried to cross the road through the village to gain touch with the 6th Royal Berkshire Regiment, Backhouse being shot dead. After vainly striving to advance, further operations were abandoned. The battalion sustained 232 casualties, including Captain H. J. P. Creagh, Lieuts. L. H. Furniss, and G. H. Walker, and 2nd Lieut. H. H. Walters, wounded. The difficulty of dealing with so large a number of stretcher-cases on such ground can only be realised by eye-witnesses. The battalion M.O., Captain A. C. B. Biggs, M.C., was most gallant and untiring in his efforts.

After relief, on October 13, the battalion made its way to Canal Bank dugouts, moving on the following day by lorry to Tunnelling camp, St. Jan ter Biezen. On October 30 they marched to Plumerdon camp. A few days later they proceeded by rail from Proven to Boesinghe, marching on to Baboon camp. Major H. A. Angier, M.C., left the battalion in October, proceeding to the United States with the British Military Mission. On November 6 the battalion went into the line in the devastated and ghastly area of Houthulst forest, and after a wet, uncomfortable spell, trudged in cold, blinding rain to shelters near Boesinghe. Thus in camp and trench the days dragged on till, in mid-December, the battalion was railed to Herzeele where Christmas was spent. On January 25 they moved from Larry camp to Chaud Chapp near Rousbrugge, where on January 28 the battalion learned to the great regret of all ranks that it was to be disbanded. On February 7 three drafts aggregating over 600 officers and men left camp to join the 2nd, 4th, and 7th Battalions respectively. The remainder with the transport marched to Proven and entrained for Noyon. Lieut.-Colonel Hill, after leading the battalion with conspicuous success through two years of hard fighting, went to command the 7th Battalion, Major P. C. Bull, D.S.O., with much excellent service to his credit, being appointed second-in-command. Major Fache, and Captains Bolingbroke and Hull, honourably mentioned in so many of Lieut.-Colonel Hill's reports, were also posted to the 7th Battalion.

February 8 was spent in the train, passing through Arras and the Somme battlefields, Thiepval, Miraumont, Boom Ravine, Mericourt, and other scenes of the 8th Battalion's great achievements.

Reaching Noyon that evening, they marched in darkness and intermittent rain to the village of Grandru. On February 12 they marched to Quesmy, becoming part of the IIIrd Corps reinforcement camp. Entraining at Ham on the 22nd, they reached Estaires two days later and joined the 7th Battalion, then in the line.

9th Battalion

The Loos-Hulluch sector—Raids and counter-raids—The 6th Division resting at Frevillers—The Cambrai operations—Christmas at Bailleulmont—The 9th Battalion receives orders for disbandment—Farewell dinner at Lebucquière—Disbanded at Courcelles-le-Comte

In March the 6th Division took over a front extending northwards from the Double Crassier at Loos northwards for a distance of over six miles, remaining there through a long and trying period of raids and bombardments. The first of these raids of any importance was carried out by "D" Company on April 10, 2nd Lieut. C. H. Miller and several other ranks being wounded. For gallantry on that occasion 2nd Lieut. Miller was awarded the M.C., Cpl. W. Goshawk and Pte. C. Andrews receiving the M.M. During the months of April and May—a period of almost incessant minor attacks—four other officers were wounded, namely, Lieut. W. F. Fitch, M.C., and 2nd Lieuts. A. H. L. Howell, F. N. Palmer, and P. Brain.

During the night of June 8–9 the enemy attempted a raid on Newport sap, but were repulsed by a platoon of "A" Company, commanded by C.S.M. F. Potter, leaving four dead on our wire. C.S.M. Potter was awarded the D.C.M. for gallantry on this occasion. Two nights later "B" Company, under Captain C. V. Canning, raided as far as the enemy's support trenches in front of Cité St. Elie, but found them empty. A certain amount of information was, however, obtained and much material damage done. On June 25 C.S.M. S. H. Mason was killed. On July 25 the 6th Division was withdrawn from the line for a month's rest, the battalion proceeding to Frevillers. During this period Major-General T. O. Marden, C.M.G., succeeded Major-General C. Ross in command of the 6th Division, Brig.-General P. W. Brown, D.S.O., succeeding Brig.-General E. Feetham, C.B., C.M.G., in command of the 71st Brigade. At the divisional rifle meeting the battalion won the Lewis gun competition. On August 8 the Corps Commander presented medal ribbons to several non-commissioned officers and men belonging to the battalion.

On September 20 a shell fell into the transport lines at Les Brebis, killing two men and wounding seven others. Telegraph wires, cut and twisted, had fallen about the horse lines, and a stampede was imminent. For gallant conduct on this occasion Sgt. Last was awarded the M.M. On September 30 2nd Lieut. S. H. Phillips was wounded, but remained at duty. On October 19 the battalion in the front line in the Lens area was subjected to a violent bombardment which lasted for four hours, obliterating their trenches and causing about thirty casualties, including the following officers—*Killed:*

2nd Lieut. B. F. Packer. *Wounded :* 2nd Lieuts. C. C. Dew, C. Sneesby, F. Goatcher, and C. H. Miller, M.C. A few days later the 6th Division, having been withdrawn from the line, the battalion marched to Nœux-les-Mines, proceeding to Lillers by train and subsequently to Denier and neighbourhood by road. On October 31 2nd Lieut. F. Goatcher died of his wounds.

On November 15 the battalion left Denier, travelling by road and rail to Moislains, and marching the next evening to a canvas camp in Dessart wood. On the 19th, moving after dark, they slipped noiselessly into their assembly positions preparatory to a surprise attack on a large scale, in conjunction with tanks, on the Hindenburg line. During the night the tanks crawled out of their shelters where they had been in hiding, and moving slowly along white tapes laid to guide them to their starting-points, formed up in order of battle. The battalion, deployed into line, lay down in the open behind them. The stillness of the night was broken only by a random shell or a short desultory burst of machine-gun fire.

The attack, kept secret until the last moment, started at 6.20 a.m. on November 20 with 324 tanks and six divisions operating on a six-mile front. The particular sector allotted to the 6th Division (Major-General T. O. Marden), to which the 9th Battalion belonged, lay between Villers Plouich and Beaucamp. At zero hour the tanks began lumbering slowly forward in the twilight, with the infantry following closely in their wake. Suddenly a German machine-gun rapped out a few rounds, and as the sound died away in the mist a thousand British guns thundered forth in answer. The formidable array of tanks, crashing through everything that lay in their path, soon drove the enemy to ground. The 9th Battalion, under Lieut.-Colonel Latham with a flag-stick in his hand, crossed No Man's Land and quickly reached the lightly held German front line. Here Lieut. E. W. N. Tayler was wounded after rescuing, with the aid of his batman, Pte. H. J. Smith, a tank which had caught up a knife-rest in its tread and was helpless. The enemy, taken completely by surprise, had only time to fire a few shells, his machine-gun nests on the flanks being destroyed by the tanks before they were able to render any considerable account of themselves. By nine o'clock in the morning the battalion had seized its objective and was in touch with both flank battalions, with its headquarters in the original German front line. The villages of Ribécourt fell easily to the 6th Division.

After the capture of the German front and close support trenches "C" Company pressed forward to Marcoing with orders to seize the cross-roads in front of the village and the bridges over the river and canal in the village itself. When, at about 11 a.m., the company began to advance, it was found that two platoons, under 2nd Lieut. A. C. J. Taylor, had already moved off, and 2nd Lieut. G. Hopkins went ahead with his batman (Pte. A. Mingay) to try and stop them. Passing some divisional snipers under 2nd Lieut. G. G. Cooper, 2nd Lieut. Hopkins reached the cross-roads, where he found four of the enemy, who surrendered. Observing 2nd Lieut. Taylor and his men about four hundred yards away to the right he signalled to them, and the two platoons closing in, joined with the rest of the company under Lieut. Bryant, who now came up. "C" Company then advanced and entered Marcoing. Shortly afterwards a tank arrived, and at the same time some 29th Divisional troops were seen entering the village from the north. "C" Company, marching back through Ribécourt, did not reach headquarters till after dark, having captured a village, with about 100 prisoners and a machine-gun, at a cost of only two casualties—an exceptional performance. At nightfall the battalion—now held in reserve—occupied the line of trenches captured by them in the morning. Altogether they had captured 150 prisoners and 3 machine-guns, sustaining only 70 casualties, amongst whom were 2nd Lieuts. E. W. N. Tayler, W. A. Bridewell, and G. M. T. Head, wounded.

Sir Douglas Haig relates a thrilling episode of the 51st Division front. He states that "many of the hits upon our tanks at Flesquières were obtained by a German artillery officer who, remaining alone at his battery, served a field-gun single-handed until killed at his gun. The great bravery of this officer aroused the admiration of all ranks." Another incident mentioned by the Commander-in-Chief is that at Masnières the retreating enemy had succeeded in destroying partially the bridge carrying the main road, and that one of our tanks in endeavouring to cross at this point fell through the bridge, completing its destruction.

November 21 was spent in consolidating captured trenches, the battalion moving up the next day to the Hindenburg support system. After being three days in reserve they moved, on the 27th, into support positions in Bois Neuf, with one company in front-line trenches at Noyelles, sustaining a few casualties daily.

On November 30, in the great German counter-attack, the 29th and 6th Divisions held the centre of the line and were the solid nucleus upon which the whole battle hinged, both to left and right. Although in front-line trenches the casualties in the battalion were extraordinarily light, not even exceeding a score. Major W. R. Whitson was killed, and Lieut. G. F. Bryant and 2nd Lieut. A. C. J. Taylor were wounded in re-establishing a platoon post which had been lost.

At Gouzeaucourt the brigade transport and details, in scattered groups near the Villers Plouich road, were engaged in their ordinary daily work when, soon after nine o'clock in the morning, the village of Gonnelieu was suddenly observed to be in flames, with the enemy advancing on Gouzeaucourt. The battalion transport, hurriedly horsing up and taking whatever stores were at hand, bustled down the Metz road out of immediate danger of capture. An hour later the enemy entered Gouzeaucourt, the few remaining details of the battalion being collected at the south-west corner of the village to check his further progress. About noon the German onrush having been stopped, a battalion of the Guards advanced and cleared the village; later, all the battalion stores were secured and taken to a new camp near Dessart wood. That evening Lieut. Vernon Lee, who with his groom and a four-mule limber was bringing back some wounded men and the body of Major Whitson, was heavily shelled near Ribécourt, his own horse and that of his groom, together with three of the mules, being literally blown to pieces, though none of the party was touched.

On December 1 the battalion concentrated in Bois Neuf, afterwards withdrawing to the Hindenburg support line, where Captain R. B. Christophers was wounded. Mid-December found the battalion in Bailleulmont, where they spent a happy and restful Christmas, the reality of which was enhanced by the frost and snow and the Christmas-card colouring of the old French village.

On January 1, 1918, the battalion marched to Courcelles-le-Comte, where the following honours and rewards were announced—Captain (T/Lieut.-Colonel) F. Latham, D.S.O., to be brevet-major. *M.C.:* Captain C. V. Canning; Lieut. J. V. Lee; 2nd Lieut. G. M. T. Head. *M.S.M.:* Sgt. R. F. Hurle. The interpreter to the 71st Brigade received the Croix de Guerre.

After a short spell in the line the battalion moved back, on January 22, to Lebucquière, where a week later a farewell dinner was held in consequence of the impending disbandment of the battalion. The following officers were present: Lieut.-Colonel F. Latham, D.S.O., Major T. B. Hall; Captains H. C. Stanford, P. L. Scudamore, C. Allerton, D.S.O. (Adjutant), R. England, M.C., L. Wilmot-Johnson, W. F. Fitch, M.C., and C. V. Canning, M.C.; Lieuts. C. H. Woods, J. C. Rowbotham, H. L. Hayne, H. E. Falkner, and A. G. Douglas; 2nd Lieuts. A. H. Stoyle, G. Hopkins, F. Bullen, J. A. Blanch, J. W. Harding, R. E. Cook, E. L. Turner, J. A. Bramley, J. A. Simmons, G. G. Cooper, S. H. Phillips, and S. H. Habershon; Captain and Quartermaster Starling; Captain F. C. Lees, R.A.M.C.; Rev. E. F. Blackburne, C.F.; Lieut. J. V. Lee, M.C. (attd.).

On February 5 drafts of the 9th Battalion left Lebucquière for the 11th and 12th Battalions. These drafts were fortunate, inasmuch as they fell amongst friends and remained links in the regimental chain. As mementos bugles were presented to Major-General T. O. Marden (G.O.C. 6th Division); Brig.-General P. W. Brown, D.S.O., commanding the 71st Brigade; to the brigade-major and the staff captain, the company commanders; Captain and Quartermaster Starling; and to the oldest members of the battalion. The silver bugle won by the battalion at the divisional rifle meeting was presented to Lieut.-Colonel F. Latham.

On February 9 the remainder of the battalion marched to Courcelles-le-Comte, where, on the 16th, after two and a half years of splendid service on the western front, the 9th Battalion ceased to exist as such. Lieut.-Colonel Latham rejoined the 1st Leicestershire Regiment. The adjutant, Captain Allerton, went to the 6th Divisional staff. Captain Starling went as quartermaster successively to the 5th Entrenching Battalion, the 11th Lancashire Fusiliers, and early in May,

1918, to the 20th Middlesex Regiment, with which he remained until the end of the war. On the King's birthday, 1918, he was awarded the M.C., a 9th Battalion honour. Lieuts. Rowbotham and Tailby, brigade transport and machine-gun officers respectively, and a few other ranks, remained with the 71st Brigade. The surplus, together with that of the other disbanded units, was formed into the 5th Entrenching Battalion, which on March 21 became a fighting unit of the 25th Division, engaged with old comrades of the 6th Division in the desperate struggle round Bapaume. Withdrawn from the Somme fighting on March 27, the remnants of the 5th Entrenching Battalion were parcelled out to the 74th Brigade, being caught a fortnight later in the German attack along the river Lys, north-west of Armentières. Thus the remnant of the 9th Battalion, ever decreasing in numbers, continued to exist until the war ended.

11TH BATTALION

Arras—The First and Second Battles of the Scarpe—Arleux—Severe fighting at the chemical works at Roeux—Hargicourt—Corporal Day wins the V.C. —The battalion goes to Gough's Army—Poelcappelle—With Byng's Army in front of Cherisy—In the VIth Corps front on the Sensee

On April 8 the 11th Battalion moved into its assembly positions half a mile south-east of Roclincourt. The next morning, at half-past five, the guns began to roar, and the battalion, six hundred strong with twenty officers, under Lieut.-Colonel Kendrick, advanced to the attack on the first German system of trenches. The progress of the 11th Suffolk Regiment—one of the two leading battalions of the 101st Brigade—was checked but not delayed by the hostile machine-gun fire, and within the allotted time the first goal was reached, "A" Company reporting the Black Line captured without loss. Shortly after eight o'clock battalion headquarters moved forward to the German second line, where they established themselves in a dugout, five of the battalion runners and the orderly-room sergeant capturing a batch of twenty German prisoners who showed little inclination to fight. As soon as the Blue Line had been occupied the battalion set to work consolidating their position and reorganising. After dusk they were sent off to the assistance of the 27th Northumberland Fusiliers (Lieut.-Colonel E. Moulton-Barrett), but on arrival found that the enemy counter-attack had been easily repulsed. Battalion headquarters and two companies then returned to their original positions where the remaining companies joined them at dawn. Weather conditions were now very bad, with occasional heavy snowstorms. On the 13th the battalion moved forward, taking over Brown and Green Lines and Towy trench. At one o'clock in the morning our line was heavily bombarded with gas shells, and that night after dark the battalion moved back to billets in Arras. Their casualties in the first battle of the Scarpe (April 9–14) amounted to about 150, including the following officers—*Killed:* A/Lieut. A. H. Woodgate; 2nd Lieut. O. B. G. Johnson. *Wounded:* Captain W. E. Harrison; Lieuts. G. R. Hattersley and R. Theobald, M.C.; 2nd Lieuts. F. L. Pulleyn, G. E. Hamill, E. T. Bolton, and T. J. Pulley.

After resting in billets at Moncheaux, Monts-en-Ternois, and Hermaville the battalion (less a party to Capelle Fermont) returned to Arras. During the evening of April 23 they moved off to a position in the railway cutting in the Blue Line of April 9th. The following day the 34th Division began to relieve the 51st Division on a front extending from the Arras–Douai railway to the Scarpe, the battalion marching that night along the towpath to Athies, and thence by the railway cutting to a position facing the chemical works in Roeux. As it grew dark on April 25 the support line was heavily bombarded, especially round battalion headquarters, and at 10 p.m. Major Tuck arrived and took over command of the battalion from Lieut.-Colonel Kendrick, sick. The next night the battalion moved into the railway cutting south-west of Fampoux.

On April 28 at 4.27 a.m. the 11th Suffolk Regiment, forming the left battalion of the 101st Brigade, attacked the chemical works north of Roeux and immediately south of the railway. It was soon held up, and then driven back by intense machine-gun fire from a trench which appeared to have been missed by our barrage, but a few men actually got right through and into a quarry to the east of the works, coming back in the evening with two or three prisoners. At 9.45 a.m. the enemy counter-attacked from the direction of

Roeux, capturing Mount Pleasant wood and part of Ceylon (communication) trench. Major Tuck then went up into the line again and found the battalion front intact, Ceylon trench once more in our hands and the enemy in the process of being driven out of Mount Pleasant wood.

At ten o'clock that night the battalion was withdrawn from the front to the support-line trenches for two hours to enable our heavy artillery to bombard the chemical works, which were attacked—but again unsuccessfully—by a fresh unit shortly afterwards. On April 30, under cover of darkness, the battalion moved back to camp in S. Nicolas. The enemy having successfully resisted the attacks on Roeux, the bitter, ugly fighting of April 27–30 in that part of the battlefield of Arleux had produced little change in the situation, though it had cost the battalion nearly three hundred casualties, including the following officers—*Killed:* Lieut. D. M. Miller; 2nd Lieuts. R. N. Durtnell and H. S. Grand. *Died of wounds:* Lieut. J. V. FitzG. Prestidge; 2nd Lieut. C. Sheen. *Wounded:* 2nd Lieut. G. Smith. *Missing:* Lieut. J. N. Harmer; 2nd Lieuts. J. W. R. Hunt and W. A. Mudd. It was afterwards ascertained that 2nd Lieut. Hunt had been killed.

On May 1 the battalion proceeded by bus from Octoi to Ivergny, afterwards marching to Occoches and Pernois. By the end of the month they were back again in the Arras sector and once more on the right of the 34th Divisional front. The period between May 1–30 was the first considerable opportunity the division had had of rest and training since its relief from the Somme fighting, the result making a marked improvement upon all battalions.

June 1–18 was spent in the lively Gavrelle sector, where much hard work was done in the Green Line and a number of casualties sustained. Returning to Arras, the battalion went by bus to Houvin–Houvigneul, but early in July, having been transferred from the XVIIth to the IIIrd Corps, they proceeded by road and rail to Péronne, the division occupying a line about twelve miles east of that town, the centre being three miles west of the Hindenburg line at Bellenglise.

On August 24 the battalion moved into the front and Brown Lines, with two companies in Priel wood, taking part two days later in a most successful attack on Malakhoff farm and trench system in front of Hargicourt, in which all the objectives were quickly gained. One account[1] says: "This battalion had some hand-to-hand fighting at the junction of Sugar and Malakhoff trenches, and suffered from a machine-gun's fire till its crew was killed. The centre company, 'B,' lost ground getting through Malakhoff farm, but this had been anticipated, and the troops on the right and left bombed inwards down the support trench, so that the Red Line was occupied up to time. The officer commanding 'D' Company[2] materially facilitated the consolidation of this part of the objective by seizing the adjacent portion of Triangle trench, in which he took thirty prisoners."

It was in this action that Cpl. Day of the 11th Battalion won the V.C. under circumstances thus described in the *London Gazette* of October 17, 1917:

"No. 15092 Cpl. Sidney James Day, Suffolk Regiment (Norwich). For most conspicuous bravery. Cpl. Day was in command of a bombing section detailed to clear a maze of trenches still held by the enemy. This he did, killing two machine gunners and taking four prisoners. On reaching a point where the trench had been levelled he went alone and bombed his way through to the left in order to gain touch with the neighbouring troops. Immediately on his return to his section a stick-bomb fell into the trench occupied by two officers (one badly wounded[3]) and three other ranks. Cpl. Day seized the bomb and threw it over the trench, where it immediately exploded. This prompt action saved the lives of those in the trench. He afterwards completed the clearing of the trench and established himself in an advanced position, remaining for sixty-six hours at his post, which came under intense hostile shell, grenade, and rifle fire. Throughout the whole operations his conduct was an inspiration to all."

Other recipients of honours falling to the battalion included: Captains A. B. Wright and R. V. Burrowes, and Lieut. W. R. Hall, awarded the M.C.; Sgt. J. P. Negus the D.C.M.; and several others the M.M. and cards of honour.

On September 25 the battalion moved from the neighbourhood of Vandencourt Château to Péronne, proceeding by rail and road to Bienvillers-au-Bois.

The fighting in the Péronne sector in July–September,

[1] *The Thirty-fourth Division*, 1915–19. [2] Captain A. B. Wright.
[3] Lieut. F. Maxwell-Lawford.

Corporal S. J. DAY, V.C.

though not belonging to any group of classified operations, cost the 11th Battalion 230 casualties, including the following officers: *Killed:* 2nd Lieuts. O. L. Buckoke (July 8) and J. D. Maxwell (July 18); E. E. G. Alderwick and R. W. F. Danvers (August 26). *Wounded:* Captain R. V. Burrowes; Lieut. J. B. M. Wilson; 2nd Lieuts. W. F. F. Sharp, F. G. Oakey, F. Maxwell-Lawford, C. J. Cavaliero, and W. G. Gentle. *Missing (killed):* 2nd Lieut. R. C. Waitt.

Early in October the battalion was sent up to Flanders, detraining by night on October 8 at Elverdinghe, whence they marched into Soult and Leipsic camps.

The 34th Division, suddenly transferred to the Vth Army (General Sir Hubert Gough), now joined the XIVth Corps (Lord Cavan), and by the night of October 8–9 had concentrated in and around Proven. Within a few hours of its arrival in the Salient the 101st Brigade moved north, and for the next three days was engaged in repairing roads in the forward area close to the front line to facilitate further advance. This severe and unpleasant task, carried out in daylight and vile weather, under constant shell and machine-gun fire, cost the battalion over fifty casualties, including Captain J. W. Wootton and 2nd Lieut. C. P. Joscelyne, both of whom died of wounds, and Major G. L. J. Tuck (in temporary command) wounded. The work was accomplished with complete success, and formed one of their most praiseworthy achievements in the war. The 34th Division did not take part in the attack on the 12th. On the night of the 18th–19th, while in camp near Stray farm, the battalion was bombarded with gas-shells, Lieut. F. Ashworth, 2nd Lieut. S. J. W. Boggis, and a score of others being badly gassed and the whole battalion more or less affected. On October 19 2nd Lieut. H. Chaplin was killed.

The conditions under which the troops were now existing were beyond description. The shelling was heavy and continuous, and the whole countryside a dreary waste of shell-holes, mostly full of water. A single duckboard track led to battalion headquarters at Olga House. Beyond that there was nothing to show routes to any given point, one pill-box being much like another. On October 20 the battalion on relief moved back to old trenches at Schreiboom, with headquarters in Kortabeek farm. This pill-box smelt so strongly that the floor was dug up, when the bodies of several Germans were found under the mud. At the feet of one was a bottle of beer unopened. While here a big shell landed just above the doorway, which faced the enemy. Had it struck the pill-box a foot lower everyone inside would have been killed.

During the night of October 22–23 the battalion took over the line between Aden House and the Broembeek stream, without guides and under the usual fire, earning the special congratulations of the divisional commander (Major-General C. L. Nicholson), who was quick to recognise the difficulties of such an operation. In the unsuccessful attack on the 22nd the battalion was not involved. The 34th Division now received the welcome order to leave the ruthless Salient and proceed to the Arras area, a change that could but be for the better. "It may safely be asserted that no division ever left the Ypres Salient with regret."[1] Towards the end of October the division took over the sector between the Arras–Cambrai road and Fontaine-lez-Croisilles, joining the IIIrd Army (General Hon. Sir Julian Byng), VIth Corps (Lieut.-General Sir J. A. L. Haldane), where they remained for three months.

The battalion reached Achiet-le-Petit on October 28, moving shortly to Boisleux-au-Mont, and then went into the line opposite Cherisy. During the last month of their stay in these parts all three brigades of the 34th Division were in the front line. Christmas was spent in reasonable comfort, though the weather was bitterly cold. On relief, the division went back to the Gomiecourt area. Lieut.-Colonel E. H. Kendrick, D.S.O., who had been in command of the battalion for the past fifteen months, was now appointed to that of the 34th Machine-gun Battalion, and Major A. B. Wright, M.C., commanded temporarily. At the close of December Major Leith-Hay-Clark left the 11th Battalion to take over command of the 25th Northumberland Fusiliers. The battalion next proceeded to Hamelincourt, where a draft of fifteen officers (including Captains W. F. Fitch, M.C., and C. V. Canning, M.C.) and three hundred other ranks joined from the 9th Battalion. On February 9 the division went into G.H.Q. reserve in the Le Cauroy area. Lieut.-Colonel M. E. Richardson, D.S.O., 20th Hussars, assumed command of the battalion from February 16. Ten days later the battalion, having been

[1] *The Thirty-fourth Division.*

inspected by the Corps Commander, received orders to move into the line, and at the end of the month was in Mercatel. At the beginning of March, in wind and snow, the 34th Division took over the centre sector of the VIth Corps' front, the battalion moving into trenches overlooking Fontaine-lez-Croisilles. On March 20 Lieut.-Colonel Richardson left the battalion on appointment to the command of a brigade, being succeeded by Major G. L. J. Tuck, D.S.O., who had hastened back from England after being wounded during the previous October. The same night the battalion took over front-line trenches just north of the Sensee river.

12th Battalion

Gouzeaucourt—The capture of Villers Plouich—The raid at La Vacquerie—Death of Regimental Sergeant-Major Macey—Major-General J. Ponsonby takes command of the 40th Division—The raid at Gonnelieu—The capture of Bourlon Wood—Sharp fighting at Bullecourt—The 121st Brigade resting at Ervillers and Hamelincourt

On April 12 the 12th Battalion, acting as outposts to the 121st Brigade, moved forward, covering the advance of the division to its new position between Gouzeaucourt and the wood of the same name, which was occupied and consolidated a week later. It then took over the Queen's Cross sector, remaining there till the end of the month. During this period the 40th Division attacked and captured Villers Plouich, a notable exploit in which, however, the 121st Brigade was scarcely involved at all. On May 2 the battalion, moving forward again, occupied a new position opposite the Hindenburg line.

On May 5 a raid on a large scale was carried out by the 119th and 121st Brigades on the village of La Vacquerie, the 8th Division making a similar effort on the right. The 12th Battalion furnished two companies, each a hundred strong, "C" Company (Captain F. Miskin), on the left, making for an isolated group of trenches, which they found unoccupied, and "D" Company (Captain A. V. Crump), on the right, for the trenches in front of La Vacquerie. "D" Company's right boundary was a partly sunken road, in which the Germans had concealed a machine-gun. This company, held up by stretches of uncut wire, and by violent rifle and machine-gun fire, was forced to retire, the casualties including Captain A. V. Crump, wounded. On the way back a section, under Sgt. J. F. Lovell, encountered a German patrol, four of whom were captured and brought in, for which exploit he was awarded the D.C.M. The vigorous nature of the opposition met with on this occasion showed that the Germans intended to cling to the Hindenburg line with all the means in their power.

In the middle of May 2nd Lieut. A. N. Rucker was wounded, and on the 23rd R.S.M. C. W. Macey died of his wounds. This warrant officer, formerly of the Essex Regiment, had played a most important part in the making of the battalion. He was posthumously awarded the D.C.M., being succeeded by C.S.M. A. Goody.

On May 22 the battalion was involved in another raid, this one being conducted by 2nd Lieut. H. Leeming. The enemy lines were a long distance away, perhaps a thousand yards or more, the object of the raid being to rush an advanced post and if possible bring back a prisoner. Leaving sections of his party at intervals in No Man's Land under the command of 2nd Lieut. L. H. Knowles, 2nd Lieut. Leeming went forward with about twenty men. With great dash they contrived, by means of Bangalore torpedoes, to blow three large gaps in the enemy wire ; they also succeeded in bringing in a prisoner belonging to the 124th Ersatz Regmient, thus obtaining an important identification. After a few days in Dessart wood the battalion returned to Gouzeaucourt. On June 2, while in the Villers Plouich sector, Captain A. H. M. Jackson was severely wounded.

The 40th Division was now allotted to the IIIrd Corps. June and July, spent in the trenches at Gonnelieu, fell within the category of quiet months. The weather was perfect and the sector quiet, the village providing fruit and vegetables for those who sought. Amid surroundings where the rigour of war could at times be almost forgotten, it was perhaps only fitting that the battalion should receive a rude reminder of the enemy's presence, when one day in the early morning mist a section of the front line was gas-shelled, causing a score of casualties—mostly fatal—before the presence of gas was detected.

In August Major-General John Ponsonby, who at the beginning of the war commanded the 1st Coldstream Guards, was appointed to the command of the 40th Division in place of Major-General H. G. Ruggles-Brise, transferred to the 3rd Division in a similar capacity. The new divisional commander quickly made himself known to all ranks of the battalion by taking the first opportunity of visiting it in the front line. On August 3 2nd Lieut. A. I. Griffiths was killed, and later in the month 2nd Lieut. R. Tricker wounded.

On September 25 at dusk, after artillery preparation, two companies, under Captains Schiff and Redding respectively, set out upon a raid at Gonnelieu, sappers co-operating with smoke-screens and thermite. The lynx-eyed enemy, having observed these companies getting out of the trenches, put down a barrage five minutes ahead of theirs. As the party advanced in the moonlight they were followed across by this barrage, but in spite of these difficulties succeeded in reaching their objective. Besides killing many Germans in the trenches they bombed several dugouts, blowing in the entrance of those from which the enemy refused to come out, and returning at the end of an hour with five prisoners and a machine-gun. Such results are not achieved without cost, and out of a total of eight officers and rather more than two hundred other ranks, these intrepid raiders sustained very nearly a hundred casualties, including the following officers—*Missing (killed):* Captain M. E. H. Schiff. *Wounded:* 2nd Lieuts. R. T. Robins, M.C., G. Hallsmith, J. T. Suttle, and J. Fryett. For gallantry in this raid the following awards were made—*Bar to M.C.:* Captain H. A. Redding, M.C.; 2nd Lieut. R. T. Robins, M.C. *M.C.:* 2nd Lieut. H. Williams. *D.C.M.:* Sgts. C. Blinco and J. McMahon; Pte. W. Pratt. Several military medals were also bestowed. In October Captain F. Miskin left the battalion on being appointed second-in-command of the 20th Middlesex Regt.

Early in October the 40th Division moved out of the line, concentrating round Fosseux and Bavincourt. Towards the end of the month they went still further west, the battalion proceeding to Sus St. Leger, much of the time being devoted to training in the wooded valleys round Lucheux. In mid-November the division began moving towards Beaumetz to participate in the Cambrai operations, and on the 22nd relieved the 62nd Division in the freshly won line south of Bourlon Wood. On November 23 the 40th Division, recently transferred to the IVth Corps (Lieut.-General Sir C. L. Woollcombe), attacked Bourlon wood and village, with the 119th Brigade on the right and the 121st Brigade on the left, the battalion being in brigade reserve. This operation formed a brilliant military exploit, and in describing the great struggle for these highly important tactical points Sir Douglas Haig in his despatches says: "At 10.30 a.m. the 40th Division (Major-General J. Ponsonby) attacked Bourlon wood and, after four and a half hours of hard fighting, in which tanks again rendered valuable assistance to our infantry, captured the whole of the wood and entered Bourlon village." The troops were, however, unable to retain their partial hold on the latter, and the next day the 121st Brigade attacked it again. By noon the companies were all in position, battalion headquarters moving into the quarry just north of the main Cambrai road. At the close of another arduous day of severe and difficult fighting, in the course of which two companies of the 12th Battalion penetrated to the north of Bourlon, that village still remained virtually in the hands of the enemy. On the 25th the division was relieved and withdrew to the Hindenburg line, the battalion having sustained 150 casualties, including the following officers—*Died of wounds:* 2nd Lieut. W. E. Whymark. *Wounded:* Lieut. H. W. Robinson; 2nd Lieuts. G. Miller, F. T. Verry, J. Fryett, and G. Hallsmith (at duty). *Wounded and prisoner:* 2nd Lieut. K. Pearce.

Early in December the battalion went into the front line in the Croisilles–Bullecourt sector, occupying the Tunnel trench, so called because of a large tunnel which ran under it lighted throughout by electricity. After spending Christmas in camp at Hamelincourt they returned to the neighbourhood of Bullecourt, where, in the closing days of the year, Lieut. B. E. Pledger and 2nd Lieut. F. W. Leeman were wounded.

On January 5 the enemy, under cover of a heavy barrage on the battalion front, attacked the right company of the three in the front line, rushing an advanced post of Lieut. H. C. Mathew's company with the aid of *flammenwerfer*. The men at the post resisted with great vigour until they were all killed. The enemy obtained a footing in a sap leading out of the battalion's front line, but a counter-attack at night restored the sap to its possession and resulted in the capture of about thirty Germans. Fighting continued till the 8th, but the position remained intact. The next day Lieut. C. J. Postlethwaite was killed, and the battalion, after an exhausting spell in the line, went back to Mory in reserve.

During January Captain A. M. W. Proctor, 2nd Lieut. R. P. Hughes, Lieut. H. C. Mathew, and 2nd Lieuts. J. Dunn and E. H. Hammonds were wounded, the three last-named remaining at duty. In the New Year's honours list Captains A. M. Cross and F. Miskin, and Lieut. M. F. Richards were awarded the M.C., and shortly afterwards the following immediate rewards were announced—*D.S.O.:* Major L. Lloyd; 2nd Lieut. G. Hallsmith. *2nd Bar to M.C.:* Captain H. A. Redding, M.C. *M.C.:* Captain A. M. W. Proctor; Lieut. H. C. Mathew; and 2nd Lieut. L. H. Knowles. *D.C.M.:* Sgts. C. Lacey and F. D. Baker; Cpl. A. W. Larwood; and Pte. J. T. Hunt. Several military medals were also awarded.

On February 12 the 121st Brigade went back to Ervillers and Hamelincourt for a month's rest. March opened with the battalion in billets in Bailleulmont, after which they proceeded to a camp in Blairville for training.

CHAPTER XVI

2ND BATTALION

The transition from an offensive to a defensive policy—Fresh commitments—An unpopular measure—The great German offensive—The battle of St. Quentin and Bapaume—The battle of Wancourt—The 3rd Division transferred to Horne's Army—The battles of Estaires, Hazebrouck, and Bethune The night attack at La Pannerie

TOWARDS the end of September, 1917, it was decided to accede to the request of the French that a further twenty-eight miles of front should be taken over by the British. This additional commitment did not actually take effect, however, until the end of the following January, when the total length of active front held by the British Army amounted to one hundred and twenty-five miles.

About this time a great many battalions were disbanded, and under instructions from the Cabinet the reorganisation of divisions on a ten (instead of a thirteen) battalion basis was completed during the month of February. Sir Douglas Haig lays stress on the fact that, apart from the reduction in fighting strength involved by the innovation, the fighting efficiency of units was also reduced. The reason is not far to seek. Each brigade, instead of having two battalions in the line and two out, had now only one out, involving two tours of duty in the line to one of rest.

The British Commander-in-Chief, in his despatch dealing with the German offensives in Picardy and Flanders, pointed out that the disappearance of Russia as a belligerent country on the side of the Entente Powers had set free the great bulk of the German and Austrian divisions on the eastern front; and that as early as the first week in November, 1917, the transfer of divisions from the eastern to the western theatres had begun. Prior to that time many thousands of fresh troops also had been brought from the eastern front as drafts. The character and vigour of the German counter-attacks at the close of the battle of Cambrai were in themselves indications of his accession of strength.

The numerous new identifications obtained by means of raids, and the mass of information gleaned from air reconnaissances and many other sources, showed clearly that the Germans were preparing for an offensive on a colossal scale. The British high command had even anticipated that such offensive would be directed down the line of the Somme towards Amiens. Accordingly, in Gough's and Byng's armies all possible arrangements were made as regards defence in depth, though the actual troops necessary for that purpose were not available.

The fighting throughout this great German offensive was of so confused and complex a character, extending over such a long period and vast area, that it is almost impossible to form any clear conception of it. It is, however, hoped that this brief prelude may help the reader to appreciate some of the difficulties which beset our troops during that crisis, and to follow the fortunes of the Suffolk battalions through the greatest battle in the history of the world.

At the beginning of March, 1918, the 3rd Division was holding the line immediately south of the Arras–Cambrai road. All three brigades were in the line, the front of each being held by one battalion. The 76th Brigade was on the left, the 2nd Battalion being therefore on familiar ground, over which it had fought in April of the previous year. However, instead of being the attackers as on that occasion, they were now definitely on the defensive, and as March wore on it became increasingly clear that a great German offensive was imminent.

On March 12 the battalion moved up into the battle zone, with headquarters in Wancourt. Actually the next few days were quiet, though the strain of waiting for the storm to break was intense. A few days later the battalion went into the line on the extreme left of the division, with its left on the Arras–Cambrai road at Cavalry farm, everything remaining suspiciously peaceful.

On March 21, just before five o'clock in the morning, an exceptionally loud explosion occurred away to the left of the battalion front, rightly judged to be that of a projector discharge. This was the signal for the bursting of a storm to which the history of the world affords no parallel. The great battle had begun. Within a few moments a terrific bombardment with gas and high-explosive shells from all types of artillery and trench-mortars thundered along the fronts of the Vth and IIIrd British Armies, a distance of fifty-four miles. Wide sectors of the French line were also swept by shell-fire, and Dunkirk was bombarded. Indeed, the battle-front might almost be said to have extended from the North Sea to the Swiss frontier. In all at least sixty-four German divisions took part in the first day's fighting alone. The battle, thus opened, lasted for four months.

The 2nd Battalion, under Lieut.-Colonel J. L. Likeman, had been working for weeks on the front with such good effect that they suffered very few casualties from this bombardment. No infantry action developed on its immediate front. Three times during the day the enemy delivered attacks on the brigade on the right, threatening to embroil the battalion which was kept under bombardment. The first of these took place four hours after zero, the others following at regular intervals of four hours. All these were repulsed with heavy loss, the enemy being subjected to enfilade fire from the machine-guns and Lewis guns of the battalion. Gas was put down at intervals, causing a few casualties, including 2nd Lieut. N. A. Bott.

The night was fairly quiet and the line, though badly knocked about, was still in a good defencible condition. On the 22nd the shelling of the back areas continued, but the battalion was not attacked; for the moment it was in the calm centre of the cyclone. At 2 p.m. the enemy in very large numbers were observed coming across the Dury–Hendecourt road and moving in a north-westerly direction. At 5 p.m. they shelled the Wancourt ridge heavily and later the vicinity of battalion headquarters. The right brigade of the 3rd Division was brought back to a line facing south-east between Heninel and Henin and in that position successfully beat off a heavy attack. The night was again quiet.

Having no knowledge of the course of events outside the fronts of the 3rd and 15th Divisions, where everything was going satisfactorily, the battalion was disappointed at being ordered, at about 1.30 a.m. on the 23rd, to withdraw to the front line of the reserve system immediately to the north-west of Wancourt village. That same night, however, at about ten o'clock, before the orders for withdrawal had been received, the Germans carried out a "stealth raid" on the front left company. A party of about six of the enemy crept through the wire and captured a lance-corporal, who happened to be passing along the trench alone. This raid was obviously carried out with the object of finding out whether the line had been, or was about to be, evacuated. The lance-corporal had, of course, no idea that later on in the night this would be effected, and his information, together with the fact that a platoon was left behind to make " war noises " until just before dawn completely misled the Germans, who, at day-break, put down a heavy barrage and then attacked the empty trench in mass formation. This bombardment was witnessed with much glee by the men in the front line of the new position, which was about a mile in rear of the old one.

On the 24th the 9th Brigade relieved the 76th and the battalion moved back to the old German trenches north of Neuville Vitasse. The 25th and 26th were spent in digging a new switch line from Telegraph hill to Ficheux. On the 27th the battalion again went into the front line overlooking Wancourt. The relief was not completed till late, and the companies had no time to settle in before being attacked. Unluckily, that very morning the battalion had received a heavy Easter parcel mail which, as events turned out, fell practically unopened into the hands of the Germans. It will be appropriate here to mention that the reserve system had been traced out some weeks beforehand, the trenches being dug about seven feet wide and six inches deep—sufficient to expose the chalk—and then left. These had all been carefully photographed by the enemy. Except for a little work done by the 9th Brigade during the night of the 25th–26th, this was the state of the front line when the battalion moved in on the 27th. Nowhere were the trenches as much as three feet deep in the front line, and in many places they were not joined up. The battalion, setting to work to improve the new trenches, reflected regretfully upon the good ones they had vacated.

Work had only just begun when, at 3 a.m. on the 28th, a violent bombardment opened on the back areas, falling an hour later on to the front trenches, which were swept with such a tornado of shells and trench-mortar bombs that it seemed impossible for anyone in the battalion to survive. This continued until about 6.45 a.m., when the barrage lengthened and fell on a line just in rear of battalion headquarters. The enemy were seen attacking in great strength along the rivers Cojeul and Scarpe on the front of the 3rd and 15th Divisions. At the moment the attack fell on the front of the battalion the 15th Division was observed to be retiring, closely followed by the enemy. The company, under Captain L. J. Baker, on the left of the front line, was immediately outflanked, and although that officer succeeded with great skill in forming a temporary flank to the left, his men were soon very hard pressed. By this time the 15th Division had been forced back still further, uncovering the whole of the left of the battalion. The left support company, under Captain T. S. Wynn, was ordered to form a flank to the left, and as many as possible from battalion headquarters continued the line round the rear of the battalion, the reorganisation being supervised by the adjutant, Captain V. C. Russell. About 11 a.m. the enemy succeeded in penetrating the front of the battalion on the right, and, pressing forward, were stopped by the right support company within a hundred yards of battalion headquarters. The two front companies, under Captains W. L. Simpson and L. J. Baker, were now outflanked and fighting desperately. Several attempts were made to get into touch with them, but the runners sent up never returned, nor did any arrive from the companies. From battalion headquarters small parties could be seen still holding out, and these were supported as far as possible by machine-gun fire. The enemy now brought two batteries into action, one on either flank, enfilading the position at point-blank range, and knocking out one after another of the machine-guns at battalion headquarters.

Deprived of covering fire, with their supply of grenades exhausted and their Lewis guns knocked out, and with no ammunition save such as they were able to collect from the dead, the two front companies were eventually surrounded and forced to surrender, but not before they had so mauled the enemy on their front that he had no heart to attempt a further advance, though a large gap now existed between the two support companies who, with sorely reduced numbers, were fighting one on either flank.

By two o'clock in the afternoon the situation had become extremely serious. The general line of the 15th Division was some two thousand yards in rear of Telegraph hill, the enemy filling the breach on the left and in rear of the battalion, despite the excellent shooting of the left support company. On the right the neighbouring battalion had been beaten back, and the enemy were fast approaching Neuville Vitasse. The two front companies had ceased to exist; a gap of about three hundred yards lay between the support companies, and the enemy were pressing heavily on all sides. No support was available from any direction. Moreover, the artillery was being mainly employed in counter-battery work, from which the infantry only derive indirect assistance.

About 4 p.m. orders were received to withdraw to a line north of Neuville Vitasse. The remnants of the battalion, already being fired on by machine-guns from behind, only accomplished the withdrawal with extreme difficulty, the adjutant with the last party shortly before dusk being almost cut off. A new position was taken up in what was known as the Army Line, in loose touch with the rest of the brigade in rear, but not with the 15th Division on the left.

With its right resting on the village of Neuville Vitasse, which the enemy had already occupied, and the left still in the air, the outlook was far from promising, but the Germans had been so roughly handled that they were in no condition to take advantage of the state of affairs. During the night grenades were seized from the brigade reserve dump in Neuville Vitasse, which was in the hands of the enemy, and with this help he was balked in his half-hearted attempts to extend his position.

During the night of the 28th–29th the transport, after heading straight for the enemy, managed to extricate itself and dump rations near the battalion. Word was passed round, and during the morning rations were distributed, a remarkably fine effort under the circumstances. On March 30 the battalion, having been relieved by Canadian troops, marched back to billets in Sombrin in a completely exhausted condition, the last arriving about 9 a.m. on the 31st.

Their losses on March 21st in the battle of Wancourt amounted to 428, including the following officers—*Wounded:* Captain T. S. Wynn, M.C.; Lieut. C. G. Gardner; 2nd Lieuts. A. W. C. Major, M.C., R. C. Gibbs, H. P. Talbot, L. Twiddy, and A. Harrison, M.C. (at duty). *Missing:* Captains W. L.

Simpson, M.C., and L. J. Baker, M.C., and R. A. Leembruggen, R.A.M.C.; 2nd Lieuts. A. H. Ward, H. J. Baylis, D. U. Stonehouse, and H. W. White.

One of the London newspapers,[1] in dealing out praise to the 3rd Division for the splendid manner in which it fought in the Croisilles–Henin region, says: "That night they fell back again to the Wancourt–Henin line to conform to the general movement, and on that line they stayed, fighting every day and beating off attacks day and night, from the 22nd to the 28th, not giving a yard of ground. It was a tremendous test of endurance, rendered none the less heavy by the fact that this division had already been in the line for fifty-two days when the battle began." The same newspaper contained the following reference to the stand made by the two companies under Captains Simpson and Baker: "There is a story, such as painters ought to make immortal and historians to celebrate, of how certain Suffolks, cut off and surrounded, fought back to back on the Wancourt–Tilloy road."

After the battle of Wancourt, or the first battle of Arras, 1918, to give it its official title, the 3rd Division was transferred to the First Army. On April 1 the battalion moved to Camblain-Chatelain, where Lieut.-Colonel Stubbs, having returned to the battalion, resumed command, Lieut.-Colonel Likeman being transferred to that of the 8th King's Own (Royal Lancaster Regiment).

Turning now to the Flanders offensive, the part played by the battalion was comparatively small as far as actual fighting was concerned, though now and again they helped to maintain the line at threatened points. It was, however, a period of intense and prolonged strain. When the battles of the Lys began on April 9 the battalion was at Les Brebis, a mining town in the Loos sector, and was consequently little affected. On the 10th the area was bombed with gas-shells, a number of civilians being asphyxiated. The next day the battalion was transferred by bus to the neighbourhood of Hinges to reinforce the line of the La Bassée canal. Arriving at dusk, it established its headquarters in some huts recently occupied by the H.Q. of the XIth Corps, and evidently very hurriedly

[1] *The Times*, April 2, 1918. The *Morning Post* of the same date also contained a very complimentary reference to the stand made by the 2nd Suffolk Regiment on this occasion.

vacated. The next morning two companies were sent up to some of the canal bridge-heads, the other two moving with headquarters to Bellerive. The troops of the 51st Highland Division, also on the canal, having recently put up a magnificent fight, were in a state of utter exhaustion and mostly asleep. The enemy, however, in an even worse plight, were unable to take any advantage of the opportunity ; no serious attempt was made to cross the canal, and except for some machine-gun fire they gave no trouble. The battalion was soon relieved, resuming the normal routine of trench life in the neighbourhood of Hinges and Locon.

On April 24 2nd Lieut. A. K. Baylis died of wounds received on the 17th, and on the 26th 2nd Lieut. G. E. M. Michael was wounded while the battalion was in reserve at Annezin. Early in May Lieut.-Colonel Stubbs and 2nd Lieut. G. Wainwright were slightly wounded, both remaining at duty. On May 24 2nd Lieuts. H. C. Franks and C. G. Davall carried out a raid in which the latter officer and several other ranks were wounded. During the month the enemy made an increasing and annoying use of gas-shell, mostly mustard, the British retaliating with gas projectors, weapons greatly feared by the Germans. One day Sgt. Garrod, of the 2nd Battalion, worked for an hour and a half in a gas-mask filling in gas-shell holes.

This period of comparative quiet was only a breathing space, during which preparations were being made for the opening of the Allied counter-offensive. The turn of the tide was signalled by a series of minor attacks all along the line, showing that the British Army had recovered from the hard times of March and April, and were ready to strike again. One of these occurred on June 14, the anniversary of the capture of Infantry Hill, the battalion taking part in a night-attack on the German forward system at La Pannerie, near Hinges. This operation, designed to provide greater depth along the canal at that point, had been carefully rehearsed in the reserve area over ground marked out to represent the enemy trenches. After dark two companies moved across the canal and took up their positions, and shortly before midnight the barrage came down. In conjunction with the 1st Gordon Highlanders, they took all objectives. The attack was a complete success, the German line being pushed back some hundreds of yards and a considerable number of prisoners captured. The battalion sustained about a hundred casualties, including the following officers—*Killed:* 2nd Lieut. H. C. Franks. *Wounded:* Captain W. J. Nagle; Lieut. H. P. Gardham; 2nd Lieuts. A. Holloway, G. M. Aird, and F. C. Emeny.

In retaliation for this attack the enemy heavily shelled the canal bank and vicinity on several occasions during the next few days. On June 30 a hostile balloon was brought down in flames in the direction of Lestrem church.

4th Battalion

The German offensive in Picardy—The battle of St. Quentin—The battle of the Ancre, 1918—The actions of Villers Bretonneux—Digging trenches by the Albert-Amiens road.

On March 20 one company of the 4th Battalion was working on a cable trench at La Fortelle, the other two resting. Early that afternoon the battalion was warned to be ready to act at an hour's notice in case of attack, and at sunset was ordered to man its battle stations. The 58th Division was on the Oise in front of Tergnier and opposite to the extreme left of the German attack. The battalion being a pioneer unit belonged to the divisional troops; all three companies were attached to different brigades.

When the offensive began, "A" Company, under Captain H. K. Staddon (the 2nd captain), and attached to the 173rd Brigade, were in their battle stations at Quessy and were soon in action, using their rifles and Lewis guns freely on Germans in masses blocked by the wire. After maintaining his position throughout the day, Captain Staddon, finding his company somewhat in the air, referred to brigade headquarters for instructions and was ordered to fall back across the canal. Accordingly at sunset he withdrew the bulk of his company, occupying for the night a line in front of the *butte* near Noureuil. "B" Company, attached to the 175th Brigade, remained at Sinceny until the evening, when three of its platoons were moved to Condren and one to Amigny-Rouy, attached to the 173rd and 174th Brigades respectively. "D" Company, attached to the 174th Brigade, was in position at

Rond d'Orleans, battalion headquarters remaining at Bichancourt. "C" Company had been broken up at the reorganisation.

On the 22nd "A" Company took part in the fighting on the north bank of the Oise, and "B" in that in and around Condren. During the forenoon Lieut.-Colonel Copeman rode forward to the Butte Noureuil, going thence on foot to Tergnier, and finding that place under rifle fire, withdrew the depot of "A" Company to battalion headquarters. Sir Douglas Haig, in his despatches, says: "At 1 p.m. (March 22) the enemy succeeded in making the passage of the Crozat canal at Quessy, progressing towards Vouel. His further advance in this sector, however, was delayed by the gallant resistance of troops of the 58th Division (Major-General A. B. E. Cator) at Tergnier; and not till evening, after much fighting, did the enemy gain that village."

On the 23rd, a day of rumours at battalion headquarters, "A" Company, under 2nd Lieut. H. B. Hutcherson (Captain Staddon being in charge of the rearguard of the brigade), took part in the fighting on the north of the Oise, as well as three platoons of "B" Company, the fourth being still at Condren on the south bank. On March 24 battalion headquarters and one company started for Varesnes, but at Quierzy were ordered to Besme, 2nd Lieut. A. Potter being wounded. The next day they moved to Pierremande, delayed on the march by an alarmist report that Manicamp was held by the enemy. During a halt a plane passed very low over the battalion and hunted Major Pretty round a tree. On arrival at Pierremande they immediately started work on fresh posts and trenches, three platoons of "B" Company going into the line at Manicamp. On the 26th the battalion, in conjunction with other troops, moved to St. Paul-aux-Bois, companies being employed in digging trenches to hold the line of the Aisne–Oise canal. On April 2 they marched to Le Mesnil, and the next day to St. Pierre Aigle. Starting at three o'clock in the morning of the 5th, they marched to Villers Cotterets, seven miles of the journey lying through a beech forest—a dreary business; and shortly after their arrival left by train for Longueau, a shell or two dropping near the train on the way. Here they awaited orders for three hours, to the concern of the Railway Transport Officer, who protested that the station would probably be bombed in consequence. Marching through St. Nicolas (Boves), they halted for a meal near Bois Gentelles, in front of which they went into position. A forester's hut built of wood was used as battalion headquarters' mess, the remainder of the *personnel* being in a dell not far away. The actual position occupied by the battalion extended from Bois l'Abbé to Cachy. On the afternoon of the 13th the companies were relieved and placed in support of the Blue Line south of Gentelles. Other trenches were dug forward by Domat, lest the French should be forced back from Hangard wood. On the 14th Lieut. H. M. Brown, M.C., employed with the 33rd Division headquarters, died of wounds.

The 58th Division had not possessed a pioneer battalion before, and was undecided how such a unit should be employed, the tendency being always to keep it as close as possible to the front line. Especially was this the case while the division was in rear of Villers Bretonneux, where the companies were in trenches so near the front line that they had no peace by day and could not move back to bathe or change their clothing. Brigades came in and went out ; but there the 4th Battalion remained, to their own discomfort and the dismay of others. Whenever there was a shortage of men the battalion took its turn of duty in the front line.

Between the Avre and the Somme the 23rd was a noisy day, and during the two following days severe fighting took place, especially in the neighbourhood of Villers Bretonneux. On the 24th, at about 2.40 a.m., Lieut.-Colonel Copeman got up to put a few things into his haversack when a shell blew in the corner of the hut where he had been lying. Another, a gas-shell, hit the roof, and so the hut was vacated in favour of some shell-slits, where headquarters remained for three hours, when the storm abated. The servants' tent was hit by a 5·9-inch shell and blown skywards, the occupants being also in a shell-slit, and a large tree near it was felled. Curiously enough, the dell in which the rest of the battalion headquarters were living was untouched, though the wood was thoroughly searched by shells and many of the trees destroyed. After a discussion as to a move forward, or else back out of the wood altogether, the C.O. agreed to try this dell, which next morning came in for its share of attention. At breakfast a shell burst in it, wounding his servant, who was serving the meal, killing L/Cpl. G. Whiting, M.M. (and bar), a most efficient battalion runner in every way, and severely wounding another man. A small fragment actually went through the doctor's cup on the table in the newly made shelter. Another shell following, the C.O. ordered a move to a fresh position in some trenches to the rear, and none too soon, for shortly afterwards everything left in the dell was practically destroyed. The companies themselves escaped with a certain amount of gas-shelling. Other casualties during this period included 2nd Lieut. G. F. P. Nobbs, wounded on the 25th. On that day "D" Company, under Captain N. Bolingbroke, assisted in the repulse of an enemy tank attack near Cachy.

Early on the 27th orders came to move. The battalion collected in a wood for breakfast, marched to Cagny for their packs, and then to near the lunatic asylum, south of Amiens, buses taking them on to Maison Roland, where they enjoyed a pleasant rest for ten days. Leaving again by bus from Coulonvillers for Molliens-aux-Bois, they camped in a wood to the east of the town on the night of May 8–9, and the next day moved to Bois Robert, south-west of Baizieux, with nightingales galore, and a big British gun or so to boom a jarring interlude. Here Pte. J. H. Chaplin, M.M., learned that he had been awarded a bar to his military medal.

The companies were now employed on the Baizieux reserve line. On May 16 the battalion went into some dugouts above Warloy, and the next day headquarters moved to the north of the park wall of Henencourt Château, where they rigged up some shelters. It was a noisy quarter, being near a battery of howitzers, and none too safe from the same cause; this was soon proved, as on the 22nd two casualties occurred, including L/Cpl. Lee, an orderly-room clerk, wounded.

On May 20, while the companies were holding trenches in front of Millencourt, 2nd Lieut. A. H. H. Sykes was wounded, and three days later Major L. C. Arbuthnot joined. The next move took the battalion to a wood north of Baizieux, two companies being sent to Bois Robert, when the awards of a military cross to 2nd Lieut. H. B. Hutcherson, and military medals to several other ranks were announced. Early in June the battalion marched to Daily Mail wood, near Agnicourt, and on the 10th, after travelling by bus from Herissart to a point beyond Picquigny, proceeded to Crouy for a week's rest. Major-General F. W. Ramsay, C.M.G., D.S.O., now assumed command of the 58th Division from Major-General N. M. Smyth, V.C., who had temporarily succeeded Major-General A. B. E. Cator, D.S.O.

Returning to Bois Robert, the battalion next took over trenches south of the Amiens–Albert road, between Bresle and Dernancourt, headquarters being in good dugouts made for a brigade headquarters, and situated in a cutting on the main road. Here the battalion was engaged in digging a new trench north of the road and in constructing a maze of wire covered by machine-guns, as a trap for the enemy should he advance. Though little occurred outside the usual trench routine, it was a period of continuous trial for the companies and their officers, working parties having to function nightly close up to the front line, and often subjected to shell-fire and gas. Bombs were also dropped, once on a working party, causing several casualties, and twice on battalion headquarters, some R.E. signallers being hit on the first occasion, while on the second Lieut. E. H. Enraght was slightly wounded and an American transport driver and his two mules killed. Other casualties during this period included 2nd Lieuts. J. W. Barrett and G. P. Hartley, wounded.

7th Battalion

The actions at the Somme crossings—The First Battle of Bapaume—Desperate fighting for the Albert bridge-heads—The battle of the Ancre—The critical 6th of April—In front of Beaumont Hamel—Farewell to the line—The 7th Battalion undergoes amalgamation—Becomes a cadre battalion—Affiliated to American troops

The 7th Battalion swung into Estaires on March 20 just before midnight in reasonable expectation of enjoying a certain period of rest. However, within a few hours of its arrival the long-foretold German offensive began in Picardy; warning orders quickly followed, and during the night of the 24th–25th the 12th Division, having concentrated in the Busnes area, was rushed south into the Albert sector. The battalion started about midnight from a point on the main road near Lillers. The night was very bright and clear, the moon being almost full, and hostile aircraft, taking advantage of the weather conditions, were busily bombing that town as the convoy passed through. The road on which the 35th Brigade assembled was, however, untouched, owing no doubt to the skilful manner in which the motor transport had been parked in the black shadows of the trees. On arrival in the Albert sector the next morning, the battalion was told off to billets in Senlis. That afternoon the 12th Division, which had now been allotted to the VIIth Corps (Congreve) of Byng's army, was sent up to occupy the line Bazentin-le-Grand–Montauban; but these orders were soon cancelled and the battalion, on nearing Fricourt, was sent back to Albert.

On the morning of the 26th the battalion found itself engaged in the defence of the Albert bridge-heads, and those of the 7th Battalion who had served in the 8th Battalion in the spring of 1916 had the curious experience of taking up defensive positions which they had helped to construct two years previously. The fighting which had been in progress for five days had now assumed a confused and desperate character. The 7th Battalion, like every other unit in this stricken area, had their backs to the wall, striving without artillery support, without bombs, rifle grenades, or trench-mortars, and with scarcely any shovels, to stem the onrush of overwhelming numbers.

The actual position taken up by the battalion that morning ran along the railway, the left company resting on the Albert railway station, and the right extending to a point about three hundred yards south of the Albert–Amiens road. The battalion moved from billets in Albert at half-past nine in the morning, and having taken up their allotted positions, dug themselves in. All preparations were completed by 3 p.m.; at 4.30 p.m. the enemy was seen advancing in waves towards Albert and, an hour later, marching in column of route up the Albert–Millencourt road. A Lewis gun, covering this approach, opened fire at a range of about a hundred yards, inflicting very heavy casualties, but unfortunately this gun was soon put out of action. Attacks along the railway were twice beaten off by No. 3 Platoon ("A" Company), while the Lewis gun of No. 2 Platoon, supported by a gun belonging to the M.G.C., swept the bridge-head on the Albert–Amiens road with deadly effect.

At 10.20 p.m. the enemy in great strength attacked this

position, using quantities of trench-mortars and hand-grenades. Ten minutes later the bridge-head was lost, the enemy pushing on and establishing a machine-gun in a house just west of the bridge. At 11.15 p.m. a counter-attack was launched by "C" Company, under Captain Green, and the line retaken with the exception of the bridge-head itself. Before midnight another counter-attack was attempted by the remnants of No. 2 Platoon and a platoon of the 5th Northamptonshire Regiment, under Captain Hull, with the object of recapturing the house and the bridge-head, but this failed owing to the entire lack of grenades and bombs, rifle fire alone being useless in such circumstances. The line was then withdrawn about three hundred yards and at last stabilised, this position being maintained in spite of heavy casualties, great exhaustion, and the lack of food and water, until the battalion was relieved shortly before dawn on the 28th. The severity of the fighting may be gauged from the fact that one of Captain Hull's platoons was reduced to three men. The battalion then went back to Henencourt to rest and reorganise, having sustained 256 casualties, including the following twelve officers—*Killed :* Captain D. S. Black, M.C. ; 2nd Lieuts. T. Blackwell and B. E. Abbs. *Died of wounds :* Captain G. T. Waters. *Wounded :* Captains C. A. C. Argles, M.C. ; Lieut. J. M. Cunningham ; 2nd Lieuts. J. A. Robertson, C. T. Maltby, P. Malby, R. W. King, C. S. Semmens, and S. T. Marchant. For conspicuous gallantry during these attacks Captain G. L. Crandon was awarded a bar to his M.C.

The critical operations of these three days brought a great strain upon all concerned. The battalion consisted largely of drafts recently arrived, most of the officers being themselves new arrivals who had had no opportunity of getting to know their men. All this was the fruit of a scheme of reorganisation and disbandment, ill-timed and ill-conceived, and thrust by politicians upon the army in the face of expert opinion.

A remarkable feature of this fighting was the presence in Albert of a large number of persons in civilian clothes, wandering about the town up to the moment of the enemy occupation. Instances occurred of battalion runners being attacked by them, and there is not the least doubt they were German spies, others again being even disguised as British officers.

On April 2 the battalion, after having been heavily shelled

in Henencourt during the day, moved into the front line opposite Albert. Two days later, in heavy rain and under cover of a violent bombardment, the Germans tried to rush the works and trenches held by the 7th Battalion and the unit next to it. The attack was beaten off, the enemy gaining a small post which later in the day was retaken by " D " Company, under Captain Crandon. On the evening of April 5 battalion headquarters received a message from that of the IVth Army that a big German attack would take place at 7 o'clock on the following morning between Moyenville and Dernancourt. Preparations were accordingly made to deal with it, the battalion being rapidly organised in depth on a front extending roughly from the Albert–Amiens road to the railway station, with a support line running along the high ground a quarter of a mile west of Albert. Subsequent developments showed these dispositions to have been most fortunate, and probably prevented a break through in that important sector along the main Amiens road.

The morning of the 6th broke clear and still, so much so that some began to scoff at the IVth Army's warning. Punctually at seven o'clock, however, a most intense barrage came down on all the battery positions about a mile behind the line and then rolled forward until it reached the front line, where it rested. Fortunately, in spite of its intensity, the line was so situated that direct observation was not possible, and the casualties were much lighter than might have been expected. The barrage was very severe, far more so than that of the 26th, and directly it ceased numerous German attacks were launched along the battle front, but were completely broken up at every point. The resulting operations presented an extraordinary spectacle, resembling a rabbit shoot, men standing up and shooting right and left with complete disregard of their own safety. Along the battalion front no enemy troops were successful in debouching from Albert; but on either flank the situation was not so satisfactory. The battalion on the right was forced back to the reserve line along the heights, but the conformation of the ground and the circumstance of the 7th Battalion being disposed in depth, prevented the enemy from exploiting his advantage. A more serious state of affairs arose in the afternoon when the Australians, who were on the right of the battalion, were ordered to withdraw to the high ground to the west, the 7th Battalion being thus left with both flanks exposed. The Germans, of course, immediately occupied the positions vacated by the Australians and the situation became critical, the whole advanced position of the 7th Battalion being then in enfilade. Indeed, a rapid and resolute initiative on the part of the German machine-gunners would have resulted in the annihilation of the battalion. Fortunately, however, the Lewis gunners of the 7th Battalion, posted at various points on that flank, managed to keep the Germans at bay until after dark.

About this time a message was received from brigade headquarters, delivered by a hot and dishevelled runner who had had to run the gauntlet of the enemy's fire. The message read as follows : " Form a defensive flank. Hold on, and the best of luck to you." This advice had fortunately been carried out some eight hours previously, the good wishes being somewhat sardonically appreciated. At dusk the Germans made a half-hearted attack on the threatened flank, but it was easily beaten off, the night closing quietly. As it was obvious that the position would be untenable the next day, Lieut.-Colonel Hill sent Major Bull back to brigade headquarters to explain the situation and suggest the best methods of coping with it, with the result that the line was established on the high ground during the night.

The battle of April 6 showed a great contrast to that of March 26. In spite of an almost complete absence of organised defences every man remained at his post and did his duty. A highly critical situation was thereby averted, proving that all ranks had profited by the experiences of Bapaume, and that the welding of the 7th and 8th Battalions had been satisfactorily completed.

By dawn on the 7th the battalion, having been relieved, had successfully withdrawn once more to Henencourt, where they bivouacked in heavy rain, all ranks being completely exhausted ; and on the evening of the 10th they went back to Toutencourt. During these operations, which included the battle of the Ancre, 1918—the last battle honour gained by the battalion—they sustained ninety-one casualties, including R.S.M. W. Goody, M.C., M.M., who died of wounds, and Lieut. H. A. Williams and 2nd Lieut. H. A. Hobson, wounded. Referring to the first-named, Lieut.-Colonel Hill said that the splendid services rendered by this warrant officer were always characterised by great coolness and disregard of personal safety.

On April 24 the battalion returned to the line in front of Beaumont-Hamel, and a fortnight later, while at Acheux, they received orders to amalgamate with the 1/1st Cambridgeshire Regiment, a change involving nearly all the men and many of the officers. Between May 11 and 17 the battalion did its last tour of duty in the trenches. The 7th Battalion was not disbanded, but became a cadre unit, with Lieut.-Colonel Hill in command, Major Bull as second-in-command, and Major Fache as adjutant, the company commanders being Captains Crandon, Brown, Bolingbroke, and Hull. Captain Kean became machine-gun officer, Lieut. Turner signalling officer, and Captain Hearne quartermaster. The last-named was succeeded by Captain Ridley, who had served with the 8th Battalion in a similar capacity. About fifty other ranks joined the cadre, including R.S.M. Fookes and R.Q.M.S. Ransford.

The cadre battalion proceeded from Acheux to the base, and on May 24 the training staff, having been turned over to the 39th Division, arrived at Nielles, marching at the end of the month to Sanghem, where it was affiliated to American troops for the purpose of giving them instruction. It should be noted that an American division consisted of two brigades, each of two regiments of three battalions; there were therefore twelve battalions in a division. To each brigade was affiliated the headquarters of a British brigade and to each regiment a British battalion cadre. The 7th Battalion cadre was at first affiliated to a division from New York and then to one from South Carolina.

11th Battalion

The great German offensive—The battle of St. Quentin—The defence of Henin hill—The battalion goes to Armentières—The Flanders offensive—The battles of the Lys—The 10th April—Hard fighting—Estaires—Bailleul—Kemmel—Scherpenberg—Digging defences near Poperinghe—The battalion joins the 61st Division at Aire—Goes to the St. Floris sector

When the sun went down on March 20 such peace and quietness reigned over the British front that those actually in the line found it hard to believe that a great battle was imminent. Certainly the 34th Division could see no reason for alarm. The Sensee valley looked restful enough. At intervals the sound of men at work rose faintly from the German trenches, but throughout the night officer patrols failed to discover any trace of the enemy. However, day dawned upon a scene vastly different.

The battalion order of battle was as follows—*Front line:* "A" Company (Captain W. E. Harrison) right, and "C" Company (Captain C. V. Canning, M.C.) left. *In support:* "B" Company (Captain L. H. Rodwell) right, and "D" Company (Captain G. F. Reid) left. At five o'clock on the morning of the 21st the Germans opened a general bombardment, heavy *minenwerfer* being used against the battalion area, which was also strongly gassed. The bombardment diminished as the morning wore on, and though materially destructive, caused but few casualties. The enemy soon forced an entry into the trenches of the unit on the immediate left of the 11th Battalion, but by 7 a.m. had been driven out, leaving several dead behind them. At three o'clock in the afternoon the enemy again opened an intense bombardment, lasting half an hour, on the battalion area, at the end of which the Germans, advancing northwards in waves across the front of "C" Company, attacked the battalion on the left, that is to say the right battalion of the 3rd Division. "C" Company, at decisive ranges, and "B" Company and battalion headquarters at about a thousand yards, enfiladed the attackers, taking a goodly toll of their numbers. All this time hostile infantry, in great strength and in all kinds of formations, was observed manœuvring. Everywhere batteries were bustling into new positions, while low-flying planes, delivering bursts of machine-gunfire, skimmed over the British trenches. It was apparent to all that a serious engagement was developing. Before sunset "C" Company's line, which had been temporarily broken, was completely re-established. The official despatches record that by nightfall "the enemy had reached the outskirts of St. Leger and was attacking the 34th Division, under command of Major-General C. L. Nicholson, about Croisilles heavily from the south-west." Orders were now received from the brigade to retire to the second system, with an outpost line abreast of Croisilles, and at half-past eight that night the withdrawal began. The battalion front line was formed of the original Hindenburg support line and the tunnel, which the engineers on leaving endeavoured to wreck, saturating the woodwork with petrol and setting fire to it. As the battalion fell back dense columns of smoke, followed by tongues of flame thirty feet high, shot up into the sky from the tunnel entrances, providing a remarkable spectacle that was enhanced by the eerie portents of the night. The German batteries, busily engaged in changing position, did not open fire.

Severe fighting continued uninterruptedly all through the night and, on the following morning, the battalion was subjected to the heaviest and most concentrated bombardment it ever experienced. Throughout the 22nd, from dawn till dusk, the 11th Battalion struggled desperately to defend Henin hill. In the course of the afternoon the enemy tried again and again to force his way into the trenches of the second system. A block was formed by Lieut. W. R. Hall, M.C., who beat off repeated attacks with great coolness and determination, being wounded and subsequently killed. At seven o'clock that evening one of the companies began to give ground, and Lieut. T. C. H. Woods, who displayed exceptional courage and contributed largely to the success of the withdrawal, was killed. During the retreat "C" Company headquarters met eight Germans with five prisoners, and having killed all the Germans, released the prisoners and brought them in. An hour later battalion headquarters and two platoons of "A" Company moved under cover of darkness into the third system in front of Boyelles. A party of details under the adjutant (Captain J. H. Brett) remained in the neighbourhood of the Crucifix until 2.30 a.m., covering the withdrawal to Henin of the 9th Brigade. The remainder of the battalion, under orders received through the 3rd Division, rejoined battalion headquarters at Hamelincourt on the morning of the 23rd. The battalion then moved back to Ayette and, having been complimented by their divisional commander, bivouacked for the night in artillery formation. The casualties sustained during March—the great bulk occurring on the 21st and 22nd—exceeded two hundred, including the following officers—*Killed:* Lieuts. T. C. H. Woods and W. R. Hall, M.C. *Wounded:* Captain G. F. Reid, M.C.; 2nd Lieuts. F. L. Baldock, L. W. H. Byron, J. Rowland,

and W. H. Tuck. *Prisoner of war :* 2nd Lieut. F. W. Bennett (attd. T.M.B.).

After a series of marches and a railway journey the battalion arrived at Erquinghem, billeting in La Rolanderie farm, the brigade reserve position, and on March 30 went into the front line in the Houplines sector, the 34th Division holding a line of some 8000 yards in front of Armentières. Shortly after sunset on April 7 the Germans bombarded the town with gas-shells, causing heavy casualties. The 101st Brigade being now in corps reserve, the 8th was spent at La Rolanderie, with the 12th Battalion close by at Fleurbaix. Before dawn on the 9th the enemy opened an intense bombardment south of the Lille railway, but no attack developed along the 34th Division front. At 10 a.m. the 101st Brigade as corps reserve was sent off to the south of Bac St. Maur ; but an hour later the corps commander came to divisional headquarters and, hearing that the enemy had broken the Portuguese front and entered the battle zone of the 40th Division, told Major-General Nicholson to use the brigade to cover his own flank. On approaching Bac St. Maur and finding that village in possession of the Germans, the 101st Brigade took up a position facing west and south-west near Fort Rompu, when fighting began immediately. Thus the first troops of the 34th Division to enter the general engagement were those who, almost up to that very moment, had formed the corps reserve, a rare tactical anomaly.

Terrific fighting followed. On the 10th the battalion, having formed a defensive flank, beat off attack after attack. Twice the Germans broke through, but on one occasion the breach was closed by Captain Rodwell and his company, and on the other by Captain Canning and his company, assisted by Major Wright.

At 3.20 p.m. Lieut.-Colonel Tuck received orders to withdraw behind the river Lys. Speaking on the telephone, the officer commanding the battalion next on the left, which was still in the front line, explained that he could not possibly get clear in less than two hours. Colonel Tuck replied that in those circumstances he would do his best to hold on till five o'clock. He did so ; and though the casualties in those two extra hours were heavy, this noble imposition helped materially to save two brigades.

Thus, without intermission, the struggle continued. On the 14th Brig.-General R. C. Gore, C.B., C.M.G., who had commanded the 101st Brigade since its arrival in France, was killed in action. He was succeeded by Brig.-General W. J. Woodcock, D.S.O. The next day the 59th Division having been overwhelmed, the 11th Battalion once more became part of the front line. On the night of the 17th–18th the battalion was relieved, moving at first into reserve trenches and three days later back to Boeschepe. The casualties in the battles of the Lys amounted to nearly five hundred, including the following officers—*Killed:* Captain G. K. Moseley; Lieut. E. T. Bolton; 2nd Lieuts. G. L. A. Duddy, R. C. Foster, and R. Theobald, M.C. *Died of wounds:* Captain W. E. Harrison, M.C.; 2nd Lieuts. R. E. Cook, H. A. Reed, M.C., and W. H. Roxbrough, M.C. *Wounded:* 2nd Lieuts. W. P. Anness, G. L. Bryant, M.C., J. E. Garnett, G. W. Harvey, H. D. S. Page, S. H. Phillips, H. E. Rowe, G. D. W. Thacker, and Lieut. and Quartermaster H. Cranfield. *Prisoners of war:* Captain L. H. Rodwell, M.C.; 2nd Lieuts. G. S. Keightley, G. T. Lloyd, R. S. Shepherd, and J. A. Simmons.

After the first battle of Kemmel Ridge the 34th Division came out of the line and was employed in digging defence lines near Poperinghe, being twice called upon to stand and prepare to defend the line it was digging, namely, during the second battle of Kemmel and also the battle of Scherpenberg Ridge. On neither occasion, however, were the services of the division actually required.

In the middle of May, owing to exhaustion of man-power, most of the infantry battalions of the 34th Division were reduced to cadre strength. The 11th Battalion, however, was not included in the order for reduction, and on May 26 proceeded to Aire to join the 61st Division (Major-General C. J. Mackenzie, C.B.) which, though in the line, had not yet been made up to establishment. In May Sgt. W. J. Matthews, D.C.M., M.M., was promoted 2nd Lieut. in his own battalion, and on June 1 Captain C. V. Canning, M.C., took over the adjutancy from Captain J. H. Brett, promoted. After a spell of training at Guarbecque the battalion went into the line in the St. Floris sector, and on June 30 into brigade reserve at Hamet Billet.

The honours bestowed on the battalion for the battle of

St. Quentin included the following—*Bar to D.S.O.:* Lieut.-Colonel G. L. J. Tuck, D.S.O. *Bar to M.C.:* Captain C. V. Canning, M.C. *M.C.:* Captains W. E. Harrison, L. H. Rodwell, and G. F. Reid; Lieut. D. B. Johnson; 2nd Lieut. W. H. Roxbrough. *D.C.M.:* R.S.M. J. Crissall; Sgt. W. D. Taylor; and C.S.M.'s E. Spalding and G. Turner. *Bar to M.M.:* Cpl. D. Barrett. Eleven military medals were also awarded.

For the battles of the Lys the battalion honours included—*Bar to M.C.:* Major A. B. Wright, M.C. *M.C.:* Lieuts. C. L. Bryant and H. A. Reed. *Bar to D.C.M.:* C.S.M. E. Spalding. *D.C.M.:* C.S.M.'s C. J. Connor and S. W. Mead, M.M.; Sgt. F. Meadows; and A/Sgt. W. J. Matthews, M.M. *M.S.M.:* C.S.M. C. J. Connor; Sgt. F. Meadows. *Bar to M.M.:* L/Cpl. H. Searle, M.M. Ten military medals were also awarded.

12th Battalion

The Great German offensive—The Somme, 1918—The battle of Bapaume—The death of Lieut.-Colonel Eardley-Wilmot—The battles of the Lys—Estaires—The defence of Fleurbaix—Hazebrouck—The battalion is broken up—The cadre returns to England

When the great German offensive began on the memorable March 21, the 3rd, 34th, and 59th Divisions of the VIth Corps (Haldane) were holding the line between Guemappe and Noreuil, the 40th Division being in camp about Blairville, Hendecourt, and Boisleux. The preceding week had been one of nimble rumour and intense strain, the great attack being expected hourly. It was just then that the news was received of the birth of a son and heir to Sir Douglas Haig, which evoked from Major-General Ponsonby the following telegram: "All ranks offer their congratulations on the arrival of your latest reinforcement."

At last the attack came, and very soon the Germans began surging into the area held by the 59th Division. The 40th Division was then ordered to move up towards St. Leger, whereupon the 12th Battalion, after standing-to for two hours some seven miles behind the line, marched to Hamelincourt and thence across country to the road at l'Homme Mort, where battalion headquarters were established. The 121st

Brigade then took up a position in the third system, between St. Leger and the Mory–Ecoust road, the line being marked out, but the trenches not actually dug. This position was taken over from the headquarters of two brigades, who had been holding on to it with details collected from all the units in their commands. Parties of Germans kept showing themselves everywhere, and already the battalions in front had ceased to exist. The front of the 121st Brigade was held by the 12th Battalion on the right, and the 13th Yorkshire Regiment on the left, but the two were not in touch, the enemy holding a strip of trench in between them. The 12th Battalion was, however, in touch with the H.L.I. on its right. At dusk the Germans were observed moving round the left flank of the battalion in large numbers. During the evening the 13th Yorkshire Regiment counter-attacked gallantly, but the situation, though restored temporarily, continued to be critical.

March 22 dawned with the enemy in great strength in front of the brigade, and still pouring in on the left of the 12th Battalion, with heavy fighting going on to the left rear. The battalion, practically surrounded, formed defensive flanks as best it could. In order to fill up the dangerous gap on the left Lieut.-Colonel Eardley-Wilmot decided to take a platoon out of the front line and place it in a suitable forward position, and with this object in view went out about six o'clock in the morning to make a personal reconnaissance. There was a thick ground mist at the time, and within a few minutes Lieut.-Colonel Eardley-Wilmot and the artillery liaison officer with him fell riddled with bullets. The 12th Suffolk Regiment was thus deprived of its able and gallant leader, and the service at large of an exceptionally fine soldier. The battalion continued to suffer heavy casualties from hostile machine-gun fire and that of its own artillery.

During the afternoon three mass attacks were launched against the left, front, and right of the brigade respectively, all three being repulsed with heavy loss to the enemy. About half-past five in the evening the unit on the right was forced back. The battalion, now under the command of Captain A. M. Cross, M.C., again formed a defensive flank, aided by the reserve platoon, the headquarter orderlies, and some Lewis guns. Half an hour later the flank was turned and the situation being hopeless, the companies were ordered to fall back on the Army line. The message was duly delivered, but arrived too late, practically the whole of the three companies being either killed or captured. The remainder of the battalion withdrew to the Army line, battalion headquarters being established in Mory copse. At nine o'clock that night Major Lloyd arrived and assumed command. Two companies of another unit having come up, a position was improvised from the Army line in front of Mory copse to the sunken road in rear of it.

The enemy, who had already gained a footing in the Army line on both flanks, now returned to the attack. The battalion was ordered to withdraw behind the sunken road, and only with the greatest difficulty, under very heavy machine-gun and rifle fire, was this move accomplished. A trench running at right angles to the sunken road was then occupied, those in it facing in both directions. On the 23rd, soon after midnight, rations and ammunition arrived in limbers, which were surrounded by the enemy almost before they could be unloaded. The limbers, however, broke through the cordon at a canter and got safely away, with four quartermaster-sergeants clinging to the tail-boards. All touch having again been lost, the troops marched in column of route right through the enemy, fortunately unobserved in the darkness, and in the early dawn began to dig in on the Ervillers–Mory road. Heavy fighting continued throughout that day and the next. During the night of the 24th–25th R.S.M. A. Goody, D.C.M., collected men belonging to different units from various detached and isolated posts and organised a line in front of the Ervillers–Behagnies road, which undoubtedly held up the enemy advance for about twelve hours. The remnants of the battalion were withdrawn from action on the 26th and sent to Neuf Berquin, being made up to strength on the way. The casualties in the battalion during March, mostly occurring at the battle of Bapaume, amounted to 367, including the following twenty-one officers—*Killed:* Lieut.-Colonel T. Eardley-Wilmot, D.S.O.; Lieut. J. E. Hamblin; 2nd Lieuts. L. Scott and C. R. Pedrick. *Wounded and missing:* 2nd Lieuts. E. L. Turner and A. W. Barnard. *Wounded:* Captain A. M. Cross, M.C.; 2nd Lieuts. G. F. Franklin, R. Tricker, R. E. Gooch, L. H. Knowles, M.C.; and C. H. Cockerton. *Missing:* Captain R. England, M.C.; Lieuts. H. C. Mathew, M.C., and G. Hopkins; 2nd Lieuts.

Lieutenant-Colonel T. EARDLEY-WILMOT, D.S.O.

A. J. Wells, J. A. Blanch, S. E. Clark, G. Hallsmith, D.S.O., G. T. Taylor, and C. H. Hitchcock. With the exception of Major Lloyd and the doctor, every officer who went into action with the battalion was either killed, wounded, or missing.

Towards the end of March the 40th Division moved by bus and lorry into the Merville area to join the XVth Corps (Du Cane) of the Ist Army, which corps—now consisting of the 40th and 34th Divisions only—was holding a front of about eight miles between Armentières and Fleurbaix, with a Portuguese division on the right. The 121st Brigade was on the left of the divisional front, the 12th Battalion being in reserve. At the beginning of April the battalion went into line in the Bois Grenier sector, and a few days later into billets in Fleurbaix in support.

On April 9, at 4.15 a.m., the enemy attacked, a very heavy bombardment being accompanied by gas in exceptional quantities. Within three hours the battalion had manned the Fleurbaix defences and, though nominally in reserve, was hotly engaged, inflicting severe losses on the Germans moving across its front from left to right. The battalion held on until half-past four in the afternoon, putting up a magnificent defence. It then withdrew, fighting a rearguard action, to the railway east of Fort Rompu, where it dug itself in for the night between the 16th Royal Scots on the right and the 11th Suffolk Regiment on the left. The 12th Battalion was now amalgamated with the 16th Royal Scots and placed under the orders of the 101st Brigade. The casualties, particularly in " B " and " C " Companies, had already been very heavy. At nightfall battalion headquarters, which had been cut off from the remainder of the battalion, were established in Fort Rompu. On the afternoon of April 10 the battalion was ordered to retire across the Lys and then, having rejoined the 121st Brigade, to make its way to Nieppe and dig itself in. After a series of attacks and counter-attacks the battalion was withdrawn on the 13th to Strazeele, and later to Proven.

The defence of Fleurbaix by the 12th Battalion, which is described in glowing terms in the history of the 40th Division, was thus referred to in Sir Douglas Haig's despatches: " In this fighting very gallant service was rendered by the 12th Battalion Suffolk Regiment, 40th Division, who held out in

Fleurbaix until the evening, though heavily attacked on three sides."

The casualties in these desperate operations amounted to 423, including the following officers—*Killed :* 2nd Lieut. C. F. Smith (attd. T.M.B.). *Wounded :* Captain H. A. Redding, M.C. ; 2nd Lieuts. L. C. Williams, M.C., H. A. Panton, and A. Johnson. *Missing (killed) :* 2nd Lieut. S. H. Habershon.

Captain H. A. Redding, M.C. (and two bars), was here wounded for the third time. This heroic officer, after having distinguished himself on so many occasions in France, joined the King's Regiment, and was drowned on March 16, 1926, while crossing the Diyala river in Iraq.

On May 3 the battalion marched to camp at Klinderbelk, where three days later it was reduced to a training cadre, twenty-one officers and six hundred and seventy other ranks being despatched to the base depot for re-posting. The cadre remained in the neighbourhood of Cassel till June, when it proceeded to England. The awards to the battalion during May and June included—*Bar to D.S.O. :* Lieut.-Colonel L. Lloyd, D.S.O. *M.C. :* Captains A. A. Smee and F. O. H. Goss, R.A.M.C. *Bar to M.C. :* Captain A. A. Smee, M.C. *D.C.M. :* Sgt. A. C. Smith ; Pte. M. Hearne. *M.S.M. :* R.S.M. A. Goody, D.C.M. ; C.S.M. J. Pateman.

CHAPTER XVII

2ND BATTALION

In the Hinges sector—The advance to victory—The Second Battle of the Somme, 1918—Albert, 1918—The capture of Gomiecourt—The attack at Ecoust St. Mein—The gallantry of Captain Nagle at Noreuil switch—The breaking of the Hindenburg line—The battle of Canal du Nord—The Second battle of Le Cateau—The battle of the Selle

AS far as the 2nd Battalion was concerned, July passed uneventfully, although in the middle of that month the Germans reached the limit of their advance. In front of Hinges the hostile artillery was periodically active, and German aeroplanes flew up and down the canal continually; but no attacks materialised.

July 18 was marked by an unusual incident. A fragment of shell struck the steel helmet of a man named Parkinson, knocking it forward with such force that his nose was almost completely severed. Pte. F. Thompson, who was close at hand, quickly replaced the man's nose, bound it up, and took him back in broad daylight to the battalion aid post at Hinges. On the way Pte. Parkinson fainted, his comrade carrying him on his back for the remainder of the journey. Pte. Thompson was awarded the Military Medal.

On July 22nd and 23rd the enemy shelled Chocques, Fouquereuil, and Labeuvrière. Early in August, after a spell of nearly four months in that sector, the 3rd Division was relieved by the 19th Division, the battalion—under Lieut.-Colonel G. C. Stubbs, D.S.O.—marching to Chocques and going on by bus to Faucquenham. On the 10th they marched out to Bellery and lined the road to cheer H.M. the King as he passed through to Ferfay. The XIIIth Corps horse show—a thoroughly well-organised affair—which took place at the latter town on the 12th, was attended by all ranks. Two days later the battalion marched to Pernes, and then, having been railed as far as Mendicourt, marched on to Sus St. Leger, where they joined the VIth Corps. Here a parade service was held, followed by a presentation of medals by Brig.-General C. L. Porter, C.M.G., D.S.O. On the night of the 19th–20th the battalion marched to Berles au Bois to take part in the forthcoming operations.

On August 21 the second battles of the Somme, 1918, began, when the advance in Picardy was resumed. At dawn on that date the IVth and VIth Corps of Byng's Army attacked on a front of about nine miles north of the Ancre from Miraumont to Moyenneville. The initial assault having been delivered, two divisions of the IVth Corps and the 3rd Division of the VIth Corps passed through and continued the advance, the 76th Brigade being in divisional reserve. The thick mist which hung about during the early stages of the attack was intensified by the smoke of shells and tank gun-fire, rendering advance only practicable by compass bearing. This condition of invisibility was responsible for some loss of direction, and on reaching Courcelles-le-Comte a smoke barrage was encountered, adding to the confusion; but in spite of these difficulties the 3rd Division attained their objective, namely, the Albert–Arras railway. On the right flank, however, outside the front of the 3rd Division, parties of enemies still held out, making movement along the railway line a matter of difficulty. During the night the battalion withdrew to trenches between Courcelles and Ayette, where they reorganised and rested. The casualties included the Rev. G. C. Danvers, M.C., C.F., Lieut. G. A. B. Gilbert, and 2nd Lieut. M. C. Ayton, M.C., wounded.

On the night of August 22–23 the battalion marched to its assembly position for the attack on Gomiecourt. At four a.m. the 76th Brigade attacked with the 2nd Suffolk Regiment on the right and the 8th K.O.R.L. on the left. The operation was a brilliant success, Gomiecourt being captured with 500 prisoners. A special order of the day was published by the Commander-in-Chief congratulating the Brigade on its magnificent achievement. The casualties at the battle of Albert, amounting to 188, included the following officers—*Killed:* Lieut. P. C. Layard; 2nd Lieut. C. G. Davall. *Wounded:* 2nd Lieuts. A. Martin, H. E. Coltman, H. F. Bennett, and H. G. Teverson, M.C., M.M., the last-named remaining at duty. For gallantry at Courcelles-le-Comte and at Gomiecourt, on August 21 and 23, A/Capt. W. M. Lummis,

COURCELLES-LE-COMTE

and 2nd Lieuts. E. R. Pond, T. Mealand, and C. Hills were awarded the Military Cross.

The battalion, having consolidated the position at Gomiecourt, marched back to Caruso copse, between Ayette and Douchy, and on the night of the 26th–27th took over trenches south of Hamelincourt, the 76th Brigade becoming the supporting brigade to the Guards Division. After sustaining a few casualties here the battalion moved up to Banks trench, on the line of the St. Leger–Vraucourt road, and on the night of the 29th–30th into assembly positions for the attack on the villages of Ecoust St. Mein and Noreuil.

At dawn on August 30 the battalion, under Lieut.-Colonel Stubbs, attacked, the four company commanders being A/Capt G. H. Wainwright, 2nd Lieuts. H. H. Hammonds, and C. Hills, M.C., and A/Capt. W. J. Nagle, M.C. It appears that the village of Ecoust was taken easily, but that the battalion, unable to maintain itself in its advanced position, was compelled at the end of about six hours to fall back on the line of the Ecoust trench. In this action great gallantry was displayed by C.S.M. J. H. Jones, M.M., and Pte. H. H. Roberts, who held on to their ground for five hours after the battalion had withdrawn. This warrant officer and man were awarded the D.C.M. and M.M. respectively. Pte. Roberts, who had previously distinguished himself by stalking a machine-gun post and putting a bullet through the gun, was afterwards badly wounded at Flesquières. The casualties, amounting to over 200, included the following—*Killed:* Lieut. K. G. Passman. *Died of wounds:* Captain G. H. Wainwright and 2nd Lieut. C. Hills, M.C. *Wounded and missing (prisoner):* 2nd Lieut. H. H. Hammonds. *Wounded:* Lieut. C. Coley; 2nd Lieuts. A. J. Courtney, L. Fricker, S. E. Leighton, T. Mealand, and A. Tomkins. 2nd Lieut. Hills had been given a commission in the previous May for gallantry in the field with the 11th Battalion.

At nightfall on August 31 the battalion was resting in Mory Switch trench. On September 1 a message was received that on the following day an advance would be made on the whole British front, and that the battalion would be in reserve to the 8th Infantry Brigade. Early in the morning of the 2nd the battalion moved forward, headquarters being established with that of the 8th Brigade. At 10 a.m. one company, under Captain W. J. Nagle, M.C., having been placed at the disposal of the officer commanding K.S.L.I., was ordered to advance and clear up Vraucourt switch, Macaulay avenue, and the sunken roads. This was effected in a brilliant manner. With only nine casualties they captured over a mile of trench, 400 prisoners, and many machine-guns. The divisional commander sent a message of congratulation on the gallant performance of Captain Nagle's company, published as a special order of the day. Captain Nagle, awarded the D.S.O. for this exploit, was ably assisted by Lieut. H. G. Teverson, M.C., M.M., an officer of great coolness, sound judgment, and a most modest disposition. The casualties included Lieut. K. M. Walker, wounded. After these operations the battalion withdrew to the Moyenneville area. In mid-September the battalion marched to some huts in Fremicourt and Mancourt. Here Lieut.-Colonel G. C. Stubbs, D.S.O., relinquished command of the battalion to take over that of the 121st Brigade, being succeeded by Major W. G. Chandler. On September 18 T/Lieut.-Colonel G. G. Carpenter arrived and assumed command of the battalion, which was occupying a sunken road at Beaumetz-lez-Cambrai, astride the Bapaume–Cambrai road. While in this position a large sand-model of Flesquières and vicinity was prepared by the 76th Brigade. It was only the close study devoted to that model that enabled the 2nd Battalion to maintain direction in the mist after crossing the Canal du Nord on September 27.

After dark on the 26th the battalion moved to assembly positions west of the canal, arriving shortly before midnight. The bed of the canal was dry, with steep bricked sides, which could only be negotiated with the help of ladders, and during the night it was decided that this obstacle should be crossed before zero hour. Accordingly, the battalion began moving off just before 4 a.m. Two companies got over comfortably, but as the third, under Captain Lummis, was about to cross, the barrage began to drop, machine-gun fire being followed by shell-fire. Lieut.-Colonel Carpenter and the adjutant (Captain Burman) assisted in getting the remainder of the battalion over. For gallantry on this occasion A/C.S.M. C. G. Wiggett, M.M., was awarded a bar to his Military Medal.

In spite of this barrage, which fortunately only caught two companies, the battalion moved forward punctually at zero (5.20 a.m.) in support to the 1st Gordon Highlanders and the 8th K.O.R.L., the objective being the village of Flesquières, which had held up the battalion's advance in the battle of Cambrai in 1917. On this occasion it was quickly seized. The whole attack was carried out with great dash and determination, large numbers of prisoners and guns being captured.

Sgt. F. G. Meen, M.M., pushing forward with his platoon, was amongst the first to enter the village of Flesquières, his splendid example gaining for him a bar to his M.M. In the report of these operations Lieut.-Colonel Carpenter brought into prominence the fine leadership and initiative of 2nd Lieut. F. W. Cook, M.C., Captain W. M. Lummis, and 2nd Lieut. H. G. Teverson, M.C., M.M., who were commanding companies. The casualties amounted to 150, including the following officers—*Killed:* 2nd Lieut. A. P. Baldwin. *Died of wounds:* 2nd Lieuts. W. L. Gray and D. W. Campbell. *Wounded:* Captain J. T. M. Mee; 2nd Lieuts. F. W. Bailey, H. G. Teverson, and E. M. Smith.

After this battle of the Canal du Nord the battalion went back to the Hindenburg support line, occupying dugouts in the vast Hindenburg tunnel system. From that position they could obtain a good view of Cambrai, then on fire in four places. On September 30 the battalion moved up to trenches between Ribecourt and Marcoing in readiness for the attack on Rumilly on the following morning. The 76th Brigade attacked with the 8th K.O.R.L. on the right and the 2nd Suffolk Regiment on the left. Severe fighting followed, but the attack was only partially successful. The front and support trenches at Rumilly were found to be full of Germans and machine-guns. Over three hundred prisoners were taken and many Germans killed, but by the time these trenches had been dealt with the attacking troops had lost the barrage, and the left company came under very heavy machine-gun fire from the front and flanks, making further advance impossible. The right company, shielded by the ground from flanking fire, pushed through the village to a trench on the far side, killing and capturing many Germans. Not until evening, and then only after much bitter fighting was the village cleared. The casualties amounted to about 180, including the following officers—*Killed:* 2nd Lieut. A. Barnard.

Wounded: Lieut. J. W. Harding; 2nd Lieuts. C. P. Blowers and P. H. Hancock. During the night of October 5th–6th the battalion came out of the line to Masnières and on the following afternoon was attached to the 9th Brigade for the attack on Seranvillers on October 8. The 2nd Suffolk Regiment and another battalion, who were in support, were to pass through the attacking battalions on the Red Line and to capture Green Line. The objective of the 2nd Battalion was the village of Seranvillers and the road into La Targette. The attack commenced at 4.30 a.m., the Red Line being captured without much resistance. The battalion then advanced to the Green Line and gained all its objectives in time, except La Targette itself. At dusk the fire died down, and the enemy evacuated La Targette, leaving a few machine-guns behind them. The casualties amounted to 135, including the following officers—*Wounded:* Lieuts. J. M. V. Percy, N. E. Cooper, H. V. Raven, F. D. V. Thursby; 2nd Lieut. T. R. Pidcock. On October 9 the battalion came out of the line to Havrincourt, and later to Marcoing. On October 16 Captain V. C. Russell, D.S.O., M.C., took over the duties of brigade-major to the 9th Brigade. On October 22 the battalion moved up from Quievy to Solesmes, where Captain W. M. Lummis, M.C., assumed command in place of Lieut.-Colonel Carpenter, sick. During the night of October 22–23 the companies left Solesmes for their assembly positions in readiness for attack on the 23rd, by the IVth and IIIrd Armies, which had opened on the 17th. At 3.20 a.m. on the 23rd the 3rd Division, on the right of the VIth Corps front, assaulted, the 2nd Battalion being on the extreme right of the corps front. Within two hours the companies had reached the outskirts of Romeries, and before sunset all objectives—no less than four—had been secured, and battalion headquarters established in Escarmain. During the day the battalion captured a German battery.

The casualties amounted to 114, including the following officers wounded: Lieut. N. G. Bray; 2nd Lieuts. F. Bartram, A. A. Browne, H. B. Rolph, W. L. K. Mann, and Captain F. W. Cook, M.C., D.C.M. The last-named officer, though wounded and gassed, remained at duty. On October 24th the battalion withdrew to Romeries, and later to Capelle-sur-Ecaillon to brigade reserve. For gallantry in the fighting at Romeries, Escarmain, and Beaudignies on October 23

2nd Lieut. W. G. Bailey, M.C., was awarded the D.S.O. and Captain A. A. Johnson and 2nd Lieut. H. B. Rolph the M.C. On October 28 Major W. G. Chandler rejoined and assumed command of the battalion. The 3rd Division was now withdrawn to corps reserve, the battalion marching in turn to St. Python, Quievy, Romeries, Frasnoy, and Carnières. On November 10 the battalion marched to La Longueville, crossing the historic Mons–Le Cateau road at Bavay, a town they had last seen in August, 1914. The 76th Brigade had been detailed to act as advance guard to the IIIrd Army from the 11th, but the order was suddenly cancelled, and at eleven o'clock on that day the Armistice began, whereupon the drums and fifes of the battalion paraded the streets playing the *Marseillaise* amid scenes of great enthusiasm.

4TH BATTALION

The advance in Picardy and the battle of Amiens—The breaking of the Hindenburg line—An unfortunate night air-raid—The battle of Epehy—The death of Captain Gaston

Early in August, 1918, the 4th Battalion was taken away from work on the Lavieville trench and the Albert road and sent back to Villers Bocage. The following night they proceeded by bus to Lahoussoye, marching on to Bois Escardonneuse, where they arrived at two o'clock in the morning. After lying down to rest for a couple of hours they began to erect bivouacs and tents. The next day was similarly spent, a few shells falling into the transport lines. On the 7th, after dark, the battalion moved forward to dugouts in a gully north-west of Sailly-le-Sec, arriving at midnight. Several of the platoons were detailed for consolidation work with the 173rd Brigade.

On the following day the 58th Division took part in the general attack of Rawlinson's Army. The IIIrd Corps, under Lieut.-General Sir R. H. K. Butler, stood on the left of the front of attack, with the 58th and 18th Divisions in line, and the 12th Division in support. Operations began at 4.20 a.m., and at 10 a.m. five platoons were sent forward to construct a line of posts to protect the left flank of the divisional front, on which the remainder of the battalion were already working. Battalion headquarters then moved forward into a valley north of Sailly Laurette. These working parties were withdrawn at 2 p.m. on the following day preparatory to a fresh attack to be launched at sunset. At midnight the battalion again went forward, digging a line of posts between the Corbie–Bray road and Gressaire wood, on the new British front line. The next evening they returned to Bois Escardonneuse, having only sustained about thirty casualties. After resting in the wood all day they went forward to a point north of the cemetery at Sailly Laurette, where battalion headquarters was established. Each company was then detailed to work with a company of Royal Engineers, carrying wire to be placed in front of a trench dug the previous night. The valley being full of gas, owing to the recent explosion of a gas-shell dump, work had to be discontinued, but was completed the next night. On August 12, at Querrieu, H.M. the King interviewed representatives from all units in the division. On the 13th the battalion again returned to Bois Escardonneuse, every man bathing in the Somme on the way. On the 20th Captain F. S. Cubitt left the battalion to take up the appointment of second-in-command of the 12th London Regiment.

On August 24 the battalion moved up to some trenches near Bois des Tailles. On the 25th, and again on the 27th, the 58th Division attacked, but the battalion, not called upon to act on either occasion, was employed in repairing roads. On the 28th they moved up into the divisional front in Bois d'en Haut, taking part in the advance and halting just short of Bois Marrières. The few casualties included Captain C. P. Parry-Crooke and 2nd Lieut. H. T. Easterley, slightly wounded but remaining at duty. At the end of the month the battalion was withdrawn, first to Petit Bois, with its memories of 1916, and later to the neighbourhood of Maricourt, where it remained for some days. At the beginning of September the battalion was congratulated by the corps commander (Lieut.-General Sir A. J. Godley) on its good work during the advance.

September 5 was a day of heavy rain and a thunderstorm, and the next evening the battalion, arriving at Rancourt by bus at nine o'clock, found themselves obliged to spend the night in the open. During the night of the 10th–11th bombs were dropped in transport lines, causing the following casualties—*Killed:* Captain D. M. French; Lieut. and Quartermaster W. Berwick. *Wounded:* Captain L. J. Richards; the Rev. F. G. Allsopp. Four other ranks were wounded, forty-two horses and mules killed and sixteen others wounded.

On September 14 the battalion, under the command of Major F. Pretty (Lieut.-Colonel Copeman being away on ten days' leave), moved into front-line trenches near Peizière, on the north side of Epehy. Throughout the 18th the battalion stood in front of Nurlu in readiness to join in the attack, though not called upon to do so. On the 22nd, under Lieut.-Colonel Copeman, the battalion took part in a successful night attack, designed with the object of straightening out the line after the capture of Epehy and of a deep railway cutting in the neighbourhood which had held up the advance for some time. The particular length of trench forming the objective of the attack had caused considerable trouble, previous attempts to capture it by frontal attack having been frustrated by machine-gun fire. On this occasion therefore a fresh plan was conceived. "B" Company, under Captain S. Scrimgeour, M.C., assisted by a platoon from "A" Company, were ordered to make a turning movement and to come in on the left flank of the objective along a sunken road, a frontal attack being delivered simultaneously by another battalion of the division. The scheme worked admirably. "B" Company crept along the sunken road unobserved and, falling suddenly on the enemy, seized two machine-guns, the crews however managing to escape. Some of the occupants of the trench were cut off and captured, including an officer; the remainder decamped, enabling the troops making the frontal attack to occupy the trench without casualties. 2nd Lieut B. Webb, who was wounded, remained at duty until the operation was concluded.

Towards the end of September the battalion proceeded by rail and road to Hersin and thence to Maroc. On October 3 they moved to Cité St. Pierre, where they were employed in making roads and tracks forward until the 15th, when they began to move eastwards, doing road repairs with short halts, the longest being at Rongy and neighbouring villages, and lasting nearly a fortnight. These villages were frequently shelled, especially during two successive nights, when Lieut.

R. A. Hayward and a few others were wounded. In October L/Cpl. W. J. Leggett, M.M., and Cpl. P. Hall, M.M., were awarded bars to their Military Medals.

On November 5, to the regret of all ranks, Captain James Gaston, M.C., R.A.M.C., while visiting the company at Howardries, was mortally wounded by a shell. He died at Rumegies the same evening and was buried in the churchyard with military honours. The funeral was largely attended, several of the residents—some of whom had been his patients—being amongst those present. Captain Gaston had been nearly two years with the battalion, by whom he was held in the highest esteem.

On the 10th the battalion left Rouex and marched to Wiers, finding the town *en fête* on account of the retreat of the Germans, and of strong rumours that peace was about to be declared. On the following morning, before marching off, a message announcing the Armistice was received, with general instructions that hostilities would cease at 11 a.m. About noon the battalion marched into Basecles, where they found the inhabitants in a state of unbounded delight.

11TH BATTALION

With the 61st Division in the St. Floris sector—The final advance in Picardy—The battle of the Selle—The remarkable bravery of Corporal Staden—The battle of Valenciennes—The Armistice

The 11th Battalion remained for about ten weeks in the neighbourhood of St. Floris, at the vertex of the German salient on the Lys. July was an uneventful month, marked only by minor incidents, the days being usually quiet and the nights broken only by artillery bombardments and attempts to obtain identifications, the enemy using a large number of parachute lights. During the 9th–10th the 61st Division, having been relieved by the 74th Division (to which the 15th Battalion belonged), went back to St. Hilaire in G.H.Q. reserve.

On July 22 the battalion marched to Campagne, near St. Omer, to join the XVth Corps, but at the end of that month returned to Linghem. On August 7, a report having been received that the Germans were withdrawing, it was suddenly despatched to Villora camp, being detailed as advanced guard to the 61st Division. During the night the battalion, under Lieut.-Colonel Tuck, D.S.O., took up a forward position, and at half-past six in the morning moved out to get into touch with the enemy. An hour or so later Le Sart was occupied without resistance. Eastward of that village, however, the enemy made a stand and, establishing himself in some farms in front of Merville which proved too strong for attack without preliminary bombardment, prevented the British troops from entering that town for several days. Towards sunset on the 8th the line taken up by the battalion was heavily shelled. The enemy's defence was purely passive, no counter-attacks being made. Active patrolling was maintained throughout the night and, on the 10th, the battalion went back to Villora camp in divisional reserve.

On August 14 the 183rd Brigade (Brig.-General A. H. Spooner, C.M.G., D.S.O.) took over the Arrewage sector. On the 19th Merville was evacuated, the enemy being closely followed and harassed as much as possible. On the 20th, a day of patrol encounters, the advance was resumed, the new line taken up by the battalion being subjected to a heavy bombardment for over an hour at about midnight. In the morning the battalion acted as advance guard to the brigade; one company and part of another, while moving to their assembly positions, were caught in a heavy gas-shell (yellow cross) and H.E. barrage, suffering many casualties. The advance was resumed at 3.30 p.m. under brisk machine-gun and rifle fire along the whole line from strong enemy rearguards, but by sunset the battalion had carried the line forward 2500 yards on the left and 1000 yards on the right. All movements had to be made with the greatest caution, as mines and traps had been laid everywhere. On the 22nd the battalion was placed in brigade reserve; the relief was completed at 4 a.m., and at 8 a.m. the advance continued. At four o'clock the next afternoon the brigade was ordered forward, but very strong opposition was encountered, and the division on the left being held up, scarcely any progress was made. On the 24th the battalion was withdrawn to the main line of resistance. The casualties during the month amounted to 334, including the following officers wounded: 2nd Lieuts. G. B.

Barnett, H. E. Ewing, G. S. Lewis, and A. L. Stokes. Seven other officers were gassed.

On September 1 the battalion was withdrawn to Villora camp in divisional reserve, but after a few days pushed on to Sailly-sur-la-Lys, the scene of recent severe fighting. The battalion again took up a leading position; by the night of the 9th–10th they had worked forward into the outskirts of Erquinghem, and from being the last British troops to leave in April were the first to set foot in the town in September. Erquinghem was found to be defended by a very thick belt of barbed wire. On the 11th the battalion was withdrawn to the neighbourhood of Estaires, where it remained till September 30, practising formations suitable for open warfare. During the month 2nd Lieut. J. D. Davis was wounded, and the following awards were made—*M.C.:* Captain G. F. R. Baguley. *D.C.M.:* L/Cpl. W. H. Edwards. Brig.-General B. L. Anley now took over command of the 183rd Brigade.

On October 2 the battalion marched to billets in Boesinghem, and three days later proceeded by rail from Steenbecque to Halloy, where they went into G.H.Q. reserve. On being detailed to take part in the final advance in Picardy, the battalion, travelling by road and rail, reached Cantaing on the 10th, where open warfare formations were further practised. Avesnes-lez-Aubert, in the battle area, was reached on the 19th, and on the 24th the 61st Division (Major-General F. J. Duncan, C.M.G., D.S.O.), XVIIth Corps, was brought up to join the IIIrd Army in the battle of the Selle, which had already been going on for a week.

At 4 a.m. on that date the 61st Division attacked over the river Ecaillon, and within two hours the battalion had taken all its objectives, together with 110 prisoners, some trench-mortars, and machine-guns. Shortly afterwards the brigade next on the left having been held up outside Vendegies, the enemy vigorously counter-attacked the leading company from the left rear, forcing them to form a defensive flank. Touch with the left was not regained until the evening. At nightfall the enemy withdrew from Vendegies under pressure from the 19th and 61st Divisions, and early the next morning the line of objective was established. On October 25 the battalion marched to St. Martin and La Folie to reorganise.

On the 27th the battalion was ordered to advance and

ascertain the enemy's strength on the river Rhonelle, and if possible to force a passage and form a bridge-head. The Germans were found in strength on both banks of the river, especially the north. "A" Company got a section over on the left, but these gallant men were all killed before their success could be exploited, the remainder of the company being driven back by machine-gun fire with many casualties. In this operation Cpl. S. F. Staden, M.M., displayed most conspicuous gallantry. In the face of close-range fire he led his platoon to the river—which he himself crossed carrying a Lewis gun—in a vain but heroic attempt to rush an emplacement. When the enemy had been driven back the grave of this corporal was discovered marked with a cross (with his identity disc fastened thereto) on which was inscribed in German the epitaph, "To a very brave Englishman."

The battalion then resumed its original positions. The enemy continued to be very active throughout the day, and at night heavily bombarded the river valley with gas-shells. On the 29th a direct hit on battalion headquarters resulted in two men being killed and eight wounded. The total casualties during the month—most of which occurred at the battle of the Selle—amounted to 274, including the following officers—*Killed:* 2nd Lieut. H. L. Saul. *Died of wounds:* Captain H. J. P. Creagh. *Wounded:* Captains G. F. R. Baguley, M.C., and S. W. Turner, M.C.; Lieut. G. H. Gough; 2nd Lieuts. L. A. Bemment, C. W. Mitchell, and J. C. Smee. Also Captain R. J. Coles and Lieut. E. J. G. Wilkinson (attd. T.M.B.).

There being every reason to suppose that the retreating enemy had elaborated a system of mining dugouts, buildings, and cross-roads, the troops were warned carefully to avoid all such places. On November 1 the battalion stood-to in readiness to support the attack along the high ground east of Somaing, but in the afternoon was ordered to withdraw to Somaing in reserve. On the 2nd they marched to Avesnes-lez-Aubert, and on the 8th to Bermerain. There the battalion was resting in billets when, on November 11, they received a message from the XVIIth Corps to the effect that hostilities would cease at eleven o'clock that morning.

The following honours were awarded during the month—*Bar to M.C.:* Captains S. W. Turner, M.C., and G. F. R. Baguley, M.C. *M.C.:* Captain H. J. P. Creagh; Lieuts.

W. G. Gentle and G. Turner. *D.C.M.:* C.S.M. C. Causton; C.Q.M.S. H. E. Mann, M.M. *Croix de Guerre:* Sgt. H. E. Jeffrey. Fourteen Military Medals were also awarded.

12TH BATTALION

Lands in England—Returns to France—Transferred to the 14th Division—Goes into the Salient—The battle of Ypres, 1918—Courtrai—The battalion at Molembaix when hostilities cease

Landing in England on June 17, the 12th Battalion proceeded by train to Brookwood, marching at once to Stonycastle, and on the 18th to Bullswater camp. On the following day drafts aggregating nearly seven hundred men, all of B 2 category, arrived, the remainder of the month being occupied in trying to arrange them in a human mosaic of the regulation pattern. On July 5 the battalion returned to France after barely three weeks in England, reaching Bayenghem-lez-Eperlecques on the 13th after a series of marches. Here they joined the 43rd Brigade (Brig.-General G. Pereira), 14th Division (Major-General P. C. B. Skinner). A month later they set out for the Salient, shortly taking over front-line trenches on the right of the brigade sector along the eastern side of Zillebeke lake, which had no water in it.

On September 14 they moved to camp in St. Jan ter Biezen, and later to St. Laurent, near Steenwoorde. On the 25th the battalion was again in the front line in the canal sector near the Bluff.

Sir Douglas Haig informs us that early in the month it had been decided to undertake operations on the Flanders front. The force to be engaged was to be placed under the command of the King of the Belgians and was to consist of the Belgian Army, some French divisions, and a number of divisions belonging to Plumer's Army. Accordingly, at 5.30 a.m. on September 28, the British XIXth and IInd Corps attacked without preliminary bombardment on a front of four or five miles south of the Ypres–Zonnebeke road. The 14th Division and three others delivered the initial assault, being supported in the later stages of the battle by two more. In greater detail and with regard to the 43rd Brigade, the attack was carried out by the 20th Middlesex Regiment (right) and the 12th Suffolk Regiment (left), each battalion attacking with two companies in front and two in support, the attacking waves being in lines of "worms." The Ypres–Comines canal, which formed the boundary between the two leading battalions, naturally interfered with lateral communication. The most important feature in the immediate battle area was the Bluff, taken by the 2nd Battalion in March, 1916, but now in the hands of the enemy; it bristled with machine-guns and trench-mortars, and had it been held by Germans of the 1914 type would have proved an insurmountable obstacle.

In describing this most successful operation, Brig.-General George Pereira says that although the battalions were very weak, and the men almost entirely of "B" category, still they attacked with keenness and confidence. The chief incident in the day's fighting was the capture of the Bluff, "A" Company tackling it in front, and "B" wheeling round and encircling it from the left. The brigade commander wrote: "I think the greatest praise is due to Captain Leeming for the handling of the left company. He acted with great promptness, coolness, and skill, and his enveloping move was the great event of the day." Brig.-General Pereira also drew special attention to the able manner in which Lieut.-Colonel Lloyd handled the 12th Battalion. The battalion captured 200 prisoners, one 77 mm. gun, two 6-inch trench-mortars, and thirteen machine-guns. The casualties amounted to 122, including the following officers wounded: 2nd Lieuts. F. J. Doouss, M.C., W. T. Carlisle, and A. M. Chequer.

After this battle the battalion went back to Dickebusch, moving a few days later to the east of Ypres, where they set to work remaking the Menin road near Hooge. On October 12 they were despatched by train to Wulverghem, joining the XVth Corps, and on the 15th marched to front-line positions at Wervicq, on the river Lys, the offensive in Flanders having been again resumed the day before. The 14th Division was in the line. On the 16th the battalion crossed the river Lys, and for the next four days continued to advance steadily. On the 20th they attacked the enemy in the neighbourhood of Dottignies, and then having crossed the canal and driven the Germans beyond the Scheldt, took up a line along the west bank of that river between Warcoing and Espierres. On

October 21 the battalion, having been relieved, marched back to Evregnies.

On November 8 the battalion returned to the Scheldt; during the night one company crossed the river to Herinnes, and the remainder at Warcoing the following morning. The advance was then continued to within about a thousand yards of Molembaix, but the 14th Division having been squeezed out by the 29th and 40th Divisions crossing its front, the battalion was still billeted in farms near Molembaix when hostilities ceased. On November 15 they went back to Tourcoing. During November the following awards were announced—*Second bar to the D.S.O.:* Lieut.-Colonel L. Lloyd, D.S.O. *M.C.:* Captain H. Leeming; 2nd Lieuts. A. Searies and C. F. R. Mowatt. *D.C.M.:* Pte. W. Tingley. Several Military Medals were also awarded.

CHAPTER XVIII

1st Battalion

The 1st Battalion in Macedonia—The raid on the village of Kupri—The line of Struma evacuated—Mosquitoes and malaria—A reconnoitring party saved by woodcock—Frost and snow—Greek comedy—The battle of Monastir—Doiran—The advance into Bulgaria—Bulgaria asks for an armistice

THE first incident of importance occurring in the year 1917 was a raid on the village of Kupri, carried out by two companies of the 1st Battalion under Major D. R. A. Eley, with the co-operation of a battalion of the Northumberland Fusiliers and a troop of the Derbyshire Yeomanry. At dawn on January 3 the Fusiliers were to open fire on the enemy's trenches in front of Kupri, while the two Suffolk companies broke through his outpost line to the west of the village. Accordingly, at 3 a.m. on that date "A" and "C" Companies, under Captains J. W. Houlton and N. B. Oakes respectively, left Kumli, a village about 1500 yards in front of the Allied line at Elisan, and set out on a compass march of four or five miles, led by the battalion scouts, under Lieut. W. B. Durrands and 2nd Lieut. H. C. Carrigan.

The outpost line was quickly rushed by the vanguard platoon, under Lieut. J. R. Sturdy, M.C., which had been pushed well forward expressly for that purpose, no Bulgars being allowed to escape to give the alarm in Kupri. Unfortunately, however, the hostile firing started a stampede amongst the yeomanry horses, causing considerable confusion in the dark. The left flank guard, losing their way, returned to Elisan at dawn, bringing with them three prisoners captured when the outpost line was rushed. The two companies skilfully worked their way round to the north side of Kupri and, having signalled to the Fusiliers to cease firing, advanced on the village. The enemy, taken by surprise and also in rear, offered little resistance, but most of them escaped down the road that would have been blocked by the yeomanry had their horses not stampeded. Twenty-nine prisoners were brought in. For this raid Major Eley was awarded the D.S.O., Lieut. Durrands the M.C., and Sgt. J. Knights of the battalion scouts the Military Medal. Major-General H. L. Croker, commanding the 28th Division, held a parade to congratulate the two Suffolk companies on their achievement.

Heavy rain had now converted the Struma valley into a morass ; trenches had to be replaced by breastworks, and all dugouts abandoned. Thoroughfares became quagmires, a mule belonging to the battalion being drowned in the mud in the main street of Kopriva. Even the Seres road, on which a hundred miles of front had to depend for supplies, was unfit for any but pack transport for a distance of five-and-twenty kilometres. The roads being impracticable for wheeled traffic, the commanding officer (Lieut.-Colonel Hon. H. E. Joicey) invented a mule-sledge for bringing up rations and supplies.

The battalion next went into the line at Dolap, with headquarters at Ormanli. In that neighbourhood the enemy's trenches were closer to those of the Allies than in most sectors as they jutted out into the plain in order to protect the entrance to the Rupel Pass. Shelling, though fairly frequent in this sector, was never very effective. In February the battalion moved back to the second line on the Struma, and in March to Orljak, south of the river. Here dummy trenches were constructed representing those at the entrance to the Rupel Pass, the attack being practised over them in readiness for General Sarrail's summer offensive.

The 10th Division gradually took over the line, and by the end of the month the whole of the 84th Brigade, under Brig.-General G. A. Weir, was in training for the attack. In April Lieut.-Colonel Joicey and the company commanders made an air reconnaissance of the enemy position. The offensive was several times postponed, but patrolling was carried out continuously. Towards the end of May the battalion moved into trenches at Haznatar and Alipsa, a waterlogged part of the line where movement was only possible with the help of waders. On May 24 the G.O.C.-in-C. British Salonika Force received definite instructions from General Sarrail that offensive operations were to cease all along the front. At the beginning of June it was therefore decided to withdraw all British troops south of the Struma, evacuating the whole line of the valley. In view of the approaching withdrawal, it was arranged that on certain nights the Allies should abstain from firing and patrolling. Minor raids were carried out by the battalion scouts at intervals, but no identifications obtained. All iron stakes were removed from the wire, and by the middle of the month the whole battalion had moved back to Paprat, situated in the hills where the mosquitoes were less numerous.

The battalion spent the first few days in its new station repairing the roads which during the wet weather had become almost obliterated. It was then moved over towards lake Doiran, with headquarters at Kamberli, to relieve the 228th Brigade, composed of garrison battalions, who were holding a line in the hills consisting of a chain of small posts with strong points at intervals, the trenches not having been completed.

At first many enemy patrols were in the habit of approaching close to the battalion line, but after one or two encounters they did not venture across the Butkova river. Malaria continued to be rife, and many cases of sand-fly fever also occurred. By night scouting had to be carried out in mosquito-proof veils—difficult to see through—and special shorts which could be turned down and the ends tucked inside the puttees. The British soldier thus equipped, with white gloves up to his shoulders, and a white veil over his steel helmet and the ends tucked inside his shirt, presented a terrifying spectacle in the moonlight.

Late in August news reached the battalion that the greater part of Salonika had been destroyed by fire. At a parade held at Kamberli on September 4, Lieut.-General C. J. Briggs, commanding XVIth Corps, presented decorations as follows—*Croix de Guerre:* R.S.M. Chase. *Médaille Militaire:* Sgt. J. Knights. *Military Medal:* Sgt. A. Ince. *M.S. Medal:* R.Q.M.S. H. F. Nunn.

In October the winter line on the plain to the south of the Butkova river was reoccupied, battalion headquarters being at Sokolovo. Much work was needed to put it into a satisfactory state, the trenches being weather-beaten and the wire without iron standards. Thorough patrolling was likewise necessary before the five or six miles of No Man's Land were sufficiently known. The enemy's outpost line was lightly held and constantly changed. Several posts were located, but when visited with a view to capture had always been moved back.

Lieuts. E. A. Pickard-Cambridge and Carrigan, with a small party, while endeavouring to round up a post in front of Upper Poroi, ran into a patrol which bombed them, slightly wounding the first-named officer and eight other ranks. The Bulgar bomb, when it exploded, flew into such small fragments that seldom anyone was more than badly peppered. Attempts were made, but without success, to ambush some of the enemy patrols. The enemy employed special scouts, wearing fur round their boots, who kept well ahead of their patrols and warned them of danger by a system of bird-calls. One November morning at dawn Lieut.-Colonel Joicey took out the company commanders on a mounted reconnaissance round Poroi railway station. Having completed their task, the party dismounted and went off in pursuit of woodcock, which had been seen in remarkable numbers. These woodcock, luring the party far afield, proved to be its salvation, for in the meantime a strong Bulgar patrol had prepared an ambush for the shooting-party, and had these officers returned by the way they went out promotion in the regiment would have been very rapid. One intrepid sportsman fired both barrels at a wild boar, but the cartridges being of Greek manufacture failed to excite the boar sufficiently to make him charge.

Sport in this neighbourhood was excellent, the woodcock flying down from the hills across the battalion lines every evening at dusk. In the morning large flocks of geese, both white-fronted and grey-legged, flew along the line and many were brought down by rifle and Lewis gun fire before this agreeable practice was forbidden. Another "patrol" spending the week-end at Butkova lake, enjoyed excellent sport, the bag consisting of sixty duck of many different species, twenty geese, besides teal, snipe, woodcock, a few partridges, and a pheasant. The patrol's casualties only consisted of one officer, wounded in the nose with No. 8 shot.

The weather was now severe, the ground being frozen hard and covered with snow. In mid-January, 1918, a British field battery and a mountain battery moved out in front of the line, taking up position by sections, with two Suffolk companies as escort. It was hoped that this demonstration would lead the enemy to reinforce his forward posts and thus provide targets for the artillery; but instead of that he confined himself to counter-battery work and shelling Poroi station and the village which, on the map, bore the simple cryptic title of "M.H."[1] No infantry was seen, though several new gun positions were disclosed. Both Upper and Lower Poroi were set on fire by British shells.

At the end of January, 1918, a hostile aeroplane crashed about two miles in front of the battalion sector. The pilot was seen to run away at once, and shortly afterwards a British gun obtained a direct hit upon it. "C" Company went out to dismantle the derelict and, with the help of Royal Engineers, to destroy the engine. Captain N. B. Oakes obtained a double-barrelled 16-bore gun from the pilot's seat, which was not handed in with the instruments.

In December, 1917, General Sarrail had been recalled to France, and already offensive preparations were being resumed. The weather was cold and wet, and in mid-February there was a heavy fall of snow. A month later the battalion, relieved after being in the line for about a year, moved back to Orljak. There the 84th Brigade, now under the command of Brig.-General F. C. Nisbet, applied itself to intensive training, carried out in conjunction with artillery, trench-mortar batteries, and machine-guns. Live ammunition was used, the battalion working over the same ground as in 1917. In May, Major J. G. Lyons proceeded to France, Captain C. D. Yeatman acting as second-in-command in his stead. After being in corps reserve for three days the battalion moved into its old sector at Kumli and Elisan for a like period, and then back again for training. At that time the Struma line consisted of a system of "pill-boxes." The 84th Brigade had two battalions in the line and two out, each having two companies in the line and two in the hills in rear. During this period much anti-mosquito work was done. At the brigade horse show the battalion won the cup for the greatest number of points in all the events.

"C" Company found all patrols on the brigade front on the Struma lightly held owing to mosquitoes. In June a Greek division arrived for instruction. A certain number of

[1] In the original Austrian survey, this cluster of houses was shown as *Meierhof*, a dairy farm.—C.C.R.M.

its officers and other ranks was taken out on patrol each night by " C " Company under Captain Owen, known as the " 84th Brigade Enterprise Company." This instruction was a difficult business as all orders had to be passed through an interpreter, who carried a loaded revolver which he pointed at everyone he addressed. The only casualty occurring on this front was a Greek non-commissioned officer, who was summarily executed for firing on his own patrol and trying to desert. By July 4 the battalion, having been relieved by the Greeks, withdrew behind the Butkova line towards lake Doiran, where two months later they took over a sector with battalion headquarters near Sarakli.

When the Allied offensive began on September 14 the battalion, greatly reduced in strength owing to the ravages of malaria and influenza, was relieved in the Signal Grec Avance sector by a unit of a composite (half Greek) brigade, and on the night of September 17–18 moved out to its assembly positions on the right of the Cretan Division. This division was to seize the hills running north-east from lake Doiran, and so place itself astride the only road by which the Bulgarian troops at Doiran could retire. For a week before the actual attack opened points in the enemy's position were bombarded. Camps were pitched behind the line, in which fatigue men lit fires, while reserve units marched about in full view of the enemy, but out of artillery range. The British-Greek offensive was, in fact, thoroughly advertised so as to pin the Bulgarian reserves to the ground and keep them away from the line of the Serbian–French advance.

The task of the Cretan Division, which was only about 10,000 strong instead of double that number, was to rush the Bulgarian outposts on the Butkova plain and then to advance against a strong position which the Bulgarians, under German supervision, had been preparing for three years. The 28th Divisional Artillery was to advance as soon as the outposts had been driven in, and then to destroy the wire in the positions round Kodzagoria wood, a four-hour halt being ordered, expressly for that purpose, before the main position was to be attacked. The 84th Brigade was ordered to protect the right flank of the Cretan Division, and also the artillery, from counter-attack from the Belashitza positions.

At dawn the leading Greek brigade rushed the Bulgar

outpost position along the Salonika–Constantinople railway, the battalion advancing to Cakli station and Kodzagoria wood. The 84th Brigade was in echelon, the 2nd Cheshire Regiment being in front and the 1st Suffolk Regiment next. Officers commanding companies rode into action on their chargers, for perhaps the only occasion in the war, but hostile shell-fire from the Belashitza mountains soon persuaded them to dismount. By half-past eight in the morning the battalion was in Kodzagoria wood, facing north-west and north, under intermittent and plunging artillery fire from positions four or five thousand feet above them. The artillery of the 28th Division, galloping into action, opened fire on the main Bulgar position. Great difficulty was experienced in maintaining touch with the Greeks as the commander of their leading brigade had been wounded early in the day and his troops, flushed with success, attacked the main position without waiting for the four-hours' bombardment. The other Greek brigades also attacked piecemeal, and though some elements obtained a footing in the front line, the great bulk were held up by masses of uncut wire and then driven by machine-gun fire helter-skelter down the gullies, where trench-mortars completed their discomfort. The Greek liaison officer with the battalion was killed while endeavouring to acquaint himself with the situation.

About five o'clock in the evening the 84th Brigade moved forward again, but it was already evident that the Greek attack had collapsed. The dry grass and shrubs along the line had been set on fire and were burning fiercely. Outposts were put out to the north-west to give warning of any counter-attack, but orders were now received to cover the retirement of the Cretan Division. Soon after midnight, it having been ascertained that all the Greeks had gone back, the 2nd Cheshire Regiment passed through the 1st Suffolk Regiment which retired with advance, flank, and rear guards. The casualties had only amounted to fourteen killed and wounded. On September 20 the battalion relieved the 2nd East Yorkshire Regiment at Signal Grec Avance.

It was now obvious that the enemy were retiring, as most of their dumps behind Doiran were burning. On September 22 a patrol under Lieut. P. W. Keefer, sent out to ascertain whether the Beles positions were still occupied, was only fired on by one field-gun and one trench-mortar, showing that a general retirement was in progress. On the following day the battalion was relieved by the 2nd Greek Regiment, and the advance towards the Bulgarian frontier continued. The battalion, reduced by influenza and malaria to 350 effectives, marched along the western edge of lake Doiran, passing through the town of that name and following the road which the Cretan Division had failed to straddle. The strength of the companies was further reduced by men having to lead A.S.C. mules, the battalion transport, with one man to four mules, absorbing practically all the personnel below the rank of sergeant. When the Allies entered Bulgaria the Greeks, anxious to take advantage of this unique opportunity to pay off old scores, had to be firmly restrained when passing through villages.

The destruction caused by British aircraft in the passes and gullies by which the Bulgarians retired was colossal. The narrow defiles were choked with guns and transport, and the enemy troops, caught with cliffs on both sides, or a cliff on one side and a chasm on the other, were literally blown to pieces. As regards the Serbians, the rapidity with which they advanced over difficult country towards Uskub and Kustendil was one of the most remarkable achievements of the war. The Allied progress was still unchecked when, on September 30, the Bulgarians asked for an armistice and hostilities ceased. On that day the strength of the battalion was fourteen officers and 250 other ranks.

In October the battalion was employed in salvage work, clearing up battlefields and the like. The gentle *comitadjis*[1] were already busily acquiring stocks of rifles and ammunition for use when peace was declared. On October 13 the battalion began marching back to the base, and on the 21st reached Guvesne, some twenty miles from Salonika, where it was organised as two companies. On November 7, an armistice with Turkey having been signed on October 30, the battalion embarked in H.M.T. *Bermudian* and, escorted by destroyers, sailed for Gallipoli.

[1] Lit. Committee-men ; irregulars paid by Government.

CHAPTER XIX

5TH BATTALION

The 5th Battalion captures Bornat Hill—A cheerless Christmas—The actions of Tel Asur—The death of Lieut.-Colonel Wollaston—Order and counter-order at Ludd—The final offensive—The battles of Megiddo—The storming of Observation Hill—The collapse of the Turkish armies—The battalion reaches Haifa—The armistice with Turkey—Beirut—The armistice with Germany

WHEN Jerusalem fell on December 9 the 54th Division (Major-General S. W. Hare), less one brigade, was in the neighbourhood of Ludd, holding a portion of the line covering Jaffa. The 5th Battalion, under Lieut.-Colonel Wollaston, D.S.O., was in reserve to the 163rd Brigade (Brig.-General T. Ward), with two companies in the trenches at Yehudieh and the remainder, under Major Copinger Hill, two miles away in the direction of Beit Nabala.

On the 11th the Turks attacked Zeifizfiyeh hill and Norfolk post. The two companies, under Major Copinger Hill, moved up as local reserve, but the attack being easily repulsed were not called upon to act. That night the battalion, less these two companies, marched across to an olive grove behind Beit Nabala. On the following day six shells from a mountain battery fell right into the middle of the bivouac area, slightly wounding one man. On December 15 the whole line advanced, the battalion, under Major Copinger Hill, participating with the 163rd Brigade in the capture of Bornat hill, the highest point in the neighbourhood, and about 3000 yards distant. "A" and "C" Companies, under Captains G. G. Warnes and A. A. Maris, were in the assaulting line, with "B" Company (Captain F. R. Althaus) in support, and "D" Company (Captain H. C. Wolton) in reserve. The battalion, emerging from the wood, soon came under machine-gun fire, but managed to reach the dead ground at the foot of the slope without much difficulty or loss. The assaulting companies, making use of the cover afforded by the rocks, quickly climbed the steep slopes of the hill, but in the meantime the Turks fled, the only prisoner taken being found fast asleep in a cave. On gaining the crest-line the companies were somewhat heavily shelled, particularly " A " Company occupying the forward slope. The battalion remained on the hill until late in the night. The casualties amounted to seventy-seven, including the following officers—*Killed :* Lieut. H. B. Ryley. *Wounded :* Captains F. R. Althaus and A. A. Maris ; 2nd Lieut. C. C. Reed. Though several acts of bravery were performed in this action no awards were made owing to the recommendations being received too late.

On being relieved the battalion moved to Stone Heaps hill and, on the 23rd, in consequence of an advance having been made the previous day, to Et Tireh. In the latter a patrol of " D " Company captured a Turkish patrol consisting of a warrant officer and seven men. They made no resistance, and seemed despondent and half-hearted. Christmas Day was ushered in by a steady drizzle. Battalion headquarters were in a squalid cave, the companies being widely scattered amongst the hills lying to the eastward of Tireh village. There was no food to supplement the ordinary rations, and everyone spent the day crouching in a bivouac, now and then hammering in a peg with a stone to save it from collapse. Many, no doubt, have looked back on the Christmas of 1917 as the most cheerless in their lives.

The battalion, having gazed longingly awhile at the attractive village of Wilhelma, welcomed the move thither on December 28. In this model German settlement, with its nicely furnished houses, well-stocked farms, and abundance of firewood, a very pleasant month was spent. This was the only occasion on which the battalion occupied houses during its stay overseas. The days were passed in digging trenches and drains, making roads, and building an embankment for a light railway. Four days' emergency rations were always kept on hand in case the roads should become impassable owing to rain. But the contingency did not arise, and the A.S.C. delivered the goods with unfailing regularity. Early in January, 1918, the brigade commander presented ribbons to those awarded decorations for the third battle of Gaza. On the 23rd, while the battalion was occupying a line of posts running southwards from Rantieh, an officer patrol engaged a Turkish patrol about thirty strong, quickly dispersing them without suffering any casualties. On the same day Lieut.-Colonel Wollaston proceeded on leave to England. A week later the battalion moved to One Tree hill, near Mulebbis. During February they moved forward to the Auja stream, with posts at Northampton Castle, El Mirr, White Gates, Long Wood, and Lemon Grove. On the 20th that portion of the village of El Mirr which lay on the east bank of the Auja was cleared of its inhabitants, and all the sheep and cattle brought away. At a divisional tournament held in March the cup for the best platoon was won by No. 13 Platoon, under Sgt. Youngs. As there were 192 platoons to select from, the 5th Battalion was justly proud of Sgt. Youngs' success.

On March 16 H.R.H. The Duke of Connaught presented decorations and medals as follows—*M.C.:* Major H. T. Copinger Hill. *D.C.M.:* Sgt. J. Pearson; Pte. W. C. Allum. *M.M.:* Sgt. A. W. Freeman; A/Sgt. S. Bowman; Pte. S. G. Wells. About that time, Pte. A. M. Rosling was also awarded the D.C.M.

On March 12 the 162nd and 163rd Brigades advanced the line further to a depth of four miles, capturing Mezeirah, Khurbet Dikerin, Mejdel Yaba, and Ras-el-Ain. This advance pushed the front of the XXIst Corps (Lieut.-General E. S. Bulfin) almost up to the line on which it remained until September. While these operations—forming part of the actions of Tel Asur—were in progress the panorama from the village of El Mirr was both picturesque and grand. Little opposition was encountered and no casualty sustained, the Turks again displaying a singular lack of energy. The next day one company took over the ruined fort at Ras-el-Ain. On March 16 the battalion moved to Garnett's wood, near Fejja, in brigade reserve. While there the unexpected news was received that Lieut.-Colonel F. H. A. Wollaston, D.S.O., who was on leave, had been killed in London during an air-raid on the night of March 7–8. The whole battalion deplored the loss of a brilliant soldier and a gallant gentleman.

At the beginning of April the battalion again moved into the line at El Mirr and Ras-el-Ain; and on the 5th Major W. M. Campbell, Suffolk Regiment, recently commanding the 1/5th Norfolk Regiment, assumed command of the battalion. He had been captured at Le Cateau, but after being a prisoner in Germany for three years had effected a bold escape.

With the advent of the hot weather a period of quiet

began in Palestine and little of interest occurred during the summer months. On April 24 Brig.-General T. Ward, C.M.G., who had commanded the 163rd Brigade since Gallipoli, relinquished his command and was succeeded by Brig.-General A. J. McNeill, D.S.O. Early in May the battalion went to Dikerin, and shortly afterwards took over the right sector of the divisional front, which consisted of a chain of sangars, each holding a platoon. These sangars were situated on the forward slope of rocky hills, with steep-sided watercourses running away from them, and, being under direct enemy observation, were not occupied during the day. On June 20 the battalion moved back to the neighbourhood of Rantieh in divisional reserve. A few days later the battalion was informed that the 54th Division, following in the wake of the 52nd Division, was to proceed to France. Great were the rejoicings and great the preparations. Off the battalion marched to Surafend, and on the following day to the railway station at Ludd. With much hustle and bustle the battalion entrained, but no sooner had the baggage been loaded and all the men settled into the train than the move was cancelled, and the battalion returned ruefully to Surafend. The 54th was now the only European division remaining in the Egyptian Expeditionary Force. The battalion spent some days at Surafend, moving camp twice—on the second occasion to get away from an epidemic of influenza which had broken out in an adjoining camp. Leave to Jerusalem was reopened, and large numbers from the battalion availed themselves of the opportunity to visit the famous city.

Early in July the battalion went off to Mezeirah for three weeks' road-making, and at the end of the month to Red House wood, near Yehudieh, where it underwent a model period of training under almost ideal conditions. Night-firing was practised with ball ammunition, signal-bombs, flares, grenades and Very lights, on a scale hitherto undreamed of in the soldier's philosophy. During this training all ranks were made to pass through the gas chamber at Wilhelma to test their masks. The health of the battalion was remarkably good, the admissions to hospital being less than in any other battalion in Palestine.

September 19 was selected as the date for the next advance. Five British divisions and the French contingent were detailed

Photo by] [*Lafayette*

LIEUTENANT-COLONEL F. H. A. WOLLASTON, D.S.O.

for the main attack on the right of the Turkish line, on a front extending from the coast for a distance of about eighteen miles. The date and hour had, no doubt, been chosen partly on account of the moon, which would then be about four days from full, giving light for the move out, followed by two hours' darkness in which to prepare for the assault. On the right of the attack—on which the movement was to pivot—was the 54th Division, with three or four battalions of Algerians and Armenians attached. The right of the divisional frontage was allotted to these battalions, the 163rd Brigade being on their left. The 5th Battalion was on the right of the brigade attack, its objective—Observation hill—being intended to form the pivot for the further movement eastward, which was to begin the same day. At half-past four on the morning of the 19th, when objects could be distinguished about two hundred yards ahead, the bombardment opened. At the end of a quarter of an hour the attack was launched and broke through the Turkish defences on the coast almost without a pause. As regards the 5th Battalion, its line of advance lay across steep foothills, which rose three or four hundred feet above the dry ravines intersecting them. Wire had been located in front of Khurbet Kesfa, and immediately the barrage had lifted from the first objective two platoons, under Lieuts. G. G. Oliver and D. Green, rushed these points. Having crossed the rock-strewn ridge, the two leading companies plunged into the Wadi-el-Ayun, and while they were clambering up the rocks on the further side an effective bombardment fell upon Observation hill, which formed the second objective. Pausing under the crest-line until the barrage had lifted, they gained the summit exactly to schedule time. Numbers of the enemy were holding on to a knoll to the left which had not been attacked, whereupon Lieut. G. Hughes, gathering together a few men and directing them towards it, captured the post, together with ten prisoners and a machine-gun.

On the summit of Observation hill considerable opposition was encountered owing to the arrival of enemy reinforcements. While Captain Fox was engaging the enemy in front and on both flanks a platoon of *Tirailleurs*, under Lieut. Morisson, came up on the right flank and co-operated with great effect, shooting the enemy down as they fled from the caves in the precipice on the north-east side of the hill. Shortly after five o'clock Captain G. Kilner with his company moved across the Wadi-el-Ayun and supported the attack. The whole operation was a complete success. The battalion captured over a hundred prisoners, including five officers, with three machine-guns and much war material, and buried a number of Turks and Germans. The casualties were—*Killed:* Lieut. N. A. Mackinnon; 2nd Lieut. P. T. Clarke, and five other ranks. *Wounded:* 2nd Lieut. W. Emerson and twenty-four other ranks. The following awards were made—*D.S.O.:* Major W. M. Campbell; *M.C.:* Captain and Adjutant A. Fair; 2nd Lieut. G. Hughes, D.C.M.

The battalion remained in the positions it had captured until late in the afternoon, when it was withdrawn to the Wadi-el-Ayun. Here it anxiously awaited much-needed water. The next day was spent in salvage work, and on the 22nd the battalion moved out on to the plain near Kefr Kasim, acting as reserve to the guard over the thousands of Turkish and German prisoners who had been collected in the ruins of Ras-el-Ain.

The brigadier thanked the battalion for their work, and said that when he saw them running like hares for the top of Observation hill he did not wait to see them arrive, but wired at once: "Observation hill taken."

Some time later, after the division had returned to Egypt, this incident was recalled in the following letter:

"HEADQUARTERS 54TH DIVISION.

"MY DEAR CAMPBELL,

"As your battalion has gone to the force in Egypt for good, I am writing to thank you and them for all they have done.

"I have known them now for three years, and they have always done well, and never better than last 19th September.

"The dash with which they took Observation hill set the pace for the whole attack. I am very sorry to part with them, and wish them all the best of luck and safe home.

"Yours very sincerely,

"S. W. HARE, Major-General.

"Commanding 54th Division."

The week's rest in camp near Ras-el-Ain, which followed this battle, was very welcome as the weather was hot. Every day the men bathed in the Auja stream. During this rest the following message was received from the Commander-in-Chief:

"I desire to convey to all ranks and classes of the force under my command my admiration and thanks for their great deeds of the past week, and my appreciation of their gallantry and determination which have resulted in the total destruction of the VIIth and VIIIth Turkish Armies opposed to us. Such a complete victory has seldom been known in the history of war.

"E. H. H. ALLENBY, General C.-in-C."

The troops composing these two armies, however, could not be compared with those of the Vth Army in Gallipoli. The war-weary Ottoman soldier of 1918 was a very different type from the spirited dauntless Turk who had opposed the battalion in 1915. No doubt this was true, but to a less extent, of all the belligerent armies. Four years of war had subdued even those of the highest mettle. The thrill of pride that went through the battalion when it realised that final victory was in sight can therefore be more easily imagined than described.

On September 27, at short notice, the battalion rejoined the brigade at Hableh and set out on the march to Haifa, passing through Kakon, Kerkur, Zimmarin, and the Crusader stronghold of Athlit. At Haifa they bivouacked for four days just outside the town, which provided a surprising variety of shops and booths and seemed to require an equally surprising number of guards. Brackish water then compelled a move to another bivouac area, which acquired the name of Scorpion camp for reasons which many remembered. The battalion next spent a pleasant week near the shore of the crescent bay of Acre, and on October 24 set out for Beirut. During the march news was received that an armistice between Turkey and the Entente Powers had been signed, and that hostilities would cease at noon on October 31. On November 1 the 163rd Brigade marched through the town of Beirut and past the corps commander (Lieut.-General E. S. Bulfin), being accorded a great welcome from the people.

The march was continued to Es Safre, where news was received of the armistice with Germany. The battalion then returned to Beirut, where, on November 28, it embarked in H.M.T. *Ellenge* for Egypt.

15TH BATTALION

The attempt to recapture Jerusalem—The actions of Tel Asur—The 74th Division sails for France—The Somme, 1918—The Second Battle of Bapaume—The Hindenburg line—The battle of Epehy—The capture of Templeux-le-Guerard—The pursuit to Mons

Owing to the proximity of the enemy to Jerusalem on the northern and eastern sides it was decided to undertake further offensive operations with the object of providing greater depth to the defence of the city. After a minor set-back on December 23 the general advance was postponed till the 27th owing to bad weather. At dawn on that date, however, the Turks made determined attacks on White hill and Ras-az-Zamby, gaining possession of the former, but this position, rendered untenable by British artillery fire, was recovered after dark. On arrival at Beit Izza from Kubeibah, where they had spent a wet and cold Christmas, the battalion was ordered up to Beit Dukka, where they bivouacked for the night. Early in the morning of the 28th the 74th Division completed the capture of Hill 2450 and by dusk were holding a line from Beitania to Rafat. On the 29th the 230th Brigade occupied Rahm Allah, the battalion being on the left of the attack. The captured positions were consolidated, the division having advanced over five miles through rugged and difficult country. Thus ended the Turkish attempt to recover Jerusalem.

A period of road-making followed until March 8, when a fresh advance began, involving, as far as the 15th Battalion was concerned, three of the hardest days' fighting and the greatest test of physical endurance in the Palestine campaign. The general idea was an attack all along the line. The 74th Division advanced along both sides of the Jerusalem–Nablus road, with the 53rd Division on its right and the 10th (Irish) Division on its left, the objective assigned to the 230th Brigade being the trench system at Burj Badawil.

Leaving camp near Balua lake soon after sunset on March 8

for its assembly positions, the battalion had first of all to climb a hill by means of a steep and narrow path which, in the darkness, took two hours to accomplish. The attack commenced at dawn, and by 8 a.m., after a temporary check, the village of Yebrud had been cleared; then, crossing a ravine, the battalion advanced on the main position at Burj Badawil, which was taken by 10.30 a.m. On gaining the crest the troops were checked by machine-gun fire from both flanks. The country was the most difficult so far experienced. A series of terraced fields led down to the Wadi and to the white streak of road, and on the far side another terraced hill rose to a considerable height. As the ground was devoid of cover and its configuration prevented the artillery from giving any support, it was decided to postpone the advance till dusk. Only one track was possible for the descent. At midnight, the bridge on the road not being held, the two attacking battalions of the 230th Brigade moved forward to the assault of Hill K.12. At dawn the crest of the hill was gained and a few prisoners captured. The artillery were now able to co-operate, and during the morning the whole of Hill K.12 as well as the high ground overlooking Sinjil were secured and the position consolidated. During the remainder of the month the 15th Battalion remained either in the outpost line near Turmus Aya and Sinjil or in close support. On April 3 orders were received that the 74th Division was to embark for France; on the 6th the battalion began its march back through the country it had helped to conquer, and on the night of the 13th–14th entrained at Ludd for Kantara. After a busy period of handing in stores and equipment only used in Palestine, the 15th Battalion embarked in H.M.T. *Leasowe Castle* at Alexandria, arriving at Marseilles on May 7. On the departure of the division from the E.E.F., Major-General E. S. Girdwood received letters of a highly complimentary character from the C.-in-C. (General Allenby) and the G.O.C. XXth Corps (Lieut.-General Sir Philip Chetwode, Bart.).

The division sailed from Egypt in seven transports, escorted by eight Japanese destroyers. When off Cape Bon a submarine was sighted and believed to have been sunk. The return journey of the transports to Egypt was not so fortunate, two being torpedoed; and with the next convoy which left Alexandria for France the *Leasowe Castle* herself was sunk, the captain and some seventy officers and men being drowned.

After spending two days at Marseilles the 230th Brigade proceeded to Noyelles, near Abbeville, for training. The battalion knew a good deal about open warfare, but the country and the conditions of fighting on the Western front being entirely different from Palestine, there was naturally much to learn in other ways. During the greater part of June and July the 74th Division formed part of G.H.Q. reserve, being liable to go anywhere at a moment's notice. It was eventually sent into the line in front of St. Venant, in the Haverskerque–Amusoires sector, at the vertex of the German salient on the river Lys, arriving in time to participate in the general counter-attack which was about to take place along the British line. On August 24 the battalion went back to Busnes, and shortly afterwards entrained at Lillers for Breilly, near Amiens. On the last day of the month they proceeded by bus to Maricourt, on the Somme, relieving the 58th Division near Hind Leg wood and joining the IIIrd Corps of Rawlinson's Army. Very heavy fighting was in progress round Mont St. Quentin and Péronne. On September 2 the 74th Division took part in the operations west and south-west of Nurlu, the battalion being in support. On the 5th and two following days the battalion was engaged in the attack on the Templeux-la-Fosse and Gurlu wood system of trenches, sustaining about a hundred casualties, including the following officers wounded: Major T. De la G. Grissell and 2nd Lieut. R. Hogg (both remaining at duty); Captains G. B. Horne, M.C., and R. O. W. Pemberton; 2nd Lieuts. W. Murray, W. E. Strong, and J. Hodges. In the middle of the month the battalion took over a sector of the front line opposite Templeux-le-Guerard.

On September 18 the IVth and IIIrd Armies attacked in heavy rain on a front of about seventeen miles between Gouzeaucourt and Holnon, the Ist French Army co-operating south of the latter. The 230th Brigade (right) and the 231st Brigade (left) were detailed for the attack. The 15th Battalion in the centre attacked from the Australian area and in a short time swept through Templeux and over the Quarries, taking the enemy completely by surprise and capturing a considerable number of prisoners. Practically along the whole front objectives were gained. In this attack dummy tanks were used with great success. The offensive was not resumed until the 21st, but the battalion remained in the front line under almost continuous fire till the night of the 24th–25th, when the division was relieved by American troops, having sustained during September over 3500 casualties. On the 28th, after a long journey by rail and road, the battalion reached Allouagne, where they remained in billets for three days. Early in October the 74th Division took over from the 59th Division a sector of the front line nearly three miles in length with Neuve Chapelle in the centre. On the evening of October 3 the battalion moved up on to the Aubers ridge, and the next day occupied a line covering the villages of Lattre and Wavrin. During the night of the 13th–14th, while the battalion was in position in front of Fournes, 2nd Lieut. N. Crowther and his runner were killed by a shell. On reaching the Lille canal on the 16th strong opposition was met with, and the battalion was forced to withdraw to positions about Sante and Rosoir, a thousand yards back. During the fighting Lieut. J. J. Henderson was mortally wounded and died the following day.

The enemy were now retreating upon Lille, and by the 18th British troops had encircled that city, which was clear of the enemy. The 74th Division then took up the pursuit and, crossing the canal with the 15th Battalion as advance guard, entered Baisieux on the 20th. From October 21 to November 8 the battalion was in the line east of Orcq, the enemy holding a stone bridge-head on the Scheldt covering Tournai. That city was entered on the 9th, and while the battalion was engaged in guarding some of its exits on the eastern side news was received that hostilities would cease at 11 a.m. on November 11.

CHAPTER XX

THE 3RD (SPECIAL RESERVE) BATTALION

IT was perhaps only natural that, during a crisis such as the great war, the services rendered to the nation by the Special Reserve—once famous as the Militia—should not have been fully recognised, yet without them the armies in the field could not have been maintained. They were the axle on which the wheel of reinforcement turned. The little streams of men, hurrying to join up, that trickled into every regimental depot, flowed out again in a torrent of drafts and reinforcements. Some idea of the stupendous work performed by the Special Reserve during the war may be gained from the fact that over a thousand officers and thirty-three thousand men passed through the 3rd Suffolk Regiment alone. Three-quarters of these officers and nearly half the men were sent overseas. By the end of 1914, in spite of the outflow of drafts, the strength of the 3rd Battalion had jumped to 115 officers and 2600 men, and eventually reached the remarkable figures of 201 officers and 4285 men. The enormous miscellaneous correspondence and the continual preparation of nominal rolls, returns, indents and orders rendered necessary by such an inflation of numbers, involved an amount of clerical labour which treble the staff available could not have discharged satisfactorily. The constant demands for officers and men made continuity of work a matter of great difficulty. It is doubtful whether the arduous and sometimes disheartening duties which fell to the lot of the commanding officers and permanent staff of the Special Reserve battalions have ever received a full measure of recognition.

The order for general mobilisation, for which the London Press had fully prepared the country, reached the barracks at Bury St. Edmunds on the evening of August 4. It was at once communicated to the officers of the 3rd Battalion, all of whom joined the following morning with the single exception of one on leave in Canada. All through the night the officers and permanent staff of the depot worked unceasingly. The next morning, before the notice to join had reached them, army reservists came flocking in, but work proceeded so expeditiously that by the end of the day nearly nine hundred had been medically examined, clothed, equipped, fed, and accommodated—surely a remarkable achievement. By August 7 the mobilisation of these reservists had been completed and they had all been despatched to the 2nd Battalion at the Curragh.

In the meantime many retired officers and local gentlemen came to the depot offering their services in any capacity whatever, either as officers or otherwise. Old soldiers and recruits poured in, making work very brisk and necessitating extra staff. The rank and file of the 3rd Battalion, according to notification, joined on the 8th, and on the 9th—at half-past two in the morning—the battalion, under Lieut.-Colonel S. E. Massy Lloyd, marched away from the barrack square to entrain for Felixstowe, its war station. Even at that early hour thousands of people lined the route to the station to speed them with parting cheers. The following officers proceeded with the battalion: Lieut.-Colonel S. E. Massy Lloyd (in command); Majors C. D. Parry Crooke and F. E. Allfrey; Captains E. A. Jackson, E. F. Hausburg,[1] A. G. Taylor, V. F. Currey, H. L. Cautley, and A. H. W. Temple; Lieuts. G. B. Pollock-Hodsoll and P. C. Harris; 2nd Lieuts. R. J. O. Dowse, C. C. Roe, R. E. P. Wilder, and E. F. King. *Adjutant:* Captain G. A. L. Sinclair Thomson. *Quartermaster:* Major J. T. Potter.

The tumultuous cheering of welcoming crowds greeted the battalion as old friends on its arrival in Felixstowe, where for many years it had carried out its annual training. Battalion headquarters was established at the Ordnance Hotel, the officers and men being accommodated in billets previously requisitioned by Major W. O. Cautley. The battalion took over the duties of the 4th Essex Regiment (T.A.), which was carrying out its annual training at Felixstowe when war was declared. At first the days were spent in digging entrenchments, erecting barriers and barbed-wire entanglements, but on completion of the defences intensive training was commenced. In the meantime large numbers of recruits and re-enlisted men had joined from Bury St. Edmunds. Residents

[1] This officer afterwards changed his name to Hutchinson.

of Felixstowe and other parts of the county provided them with bedding, the army supplies of such being temporarily exhausted.

It was a strange but common sight to see the battalion on a route march, headed by the band, with perhaps eight hundred men in uniform followed by a still greater number in a medley of civilian clothes. Some wore the colours of their public schools, colleges, or clubs ; others had wisps of straw tied round their knees to keep their corduroys in due restraint. Some were in smocks, and some in silk hats and frock-coats ; others, down at heel and out at elbow, but with hearts of gold. Was there ever such a motley throng, or a more truly patriotic one ?

Musketry, of course, claimed a position of importance in the training programme, and Major Allfrey, the musketry instructor, spent many a day from dawn till dusk on the rifle range. On one occasion a British aeroplane fell into the sea about a mile from the shore, and Captain Temple, who was in command of the sea-post defence section at Felixstowe, was instrumental in saving the occupants. Great difficulty was experienced in meeting the continual demands both for overseas reinforcements and for personnel to form the nucleus of some newly-raised unit. Occasionally non-commissioned officers had to be replaced by instructors from the police force, mostly from London. These men rendered invaluable assistance, especially in the maintenance of discipline. The first reinforcement draft for France left Felixstowe as early as August 26, and ten days later, in order to replace the heavy casualties sustained by the 2nd Battalion at Le Cateau, a batch of officers proceeded overseas at very short notice.

Recruits and re-enlisted men continued to join in large numbers, but with instructors ready to teach and men anxious to learn, progress was remarkably rapid. Incessant demands on the 3rd Battalion for trained men and specialists of all kinds had depleted it in many ways, and especially as regards cooks. After much ado six cooks from London reported themselves to the battalion for duty. They demanded free board and lodging at a first-class hotel and salaries of two guineas a week. The rank and file, with visions of being served by white-hatted chefs, were quickly disillusioned, as these men turned out to be merely cooks' helps, who knew nothing whatever about cooking.

During the night of September 26th–27th a warning was received that a German airship was cruising about over the North Sea some thirty miles from Felixstowe. Everyone was anxious to get a view of it, but after watching and waiting for several hours the garrison was informed that the airship had gone back. After this incident rigid instructions came into force regarding the concealment of lights.

In November the 1st Battalion, under Lieut.-Colonel W. B. Wallace, arrived from Lichfield and was billeted alongside the 3rd Battalion. On December 22 a letter was received from the Mayor of Bury St. Edmunds wishing all ranks of the battalion a Happy Christmas. Owing to the war the great national festival was observed with the most praiseworthy moderation, but the kind message from the mayor was nevertheless much appreciated by the battalion, and gratefully acknowledged by Lieut.-Colonel Massy Lloyd. On the 28th a heavy gale swept over England, doing great damage.

On January 19, 1915, three German airships raided Yarmouth, King's Lynn, and neighbourhood, but did not visit Suffolk. Three months later a German airship, with lights burning and making a great noise, passed over Harwich and Felixstowe. This was the first Zeppelin seen by the battalion. During the first half of the war German aircraft visiting England seemed to avoid the estuary of the Thames and to fly over Suffolk, but latterly they entered by Essex or Kent and, during the last year of the war, Suffolk was but little affected.

Towards the end of January the band and six non-commissioned officers, under Major Jackson, proceeded to Tottenham to attend the funeral of R.S.M. R. Burton, M.C., late of the 2nd Battalion, in which he had served with distinction during the retreat from Mons and at Le Cateau. During March Major W. O. Cautley and Pte. R. Francis, both of the 3rd Battalion, were awarded the D.S.O. and D.C.M. respectively; and in April Sgt.-Major R. Barber and Colour-Sgt. Instructor T. Packard, both belonging to the permanent staff of the 3rd Battalion, received commissions in the Suffolk Regiment. On May 9 a memorial service was held in St. John's Church, Felixstowe, in memory of 2nd Lieut. F. E. Stantial, killed in action in France with the 1st Battalion. He was a son of the Rev. A. E. Stantial, vicar of the parish.

Towards the end of May one of the newly constituted standing medical boards visited the battalion, dividing the men into categories and, incidentally, heaping further clerical work upon the distracted staff. About this time a large draft arrived from the 13th Reserve Regiment of Cavalry at Colchester. These men, naturally resenting their transfer from cavalry, were organised as a separate company, under Captain J. A. Campbell. To meet the pressing demand for field-glasses, a fund was started to purchase a quantity of these articles, a proportion of the number of pairs purchased being sent overseas with each draft. In July both the 3rd Battalion itself and its defences were inspected, the results being entirely satisfactory. Battalion orders for August 3 contained the following appreciative announcement :

" A commanding officer at the base informed an officer of the battalion that he could pick out the drafts of the 3rd Battalion at any time. They were so well instructed, and were the smartest drafts which came down to Rouen. He also remarked that the officers were more soldierly than those from other corps, this being from his own personal observation."

On August 16 a violent thunderstorm broke over Felixstowe and neighbourhood. Pte. W. Claydon, a native of Bury St. Edmunds, was killed outright, Pte. Waters, struck by the same flash, being rendered unconscious. In November Major F. S. Cooper, Suffolk Regiment, was appointed adjutant in place of Captain Eley, who had succeeded Major Sinclair Thomson in May.

The following message from His Majesty the King was published in Battalion Orders on December 25 as a special order :

" Another Christmas finds all resources of the Empire still engaged in war, and I desire to convey on my behalf and on behalf of the Queen a heartfelt Christmas greeting and all good wishes for the New Year to all on sea and land who are upholding the honour of the British name.

" In the officers and men of my Navy, on whom the security

of the Empire depends, I repose in common with all my subjects a trust that is absolute. On the officers and men of my Armies, whether now in France, or in the East, or in other fields, I rely with an equal faith, confident that their devotion, their valour, and their heartfelt sacrifice will, under God's guidance, lead to victory and an honourable peace.

"There are many of their comrades now in hospital, and to these brave men I desire with the Queen to express our deep gratitude and our earnest prayers for their recovery.

"Officers and men of the Navy and Army, another year is drawing to a close as it began, in toil, bloodshed, and suffering, but I rejoice to know that the goal to which you are striving draws nearer into sight. May God bless you and all your undertakings. "GEORGE, R.I."

Christmas greetings were also received from the mayor, aldermen, and burgesses of Bury St. Edmunds, and from the 1st Battalion in Salonika. On January 10, 1916, Major Allfrey assumed command of the battalion in place of Lieut.-Colonel Massy Lloyd, who had gone to France on temporary duty. In May Captain C. S. Wilson succeeded Major F. S. Cooper as adjutant. On June 6 the 3rd Battalion took part in the review of the Felixstowe garrison by H.M. the King. Before His Majesty left the town the following message was received: "The King wishes to express his satisfaction with the appearance and steadiness on parade of all ranks at his inspection to-day. His Majesty was glad to have this opportunity of showing his appreciation of the services rendered by reserve units in maintaining his army in the field."

In the despatches published with the *London Gazette* of January 25, 1917, Lieut.-Colonel Massy Lloyd was promoted brevet-colonel; and in those dated February 22 the following were mentioned: Major and Quartermaster J. T. Potter; R.S.M.'s E. Dowsett and F. Meadows. Early in April Brig.-General Cunliffe Owen having proceeded overseas, Colonel Massy Lloyd was appointed to the command of the Felixstowe district. On relinquishing the command of the 3rd Battalion Brig.-General Massy Lloyd was presented with a silver inkstand by the warrant officers and sergeants, the presentation being made by R.S.M. Dowsett. Brig.-General Massy Lloyd in a few well-chosen words expressed his high appreciation of this gift. He was succeeded by Major F. E. Allfrey. In May the Field-Marshal Commanding-in-Chief the Home Forces inspected the battalion and expressed himself thoroughly satisfied.

On June 16 two Zeppelins approaching the coast were engaged by British aircraft and driven back. At eleven o'clock that night they returned, passing inland between Felixstowe and Clacton. They were immediately engaged again, and chased all round East Anglia. Some hours later one of the raiders was brought down in flames about ten miles north of Felixstowe. The sight of the falling mass, plainly visible by the garrison, raised a cheer that could be heard for miles around. But they were not left alone for long, and on July 4 a squadron of aeroplanes made a determined raid on the garrison. No sooner had the warning been received than the hostile aircraft were overhead bombing heavily, fourteen of the garrison being killed and twenty-nine wounded. On July 22 a German air squadron again raided Felixstowe, this time in broad daylight and without any warning whatever, twelve persons (including civilians) being killed and twenty-three wounded. Much material damage was done on both occasions.

Christmas came round once more, the fourth in the war, greetings being again received from H.M. the King. On January 5 Majors A. S. Peebles, D.S.O., and F. T. D. Wilson, with several other ranks, all repatriated prisoners of war, were posted to the battalion for duty. Owing to the situation on the western front the War Office telegraphed that all men belonging to the first category were to be in readiness to proceed to France by March 31. At that time the situation on the Felixstowe front also gave rise to anxiety owing to an *émeute* occurring amongst a contingent of the Women's Army Auxiliary Corps, attached to the battalion. On the morning following the outburst the defaulting W.A.A.C.'s were marched in before the commanding officer. On the charges being read out to them they all burst into tears, the case being hurriedly dismissed. The next day some of them were brought up again and fined half a crown each. They all went away quietly, but only to gather strength for the next day's eruption, when no less than six of them deserted. These desperate termagants were, however, soon captured and, with remarkable promptness, transferred to other spheres of usefulness. The situation having been restored, a test war-station scheme was opportunely carried out by the Felixstowe garrison. The operations, which began at half-past one in the morning, were conducted in a thunderstorm and witnessed by General Sir William Robertson, who commended the efficiency of the battalion and the bearing of the troops under such conditions of weather.

On November 11 news was received that the Armistice had been signed. The commanding officer was immediately besieged by people demanding the instant release of their relatives and friends, his obvious inability to comply in all cases with such requests causing some discontent. Christmas of 1918, vastly different from its four predecessors, was celebrated with the wildest rejoicings.

During the war the 3rd Battalion gave several large contributions to the Suffolk Prisoners of War Fund and, in the twelve months ending with July 31, 1918, was instrumental in collecting no less than £647 6s. 6d. for the fund. The record of the Suffolk Prisoners of War Help Committee is one in which the county will always take pride. Before the year 1914 had closed reports came through concerning the harsh treatment being meted out to the British prisoners of war in Germany, amongst whom were many of the 2nd Battalion who had been captured at Le Cateau. Discussions at once took place between persons interested, and a committee was formed to raise funds to provide and send out food and other necessaries to the Suffolk men who were prisoners of war. This committee, formed early in 1915, was one of the first, if not actually the first, of its kind, and consisted of:

Bunnell H. Burton, Esq. (Chairman).
A. M. Bernard, Esq.
F. L. Bland, Esq.
B. W. Elkington, Esq.
Colonel Hon. H. W. Lowry-Corry, D.L.
Colonel C. R. W. Hervey.
Mrs. Massy Lloyd.
A. Maitland Wilson, Esq., D.L.

Joint Honorary Secretaries

Major G. R. C. Stuart, C.B., D.L.
Richard Edwards, Esq., M.B.E.

The Committee, starting its labours with a provision for about five hundred, ended by sending parcels to over a thousand. The amount of money subscribed in the county exceeded £100,000, and the Suffolk Committee was the only one able to maintain continuous supplies to its prisoners of war without being subsidised by the central organisation in London. Many a prisoner owed his life to the efforts of these patriotic people.

On December 29 a service was held in the garrison churches in memory of those who had fallen in the war. With the opening of the New Year the demobilisation of the army began in earnest, everyone striving to be the first to go. The greatest tact had to be exercised on all occasions to prevent an open rupture. Recruiting for the standing army now opened, large numbers taking advantage of the bounties offered. In January, 1919, the band, forty strong, under Bandmaster H. E. Adkins, proceeded to France to join the 2nd Battalion. Early in February Lieut.-Colonel F. E. Allfrey was demobilised, handing over to Major R. B. Unwin, and taking away with him the best wishes of the battalion in which he had served for many years. At the end of the month Captain C. S. Wilson relinquished the adjutancy which he had held with the highest credit for nearly three years. During his tenure of that appointment his services undoubtedly contributed to the general efficiency of the Suffolk Regiment. He was succeeded by Captain N. A. Bittleston.

The battalion now received orders to proceed to Rugeley, in Staffordshire. Leaving behind 56 officers and 2385 men, under Major S. J. B. Barnardiston, D.S.O., the remainder, consisting of 38 officers and 756 men, under Major R. B. Unwin, entrained at Felixstowe on March 7. Rousing cheers from the large crowds assembled were raised as the train moved out of the station. The camp was over four miles from the town, and the battalion in vile weather, in bad huts, and amid strange surroundings, did not settle down readily. During March the battalion—belonging to the Eastern Counties Reserve Brigade—detached a company to take charge of prisoners of war in Lincolnshire, and in April furnished a draft for Egypt. This draft, parading in khaki clothing and pith helmets, at half-past one in the morning, with snow lying on the ground nearly a foot deep, presented a strangely incongruous spectacle. On May 1 Lieut.-Colonel V. C. Gauntlett, the King's Regiment, took over command of the battalion from Major R. B. Unwin.

Throughout May and June the weather was warm and dry, the bracken and grass round the camp were constantly catching fire, and it was a frequent occurrence for the battalion to be called out at night to dig trenches to prevent the flames from reaching the huts. In July Lieut.-Colonel A. S. Peebles, D.S.O., Major F. T. D. Wilson, Captain H. R. Gadd, D.S.O., M.C. (Adjutant), Captain J. Hearn (Quartermaster), Lieut. T. D. Pickard-Cambridge, and a nucleus of the 2nd Battalion arrived in Rugeley and took over the personnel and stores of the 3rd Battalion. On the 27th of that month the 3rd Battalion was demobilised after an embodiment lasting five years to within a week—the longest and most strenuous in its history. Not a single old Special Reservist remained when the battalion was disembodied. During the great war twenty-nine officers of the battalion were killed in action and forty-five other ranks killed or died at home, the remainder having been transferred or invalided. In February, 1919, the under-mentioned warrant officers and non-commissioned officer were awarded the Meritorious Service Medal: R.S.M.'s E. Dowsett and F. Meadows; Colour-Sgt. U. Dockerill. Later, Captain W. L. Llewellyn was granted the brevet rank of major for services rendered during embodiment. On July 27, 1919, the 3rd Battalion as such ceased to exist, thus sharing the fate of many others who, like themselves, had played the game.

CHAPTER XXI

Battalions of the Second and Third Lines—Battalions not proceeding overseas integrally—Ancillary formations of the Suffolk Regiment

According to the original organisation of the New Armies the supply of drafts was provided for by reserve battalions, affiliated either to the old regular and Territorial battalions or to the new Service battalions. In the autumn of 1916 a new system was introduced, namely, the training reserve. The reservoir was formed by pooling most of the former reserve battalions of the Service battalions and locally raised units of the New Armies, called respectively 2nd Reserve and Local Reserve Battalions, and diverting new recruits to the training reserve. The old militia battalions remained; with regard to the Territorial Force, the third line battalions were converted into Reserve Battalions.

When the 4th Suffolk Regiment left for France a 2/4th Battalion was formed under Colonel W. A. Churchman, V.D., with Captain E. C. Quilter as adjutant, its headquarters being at first at Stowlangtoft, near Bury St. Edmunds, and later at Cambridge, where it remained for the rest of its existence. In 1916 the battalion was disbanded, some of the personnel being sent to the 64th Provisional Battalion (afterwards the 14th Battalion Suffolk Regiment) at Holt, Norfolk, and the remainder to the 3/4th Battalion.

The 3/4th Battalion was formed in April, 1915, at Ipswich, under Colonel G. L. Bence-Lambert, C.M.G., with Captain E. P. Clarke—who had been wounded while serving with the 1/4th Battalion in France and was convalescing—as adjutant. At the end of two months or so it moved to Windsor Great Park, going under canvas by the side of the Long Walk. Later on in the year it was sent to Halton, near Tring, where it became associated with the 3/5th Battalion and the Norfolk, Cambridge, and Essex third-line battalions. Towards the close of 1916 the 3/4th and 3/5th Battalions were amalgamated, when Colonel Bence-Lambert retired. Lieut.-Colonel H. J.

Hargrave, who had been commanding the 3/5th, was then given command, the new battalion being named the 4th Reserve Battalion Suffolk Regiment. Early in 1917 Major F. W. Turner took over command from Lieut.-Colonel Hargrave, appointed to that of a military hospital.

The 2/5th Battalion was raised at Stamford in November, 1914, Lieut.-Colonel C. F. Wright being appointed to the command, with Major H. H. Johnson as second-in-command, Captain G. H. Long, adjutant, and Major A. Goat, quartermaster. In April, 1915, the battalion moved to Peterborough, in May to Cambridge, and in August to Bury St. Edmunds. The 69th Division (Major-General F. H. Kelly, C.B.), to which it belonged, concentrated at Harrogate in April, 1916, prior to proceeding overseas ; but owing to the enormous casualties in the battles of the Somme in July of that year it was retained in England as a draft-furnishing division. The battalion, now under the command of Lieut.-Colonel G. H. Long, spent the winter of 1916–17 in Doncaster, moving the following April to Thoresby Park, near Retford, Nottinghamshire. During the autumn the battalion, under Major E. C. Tillard—Lieut.-Colonel Long having proceeded overseas—was transferred to Canterbury, where at the end of 1917 it was disbanded.

The 3/5th Battalion was raised at Bury St. Edmunds in April, 1915, by Colonel G. L. Andrewes, V.D., with Major H. C. Langman as adjutant, and later on in the year was moved to Halton, near Tring. In May, 1916, Major H. J. Hargrave took over the command from Colonel Andrewes and was promoted Lieut.-Colonel, Captain L. H. Rodwell succeeding Major H. C. Langman as adjutant. Subsequently the battalion was amalgamated with the 3/4th Battalion as already stated.

The main purpose of these second and third line battalions was to provide drafts for the fighting areas, and in order to enable them to do so they were continually supplied with recruits of all ages who were called up for service, and men of their own first-line battalions who had been wounded or invalided and were getting fit for further active service. The recruits were put through an intensive form of training, and at the end of eight weeks were expected to be—and generally were—ready to go overseas. The returned men of category A 3 were hardened up as rapidly as possible and, as soon as they were passed medically fit, sent out again. Drafts were therefore going away continuously, but the particular front for which they were intended was never disclosed until the last moment. The permanent staff and instructors of these battalions were drawn almost entirely from the regular army and comprised some of the finest men in the service.

The clerical staff was composed of disabled men and those permanently unfit. The officers, passing through in a continuous stream, belonged to the following categories: (1) Young officers who had not been overseas, but had come from officers' training camps; (2) those who had served in the ranks at the front and, having received commissions, had attended officers' training camps; and (3) officers who had been wounded or invalided, but had recovered sufficiently to go out again.

6th (Cyclist) Battalion

This battalion, originally raised as a Cyclist Battalion in August, 1911, by Lieut.-Colonel W. T. Pretty, T.D., was formed from a nucleus of one company of the 4th Battalion. At the beginning of August, 1914, the battalion, at full strength, was in camp at Pakefield Cliff, near Lowestoft, undergoing its annual training. During the precautionary period immediately preceding general mobilisation the battalion garrisoned coastal stations between the rivers Deben and Waveney, mobilising on the declaration of war at its headquarters at Ipswich, and moving on August 5 to Saxmundham, its war station. Until the arrival in that neighbourhood of other cyclist battalions the 6th Battalion had charge of the whole Suffolk coastline, with the exception of the Harwich defences. Subsequently they were entrusted with the defence of the coast between the Deben and the Blyth. During the first week of August, 1914, every man of military age in the battalion volunteered for service overseas, and the 1/6th Suffolk Regiment was recognised as an Imperial Service Battalion.

The battalion never went overseas as a unit, but soon began furnishing drafts for the western front, and by degrees all the physically fit officers and men were posted to battalions overseas. The first of these drafts left in August, 1914, under

Captain C. J. F. Cobbold, joining the Ist Army Cyclist Corps. The battalion, with its headquarters at either Saxmundham or Wickham Market, continued to be employed on coast defence until the end of the war. The individual records of members of the battalion must be sought in the history of the units with which they served.

A party of the 1/6th Battalion, stationed near Corton, Lowestoft, came under fire during the German cruiser raid on Yarmouth and Lowestoft on April 25, 1916, which resulted in a score of casualties. Another party was at Southwold during the surprise bombardment of that place by a German destroyer on January 25th–26th, 1917. The only other war episode with which the battalion was connected was the descent in flames of a Zeppelin at Hollow Tree farm, Theberton, near Saxmundham, on June 17, 1917.

The 2/6th Battalion, also a cyclist unit, was raised in September, 1914, as a result of a recruiting campaign in Suffolk, promoted by Lieut.-Colonel W. T. Pretty, T.D., D.L., commanding the 1/6th Battalion, and Captain W. Rowley Elliston. The first details were assembled at the works of Messrs. Richard Garrett and Sons, Ltd., Leiston,[1] and placed under Captain W. Rowley Elliston, 1/6th Battalion, for rations, pay, and discipline. Theirs was not a life of luxury, the men being bedded down in straw in sheds. Cross-country runs, taking place in the early mornings, were often substituted for the usual physical training. These parades were conducted by a nimble-footed officer who was a keen follower of beagles and wanted—if the rumour may be believed—to win the men over to that agreeable form of sport. Towards the end of October the battalion moved to Ipswich, where it was quartered in the Diesel engine-works. A more uncomfortable billet would be hard to find, the men sleeping on the oily floors amongst huge machines, with only two blankets apiece. Lieut.-Colonel A. C. Churchman[2] was now appointed to the command; shortly afterwards those of the 1/6th who were ineligible for foreign service were turned over to the 2/6th.

Three weeks later the battalion was sent up to Louth, Lincolnshire, where they remained for about six months, with

[1] An Illustrated Memorial of the Great War in relation to Leiston and District was published by J. S. Waddell, Leiston.

[2] Afterwards Sir Arthur Churchman, Bt., M.P.

detachments at Grainthorpe and Theddlethorpe. The people of Louth soon began to display that hospitality and kindness which the Suffolk men were destined to enjoy at their hands to a remarkable degree. No soldiers were ever better cared for than the 2/6th Battalion by the good citizens of Louth.

The battalion, armed with Japanese carbines, was kept busy with training and road-patrolling. A good deal of sickness prevailed, scarlet fever being epidemic. In March, 1915, the battalion moved to the coast, with headquarters and one company at Huttoft, but were soon afterwards transferred to Marshchapel, with outstations at Tetney Lock and Donna Nook. In August the battalion, now organised as four companies, moved to Skegness, with detachments at Boston and Wainfleet. Here again they were most hospitably received. Early in 1916 the battalion went under canvas at Chapel St. Leonards, a village to the north of Skegness, where training and patrol duty continued. In June a draft of fifty men left for France, and in the following month another of two hundred which, prior to departure, was inspected by Field-Marshal Sir John French. This draft disembarked at Boulogne, moving later to Etaples, which at that time contained many thousands of troops. Before leaving England each man was presented with a silver pencil bearing the inscription, "With best wishes from A.C.C." The commanding officer, adjutant, regimental sergeant-major, and a few non-commissioned officers accompanied this draft, which was destined to great achievements in France. One of the first officers of the 2/6th Battalion to gain distinction on the western front was 2nd Lieut. F. G. Truscott, awarded a Military Cross for gallantry at Loos in September, 1915.

The following extract from battalion orders of the 1/6th Battalion, dated September 11, 1916, was republished in those of the 2/6th: "I am privileged to record in orders the following appreciation by the G.O.C. 37th Brigade of the draft recently sent to France. . . . 'The (7th) Suffolks in this (12th) Division were filled up by drafts from the Suffolk Cyclist Battalion. They arrived in the middle of operations (Somme, 1916), and are considered the best men they ever had, well trained, with great hearts in them.'"

The 1/6th and 2/6th Battalions were justly proud of this high tribute, and shortly afterwards two officers of the 2/6th, inspired by the general's burning words, composed a song entitled "In Suffolk," the words being written by Lieut. F. Elias,[1] and the music by Lieut. H. S. Middleton.

The literary talent in the 2/6th Battalion blossomed forth at the end of 1915 into an amusing and well-edited publication, prepared by Lieut. Elias, entitled *C.B., or the Christmas Bulletin of the Cyclist Battalion.* The cover, designed by Lieut. S. N. Evans (killed in an aeroplane on July 9, 1917, while flying over London), bore the following couplet:

Let none of you declare you've had no warning,
We'll give you all C.B. on Christmas morning.

Until the departure of the large draft in 1916 the 2/6th Battalion was composed almost entirely of Suffolk men. The most numerous section hailed from Lowestoft, but nearly every part of the county was represented. The use made of cyclists by the Belgians, and the emphasis laid by the authorities before the war on the value of this type of mobile force, put many expert cyclists from London and elsewhere on the look-out for an opening for their particular form of skill. Accordingly, in the first months of the war the battalion recruited a number of men from London, and on being sent to Lincolnshire, gathered further recruits from that county. Still, the battalion remained predominantly Suffolk, and when the men were on a route march one could always hear the true Suffolk speech, with its rich accent, its ample human qualities, and its salted and vigorous humour.

The departure of the big draft broke up a happy family that had always hoped to go to the front as a whole; and to those who were left behind to await their return things never seemed quite the same again. Following these men went other drafts of first-class quality. Numbers of officers on going overseas were posted to the 4th Battalion and other units, maintaining wherever they went the reputation of the battalion they had first joined. The 2/6th remembered particularly Captain Charles Stuart, son-in-law of Sir Arthur Churchman, Bt., its first commanding officer. Captain Stuart was a Fellow of Trinity College, Cambridge, who had represented his university at tennis and golf, and whose brilliant and eager mind lighted those of all with whom he came in

[1] "John Owen," the novelist. *See* Appendix V.

contact. Six weeks after landing in France he was killed in action. There was, too, Lieut. Stewart Evans, who left the battalion to join the R.F.C., and who—after some preliminary service in Egypt—was killed while flying over London. Then there was 2nd Lieut. J. J. Brooke, who for a time commanded the battalion machine-gun section; also Lieut. G. P. Cockburn. The loss of these young officers brought to their comrades at home a sense of how ruthless war can be, and how unsparing of youth and promise. The following is a list of officers of the 1/6th and 2/6th Battalions who laid down their lives in the Great War:

Brooke, J. J., 2nd Lieut. Killed in action 4.10.17.
Churchman,[1] C. H., Captain. Killed in action 3.5.17.
Cockburn, G. P., Lieut. Killed in action 23.3.18.
Evans, S. N., Lieut. Killed 9.7.17.
Fison, J. F. L., M.C., Captain. Died of wounds 2.11.17.
Moseley, G. K., Captain. Killed in action 10.4.18.
Samuel, W. G., Captain. Killed in action, 21.9.18.
Stuart, C. E., Captain. Died of wounds, 15.3.17.
Truscott, F. G., M.C., Lieut. Died of wounds 6.4.17.
Westwood, W. P., 2nd Lieut. Killed in action 26.9.17.

The Cambridge and Suffolk (Reserve) Battalion

In the spring of 1917 the 4th Reserve Battalion Suffolk Regiment, to which reference has been made in the early part of this chapter, was amalgamated with the Cambridge Reserve Battalion while both were at Halton, near Tring, the whole being renamed the Cambridge and Suffolk (Reserve) Battalion, under the command of Lieut--Colonel F. W. Turner, with Captain F. M. Wilson as adjutant. The quartermaster was Major W. Dooley, who had already rendered valuable service in the 4th Battalion in the same capacity, both at home and on the western front.

In August, 1917, the battalion went to Crowborough, where, in the following March, Lieut.-Colonel C. F. H. Greenwood, D.S.O. (28th London Regiment), who had recently returned from France, took over command from Lieut.-Colonel F. W. Turner. A few days later Field-Marshal Sir

[1] Son of Sir Arthur Churchman, Bt. *See* Appendix I.

William Robertson inspected the battalion, exhorting it to send every available man to France whenever required. A weekly though memorable event was the despatch of a draft to the western front, and in less than six months nearly nine hundred were sent. In addition, a good many officers and men volunteered for service with the King's African Rifles, their offers being in many cases accepted. During the first blast of the great German offensive all " B " men were moved up into Category A.

The average strength of the battalion was about twelve hundred, composed partly of men who had returned from expeditionary forces and partly of youths, all under a willing and hard-working staff of non-commissioned officers unfit for further active service. The average number of officers in the mess was a hundred.

In August Colonel Greenwood returned to France to resume command of the 22nd London Regiment (The Queen's), handing over that of the Cambridge and Suffolk (Reserve) Battalion temporarily to Major F. J. Rodwell,[1] who was succeeded by Lieut.-Colonel S. D. Roper. The battalion was then sent to Hastings and was still there when the Armistice was signed. In December the bulk of the officers and men were transferred to the 3rd Battalion, but the cadre remained in existence till the midsummer of 1919, and when demobilised was nominally stationed at Ipswich. On the occasion of its disbandment Field-Marshal Sir Douglas Haig, who was then Commanding-in-Chief the Forces in Great Britain, wrote to Lieut.-Colonel Roper expressing his appreciation of the high standard of the drafts sent overseas by the battalion and of its splendid service during the Great War.

10TH BATTALION

This battalion was raised at Felixstowe early in October, 1914, by Captain F. L. Stanley Clarke by breaking off two recruit companies from the 3rd Battalion. The 10th, originally raised as a Service battalion, was at first commanded by Major F. E. Allfrey. Early in October Lieut. T. A. C. Thornhill and 2nd Lieuts. G. C. Fitzherbert and G. M. Brown were gazetted

[1] Afterwards Major F. J. Rodwell, O.B.E., T.D.

thereto, other officers being detailed from the 3rd Battalion. Towards the end of that month Major T. S. Young was sent to take over the temporary command from Major Allfrey, the latter with the other officers detailed from the 3rd Battalion being withdrawn and the new unit left to function alone. Early in November Brevet-Colonel H. R. Roberts was selected to command the battalion, 2nd Lieut. G. M. Brown being appointed adjutant and promoted to lieutenant. Lieut. J. Roberts was appointed quartermaster.

The battalion was then forming part of the Special Reserve Brigade at Felixstowe, under Brig.-General J. R. M. Dalrymple-Hay, C.B., D.S.O. While there the battalion was billeted in excellent quarters along the sea-front. During November and December Captains F. Le Feuvre, L. Lloyd, and F. W. Brooke, and Major G. F. Collinson, took over command of the four companies, Lieut. E. B. Miller being appointed machine-gun officer, Lieut. R. J. M. Raven-Hart signalling officer, and 2nd Lieut. H. W. Jenks musketry instructor. Wearing old red-and-blue uniforms and issued with wooden dummy rifles the battalion experienced some difficulty as regards training owing to a cramped and unsuitable parade-ground and the constant furnishing of working parties in connection with the coastal defences. Early in 1915, owing to an outbreak of cerebral spinal meningitis, the brigade was temporarily scattered, the 10th Battalion being sent to Bury St. Edmunds, where the men, with the senior officers and the adjutant, were accommodated in the barracks and the remainder billeted in the town. While at Bury training proceeded rapidly, and it was to the great disappointment of all ranks that, in April, 1915, the battalion was converted into a reserve battalion and a draft-finding unit.

In May, 1915, the brigade reassembled at Colchester, the battalion occupying hutments in Reed Hall camp, where the depot companies of the 12th Battalion were absorbed. Following on the conversion of the battalion from a service to a reserve battalion, an intensive system of draft training was adopted, each course lasting ten weeks, carried out amid a constant change of personnel. In addition to the training of drafts the brigade had to furnish a flying column for coast defence and pickets for all main roads leading into Colchester.

In March, 1916, the brigade moved to Dovercourt, Major G. H. S. Crofton succeeding Major Young as second-in-command upon the latter's transfer to another unit. While there the battalion was responsible for the defence of the coast from the pier for a distance of three miles to the south. During the year the strength of the battalion steadily increased until at one time it was over 2000 other ranks, with from 100 to 150 officers. In August, 1916, Colonel Roberts resigned the command owing to ill health, being succeeded temporarily by Major G. H. S. Crofton. Before a new commanding officer was appointed, however, the 10th Battalion, amalgamating with the 11th Essex Regiment, became the 26th Training Reserve Battalion, and as such ceased to form part of the Suffolk Regiment.

13TH (RESERVE) BATTALION

In accordance with the scheme of grouping together reserve companies of locally raised service battalions of the same regiment and forming reserve battalions to provide reinforcements for service battalions in the field, the 13th (Reserve) Battalion was raised on September 14, 1915, from the two reserve companies of the 11th (Service) Battalion which remained when the latter left Cherryhinton in the previous June to join the 34th Division at Ripon. The companies were administered by the Cambridge and Isle of Ely Territorial Force Association. In October Major A. W. Stanley, who was in command, was promoted Lieut.-Colonel, Major W. V. Weston being appointed second-in-command, Lieut. N. K. Bell adjutant, and Lieut. H. Cranfield quartermaster.

On November 9, 1915, the battalion, over four hundred strong, proceeded to billets in Trowbridge, joining the 24th Reserve Infantry Brigade (Brig.-General E. Morton), but within three months was transferred to the 26th Reserve Infantry Brigade (Brig.-General K. E. Lean, C.B.) and sent to Leamington. On April 14, 1916, the battalion was ordered to Lessness Park, Abbey Wood, where it was quartered in huts. At the end of July it was transferred to Chohole Gate camp, Richmond Park, its strength in the meantime having increased to well over eight hundred. On September 1 the unit became the 108th Training Reserve Battalion, transferring three hundred men to the 3rd Battalion. Up to that date the 13th Battalion had sent away seven hundred men in drafts, nearly all proceeding to France.

On October 10, 1916, the unit was converted into a reserve garrison battalion and recruited about nine hundred B 1 men, all those belonging to the first category being distributed amongst the other four battalions of the brigade.

On November 3, the day after the battalion left Chohole Gate for Barnes, the camp was completely flooded out and nearly all the tents were blown down by a violent gale. The small guard, under Lieut. E. W. N. Tayler, detailed to remain behind and wind up the camp, took nearly a month to complete their task in consequence. In December Captain A. Pickles was appointed adjutant in place of Lieut. N. K. Bell, transferred to the 11th Battalion in a similar capacity.

On January 1, 1917, about a thousand men of the battalion moved into the stables of the Ranelagh Club, the remainder being billeted in Barnes. In July the battalion went into camp at Bocking, near Sittingbourne, in the Thames and Medway garrison. Two months later they were transferred to the Maida Barracks, Aldershot, and in December, 1917, were disbanded.

14th Battalion

This battalion, which first appeared under that title in the Army List for February, 1917, had its origin in the 64th Provisional Battalion. That unit, formed at Cambridge on 20th June, 1915, from home service and unfit men of the 2/4th and 2/5th Battalions, was shortly afterwards sent to Cromer for coast-defence duty. Territorially the battalion was practically a homogeneous body, all the men—with the exception of a draft of about a hundred from the Sherwood Foresters—hailing from Suffolk. The first commanding officer was Major R. E. White, V.D., who was promoted Lieut.-Colonel in September of that year, the second-in-command being Major R. C. Kay, and the adjutant Captain H. D. Mitchell. Early in 1916 the battalion volunteered for garrison service overseas, about six hundred men being passed medically fit, but as that figure fell short of the number required by regulation it was not sent abroad.

On Major Kay being appointed to the command of a battalion in 1916, Major P. W. Cobbold became second-in-command until he went to France in the summer of that year. He was succeeded by Major H. Davies, M.C., and subsequently by Major E. A. Thomas. When Captain Mitchell proceeded overseas from Cromer, Lieut. G. E. Hollond became adjutant. On April 7, 1916, the battalion was sent to Holt, but on the 11th of that month proceeded to Sheringham, and on the 21st to Salthouse. At the last-named station it was converted into a draft-supplying battalion, and in October was ordered to Weybourne.

On January 1, 1917, the 64th Provisional Battalion became the 14th Battalion Suffolk Regiment, Captain H. G. Smith-Rewse being appointed adjutant in March. In June it proceeded to Sidestrand, where Lieut.-Colonel R. E. White relinquished the command, being succeeded by Lieut.-Colonel R. L. Lees, D.S.O., T.D. In July the battalion returned to Sheringham, where, in the following October, Captain W. Adams was appointed adjutant. Shortly after the Armistice the battalion was disbanded.

1st (Reserve) Garrison Battalion

This battalion was raised in the spring of 1916, its first station being Wendover, Bucks, but in May it was sent to Tilbury, and in the following month to Gravesend. At first the battalion was commanded temporarily by Captain G. Steele, and in May Lieut.-Colonel H. R. Wallace, D.S.O., was appointed. About the same time one company was sent to France, joining the L. of C. Troops and remaining overseas until the end of the war. In 1918 this company was transferred to the reserve army, but at the signing of the Armistice belonged to the 197th Brigade.

In August, 1917, Brevet-Colonel C. F. Grantham was appointed to the command of the battalion, whose headquarters were still at Gravesend, with detachments at Tilbury, Queenborough, Leysdown, Thames Haven, Cliffe Fort, Kynock Town, Pitsea, Weedon, Harty Ferry, All Hallows, and Coal

House Fort, besides small parties along the estuary of the river.

The strength of the battalion fluctuated considerably, drafts being continually received from, and despatched to, the different fronts, but it averaged 200 officers and 1800 men.

Serving in the battalion were several eminent professional musicians. These Colonel Grantham formed into an orchestra, which by its performances raised over £1800, enabling the battalion to present pianos to three different hospitals and disburse donations to various charities.

Early in 1918 the battalion was transferred to Grain Island, returning a year later to Gravesend, where it was demobilised.

2nd (Home Service) Garrison Battalion

The strain brought upon reserve battalions in providing drafts for overseas and at the same time troops for coast defence led to the formation of garrison battalions for home service, and on May 5, 1916, the 2nd (Home Service) Garrison Battalion of the Suffolk Regiment came officially into being. The new unit, raised in the Harwich garrison area, was to complete its establishment from men of the lower categories in the local special reserve brigade and from officers unfit for service overseas. Colonel Sir Kenneth Kemp, Bt., who from 1904 to 1910 had commanded the 3rd Norfolk Regiment, was appointed to the command, with Major F. White (late East Surrey Regiment) as second-in-command; Lieut. H. W. Harrison (1st Suffolk Regiment) adjutant; Lieut. G. E. Hammond (from the 9th Suffolk Regiment) quartermaster; and J. Tann (Norfolk Regiment) as regimental sergeant-major.

The battalion, soon at full strength, was as quickly scattered to various defence posts, such diffusion leading naturally to difficulties of administration and co-ordination.

On June 4, 1916, His Majesty the King reviewed the troops of the Harwich garrison. After His Majesty had ridden down the lines the troops marched past, the 2nd Garrison Battalion presenting a steady and workmanlike appearance, and acquitting themselves with considerable credit.

On taking up their quarters the companies quickly began

to make gardens and to cultivate any adjacent waste ground. But the demon of despair, who lies in wait for mortals, especially soldiers, did not allow the Harwich garrison to escape him. Were men trained as specialists, forthwith they were despatched to the four corners of the earth. Were plots of ground round defence posts put under cultivation and made to flourish like the green bay tree, at once came orders to vacate them. When all the produce had vanished the original owners were recalled.

By the end of 1917 the strength of the battalion was so reduced, and the danger of invasion so remote, that its numbers were made up with " C " men. After having been employed with the Royal Defence Corps in the Harwich and Ipswich districts the battalion was disbanded in April, 1918.

CHAPTER XXII

The Back Areas in France—The Great Dispersal

IT must be borne in mind that the soldier in the field led a dual existence, each reacting directly on the other, and any account of the war without reference to each of these phases would be obviously inadequate. As is but natural, the actual fighting record must claim overwhelming preponderance, but as the soldier spent at least as much time out of the trenches as in them it is quite clear that some description of the back areas must be forthcoming. Before bidding final farewell, therefore, to the armies in the field, let us pass in brief review life as lived behind the line, where the war-worn soldier could laugh his laugh, play his game, sing his song, amuse himself in cinema or theatre—and forget. Unquestionably his fitness, welfare, and efficiency were almost entirely dependent upon such periods of rest. In the earlier stages of the campaign many and serious discomforts were unavoidable, but as experience had fuller play, these were gradually eliminated until in its later stages all units were admirably looked after, some almost luxuriously. A trained commanding officer, who realised the superlative importance of everything affecting the comfort of his men, and a helpful staff, were essential. The subject is far too large for a short account, as is its evolution from the earliest stages to its final and complete efficiency. The due provision of necessities and luxuries was the sphere of those in charge of the back areas. Under the heading of necessities it covers the feeding and clothing of the men, fitting and washing of clothes, housing, and transport; under luxuries, the provision of canteen stores, recreations, cinemas, leave, and many other details.

To take food, a primary essential. Never once did the Army Service Corps fail to supply the day's rations, though the link was very nearly snapped on one or two occasions in

1918. But the actual supply is only half the battle. In order to eliminate the interminable stew, the common fare of all units in the early days of the war, cooking classes and competitions were arranged. As hot food had to be cooked in the trenches without any show of smoke, hot boxes were improvised. Then came the time when men were so exhausted walking across the battlefield, as for example on the Somme, that food had to be provided half-way to the trenches. From that time onwards soup kitchens were installed at sheltered —or unsheltered—spots on the duck-board track. There, supervised by the padres, free soup was given to all. Chocolates and cigarettes could be purchased and were often given free. When troops came out of the line nothing was more appreciated than an egg or some fish. Vegetables were invaluable, but all such had to be collected, and in competition with other units unless the divisional staff were very helpful. A good quartermaster was the right-hand man of a battalion commander, and his value was reflected in the welfare of the whole unit.

Baths were almost as important, while clean clothing was an absolute necessity. Like cooking, and indeed all other administrative needs, baths went through their process of evolution. They started at La Gorgue in great vats filled with boiling water, into which half a dozen men scrambled at a time and soaped themselves. Then, through Soyer stoves, they came to showers at two minutes a time, for water and fuel were often scarce. Bath houses had to be built and pipes installed. Clothing had to be washed out and fumigated, easy matters to arrange when troops were stationary. But every few days the battalion moved, perhaps to a fresh area where fresh baths had to be constructed and fresh laundries installed. In a well-organised battalion towards the end of the war the exhausted soldier, caked with mud, who often took many hours to come from the trenches to his camp, found hot water awaiting him, clean clothes, a warm canteen and good food, and a theatre to follow. In the early days of the war a tithe of these necessities would have made a paradise.

As the war proceeded so the provision of accommodation for horses and men became more and more a problem. The barns of earlier days had disappeared; huts and stables had to be erected on the devastated land. Some time before the end of the war divisions had begun to organise gangs of brick-layers and carpenters, and already clusters of one-roomed bungalows were rising up out of the ruins of villages. All the time the reader must picture to himself an endless stream of traffic on the roads behind the lines, for necessities and luxuries depend on roads to reach their destination. In winter, however, when the roads were covered with deep liquid mud, with great yawning holes at intervals, the traffic could hardly be likened to a stream: for hours there was no movement, vehicles standing hopelessly blocked. In those early days horses often remained in harness for twenty-four hours or more, only covering perhaps half a dozen miles in that time. On the medical side, the dressing stations, hospitals, convalescent companies, rest camps, and the like form too extensive a subject to be described here; but they made up a big part in the soldier's life, for few indeed escaped them.

In modern warfare, certain luxuries actually become necessities. The value of a good laugh cannot be over-estimated. Every division had its cinema—with a constant change of the best and most comic programmes—and its theatre. In a sense their worth was greater than that of a London theatre, and their audiences were more enthusiastic. Like everything else, these theatres went through their process of evolution. The earliest performances were given in a barn, with a make-shift stage, neither chairs nor forms, no electric footlights, and no dresses worthy of the name. The final productions, remarkable in themselves, boasted all the appurtenances of the London stage. The canteen, a real necessity of to-day, was preceded by the Y.M.C.A. tent, and had by no means reached perfection by the end of the war.

As the great struggle went on, a battalion's activities were directed into various administrative channels. Economy became the order of the day. New clothes and boots could not be found to replace the old. The old had to be repaired, and shops established to carry out the repairs. Salvage parties busied themselves in collecting the flotsam and jetsam of war. Tins had to be melted down for solder and grease for fat. Back areas had to be organised so that troops coming out of the line found billets ready for them. In the earlier days there was always a scramble for accommodation—first come, first served. The Christmases of 1914 and 1915 were spent in warm farm-houses, but as the line fluctuated backwards and forwards these farms gradually disappeared, Nissen huts taking their places. In areas very far back, the château, the farm, and the village still flourished, all numbered and ticketed and presided over by a superannuated town major and some ragged veterans.

No account of life out of the line in France would be complete without a passing reference to Lucienne of Armentières, or her like in other big towns. These women ministered in cafés to many thousands of British soldiers, and their names became historic. But when the cities—Armentières, Ypres, Bethune—which saw their good works, fell into ruins, they also vanished.

. . . .

When unveiling the memorial to the men of Norfolk, Suffolk, Essex and Cambridgeshire, who fell in the Great War 1914–1919, erected at Liverpool Street Station in 1920 by the London Society of East Anglians, the Lord Mayor of London said that he could pay no better tribute to the men of East Anglia than the following, spoken by Marshal Foch two years previously: "I have heard before of the valour of the men of the East of England. There is nothing more inspiring than details of the deeds you have performed, and France will always be grateful to you for your heroic sacrifices on her account."

Let us now, therefore, hark back to the men who shared in those sacrifices, and to the five Territorial and Service Battalions of the Suffolk Regiment who were still in the field when the armistice with Germany was signed and, taking each in turn, record its movements until the world's greatest parade had been dismissed.

The 5th Battalion arrived in Cairo from Beirut on the last day of November, 1918. As usual, the close of the rainy season was marked by a good deal of sickness, influenza and malaria being especially rife. The incidence of disease in the battalion, though the lowest in the brigade, was the highest since the period following the evacuation of Gallipoli. With the cessation of hostilities a new atmosphere was created ; men were longingly eager to return to their country and their homes, to the land they had so long and so faithfully defended. Demobilisation was in the air ; but during its continuance and up to its final consummation a few incidents affecting the battalion are worthy of record.

On December 20 the 54th Division marched through Cairo, past the Commander-in-Chief, who was stationed in Opera House Square. The battalion, quartered at Helmieh and having been detailed for duty on Christmas Day, celebrated that festival on the 24th, the 1/8th Hampshire Regiment lending a magnificent marquee for the occasion. On the 29th Captain A. Fair, M.C., relinquished the adjutancy which he had held for nearly twenty months, being succeeded by Captain C. M. Fyson. On January 5, 1919, the battalion sustained a great loss by the death of R.S.M. J. J. French, D.C.M., who had served with it from before the war and had taken part in almost every one of its engagements.

With the advent of the New Year demobilisation, now in full swing, received a temporary check owing to an outbreak of rioting in Egypt. The troops were called out in aid of the civil power to protect persons and property, and to restore order, but, fortunately, the battalion never came into actual contact with the mob. Early in April the battalion went into the Abbas Hilmi barracks at Abbassia. On March 25 the 5th Battalion was selected to furnish a guard of honour for General Allenby on his return from a flying visit to Paris, the guard being commanded by Captain H. C. Wolton, M.C. The following day the Rev. E. D. Rennison and Captain H. C. Wolton left to inspect the graves of those of the battalion who were buried in Palestine and Syria. By their good offices the greater number of these graves were located and visited, photographs being sent to the next of kin. On Sunday, April 13, the battalion marched to the Cairo garrison church, the first parade of the kind it had attended at a church since leaving Thetford in 1915.

On May 5 the Commander-in-Chief inspected the battalion, sending it a message of appreciation, and on the 26th bestowed high praise on a guard of honour, under Captain E. D. Wolton and Lieut. E. E. Ladell, which had paraded at Zeitoun. During that month a draft of two hundred men arrived, an additional hundred being transferred from the

THE CENOTAPH OF THE SUFFOLK REGIMENT
St. Mary's Church, Bury St. Edmunds

5th Bedfordshire Regiment. The beginning of July saw most of the original officers and practically all the men gone. Thus was broken up a battalion with a fine record, that had lived as one big family, with little crime and general good feeling; that had earned an individual message of congratulation from the Commander-in-Chief, and that carried as its motto the burning words, addressed to the 54th Division, which fittingly close its history.

In the Peace procession held in London on July 20, 1919, the colours of the 5th Battalion were carried amongst the massed colours of the Territorial units of the kingdom. In November, 1919, the cadre of the battalion arrived home from Egypt. At short notice a party of officers and men escorted the colours to the station, Bury St. Edmunds, and handed them over to the officer commanding the cadre as the representative of the mobilised battalion. From the station the cadre proceeded to the Corn Hill, where it was officially welcomed home by the mayor on behalf of the borough. Thus ended more than five years of mobilised service, of which four years and five months had been spent overseas. On February 27, 1920, a reunion dinner was held at the Corn Exchange, Bury St. Edmunds. This proved to be the last representative gathering of the 5th Battalion and was an overwhelming success, about eight hundred of all ranks attending. During 1921 the battalion, under the command of Major B. E. Oliver, had been open for recruiting, but the area allotted to it did not include Beccles and Bungay, as was the case before the war. At the end of that year the 5th Battalion was informed that, owing to the need for national economy, it was to be disbanded, a decision naturally received with great regret. Accordingly, the battalion plate and the balance of its funds were placed in the hands of trustees. The war trophies were handed over to the officer commanding the Stowmarket company, thenceforth to form part of the 4th Battalion, but with the proviso that they should be handed back to the 5th Battalion should it ever be resuscitated.

On Sunday, December 4, 1921, the colours of the battalion were laid up in St. Mary's Church, Bury St. Edmunds, an impressive ceremony marking the conclusion of sixty-two years of service. A large party of officers and men accompanied the colours to the church, where they were laid upon the altar. Before the sermon they were removed to the cenotaph and placed in company with those of the 7th, 8th, 9th, 12th, and 1st Garrison Battalions, guarding with their folds the empty tomb of seven thousand soldiers of the Suffolk Regiment. Taking as his text, " O sword, put up thyself into thy scabbard, rest, and be still," the vicar, Dr. Gray, recounted the history of the 5th Battalion since 1859, concluding his address with this fitting epilogue : " For five fiery and then frost-bound months they suffered the ghastly rigours of Gallipoli with an endurance which reads like a chapter from the Apostle of the Gentiles—in weariness and in painfulness, in watchings often, in hunger and in thirst, in cold and nakedness, in disease more cruel than the bullet, and never out of the range of screeching shells. Such a record is best told as it was borne, in the patient dignity of silence. . . . Of its service in Sinai, Palestine, and Syria, Field-Marshal Viscount Allenby has said (referring to the 54th Division) : 'They fought through those burning deserts, through the rocky mountains of Judæa, and through the swamps of Syria ; these East Anglian men can literally be said to have gone through fire and water.' The 5th Battalion is disbanded, but its colours will remain, a token of faithful service and duty well performed."

7th Battalion

The 7th Battalion, reduced to a cadre in May, 1918, took no part in the final advance to victory. As soon as the last of the American divisions, to which it was affiliated, had been sent into the line the cadre moved to Abancourt and Haudricourt, administering a reinforcement camp for troops suffering from malaria contracted in other theatres. As these became fit they were drafted to units in the line. On September 19 the 7th Battalion cadre, together with that of another unit, proceeded to Cayeux, near the mouth of the Somme, where they took over about three thousand young soldiers. These consisted of youths under eighteen, sent out in the spring of that year, and belonging to almost every regiment and battalion on the western front.

At the beginning of October the cadre returned to Haudricourt, taking with them this great contingent of young soldiers, but shortly after the armistice proceeded to Woincourt, where Christmas was spent. From that time onwards the young soldiers were despatched in batches to their homeland. Early in 1919 the cadre staff went to Dieppe, where they were in camp at Rouxmesnil. In March, Lieut.-Colonel G. V. W. Hill, D.S.O., the distinguished commander of the 8th Battalion, left the cadre to rejoin his regiment, Major P. C. Bull, D.S.O., taking over the command, Captain G. L. Crandon, M.C., remaining as adjutant, and Captain R. M. Ridley, M.C., quartermaster. At the end of April the cadre moved to Havre, being chiefly employed in finding guards and fatigue parties. On May 1 a King's Colour was presented to the battalion, the ceremony being performed by Major-General H. C. C. Uniacke, C.B., C.M.G. In the final honours list C.S.M. Johnson was awarded the M.S.M. This warrant officer, who had done excellent work in the 7th and 8th Battalions as C.Q.M.S. and later as C.S.M., had several times been recommended. The cadre was finally broken up in Havre. A colour party, under Captain G. L. Crandon, M.C., proceeded to England and deposited the colour at the depot, whence it was later transferred to St. Mary's Church, Bury St. Edmunds and placed amongst those of the other service battalions. In the official orders of battle the 7th Battalion is shown, in July, 1918, as belonging to the 116th Brigade, 39th Division ; in August to the 66th Division, and in October to the 197th Brigade, to which it belonged when hostilities ceased.

11th Battalion

The armistice found the 11th Battalion resting in billets in Bermerain, close to the scene of its fighting on the previous October 24. It was thus able to congratulate itself that it had taken part in dealing the last hammer-blows which had completed the Allied victory. After ten days spent in Cambrai the battalion entrained for the Abbeville area. Here in the straggling village of Ailly-le-Haut-Clocher it was able to celebrate a peaceful Christmas and to begin the part-happy, part-sorrowful, and always complicated task of demobilisation. Occupation was found for the men in the mental exercises of education and the physical exercises of marching and football, while ceremonial parades were rehearsed for the official presentation of the King's Colour by the divisional commander.

While demobilisation was in progress disturbances arose in the department of Pas-de-Calais, the battalion being hastily despatched for disciplinary purposes to the important railway depot at Audruicq. Fortunately, however, during its stay no serious trouble occurred, the battalion being employed in general guard duties and controlling parties of German prisoners at work in the camps and yards. In March the rapidly dwindling ranks of the battalion were supplemented by the arrival of large drafts of officers and men from the 1st Cambridgeshire, 12th Suffolk, and other regiments. The task of welding all these different detachments into a homogeneous whole was a difficult one, but the process went on so well, both at Audruicq and later at Rouen, that the battalion was chosen as the only British unit to take part in the French Peace Review at Rouen on July 14. The fact of their being so chosen, and of their commanding officer, Lieut.-Colonel Tuck, returning from leave especially to prepare them for and command them on that occasion, gave an additional fillip to all ranks, who acquitted themselves extremely well. The battalion marched with French troops through the thronged streets of Rouen, and was reviewed by a French general, who paid it many high compliments.

During the post-armistice months the battalion transport reached a high pitch of excellence, and a very creditable band and a concert party were got together; else there is little to record. Towards the end of July the battalion left the 61st Division, Lieut.-Colonel Tuck receiving a letter of high appreciation from the divisional commander, Major-General F. J. Duncan. The last act in the battalion's history in France—from the end of July to the middle of September—was set in the area between Bethune and Péronne, with headquarters at Arras, where it was able to revive the memory of so many of its former achievements and to visit the graves of many of its fallen. It was at Arras, on the first anniversary of Armistice Day, after a final tribute paid to that great company of the dead, by whose sacrifice its honour and fame had increased and multiplied, that the battalion bade its farewell to the land of their resting-place.

By the end of October the battalion had been reduced to a cadre which, on November 15, arrived in Cambridge. The cadre, accorded a civic welcome, marched through the streets of the town to a reception given by the Cambridgeshire and Isle of Ely Territorial Force Association, who originally raised the battalion. During the next few days the personnel was dispersed and the stores and equipment were handed in, until finally Lieut.-Colonel Tuck, who had been with the battalion from its very first day, alone was left, ultimately demobilising himself just before Christmas. The following is a summary of the more important honours gained by the 11th Battalion :

Victoria Cross : Cpl. S. J. Day.

Companion of the Most Distinguished Order of St. Michael and St. George : Colonel C. W. Somerset, M.V.O. ; Lieut.-Colonel G. L. J. Tuck, D.S.O.

D.S.O. and Bar : Lieut.-Colonel G. L. J. Tuck, C.M.G.

D.S.O. : Lieut.-Colonel E. H. Kendrick ; Captain O. H. Brown.

M.C. and Bar : Major A. B. Wright ; Captains G. F. R. Baguley, C. V. Canning, and S. W. Turner.

D.C.M. and Bar : Sgt. E. Spalding.

M.M. and Bar : Sgt. J. P. Negus ; Cpl. G. H. Wilding ; Ptes. D. Barrett and H. Searle.

Legion of Honour : Lieut.-Colonel G. L. J. Tuck, C.M.G., D.S.O.

Immediate Commisions in the Field : Sgts. C. Hills and W. J. Matthews, D.C.M., M.M.

On May 11, 1922, the King's Colour of the 11th Battalion was laid up in Ely Cathedral at a memorial service attended by General the Lord Horne, the Bishop of Ely officiating.

11th (Service) Battalion the Suffolk Regiment

	Officers	O.Rs.	Officers	O.Rs.
Total served in Battalion			242	5469
Killed in action	26	527		
Died of wounds (in France) .	11	147		
Died as prisoners of war .		5		
Died of sickness . . .	1	11		
Missing, accepted as having died	4	122		
Missing, almost certainly died	1	103		
			43	915
Wounded[1]			100	2515
Prisoners of war			9	163
Total battle casualties			152	3593
Re-enlisted in the Army				83

12th Battalion

Within a day or two of the armistice the 12th Battalion returned to Evregnies, marching thence to Turcoing, where Christmas was spent. The one outstanding peculiarity about the life of a soldier in France after the armistice was the utter and uncanny peacefulness of it. In December the following awards were gazetted—*French Croix de Guerre*: Major A. M. Cross, M.C.; Ptes. W. Tingley, D.C.M., and J. Hicken, M.M. At the end of the year the strength of the battalion was forty-three officers and about eight hundred other ranks.

Early in January, 1919, the battalion marched to billets

[1] Includes "Died of Wounds." There is no record of those who died of wounds in England.

in the neighbourhood of Bondues, near Lille, and towards the end of the month to Roubaix, where a King's Colour was presented by Lieut.-General Sir Beauvoir de Lisle, K.C.B., K.C.M.G., D.S.O. After the presentation the battalion returned to Bondues. During February half a dozen officers and two hundred men were transferred to the 11th Battalion for the Army of Occupation. Throughout this period every practicable step in the direction of vocational training was taken with the object of preparing the men for their return to civil life.

During March the battalion was reduced to cadre establishment, the cadre itself being sent to Bondues and the mobilisation stores to Petit Audenarde. Captain F. Adams[1] was gazetted a Chevalier of the Order of Leopold and also awarded the Croix de Guerre. On April 3 the cadre moved into billets at Herseaux and, in July, returned to England. The King's Colour belonging to the battalion was then laid up in St. Mary's Church, Bury St. Edmunds, being placed amongst those of other battalions of the Suffolk Regiment. The cadre was then dispersed, marking the close of the battalion's four years of existence, over three of which had been spent in France. Having already achieved great fame at Bourlon Wood, at La Vacquerie, at Gonnelieu, and at Bullecourt, the 12th Battalion fought right through the great German offensive of 1918, and in the battles of the Lys gained the distinction of being mentioned by name in Field-Marshal Sir Douglas Haig's despatches.

15th Battalion

On the day following the cessation of hostilities the 15th Battalion continued its march eastwards to La Hamaide, eventually arriving, on November 18, at Herinnes, where it remained in billets until February 27, 1919. On January 26 a contingent of five officers and seventy-five men belonging to the battalion took part in a review in Brussels before H.M. the King of the Belgians. From Herinnes the battalion

[1] Like Captain Redding of the same battalion, this gallant officer has since laid down his life in the service.

moved to Grammont, where during the month of April demobilisation was practically completed. The cadre remained at Grammont until June 19, when it returned to England to be finally dispersed at Bury St. Edmunds on June 27, 1919.

Some time elapsed before any definite decision was reached with regard to the future of the Territorial Army, and especially the Yeomanry. During 1919 and 1920 many conferences were held at the War Office, the upshot being that only the fourteen senior regiments of Yeomanry were to be retained as such. This decision evoked many protests from the other less fortunate regiments, who were informed that they would be converted into Royal Artillery or into units of the Royal Tank Corps, or Royal Corps of Signals, or Scouts. In order to allay dissatisfaction, the authorities issued instructions that any of the regiments affected might continue as yeomanry for a further period of two years, when they would be required either to revert to the particular arm of the service assigned to them or else be disbanded altogether. Amongst those responsible for the future of the Suffolk Yeomanry this offer was accepted by a small majority, against the better judgment of the remainder, who foresaw little hope of ever becoming cavalry again when several regiments of regular cavalry were being amalgamated, and consequently that two years' training would be wasted. When the time was up the inevitable happened and the Suffolk Yeomanry, who in the meantime had only enlisted just over a hundred men, were informed that they must become artillery or be disbanded.

Eventually two batteries of field artillery were raised, one at Bury St. Edmunds and the other at Beccles. These were brigaded with two howitzer batteries which had formerly been brigaded with two Hertfordshire batteries. This arrangement did not prove a success and steps were taken to induce the Norfolk Yeomanry, who had not yet elected to join any particular arm of the Territorial Army on its reorganisation, to raise two batteries of field artillery in Norfolk. This having been accomplished, the four batteries became the 108th (Suffolk and Norfolk Yeomanry) Field Brigade, R.A., with headquarters at Swaffham, the batteries being numbered and located as follows: No. 411, Bury St. Edmunds; No. 412, Beccles; Nos. 429–30, Swaffham. From 1923 the brigade was commanded by Colonel the Viscount Bury, M.C., who, in

October, 1926, was succeeded by Lieut.-Colonel O. Birkbeck. All this time the brigade, in spite of many difficulties, was steadily increasing towards the required establishment.

A memorial, unveiled in May, 1928, was erected under the west window of St. Mary's Church, Bury St. Edmunds, facing the cenotaph of the Suffolk Regiment, to the memory of 14 officers and 170 non-commissioned officers and men who laid down their lives in the Great War. All were either Suffolk yeomen or belonged to the 15th (Yeomanry) Battalion Suffolk Regiment.

CHAPTER XXIII

The Suffolk Volunteers

By Major E. R. Cooper, late commanding 3rd V.B. The Suffolk Regiment.

IN writing this chapter after the lapse of eight years the great difficulty has been the collection of material. Most of those to whom application has been made appear to have kept no record nor any papers useful for the purpose; even the War Office excuse themselves on the ground that the papers are not easily accessible.

The writer has therefore had to depend largely upon the material in his possession relating to his own battalion and the account of their services which he published in various newspapers circulating in North Suffolk at the close of the war. If therefore any reader considers that undue prominence is given to the 3rd Battalion, will he please bear in mind that even in these days of substitutes it is difficult to make bricks without straw, and that, but for the 3rd Battalion records, very little could have been made of this chapter.

Owing to her insular situation England has always shunned universal military service, and the history of her wars is a chronicle of frantic efforts to improvise armies after the need for their services has arisen, and whenever during the last four hundred years the fear of invasion has reared its head almost certainly the manhood of the nation have responded by forming volunteer armies for the defence of the homeland.

About the earliest recorded Volunteer review was in 1539, when Henry VIII, having broken with the Pope and anticipating a French invasion, reviewed 15,000 London Volunteers at Westminster, and the latest London review of Volunteers was by Lord French in Hyde Park in June, 1916, in the middle of the Great War. Between those dates lies a long story of Volunteer efforts and military services rendered by civilians in times of national danger, and although their efforts have usually been derided by the idlers and superficial critics, and often discouraged by the authorities, there is not the slightest doubt that when England again stands in danger of invasion the people of this remarkable old country will arise and clamour to be trained for the defence of all they hold dear.

Suffolk has always been a stronghold for Volunteers, probably its geographical position through centuries of Continental strife has bred the frontier feeling, and certainly her sons are most amenable to discipline and make as good soldiers as can be found anywhere.

The country instantly realised its dangers in 1914, and as early as August proposals were made for a Volunteer force but were publicly vetoed by the Government. The matter was, however, pressed so strongly that the War Office were reluctantly constrained to authorise "lessons in drilling and musketry" for men over age or unfit, upon the strength of which were formed Volunteer Training Corps all over the country which were eventually brought under a central association.

Having regard to the ridicule poured upon the 1860 Volunteers by *Punch*, it is cheering to quote from the issue of July 7, 1915.

Member of V.T.C. to President of the Local Government Board: "What can I do? Ah! I'm glad they've asked me that at last. I shall tell them I'm one of the half a million Volunteer soldiers who've been waiting for a job the last six months."

Again, Mr. Archibald Hurd remarked in the *Daily Telegraph*, April 2, 1918: "At first the Volunteers were told they were not wanted, then under pressure they were grudgingly accorded recognition, and at last under further pressure they received small grants from army funds. In spite of every obstacle the force has steadily grown."

In November, 1914, it was discovered that Germany had matured plans for the invasion of England as soon as the reinforcement of the B.E.F. had sufficiently denuded her of troops. It is illuminating now to read on page 349 of the *Life and Letters of W. H. Page* a letter from a German's English wife written from Bremen, September 25, 1914, in which she says they are confident that they will land ten army corps in

England before Christmas. They mean to destroy. Towns concerned with war material to be annihilated, the men killed, and German citizens planted in their place.

Lord Kitchener then decided to make use of the V.T.C., and requested the central association to administer the force and distribute the red " G.R." brassards, which were the only Government issue to the Volunteers until 1916, everything else having to be provided by the corps. But even now they were not allowed to train men of military age, and recruiting officers were sent round to examine the registers and require the discharge of all men eligible for service. Still, in the long run the usefulness of the Volunteers became apparent, and eventually Lord Kitchener admitted that over a million men had passed through the Volunteer ranks into the army, and that the central association was a powerful recruiting organisation. After his death, of course, it became much more efficient, and partially trained large numbers of men for the army. Lord Harris stated in the House of Lords, April 18, 1918, on the authority of a commander of a pre-war Territorial division, " The Volunteer Force as it is now is superior to what the Territorial Force was before the war."

The V.T.C. in Suffolk came into being during the winter of 1914–15, and received enthusiastic support. Meetings were held and men enrolled all over the county. It was estimated that North Suffolk alone enrolled a thousand men, and in the early days it is probable there were from six to seven thousand Volunteers in Suffolk.

Early in 1915 a County Volunteer Association was formed by the Lord-Lieutenant, who appointed Lieut.-Colonel G. L. Bence-Lambert, C.M.G., county commandant, and the various corps were grouped into six battalions, roughly following the parliamentary divisions, the original distribution being as follows:

Number.	*District.*	*Commandant.*
1st Bn.	Ipswich	Colonel F. G. Bond, V.D.
2nd Bn.	Bury St. Edmunds	Sir George Agnew, Bart., M.P.
3rd Bn.	Lowestoft	Major H. R. Tamplin.
4th Bn.	Woodbridge	Lord Rendlesham.
5th Bn.	Sudbury	Brig.-Gen. J. A. Coxhead, C.B.
6th Bn.	Saxmundham	Colonel Abdy Collins, V.D.

Lieut.-Colonel Bence-Lambert was shortly after given command of the 3/4th Suffolk Regiment, and was succeeded as county commandant by Earl Cadogan.

The Volunteers were fortunate in having the use of the territorial drill-halls and ranges accorded by the Territorial Force Association, and set to work seriously to train the men and to raise funds for uniforms, equipment, and arms. A number of short Martini-Metfords of very inferior quality were obtained and contracts entered into for uniforms. The War Office having barred the use of wool or khaki dye for Volunteers, they were condemned to the use of grey cotton, most unsuitable in every way for the purpose. If an invasion had taken place at this period these grey uniforms, with the conspicuous red brassards, would have led the enemy to concentrate upon the Volunteers wherever located.

In the summer of 1915 General Sir Horace Smith-Dorrien, G.O.C. Eastern Command, inspected several battalions of Suffolk Volunteers and remarked: "On my taking over command in these parts I heard much of the zeal with which they have thrown themselves into training. I took an early opportunity of inspecting several corps, and was much impressed by their fine bearing; probably I alone have been able to gauge how enormously their work has added to the efficiency of my scheme for the protection of our coasts."

As a result of this favourable report certain railway guard duties were allocated to the Volunteers, and for a considerable period night guards were found for various bridges on the Great Eastern Railway, also continuous guards for a long time over munition stores at Ipswich, a tedious and trying duty for men who were working all day, often at high pressure.

Lord-Lieutenant's commissions were issued to the officers in September, 1915, signed by Sir Courtenay Warner as President of the Suffolk County Volunteer Regiment, and on Sunday, November 8, 1915, was held the first regimental shoot on the Bromeswell range. Five battalions sent teams, and although it was a cold, snowy day, and most of the rifles and ammunition none too good, the result was very encouraging. Ipswich were the winners, followed by the 3rd, 2nd, 4th, and 6th, the 3rd Battalion producing the best shot—Sgt. G. Clarke—of Halesworth, who collected a special prize from the Mayor of Ipswich.

On April 25, 1916, the 3rd Battalion area was under enemy fire for the first time, Lowestoft being heavily bombarded by German battle-cruisers, and some sixty 12-inch shells fired into and over the town. For want of a definite place in the scheme of local defence the Lowestoft Volunteers were unable to assist except as individuals, the position being more difficult owing to the resignation of Major Tamplin, the writer not being promoted from adjutant to the command of the 3rd Battalion until April 28, battalion strength then being about four hundred only.

At this time very useful work was being done by the 1st Battalion on Sundays in enlarging and altering the Bixley Heath rifle range, also by "C" and "D" Companies of the 3rd Battalion in assisting the Norfolk Volunteers to level and lay out the ground at the new air station at Pulham, from seventy to one hundred men from Beccles, Bungay, and Halesworth spending their Sundays at pretty stiff manual labour.

In May, 1916, the War Office at last intimated that they were prepared to take over the V.T.C. upon certain conditions. There were then 4390 of all ranks enrolled in the Suffolk V.T.C. Regiment, 3600 being required to complete the existing establishment of six battalions. The men were to be attested under the old Volunteer Act of 1863, and thereupon certain equipment and a small grant for expenses were promised from army funds.

No figures are available as to the total numbers who attested, but about this time tribunals began to order exempted men into the Volunteers to train, and sufficient were obtained to ensure the continuance of the six battalions, the 3rd Battalion attesting 712 men. Officers were to receive King's commissions, the first of which for Suffolk appeared in the *London Gazette* of September 1, 1916. This step was soon followed by permission to wear the usual khaki dress of army officers.

In the House of Lords on May 30, 1916, Lord Kitchener said the Volunteers had been most useful in meeting many emergencies, such as guards, patrols, trench digging, unloading trains, etc. They had set a fine example, and personally he welcomed the presence in the country of a large body of disciplined men who might prove of great service in case of sudden national emergency.

In 1916 Lord French spent much time inspecting Volunteers in various parts of the country, the Suffolk parade taking place on Sunday, October 22, 1916, at Gyppeswick Park, Ipswich. The various battalions paraded early, and had special trains from all over Suffolk arriving at Ipswich about 11 a.m., and on Lord French's arrival he proceeded to inspect the parade. The right-hand man of "A" Company, 3rd Battalion, a Lowestoft man named Taylor, had been the Field-Marshal's orderly in South Africa, and the latter noticing his medal at once expressed pleasure at seeing him again.

After the inspection Lord French addressed the officers, and dwelling upon the possibility of invasion, said the Government were prepared to equip the force fully, but all must sign on for the duration of the war.

Exclusive of guards and patrols requiring 300 men, there were 5074 on parade at Ipswich. The transport arrangements were very good, but the outlying battalions had to be on duty nearly twelve hours, and it was a cold day for cotton uniforms.

The parade state for Lord French's inspection was :

Battn.	*Commanding.*	*Officers.*	*N.C.O.'s*	*Men*
1st	Colonel F. G. Bond, V.D.	24	30	907
2nd	Major Sir George Agnew, M.P.	22	88	662
3rd	Major E. R. Cooper	19	77	777
4th	Major Lord Rendlesham	20	80	610
5th	Captain L. Hyde Parker	19	24	577
6th	Colonel H. A. Collins, V.D.	32	89	1019

The parade was taken by Brig.-General J. A. Coxhead, C.B., Commandant of the 5th Battalion. Lord French was attended by Lieut.-Colonel FitzGerald, Captain the Marquess of Granby, Colonel Sir Douglas Dawson, Brig.-General the Earl of Albemarle, and others.

In December the Volunteer Act of 1916 was passed, and under its provisions in the following January came out an A.C.I. providing for the formation of sections A, for men over military age ; B, for those of military age ; C, for boys of seventeen ; and D for men unwilling to sign on for the duration, thereby retaining the old 1863 right of resigning on fourteen days' notice. The drills required under the new scheme were fixed at fourteen of one hour each per month until passed efficient, and ten per month afterwards. This scheme was in some ways detrimental, as it made unnecessary distinctions between the men, and provided section D for those who were glad to slip out of accepting the full responsibility—something after the fashion of the "Conchy" created by the Military Service Acts. In due course this mistake was realised and section D revoked.

On January 25, 1917, Suffolk was attacked by the enemy from the sea for the second time, again in the 3rd Battalion area, Southwold being bombarded at 11 p.m. by German "Light Forces," who fired a parachute star-shell each side of the town and then pumped in sixty-eight shells in eight minutes and cleared out. Very little damage was done, most of the shells passing far over into the country. At the request of the Horse Guards the writer plotted the shell-holes on 6-inch ordnance sheets.

In February, 1917, the Volunteer strength was 241,191 in 242 battalions.

Early in 1917 whole-time adjutants and regimental sergeant-majors from the Army and Territorials were appointed to the Volunteers, and the force was armed with 1914 pattern magazine rifles. Full equipment and uniform were issued to those who passed the medical examination, and the home service battalions were directed to furnish instructors for the Volunteers in their neighbourhood. The course of training covered close-order drill, physical training, musketry, bombing, and bayonet fighting, on two evenings and Sunday mornings in each week, with miniature rifle practice on other evenings.

At this time exempted men were pouring into the Volunteers and as regularly passing on to the army after a few months' training. This training was a great help, and one man in particular from the 3rd Battalion was out in France in six weeks after he was called up, but of course it meant a lot of work for the Volunteer staff, not the least of which was the recovery of equipment from men who were called up. From June 1, 1916, to March 1, 1918, 236 men went from the 3rd Battalion into the Navy or Army.

In the summer of 1917 a colour-sergeant instructor of

musketry was sent to each Volunteer battalion and at once started preparing for and putting the men through their musketry practices on the open ranges, firing taking place almost always on Sundays. Courses for Volunteer officers were also inaugurated, and attendance at a course was made essential for the grant of £10 towards the officer's outfit, a most useful scheme. Hotchkiss guns were also issued, four to each battalion, and teams were trained in their use, the keenest and best officers and men undergoing courses at Hythe, and many passing out as first-class instructors. Some detachments of the 4th Battalion were also trained as Stokes Gunners.

In the autumn of 1917 regular officers were sent down to examine the Volunteers for efficiency, and October and November were spent in preparing for and attending to these inspections by detachments. A regimental shoot for the county cup took place on December 23, 1917, at Bixley Heath range; the 1st Battalion were winners with a score of 555, put on by a team of eight, followed by the 6th Battalion, 537; the 5th Battalion, 530; the 3rd Battalion, 520; the 2nd Battalion, 512; and the 4th Battalion, 493, special prizes for the highest scores being taken by Captain Sir H. Bunbury and Captain Peart.

In January, 1918, Volunteer strength was 289,137 in 313 battalions, and the same month preparations were made for a test mobilisation of the regiment at some week-end, of which thirty-six hours' notice were to be given. This never came off, but when the great push started in March there is no doubt the Volunteers were on the brink of mobilisation in real earnest. Colonel Repington records in his diary under March 25, 1918, that Lord Scarborough (Director-General of the force) told him he was in favour of calling up the Volunteers for a month's training, but later, on March 30, the author says: "Apparently the wobblers have now drawn back again and do not mean to call up the Volunteers. I suppose our fool of a War Cabinet think that untrained recruits are just as good."

However, the War Office evidently began to realise that the Volunteers were worth cultivating and now sent down officers returned from the front on the six months scheme with the rank of lieut.-colonel to supervise the training, each looking after two battalions. As the strength was much depleted by the calling up of exempted men it was also decided to endeavour to rake in the farm labourers, who had been exempted in large numbers by the country tribunals, and with the assistance of the County War Agricultural Committee all these men were circularised and the Volunteer commanding officers held recruiting meetings in all their outlying districts. Twelve meetings were held in the 3rd Battalion area, resulting in the enrolment of 155 recruits and increasing the drill centres to seventeen. There is none better than the Suffolk farm labourer when you can get him.

The following is an extract from a special order of the Field-Marshal Commanding-in-Chief Home Forces, dated May 10, 1918: "The isolated Volunteer Training Corps as they existed two years ago have developed into an organised, armed and equipped Volunteer force. The energy of the commanders, with the sympathy and assistance of the lords-lieutenant of counties and local authorities, and the keenness and intelligence of the men, is deserving of the highest commendation, and has rendered it possible to allot to the Volunteer force a definite position in the defence force of this country."

This definite position meant as regards the coastal battalions their allocation to certain strong points and road-blocking works in the supporting line; and as the result of a conference at Yarmouth on April 19 there were allotted to the 3rd Battalion seven strong points in the Lowestoft district and four in Southwold district, together with four road-blocking works in rear of these, requiring garrisons amounting to 10 officers and 305 men.

Towards the end of May things were looking serious over the water, and England was pretty well denuded of troops after the large reinforcements had been sent across to hold the western front. It is said that the authorities again considered the question of calling up the whole Volunteer force for home service, but perhaps in order not to dislocate trade too much it was eventually decided to call upon them to find 15,000 men to serve on the coast for two or three months until the Americans were fit to take their part and the crisis had been tided over.

Suffolk was asked to find 330 officers and men out of 5800

on the roll at this period. This would appear an easy task, but the conditions really made it very difficult. The service was to be voluntary; no men of "A" Category were to be taken, and only boys under eighteen and men over thirty-five were eligible. Again, no man could be taken without the consent of his employer. The greater part of the men were cut out by these restrictions, which were difficult to understand, but perhaps were laid down in the interests of the essential civilian services. It seemed to those who had to deal directly with the men that it would have been much fairer to have made a nominal call-up of the whole force, and then directed the county authorities to select 15,000 men who could best be spared. The natural result was that the willing went while the canny and unwilling stayed at home and made hay while the sun shone.

The War Office circular of June 1, 1918, regarding the formation of these special service companies stated they would be employed on the north and east coasts, and each company would be formed of 114 officers and volunteers of the infantry battalions who might volunteer for the service, and who had been passed as efficient; that they would be subject to the King's Regulations, and receive pay and allowances at ordinary army rates, but no gratuities. It wound up as follows:

"In conclusion I am to emphasize the great importance of securing the necessary numbers of efficient members of the Volunteer force for this duty, and in view of the limited duration of the service and the circumstances of exceptional national stress in which the appeal is made I am to express the hope that the response will be such as to ensure the complete success of the scheme and justify the council's confidence in the value and utility of the force as an integral part of the army."

Immediately upon receipt of this appeal parades were held all over the county and the matter pressed as strongly as possible, but the restrictions cut away many of the best men, and unpatriotic and selfish employers were able to prevent their men from joining. Exempted men were also afraid their service might prejudice any further claim on review. However, eventually 20 officers and 328 N.C.O.'s and men were accepted from Suffolk out of 5800 on the county roll.

The establishment of these companies was as follows :

No. 9 Suffolk Volunteer Company

O.C. Company : Captain H. M. Cautley. *Subalterns :* Lieuts. B. Corder, C. F. Woods, R. Newberry, and A. W. Drake ; and 74 N.C.O.s and men from the 1st Battalion.

No. 10 Suffolk Volunteer Company

O.C. Company : Major E. R. Cooper (senior officer serving). *Subalterns :* F. E. Burgess, W. U. Cookes, F. J. Ratcliffe, and F. Wayman ; and 80 N.C.O.s and men from the 2nd and 3rd Battalions.

No. 11 Suffolk Volunteer Company

O.C. Company : Captain Gordon Barratt. *Subalterns :* Davies, Bates, Soden, and Broome ; and 88 N.C.O.s and men from the 6th Battalion.

No. 12 Suffolk Volunteer Company

O.C. Company : Major Sir Collingwood Hughes, Bart. *Subalterns :* Bixby, Fox, Phillips, and Robertson ; and 86 N.C.O.s and men from the 4th Battalion.

The 3rd Battalion provided six out of the twenty officers serving, including two of the company commanders, but only thirty men.

The Special Service men proceeded by train on June 29, 1918, to Melton, near Woodbridge, whence they were transported by Volunteer motor transport twelve miles to a camp at Bawdsey Manor on the coast, where they were attached to the 2/8th Cyclist Battalion—the Essex Regiment, who were holding the coast from the river Deben to Shinglestreet, about four miles, and were, when the Volunteers arrived only about two hundred strong. The Cyclists were in huts, but the Volunteers were put under canvas, and when it set in wet a few days later there were very soon seventy cases of a mild form of influenza. The Volunteers at once went into full-time training under Essex instructors and carried on the ordinary routine of the Coast Defence units, including guards, patrols, periods of vigilance, and all the fatigues of a camp, with occasional night alarms.

The 3rd Battalion Royal Irish Fusiliers came into camp a few weeks after, but took no part in the coast defence duties.

Minden Day was observed by a special parade at which red and white roses were handed by Mrs. Cooper to all the Suffolk Volunteers on parade, the band of the 3/R.I.F. kindly assisting at the proceedings and at the subsequent march past. The afternoon was spent in games.

There were special classes for musketry, Hotchkiss gun and Stoke's gun, and all ranks had to become cyclists. Toward the end of July the battalion was inspected by Brig.-General the Earl of Albemarle, and shortly after was ordered to proceed to Colchester to fire the complete G.M.C. Accordingly at 6.30 a.m. on August 8 the four companies, under the command of Major Cooper, left by motor transport for Melton, thence by train to Colchester, marching out in full marching order four miles to Old Heath camp, where they again went under canvas.

Firing on the Middlewick range commenced on the following morning and finished on the 12th, the result being 1 marksman, 66 first, 131 second, and 60 third-class shots. The battalion average was 72·7, which was considered quite good for middle-aged men with strange rifles. The strength was already down owing to a good few farm workers being reclaimed by their employers for harvest work.

On August 13 camp was struck and the battalion marched back to Colchester, entraining for Melton, where they were met by motor transport and arrived back at Bawdsey at 5 a.m.

Towards the end of August the position in France had improved marvellously, and word came through that the Volunteers who had signed for two months would be discharged at the end of August, while those who had signed for three months could either leave then or stay their time out. A good many had signed for two months with the intention of staying longer if required, but as they were no longer needed many were glad to get back to their work at home. About half the men were dismissed on August 28, while the rest stayed on for a third month.

Mr. Macpherson, Deputy-Secretary for War, stated in the House that four-fifths of the men asked for were obtained (about 12,000) and had been trained in areas where their services were likely to be required. The men had cheerfully borne a pretty stiff military training, and it might be added that the military authorities were thoroughly satisfied with the work which the Special Service Volunteers had done, and that the behaviour of the men in novel and occasionally trying conditions had been excellent.

There is no doubt that the Suffolk Special Service Volunteer companies were a most willing and tractable body of men, and that at the end of two months' continuous training they were equal to the general run of home service troops. If the younger men had been allowed to serve, many would have been fit to go overseas at the end of their special service. The boys of seventeen were trained with an A 4 squad and soon became quite smart lads.

Lord Scarborough, Director-General of Territorial and Volunteer Forces, wrote on September 28, 1918, with regard to the termination that day of the Special Service engagements, that the Army Council keenly appreciated the patriotic response to that appeal, that it was fully realised that the Special Service Volunteers had enabled the Government to meet a critical situation and to tide over very difficult days in the history of the war, and he added that all concerned might congratulate themselves on the fact that up to the limit of their powers they had directly contributed to the improvement of the situation in France and on more distant fronts, and that it was a matter of satisfaction to know that the members of the Volunteer force could be relied on to come forward on the occasion of a crisis such as that which had recently occurred.

On September 29, 1918, a regimental shoot took place at the Bromeswell range, the cup being again won by the 1st Battalion, the 3rd Battalion being runners-up once more, while Private Tillett of the 3rd Battalion, a Special Service man, came out the best shot in the regiment. The results were as follows—teams of sixteen :

1st Battalion 812, 3rd Battalion 748, 4th Battalion 725, 6th Battalion 615, 2nd Battalion 600, and 5th Battalion 599.

An inspection of several Suffolk Battalions was fixed to take place at Norwich on November 3, but owing to the wave of influenza which swept over East Anglia at that time it was cancelled, and events soon made it clear that the active work of the Volunteers was done.

Immediately after the Armistice orders were given that Sunday parades were to cease and that attendance at other drills would in future be voluntary. This was practically the *coup de grâce,* attendance at drills became nominal and in most places ceased altogether after Christmas.

At the Armistice the regimental strength was 5188, the total number of Volunteers in the Force being 248,444, of whom 199,552 were men of military age exempted for various reasons. From June 1, 1916, when records commenced, to November, 1918, 1 officer and 323 men went from the 3rd Battalion into the Army or Navy; assuming the same average for the other battalions, this meant 1944 from the Suffolk Volunteers, and for the 281 battalions in the Force an approximate transfer during that period of 90,000 partly trained men.

Lieut.-General Pulteney, commanding the 23rd Army Corps, at Bury St. Edmunds, wrote to the county commandant on January 22, 1919, expressing his high appreciation of the excellent work carried out by the Volunteers while attached to that Corps. He desired especially to convey his appreciation of the work done by officers and men of the Special Service section who undertook the greater responsibility of two or three months' continuous training with Home Defence units in East Anglia. The War Office stated in February, 1919, that the future of the Volunteers must remain in suspense, but that as an immediate mark of appreciation of their services it was decided that officers would retain honorary rank on retirement and the right to wear uniform on special occasions, and that other ranks should retain their uniform, any further recognition of the valuable services rendered by the force to remain for later consideration.

In September, 1919, the Lord-Lieutenant received a letter from His Majesty the King acknowledging the services of the Volunteers and conveying his high appreciation of the services rendered by all ranks of the force. His Majesty added :

" I cannot forget the self-sacrifice and patriotism which inspired so many of my subjects, who from reasons of health or age were unable to serve abroad, to come forward and train themselves for any eventuality in the hour of their country's need."

The disbandment of the Volunteers was decided upon, and the men were discharged in October, 1919, receiving certificates of service in very poor style ; and the war having ended officially on January 10, 1920, the officers were gazetted out in February and March, and received letters of thanks from the Army Council.

On August 28, 1919, the following names of regimental officers of the Suffolk Volunteers were mentioned in the *London Gazette* as having been brought to the notice of the Secretary of State for War for valuable services rendered in connection with the war : Captain C. Boardman, Colonel F. G. Bond, Captain Sir H. Bunbury, Bart., 2nd Lieut. W. Clarke, Major H. A. Collins, Major E. R. Cooper, Major Sir A. C. Hughes, Bart., Captain Hon. G. Lambton, Lieut. A. H. Sadd, and Captain A. E. Tuttle.

Wheeler and Broadley remark with regard to the old Volunteers : " The part they played in the history of the stirring times in which they lived was perforce a passive one, yet they left to posterity an example of real patriotism which, if it has been equalled, can never be surpassed until the armed citizens of a future day and perhaps another generation are brought face to face with the bold individual who may attempt to succeed in an enterprise in which the great Napoleon failed."[1]

It may fairly be claimed, at any rate in the case of the coastal battalions of the Suffolk Volunteers, that the example of those old-time citizen soldiers has been excelled during the late war, having regard to the enormous advance in offensive weapons of all kinds, the varied nature of the training required under modern conditions of war, and the special risks attaching to the defence of the Suffolk shores in the face of the most determined and unscrupulous enemy the world has ever seen.

The question of any further recognition of the " valuable services rendered by the Force " (p. 22) may still be under consideration, but it seems unlikely that any further notice will be taken of them. They were the only branch of the services unrepresented in the victory parades, and even the Special Service men, who threw up everything and voluntarily proceeded on service in the dark days of 1918, remain without any adequate acknowledgment. It is only right therefore

[1] *Napoleon and the Invasion of England*, Vol. 2, p. 242.

that some authentic account of the early and protracted struggles of the Suffolk Volunteers, their ultimate recognition and appreciation by the authorities, and the part they played in the reinforcement of the army and the garrisoning of the coast should be placed on record, and the grateful acknowledgments of all who served are due to the Suffolk Regimental History Committee for allowing this little sketch to appear amongst the glorious services of one of the best of our old county regiments.

Is it too much to hope that in any similar grave emergency in the future a Volunteer force may be immediately organised and receive full recognition from the start, so that the utmost use may be made of it both in training potential recruits for the army and in providing an organised force of low category, exempted, and over-age men, available for many purposes in the scheme of home defence ? This brief story should make it plain that under such circumstances public opinion will demand a volunteer army, and that prompt recognition will save it from the ridicule and discouragement which handicapped it in the early days of the Great War and which to some extent pursued it to the end.

A more detailed history of the 3rd Battalion is in the War Museum library.

The establishment of the Suffolk Volunteers as in October, 1919 :

Hon. Commandant : Hon. Colonel Sir Courtenay Warner, Bart., Lord-Lieutenant.
County Commandant : Colonel G. O., Earl Cadogan.
County Adjutant : Major T. H. Bryant.

GROUP A. (1ST, 2ND, AND 5TH BATTALIONS)

Commandant : Lieut.-Colonel F. A. T. Lord Rendlesham.
Adjutant : Captain C. F. Cubitt.

GROUP B. (3RD, 4TH, AND 6TH BATTALIONS)

Commandant : Lieut.-Colonel H. S. Marriott.
Adjutant : Captain J. Forsdike.

1st Volunteer Battalion the Suffolk Regiment, Ipswich.

Hon. Commandant:

Lieut.-Colonel J. D. Cobbold.

Major:

Gill, G. F. C.

Captains:

Vincent Fernie, Rev. J. F.
Prentice, W. H.
Cautley, H. M.
Paul, R.

Lieutenants:

South, C.
Pretty, R.
Cazalet, E. J.
Prentice, J. M.
Jolly, W. O.
Corder, B.
Cullingham, J. B.
Francis, W. A.
Fox, G. B.
Notcutt, S. A.
Shipston, C. H.

2nd Lieuts.:

Vulliamy, L. H.
Waspe, W.
Wilson, W.
Maxwell, D. B.
Leek, F.
Turner, P.
Reed, P.
Woods, C. F.
Welburn, A. H.
Quinton, P. J.
Hollamby, E.

Adjutant:

Arbuthnot, J., Captain.

Quartermaster:

Mills, A., Lieut.

Medical Officer:

Pringle, A. Y., Captain.

Chaplain:

Douglas-Hamilton, Rev. H. A.

2nd Volunteer Battalion the Suffolk Regiment, Bury St. Edmunds.

Hon. Commandant:

Lieut.-Colonel Sir G. W. Agnew, Bart.

Major:

Keates, W. (*commanding*).

Captains:

Bunbury, Sir H. C. J. (*2nd-in-command*).
Spurgeon, J. F.
Lambert, F. C.
Lambton, Hon. G.
Naish, S.

Lieutenants :

Hales, J.
Davies, A. C.
Daking, C. F.
Childs, H. A.
Wilkinson, M. E.
Hammond, C. E.
Hay, J. D.
Hunter, J. D.
Cattle, C. F.
MacLaren, D.
Gent, A.

2nd Lieuts. :

Horne, F. W.
Saunders, A. F.
Dawson, J. A.
Wilson, J. J.
Harrison, M.
Broome, W. R.
Wayman, F.
Medcalf, W. C.
Tozer, C. W.
Roll, J. A.

Adjutant :

Ridgeway, W., Lieut.

Quartermaster :

Goldsmith, E. F., Lieut.

Medical Officer :

Wood, O. R. M., Lieut.

3RD VOLUNTEER BATTALION THE SUFFOLK REGIMENT, BECCLES.

Hon. Commandant :

Somerleyton, Hon. Lieut.-Colonel, Lord.

Major :

Cooper, E. R.

Captain (2nd-in-Command) :

Cockrell, W. F.

Captains :

Barratt, G.
Calvert, E. P.
Larke, J. S.
Huke, H. J.
Tuttle, A. E.

Lieutenants :

Grubbe, E. E.
Burgess, F. E.
Cookes, W. U.
Thompson, E. A.
Fox, F. W.
Gouldby, A.
Ratcliffe, F. J.

2nd Lieuts. :

Orford, A. J.
Hall, C. C.
Lockitt, C. H.
Critten, A. J.
Barry, G. J.
Pawlyn, A. C.
Clarke, S. E.
Smith, C. N.
Halliday, S. C.

Adjutant :

Bull, E. A., 2nd Lieut.

Quartermaster :

Culf, C. C., Lieut.

4th Volunteer Battalion the Suffolk Regiment, Woodbridge.

Hon. Commandant:

Lowther, Hon. Lieut.-Colonel J. W.

Major:

Hughes, Sir A. C.

Captain (2nd-in-command):

Rowley, C. R.

Captains:

Milbank, G. H. V.
Phillips, E. G. W.
Yorke, B. R.

Lieutenants:

Booth, W.
Caselton, C. F.
Paul, S.
Horner, H. T.
Beatton, H. J.
Phillips, A. W. R. H.
Sadd, A. H.
Timbers, H. M.

2nd Lieuts.

Bixby, P. O.
Moorson, E. R. H.
Barton, H.
Mossop, G. A.
Sproxton, F.
Creighton, G. M.
Robertson, J. G.
Rickards, Rev. J. A.
Shipston, W. R.

Adjutant:

Earnshaw, A., 2nd Lieut.

Quartermaster:

Notcutt, R. C., Lieut.

Medical Officer:

Toombs, H. G., Lieut.

Chaplain:

Pollard, Rev. L. G., Capt.

5th Volunteer Battalion the Suffolk Regiment,

Hon. Commandant:

Coxhead, J. A., Hon. Lieut.-Colonel.

Captain (2nd-in-Command):

Hyde Parker, L.

Captains:

Rumball, G. H.
Boardman, C. T.
Grimwade, H. W. F.
Scott, A. L.

Lieutenants :

Gregory, H. F.
Peachey, H. W.
Western, G. S.
Drake, A. W.
Hill, J. S.

2nd Lieuts. :

Dawson, G. A. P.
Prowse, W.
Arnold, H. A.
Sainsbury, F.
Hutchinson, J.
Wheeler, F. B.
Wilson, E. F.
Cutts, T. J.
Buckney, C.
Hustler, W. R.
Winch, E.

Adjutant :

Dunn, W. G., Captain.

Quartermaster :

Warren, W. J., Lieut.

Medical Officer :

Goodman, T. H., Lieut.

6TH VOLUNTEER BATTALION THE SUFFOLK REGIMENT.

Hon. Commandant :

Lane, Sir R. B., Hon. Lieut.-Colonel.

Major :

Collins, H. A.

Captain (2nd-in-command)

French, F. W.

Captains :

Peart, W. K. H.
Collins, E. A.
Walne, H. G.
Clarke, A. C.

Lieutenants :

Freire-Marreco, G. A.
Newberry, R.
James, F. C.
Chevallier, J. B. T.
Aldred, F. W.
Busby, W.
Murrell, H. C.
Neave, H. J.
Hayward, R. C. C.
Bates, E.
Black, D.
Clarke, W.
Eldridge, F. J. P.

2nd Lieuts. :

Soden, J. E.
Mayfield, A.
Raven-Hart, Rev. W. R.
Tattersfield, J.
Heywood, N. A.
Delap, Rev. L. B.
Goram, T. J.

Adjutant :

Roberts, W. J., Captain

Quartermaster :

Snell, G. R., Lieut.

Medical Officer :

Biden, C. W., Lieut.

Chaplain :

Farmiloe, Rev. W. T.

CHAPTER XXIV

The 1st Battalion arrives in Gallipoli—Returns to England—Sails for India—On active service with the Malabar Field Force—Sails for Gibraltar—The 1st and 2nd Battalions meet again—The 1st Battalion arrives in Colchester—The march through Suffolk

ON November 9, 1918, H.M.T. *Bermudian* anchored off Cape Helles, and on the following day the 1st Battalion—having transhipped to H.M.S. *Waterwitch*—proceeded up the Dardanelles to the Turkish fort at Soghanli Dere. Moving later to Cham Burnu, the battalion again embarked in H.M.S. *Waterwitch*, bound on this occasion for the town of Gallipoli. Here they were inspected by Lieut.-General Sir H. F. M. Wilson, Commander-in-Chief of the Allied Forces in Turkey.

On April 16, 1919, the temporary nucleus of foreign service details, which had been formed in Felixstowe, moved from Bury St. Edmunds to Thetford, and on the following day the cadre of the 1st Battalion arrived in England from the Dardanelles. On the 19th the cadre reached Thetford and, having absorbed the nucleus, resumed the dignity of a fully-fledged battalion. Thetford St. Mary, where their hutments were situated, is in the Suffolk portion of the town and, strange to say, this marked the only occasion since the year 1782 that a regular battalion of the regiment had been quartered in the county.

Shortly after the armistice Lieut.-Colonel Hon. H. E. Joicey, D.S.O., relinquished the command of the 1st Battalion which he had held throughout three eventful years, being succeeded in June, 1919, by Lieut.-Colonel A. F. Stewart, C.M.G., O.B.E. Towards the end of that month the colours, with the band and drums, were taken to Ipswich for the regimental memorial service held in the church of St. Mary-le-Tower. These colours were amongst the oldest in the army, having been presented to the 1st Battalion in 1849, and carried in action during the New Zealand war. On July 14 they were carried in the Allied victory march through Paris, the colour-party consisting of Brevet-Lieut.-Colonel F. S. Cooper,

D.S.O., Brevet-Major J. A. Campbell, D.S.O., C.Q.M.S. H. E. Mann, D.C.M., M.M., Sgt. H. Quantrill, D.C.M., and Pte. Wilson, D.C.M. The same colour-party, together with representatives from each company, under Lieut. A. A. Johnson, M.C., took part in the victory march through London a few days later.

The battalion being now under orders for India, the advance party left for Liverpool, where two months later half the battalion embarked in the S.S. *Teuca.* In September the remainder of the battalion was inspected by General Sir H. S. Horne, G.C.B., who afterwards presented a number of Mons Stars. Shortly afterwards the battalion was called out on strike duty, which happily passed without incident, and on November 6 embarked in H.M.T. *Braemar Castle* at Southampton. Landing in Bombay on the last day of the month, they reached Jubbulpore on December 3, where the remainder of the battalion was awaiting them in the Ridge barracks

On January 6, 1920, the battalion was inspected by General Sir Charles Monro, Bart., G.C.B., Commander-in-Chief in India. On September 12 Major F. T. D. Wilson was promoted to the command of the 1st Battalion, which in the following month was inspected by Lord Chelmsford, Viceroy of India. On January 1, 1921, Lieut. H. B. Monier-Williams, M.C., was appointed adjutant in place of Brevet-Major J. A. Campbell, D.S.O., a student at the Staff College. Towards the end of uneventful hot weather an interesting ceremony took place in the Old Cemetery, Jubbulpore, where a memorial service was held, wreaths being laid on the graves of Lieut.-Colonel Arthur E. V. Ponsonby[1] and others of the 2nd Battalion who died at Jubbulpore during the years 1867–71.

Owing to the prevalence of malaria in Jubbulpore it was decided to transfer the battalion to a hill station, and on September 1 Lieut.-Colonel Wilson with the headquarter wing and one company arrived in Wellington. Two of the other companies, who were following, were diverted to Madras for duty in connection with strike riots in that city. The remaining company was left behind in Jubbulpore for the time being.

[1] Uncle of Major-General Sir John Ponsonby, Colonel of the Suffolk Regiment.

The arrival of the 1st Battalion in the Nilgiri hills almost coincided with one of those outbreaks amongst the Moplahs of Malabar which the army in India, upon at least a score of occasions since the Mutiny, has been called out to suppress. The Moplahs are descendants of Arabs who, landing on the west coast of India about A.D. 800, married women of the country. Chiefly concentrated in the Ernad, Wallavanad, and Ponnani districts, where their males number a quarter of a million, the Moplahs are remarkable for the fanaticism they display towards Hindus. The rebellion of 1921–22, the most serious that had hitherto occurred, was no less than an attempt to overthrow British rule and to establish an independent Moplah state within the Khilafat. According to Lord Rawlinson, about 10,000 rebels took the field, "with several thousand half-time rebels behind them who joined in when the course of the operations brought the fighting their way."

The operations which took place between August 20, 1921, and February 25, 1922, were conducted on a much larger scale than had been necessary on any previous occasion. Altogether about seven thousand troops were employed, but the number in the area at any one time never exceeded five thousand. The operations were carried out under adverse conditions, both as regards terrain and climate. In August, as usual, the monsoon was at its height, the torrential rain increasing the difficulty of movement over the waterlogged, jungle-clad slopes of the Nilgiris. The work of the troops was further hampered by the swollen state of the rivers, the wholesale destruction of bridges, and the blocking of roads by felled trees. The guerilla tactics adopted by the rebels, admirably suited to the country and conditions, were varied by two or three organised attacks in force against detached bodies of troops when the opportunity offered. These attacks, delivered with fanatical determination, were carried out at the cost of heavy casualties. The Moplahs were armed with a wonderful variety of rifles, guns, and swords, the last-named being a kind of flimsy cutlass.

On September 13 "D" Company, under Captain H. P. Sparks, M.C., arrived in Tirur, in the Malabar area. Battalion headquarters, with H.Q., "A" and "B" Companies, followed on November 17, "C" Company—which had only rejoined

MAP OF MALABAR

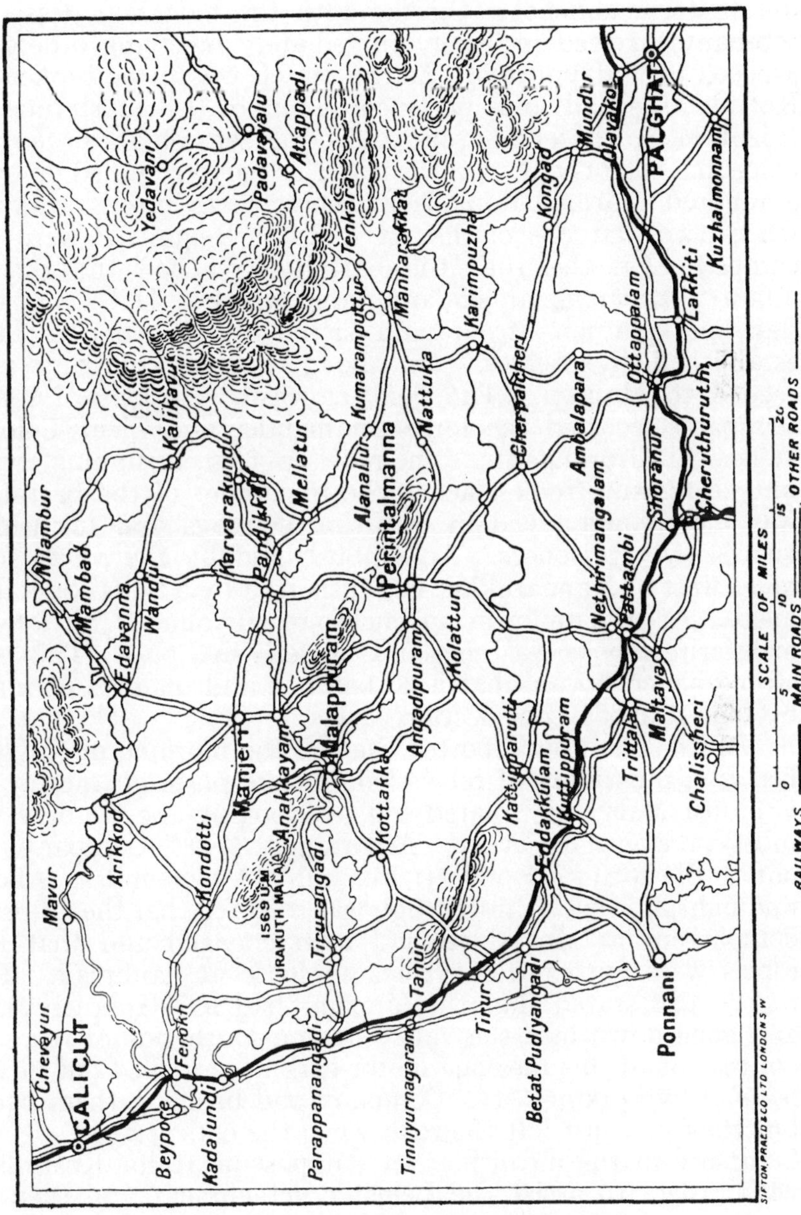

from Jubbulpore on the previous day—remaining at Wellington to form a depot. On the 18th the battalion (less one company) arrived in Tirur, immediately receiving orders to proceed to Malappuram. As the march was to be broken at Kottakkal, an advance party consisting of the quartermaster (Lieut. M. S. Chase) and four cooks, was sent on ahead to that place in a motor-van. On the way this party rounded up over a hundred unarmed Moplahs, marching them in to Kottakkal, where two platoons of the 1st Leinster Regiment[1] were encamped. On the 19th the battalion reached the British infantry barracks at Malappuram, where "D" Company (less one platoon at Otapara signal station) had already established themselves. On the 20th that company proceeded to Manjeri. The next day two platoons of "A" Company escorted the force commander and Lieut.-Colonel Wilson to Tirurangadi; some rebels were seen running away, but no fighting took place. The remainder of the battalion was mainly employed in escorting convoys and furnishing guards over prisoners. An ambush laid by the rebels four miles west of Mannarakkat was dispersed by a Suffolk detachment. At Malappuram an enclosure surrounded by a wall of laterite blocks was chosen as a defensive post. This was strengthened by an abattis of bamboo and manned at night by four guards of one section each.

Police spies now reported that on the morning of November 27 a mustering of rebels would take place on the top of Urakuth Mala, an isolated hill overlooking the country for miles in every direction. Accordingly "D" Company set out on the 26th for Kondotti, a march of twelve miles. About midnight, however, information was received that the Leinster detachment at Kottakkal had been engaged and that the rebels were expected to attack in force at daybreak. The report also stated that the Moplahs had left Urakuth Mala and gone down into the valley on the south side of the hill. On receipt of this message motor-cars were rushed out in the hope of overtaking "D" Company and bringing them back, but they had just left the road when the cars arrived. "A" Company in the meantime set out post-haste for Kottakkal with orders to assist the Leinster detachment and then to

[1] During these operations in Malabar, the Leinster Regiment, one of the old East India Company's regiments, made its last appearance in action.

drive northwards to the river in the direction of Urakuth Mala. After an exhausting march they met some of the notorious Vengara gang near that village; these promptly fled, but three were killed, several wounded, and two captured. One of the prisoners turned out to be a police spy. Unfortunately, "D" Company drew blank; after a most strenuous climb they reached the summit of the hill only to find it deserted.

The rebel country was now divided up into areas, that allotted to the Suffolk Regiment being about twenty miles long by eight broad. In preparation for a big drive fixed for the end of November, "A" Company was sent off to Valakolam, and a signalling station, under Lieut. L. J. Baker, M.C., established on the top of Urakuth Mala. Late at night on the 29th it was reported that Malappuram was about to be attacked. This rumour, no doubt circulated with the object of immobilising troops during the next day's operations, was discredited, and "D" Company, in accordance with the original scheme, left barracks at midnight, headquarters starting for Urakuth Mala three hours later. The drive resulted in thirty-six Moplahs being killed, a considerable number wounded, and half a dozen captured. Thus ended a very successful day. In February, the rebellion having been stamped out, the Malabar Field Force was broken up. Ten thousand Moplars had been killed, wounded, or captured, while forty thousand others had surrendered. The British casualties amounted to forty-three killed and 126 wounded. Early in the New Year battalion headquarters and two companies returned to Wellington, one and a half companies being left at Malappuram and a half company at Calicut, until the battalion left for Bombay.

The year 1922 was a very successful one for the battalion, both as regards work and sport. At all its inspections, at rifle meetings, assaults-at-arms, tournaments, and competitions the battalion came out with flying colours. During the summer months it was inspected by general officers as follows: April 12, Major-General J. T. Burnett-Stuart, commanding the Madras district; July 12, Lieut.-General Sir William Marshall, G.O.C.-in-C. Southern Command; August 21, Major General J. Ponsonby, who had been recently appointed to the command of the Madras district; August 23, General Lord Rawlinson, Commander-in-Chief in India. On all four occasions the reports were eminently satisfactory. In 1922 and 1923 the battalion was remarkably successful in the Army Rifle Association competitions, winning the coveted Queen Victoria trophy and the King George cup each year, as well as many other important prizes.[1]

In May Brevet-Lieut.-Colonel F. S. Cooper, D.S.O., came home on eight months' leave, during which he was placed on half-pay, having attained the age limit. In September, Captain J. G. Frere, D.S.O., M.C., was appointed adjutant in place of Lieut. H. B. Monier-Williams, M.C., whose tenure of that appointment had expired. On December 30, after two years of success in all directions, the battalion left Wellington for Bombay and Deolali, and on April 4, 1924, arrived in Gibraltar. On September 12 Lieut.-Colonel F. T. D. Wilson, having completed his tenure of that appointment, gave up the command, and was succeeded by Lieut.-Colonel R. G. Coles. During Lieut.-Colonel Wilson's four years of office the 1st Battalion attained a standard of all-round efficiency which has probably never been surpassed by any regiment of the line. Early in 1924 the award of the Indian General Service medal, 1908, with clasp "Malabar, 1921–22," was announced. Approximately six hundred officers and men of the 1st Battalion had taken part in the operations concerned. On May 21, 1925, General Sir Thomas Morland, K.C.B., K.C.M.G., D.S.O., A.D.C., Colonel of the Suffolk Regiment, died in Switzerland. He was succeeded by Major-General J. Ponsonby, C.B., C.M.G., D.S.O., appointed on May 22.

On January 19, 1926, the 2nd Battalion arrived in Gibraltar to relieve the 1st Battalion, the two remaining together for nearly a month—a unique event. Prior to the departure of the 1st Battalion from Gibraltar the ceremony of trooping the colour was performed, both the 1st and 2nd Battalions being on parade. At the conclusion of the ceremony H. E. the Governor (General Sir Charles Monro, Bart.) addressed the 1st Battalion, while the 2nd marched back to quarters. Another interesting function performed by the regiment was the parading of the keys of Gibraltar. With the permission of the Governor the keys, locked in a glass case, were taken from Government House, and then, having been placed in charge of a guard with fixed bayonets and headed by the bands

[1] See Appendix IV.

and drums of both battalions, were carried through the main streets of the town.

On February 15 the 1st Battalion sailed for England. As the transport left the harbour the crews of the battleships *Revenge*, *Resolution*, and *Ramillies* successively dressed ship and gave three hearty cheers, which resounded in echo from the Rock. After a pleasant voyage H.M.T. *Nevasa* dropped anchor in Southampton Water on the evening of the 19th, and twenty-four hours later the battalion arrived at St. Botolph's station, Colchester, where a large crowd had assembled to welcome them home. Thus ended a remarkable foreign service tour of nineteen eventful years, during which the battalion had served in Malta, Egypt, Soudan, France, Belgium, Macedonia, Gallipoli, India, and Gibraltar.

In July, 1926, a pageant entitled "Through the Ages" was presented by the 1st Battalion at a military tattoo held in Colchester. The display introduced the uniforms of the regiment in the years 1685, 1759, 1799, 1850, and 1899. On October 1 Lieut. T. Hume was appointed adjutant vice Captain J. G. Frere, D.S.O., M.C., a student at the Staff College. Later in the month the 16th Annual Dinner of the Sergeants' Dinner Club was held at the Moot Hall, Colchester, Lieut.-Colonel F. T. D. Wilson being in the chair.

On December 23 Brevet-Lieut.-Colonel W. N. Nicholson, C.M.G., D.S.O., was promoted Lieut.-Colonel and appointed to the command of the 1st Battalion in place of Lieut.-Colonel R. G. Coles, retired. During the year the A.R.A. Machine Gun cup was won by the machine-gun section of the 1st Battalion, the Company Shield (at home) being won by "D" (Captain Leith-Hay-Clark's) Company. This latter trophy was retained in the battalion in 1927, when it was won by "C" (Major J. L. Likeman's) Company. On March 22, 1927, the Army Cross-Country Championships were held at Colchester. Pte. G. H. Bendall, 1st Battalion, almost succeeded in winning the championship, coming n second and being beaten by two seconds only. Ptes. Bendall and Harwood, both of the 1st Battalion, had previously attained first and second places in the Eastern Command Championships. In April Pte. Bendall won the Markham Cup with the Colchester Harriers for the second year, finishing in record time. A few days later he ran a dead-heat for first place for the army in the Services Cross-Country Race at Portsmouth.

In the King's Birthday honours Major-General J. Ponsonby, Colonel of the Suffolk Regiment, was created a K.C.B. At Bisley Lieut. A. G. Rumbelow, M.B.E., won the Revolver Thirty Cup, a trophy for which he had tied in previous years, and in 1926 had received the silver medal. He also won the Revolver Gold Medal and the Revolver Cup (non-central match) for 1927. During July the 1st Battalion produced a pageant entitled "Lodging the Colour (1685)" at the Colchester military tattoo in Castle Park.

In August, 1927, the 1st Battalion, under Lieut.-Colonel Nicholson, carried out a recruiting march through Suffolk, the first of the kind it had ever made in the county. For nearly two and a half centuries the Suffolk Regiment had prided itself upon, and had maintained, its territorial character, and no commanding officer could ever wish anything better than a continuance of the supply of Suffolk men for the Suffolk Regiment. Leaving Colchester on August 16, the battalion crossed the Stour and entered Suffolk, ending the first day's march at Stratford St. Mary. On the 17th the march was continued to Ipswich, where the battalion received a civic welcome from the mayor and corporation. This over, the time-honoured ceremony of trooping the colour was performed in Christchurch Park. The next day all ranks of the battalion were fêted in the Corn Exchange by the mayor and corporation and the townsfolk of Ipswich. On the 19th, striking into the heart of Suffolk, the battalion set out along the Norwich road for Stowmarket. A short halt was made near Baylham House —until recently the residence of Lieut.-Colonel A. S. Peebles, D.S.O., Suffolk Regiment, and at one time that of William Dowsing, a notorious character of the Commonwealth period. From the tower of Shrubland Hall, the stately seat of Lord de Saumarez, floated the Union Jack, whilst all along the route the houses were hung with flags and bunting. In Needham Market, where the troops were warmly welcomed, decorations were lavishly displayed. On arrival at Stowmarket the battalion was accorded a splendid welcome. Hollow square was formed in front of the Memorial Pavilion, upon whose gates hung a wreath designed in the colours of the regiment. On the dais were assembled the Chairman and members of the Urban District Council, the Lord-Lieutenant of Suffolk (Colonel Sir Courtenay Warner, Bart.), the Colonel of the Suffolk Regiment (Major-General Sir John Ponsonby), Brig.-General S. E. Massy Lloyd, and many others.

The battalion, having been inspected by the Lord-Lieutenant and the Chairman of the Council, received an address of welcome to the town. An interesting ceremony followed, the Lord-Lieutenant presenting to the battalion two colour-belts and a set of flutes, provided by subscriptions in the county. In making the presentation, Sir Courtenay Warner said that the belts and flutes were a small symbol showing that the county did not forget its boys who went out to fight, but looked on them with love and interest, watching their careers as it watched those of its children. After presenting the flutes the Lord-Lieutenant concluded with these words: "May the drums and fifes of the old 12th Foot play you to as great glory in the future as they have in the past." In the evening the officers of the battalion were the guests of the Lord-Lieutenant at Brettenham Park. After dinner Sir Courtenay Warner announced that the following telegram had been despatched to His Majesty the King on behalf of the battalion:

"To His Majesty's Equerry-in-Waiting, Abbeystead, Lancashire.

"1st Battalion Suffolk Regiment now on its march through the county sends humble and respectful greetings to His Majesty. COURTENAY WARNER,

"H.M. Lieutenant, County Suffolk."

To which he had received the following reply from His Majesty:

"Colonel Sir Courtenay Warner, Brettenham Park, Stowmarket, Suffolk.

"I have received with much pleasure the message of greeting you sent me from the 1st Battalion Suffolk Regiment. In thanking all ranks, please tell them how glad I am to hear that they are having this opportunity of visiting their county, and I am sure they have met with a hearty welcome everywhere." "GEORGE R.I."

On the 20th the battalion left Stowmarket and began its march to Bury St. Edmunds. At Tostock the Girl Guides turned out in uniform to greet the battalion. The weather now broke, and Rougham Park was reached in a regular downpour. Here the midday halt was arranged, the park having been placed at the disposal of the battalion by Sir George Agnew, Bart. During this halt the Mayor of Bury St. Edmunds (Major E. L. D. Lake) motored over to tell the commanding officer that, owing to the rain, all outdoor arrangements for the welcome of the battalion in Bury had been postponed until the following day. Accordingly on Sunday the 21st the battalion was officially welcomed to the ancient borough of Bury St. Edmunds by the Lord-Lieutenant of the county and the mayor and corporation. In the afternoon a crowd of some ten thousand people assembled to witness the ceremony of the trooping the colour on the recreation ground, many former officers of the regiment being present. On the 22nd the battalion marched to Sudbury, where it enjoyed another splendid welcome, and on the 23rd returned to Colchester. The march from beginning to end had been an unqualified success.

During September the battalion took part in the concentration of the 4th Division in East Kent and was encamped on Dibgate Plateau, Shorncliffe. Owing to excessive rain the manœuvres were curtailed. Early in the month a party under an officer proceeded to Portsmouth to watch the speed trials of H.M.S. *Suffolk.* On October 7, 1927, Captain T. Hume was obliged to resign his commission owing to ill-health. He was succeeded as adjutant by Captain H. P. Sparks, M.C. The 17th Annual Dinner of the Sergeants' Dinner Club took place at the Moot Hall, Colchester, on October 8, Major-General Sir John Ponsonby presiding. On November 13 the first of a series of regimental reunions to be held in Suffolk was arranged at the Drill Hall, Portman Road, Ipswich, the chair being taken by Brig.-General S. E. Massy Lloyd.

CHAPTER XXV

2ND BATTALION

The 2nd Battalion marches into Germany—Is reincarnated in England—Back again in Ireland—Death of Lieut.-Colonel Barnardiston—Unveiling of the Le Cateau Memorial—The battalion goes to China

AFTER halting for a few days at La Longueville the battalion, under Major W. G. Chandler, took part in the advance to the Rhine. On December 11, with bayonets fixed, colours flying, and the drums and fifes playing the regimental march, the battalion crossed the frontier and entered Germany, marching past the corps and divisional commanders assembled to receive them. On December 19, with equal pomp and ceremony, the battalion marched into Gymnich, its permanent station, where Christmas was spent. In January, 1919, Lieut.-Colonel G. G. Carpenter took over the command of the battalion from Major W. G. Chandler, who was proceeding to the Senior Officers' School at Aldershot. Towards the end of February, after a stay of nearly ten weeks at Gymnich, the battalion marched to Cologne. Early in March several officers and a good many other ranks left the 2nd Battalion to join the 4th Battalion at Troisdorf for service with the Army of Occupation. On April 8 the battalion moved to Dansweiler. In the meantime the demobilisation of the 2nd Battalion which had begun at Christmas, proceeded apace.

On June 5 a nucleus from the 2nd Battalion arrived at Bury St. Edmunds from the Army of the Rhine, and a few days later a cadre was formed there, with Lieut.-Colonel A. S. Peebles, D.S.O., in command, Major F. T. D. Wilson second-in-command, and Captain H. R. Gadd, D.S.O., M.C., adjutant. On July 24 the cadre, having absorbed the nucleus, proceeded to Rugeley, taking over the personnel of the 3rd Battalion, and joining the Eastern Reserve Brigade. On the 29th the battalion proceeded to Wolverhampton on strike duty, which happily passed off without incident. On December 4 the battalion left Rugeley for the Meeanee Barracks, Colchester, joining the 11th Infantry Brigade. In July, 1920, Brevet-Major H. R. Gadd, D.S.O., M.C., resigned the adjutancy on being appointed an instructor at the Royal Military College. He was succeeded by Captain H. C. N. Trollope, D.S.O., M.C. In September Major F. T. D. Wilson was promoted to the command of the 1st Battalion.

On December 28 the 2nd Battalion left Colchester to join the Interim Expeditionary Force in Ireland, landing in Dublin on the following day. On arrival it was split up into detachments, two companies with battalion headquarters going to Boyle, co. Roscommon, one to Galway and Oranmore, and the other to Carrick-on-Shannon. The first party, after a stay of two months, went to French Furze Camp, Curragh, where it was joined by the other two at the end of July.

On March 22 the battalion moved to Ballykinlar, co. Down, but a few days later was transferred to Belfast and quartered in the Ulster Hall. In June the battalion returned to Ballykinlar, and in July Brevet-Lieut.-Colonel G. A. L. Sinclair Thomson retired. On August 16, 1922, Lieut.-Colonel A. S. Peebles, D.S.O., was placed on half-pay on completion of his period in command of the 2nd Battalion, and was succeeded by Lieut.-Colonel S. J. B. Barnardiston, D.S.O. On January 1, 1923, another change was introduced to the organisation of a battalion, a wing being formed consisting of battalion headquarters and four groups, including the machine-gunners, and known as the H.Q. Wing. The band, drums, signallers, transport, and all those in regimental employ were transferred to the new formation. On January 31 the battalion left Ballykinlar for Colchester after a spell of two years in Ireland.

On May 20 the Colchester town War Memorial was unveiled by Field-Marshal Sir William Robertson, a detachment of the battalion, with the colours, attending. In June the drums carried by the 8th (Service) Battalion in the Great War were received on presentation by Brevet-Lieut.-Colonel G. V. W. Hill, D.S.O., Royal Irish Fusiliers. On July 26 Lieut. R. H. Maxwell was appointed adjutant vice Captain H. C. N. Trollope, D.S.O., M.C., whose tenure had expired. On October 17 the Grierson Shield, won by the machine-gun platoon of the 2nd Battalion, was presented by the G.O.C.-in-C. Eastern Command.[1]

[1] For the musketry successes of the 2nd Battalion see Appendix IV.

On January 31, 1924, Lieut.-Colonel S. J. B. Barnardiston, D.S.O., died at Colchester from pneumonia, to the profound sorrow of all ranks and the wide circle of his friends. The funeral, which took place at Great Henry, Sudbury, on February 3, was largely attended. On March 10 Brevet-Lieut.-Colonel F. S. Cooper, D.S.O., joined the battalion from half-pay on promotion and assumed command. Early in May the Ipswich War Memorial was unveiled, the colours, band, and drums of the battalion attending the ceremony. On June 20 Captain E. D. C. Hunt, M.C., died at King Edward VII Hospital. He had served with distinction with the 2nd Battalion in the Great War, being twice wounded, and gaining the Military Cross and bar. Towards the end of August the battalion proceeded to East Blatchington, Seaford, for battalion and brigade training, returning to Colchester in mid-September. On November 19 Major and Brevet-Lieut.-Colonel J. H. Robinson was promoted Lieut.-Colonel on the half-pay list from the Suffolk Regiment, retaining his appointment at the War Office as Deputy Assistant Director of Artillery.

On January 15, 1926, the battalion, over six hundred strong, with families, embarked at Southampton in H.M.T. *Nevasa* for Gibraltar to relieve the 1st Battalion. From January 19 the two battalions remained together on the Rock until February 15, when the 1st Battalion sailed for England, leaving behind over two hundred men to bring the 2nd Battalion up to full colonial establishment.

An impressive ceremony, of deep interest to the 2nd Battalion, took place on May 29 at the unveiling of the British IInd Corps Memorial at Le Cateau by General Sir Horace Smith-Dorrien. The memorial, in the form of a cenotaph and made of stone quarried near Paris, is situated to the south-west of the town of Le Cateau, on the extreme right of the position occupied by the rear-guard of the IInd Corps in the stand made against Von Kluck on August 26, 1914. The names of those of the 2nd Battalion who fell on that occasion are inscribed on the north face of the monument.

Amongst those present at the ceremony were the mayor (M. Sylvère Lebeau) and corporation of Le Cateau, the mayor of Briastre, and the mayors of the Canton. M. Moury-Muset, sous-Préfet de l'Arrondissement de Cambrai, representing M. le Préfet du Nord; M. Paul Bersez, Sénateur du Nord;

General Frid, representing the General Officer Commanding the 1st French Army Corps. The Suffolk Regiment was represented by the following past and present officers: Lieut.-Colonel A. S. Peebles, D.S.O., Lieut.-Colonel F. T. D. Wilson, Major E. E. Orford, and Captain N. B. Oakes. The 1st Battalion was represented by a party of non-commissioned officers.

At the close of a stirring address General Sir Horace Smith-Dorrien formally unveiled the cenotaph. M. Moury-Muset, after expressing regret at the unavoidable absence of the Prefect of the Nord Department, paid a graceful tribute to the great part played by the British Empire in the war. Lord Balfour of Burleigh, on behalf of the monuments committee, speaking in the purest French with great eloquence, then handed over the memorial to the care of the municipality of Le Cateau. Amongst the large number of wreaths placed on the cenotaph at the conclusion of the ceremony were several from the 1st and 2nd Battalions and the Suffolk Old Comrades' Association.

The year 1926 passed uneventfully until December 12, when the battalion received sudden and unexpected orders to proceed to Hong Kong. On the 31st 13 officers and 818 other ranks sailed in the s.s. *Achilles* under Major A. G. Taylor, Lieut.-Colonel Cooper being sick. At Penang and at Fort Swettenham the battalion went ashore for exercise, and at Singapore they spent four days at Fort Canning. On February 4 the battalion disembarked at Hong Kong, joining the South China Command, under Major-General C. C. Luard, C.B., C.M.G. Within a fortnight, however, they were transferred to Shanghai, where they landed on February 22, being accommodated in the buildings of the Shanghai Race Club. The battalion, now forming part of the Shanghai Defence Force (Major-General J. Duncan, C.B., C.M.G., C.V.O., D.S.O.), took up the duties of internal security in concert with the international force. On April 28 Major A. G. Taylor was granted the local rank of Lieut.-Colonel while commanding the battalion.

On September 5, to the deep regret of all ranks, Captain E. H. Faulconer-Wright died of pneumonia in the Royal Hospital, Shanghai, after a very brief illness. The deceased officer joined the Suffolk Regiment from Sandhurst in August,

Photo by] [*Central News*

THE UNVEILING OF THE LE CATEAU MEMORIAL
BY GENERAL SIR HORACE SMITH-DORRIEN, G.C.B., G.C.M.G., D.S.O.

1914. In February, 1928, Lieut.-Colonel F. S. Cooper, D.S.O., who had rejoined during the previous August from sick leave, was placed on half-pay on completion of four years in command of the battalion, being succeeded by Lieut.-Colonel W. M. Campbell, D.S.O., M.C. Colonel Cooper, a fine type of commanding officer, who had served with distinction in many parts of the world, joined the 2nd Battalion while they were in camp at Marichuk, near Quetta, at the end of October, 1899.

CHAPTER XXVI

4TH BATTALION

The battalion spends another Christmas in France—Joins the Army of Occupation in Germany—The cadre returns to Ipswich—The reaction of the war recalls the labour of Sisyphus

VERY shortly after the armistice all work, such as the repairing of bridges and permanent ways, and the filling up of road craters, on which the 4th Battalion had been employed for some time, was abandoned, giving place to that of vocational training and educational classes. But now that the war had ended and all the excitement was over, everyone was seized with a longing to return to his native land and lay his arms aside. Even the most conscientious soldier did his duty perfunctorily.

On November 14 the battalion left Basecles for Ecacheries, and while billeted there the award of a Military Cross to Lieut. B. Webb was announced. On December 2 they marched out to the aviation ground at Grandglise, where the 58th Division was inspected by General Sir H. S. Horne, commanding the Ist Army. On the 5th His Majesty The King drove through the divisional area, the battalion assembling near Stambruges to cheer him as he passed. A fortnight later the battalion moved into billets in Stambruges, where Christmas was spent. With the opening of the New Year demobilisation began in earnest. In January, 1919, the Meritorious Service Medal was awarded to Sgts. L. K. Roe, W. F. Olley, and R. C. Bonny, and Belgian decorations to Cpl. Smith and L/Cpl. Neal. In March the battalion, having been posted to the Army of Occupation in Germany, proceeded to Troisdorf, Cologne, where early in April Lieut.-Colonel G. C. Stubbs, D.S.O., took over the command of the battalion from Lieut.-Colonel H. C. Copeman, C.M.G., D.S.O., who had held that appointment with great distinction throughout three years of storm and stress. Towards the end of the month General Sir William Robertson, Commander-in-Chief of the Army of the Rhine, inspected the battalion at Siegburg.

The cadre of the 4th Battalion, Lieut.-Colonel Stubbs commanding, having returned to England with the Eastern Division (Major-General Sir Lothian Nicholson, K.C.B.), arrived in Ipswich on October 11, 1919, and were received by the mayor and corporation at the steps of the Town Hall. Afterwards they were entertained in the Council Chamber by the mayor. At night there was a concert in the Public Hall, followed by a torchlight procession. The cadre was then sent to Ripon, where rapid demobilisation took place. While there it was addressed by Sir John Ganzoni, M.P., who had served with the 4th Battalion in France.

Recruiting for the Territorial Army was closed till February, 1920, by which time Major W. M. Campbell, D.S.O., M.C., had taken over the adjutancy from Major Cubitt. When it reopened Major F. Pretty, T.D., was asked to undertake the re-formation of the battalion, some half-dozen officers, who had served with it in France, immediately coming forward, including Lieut.-Colonel E. P. Clarke, D.S.O., T.D., with already more than twenty years' service in the battalion to his credit. At such a period, with everyone heartily sick of war, camp was out of the question, and in 1920 none was held. As a result, however, of Lieut.-Colonel Pretty's personal effort in recruiting, officers from various battalions of the regiment, and also from other units, offered their services. The response from warrant and non-commissioned officers was even more encouraging, practically every appointment from R.Q.M.S. to corporal being filled by men who had served overseas with the battalion. The strength of the battalion which, in January, 1921, was only 15 officers and 46 men, by March had risen to 16 officers and 150 men. Further development was checked by the coal strike which, however, ended in time to allow the battalion to hold, at Great Yarmouth between July 23 and August 6, its first post-war camp, when 14 officers and 316 other ranks attended. The 4th Battalion was the only unit in the brigade in camp. The following season's camp at Lowestoft witnessed further progress. A photograph of the sergeants taken on that occasion showed 147 medal ribbons amongst 42 of them.

On June 17, 1922, Lieut.-General Sir E. P. Strickland, K.C.B., K.B.E., C.M.G., D.S.O., was appointed honorary colonel of the 4th Battalion.

To assist in the uphill work of overcoming the general war weariness and inspiring fresh interest in the Territorial movement the battalion went to Felixstowe at the end of July for a fortnight's annual training, 16 officers and 438 other ranks attending. Towards the close of the year Captain D. R. A. Eley, D.S.O., took over the duties of adjutant from Major W. M. Campbell, D.S.O., M.C. The gradual swelling of the ranks continued, testifying to the efforts made by Lieut.-Colonel F. Pretty, who on April 10, 1924, handed over the command to Lieut.-Colonel E. P. Clarke, D.S.O., T.D., the strength of the battalion at that time having increased to 21 officers and 618 other ranks. This satisfactory state of affairs was not only maintained but actually improved, and during the following month the 4th Battalion gained the distinction of being the first infantry unit in the Eastern Command to reach establishment. That year a brigade camp held at Dover marked the commencement of a new spirit in the training of Territorial battalions. This system was found to lead to increased efficiency, and similar camps were held in 1925, 1926, and 1927 at Canterbury, Felixstowe, and West Runton respectively.

In 1925 the new Drill Hall and offices at battalion headquarters in Ipswich were completed, being formally opened on June 20 by the Director-General of the Territorial Army (Lieut.-General Sir Hugh Jeudwine, K.C.B., K.B.E.). The general strike of 1926 involved the cancellation of the annual training for that year, but a camp lasting for six days was arranged at Felixstowe. During 1926 and 1927 the strength of the battalion fluctuated considerably, a general falling-off in recruiting being recorded throughout the country. The new Drill Hall at Woodbridge was opened on January 15th, 1927, by Field-Marshal Sir Claude Jacob, G.C.B., K.C.S.I., K.C.M.G., the guard of honour, commanded by Captain H. R. Hooper, M.C., being furnished by the Woodbridge detachment, 4th Battalion Suffolk Regiment. On December 11 of that year Captain H. B. Monier-Williams, M.C., took over the adjutancy from Captain D. R. A. Eley, D.S.O.

APPENDICES

APPENDIX I

OFFICERS OF THE SUFFOLK REGIMENT KILLED IN THE GREAT WAR WHILE SERVING WITH OTHER REGIMENTS

Major H. E. Thomas	25th N.F.	18.4.18
„ H. Pretty, M.C.	10th D.C.L.I.	24.3.18
„ W. O. Cautley, D.S.O.	1st Northants	9.5.15
Captain C. D. Hempson, D.S.O.	6th K.O.R.L.	8.3.17
„ C. H. Churchman	1/5th W. Yorks	3.5.17
„ W. G. Samuel	2nd Bedford	21.9.18
„ C. A. Fry	6th Essex	1.4.18
Lieut. G. P. Cockburn	7th R.W. Surrey	23.3.18
„ J. C. Grimwood	2/5th R. Warwick	3.12.17
„ H. O. Ashton	15th R. Warwick	29.8.18
„ V. B. Llewellyn-Jones	1st Welch	4.5.15
„ W. M. Vincent	1/4th Essex	26.3.17
„ W. Cropley	10th Essex	29.1.18
„ C. T. Cockle	R. Warwick	10.9.18
2nd Lieut. C. B. Brooke, D.S.O.[1]	Green Howards	1.7.16
„ J. J. Brooke	3/4th R. W. Surrey	4.10.17
„ H. L. Chippington	16th R. Warwick	23.8.18
„ F. E. Ablett	1/8th King's	20.9.17
„ A. Newman	1/9th King's	20.9.17
„ H. J. Dawes	Green Howards	8.5.18
„ F. H. Isaacs	11th R.S. Fus.	30.9.18
„ H. L. S. Savory[2]	3rd Worc.	26.4.18
„ C. S. Kemble	2/4th R. Berks	27.5.18
„ C. J. Harmsworth	3rd Middx.	9.1.17
„ A. W. Rash[3]	1/1st Cambs.	31.7.17
„ G. G. R. Nock	1/1st Cambs.	5.9.18
„ H. W. Fuller	1/1st Cambs.	18.9.18
„ W. R. Harris	1/1st Camb.	10.10.18

[1] Acting Captain. [2] Died of wounds. [3] Died of wounds.

APPENDIX II

A DIGEST of some of the more important honours gained by the Suffolk Regiment in the Great War, with the addition of a few of those not mentioned in the text.

V.C. Sgt. A. F. Saunders and Corp. S. J. Day.

C.B. Brig.-Genls. C. H. C. Van Straubenzee and G. H. S. Browne.

C.M.G. Colonel C. W. Somerset, M.V.O.; Lieut.-Colonels H. C. Copeman, D.S.O., C. Parry Crooke, W. N. Nicholson, D.S.O., G. L. J. Tuck, D.S.O., and W. B. Wallace.

C.B.E. Brig.-General S. E. Massy Lloyd.

D.S.O. and two bars. Lieut.-Colonels G. V. W. Hill and L. Lloyd.

D.S.O. and bar. Lieut.-Colonels G. C. Stubbs and G. L. J. Tuck; Captain J. A. Campbell.

D.S.O. Lieut.-Colonels F. W. Jarvis, J. Josselyn, A. F. Randolph and M. F. Mason; Majors R. M. B. Needham and Miles Barne; and Lieut. J. G. Frere, M.C.

M.C. and two bars. Captain H. A. Redding; 2nd Lieut. H. G. Teverson, M.M., F. W. Cook, D.C.M., and W. G. Bailey, D.S.O.

M.C. and Bar. Captains G. L. M. Fache, E. J. Greene, A. A. Smee, G. L. Crandon, E. D. C. Hunt, C. V. Canning, S. Scrimgeour, A. B. Wright, A. W. C. Major, S. W. Turner, and G. F. R. Baguley; Lieuts. V. C. Russell, J. C. G. Matthews, H. B. Monier-Williams, A. G. Burrows and A. E. M. Coles; 2nd Lieut R. T. Robins.

M.C. Captains D. V. M. Balders; Lieut.-Colonel T. De la G. Grissell; Captains G. Fraser, C. W. Merison, R. M. Ridley, R. Starling, L. G. S. Payne, H. Hannay, F. S. Cubitt, G. B. Horne, and T. Wilson; Lieuts. H. F. Horton, N. M. Gordon, D. Green and H. L. Hayne; 2nd Lieuts. H. V. C. de Crespigny and H. A. Reed; C.S.M. S. C. Green.

D.C.M. and bar. Sgt. E. Spalding

D.C.M. C.S.M.'s J. C. Parsons and C. Causton; Sgt. J. H. Watkins (attd. Nigeria Regt.), W. G. Beadon, and E. H. Lingley.

M.M. and two bars. A/Sgt. R. Tyler.

The following awards were gazetted in recognition of valuable services rendered whilst prisoners of war or interned—

M.S.M. C.S.M. (T/R.S.M.) W. A. Read. *Mentions:* C.S.M. W. Crack; Pte. W. J. Goddard.

The following rewards were gazetted in recognition of gallant conduct and determination displayed in escaping or attempting to escape from captivity—*M.C.:* Captain (now Major) (A/Lieut.-Colonel) W. M. Campbell, D.S.O. *M.M.:* Sgt. T. A. Bloomfield; Ptes. G. Cox, L. Rudd, and R. C. Waller. *Mention:* Captain F. Moysey.

CAMEROONS. *D.S.O.*

Captain M. H. S. Willis, Suffolk Regiment (attd. Nigeria Regt.).

APPENDIX III

POSITIONS OF SUFFOLK BATTALIONS ON THE WESTERN FRONT AT THE TIME OF THE ARMISTICE

Battalion	*Station*	*Division*	*Army Corps*	*Army*
2nd	La Longueville	3	VI	Third
4th	Basecles	58	I	Fifth
7th	Haudricourt		197th Brigade	Reserve
11th	Bermerain	61	XVII	Third
12th	Molembaix	14	XV	Second
15th	Tournai	74	III	Fifth

APPENDIX IV

MUSKETRY SUCCESSES

1ST BATTALION *A.R.A. Competitions*

Queen Victoria Trophy, 1922, 1923 and 1924
King George Cup, 1922 and 1923
Whitehead Cup, 1923
Royal Irish Cup, 1923
1st Army Cup, 1922
Hopton Cup, 1922, 1923 and 1924
Company Shield, 1922, 1923, 1924 and 1925
The India Cup, 1922 and 1923
Lewis Gun Championship, 1922. Corporal E. C. Spinks, M.M.
18th Hussar Cup, 1922 and 1925
Revolver Cup, 1923. Lieut. A. G. Rumbelow

2ND BATTALION

A.R.A. Competitions

1922–23

Queen Victoria Trophy, 2nd
King George Cup, 3rd
Whitehead Cup, 2nd
Young Soldiers' Cup, 3rd
Company Match, 3rd
Lewis Gun Championship, 2nd. Corporal Squirrell
Revolver Cup, 3rd. 2nd Lieut. G. W. Browning

All Ireland Rifle Meeting

Queen Victoria Cup, 1st
Private Soldier's Cup, 1st
Young Soldiers' 113, 1st
Curragh Cup, 2nd

APPENDIX V

SUFFOLK REGIMENTAL SONGS

" STABILIS."

YOU will find an ancient colour in the Twelfth Foot of the line
That bears the motto " Stabilis " in memory of the time
When " Steady " was their watchword, though all was touch and go,
And steadfastly they bore it, for all the world to know.
It was " Steady," but they didn't need no steadying ;
" Steady, Twelfth ! " they stood there firm, yes, firm and true.
And they made a watchword then, for all future Suffolk men,
So they passed it on to chaps like me and you.

A hundred odd years take, and again it's touch and go,
The Suffolks guard the British right not far from Le Cateau,
When, though all hope had vanished, and the shells are falling fast,
They remember the old motto and are " Steady " to the last.
Is it " Steady " ? No, they aren't in need of steadying ;
It is " Stabilis " by nature through and through.
So they kept the watchword well, as the numbers left can tell,
And they passed it on to chaps like me and you.

You will find this old tradition in the Twelfth Foot of the line,
Perhaps it isn't talked of, but it's with them all the time;
Though the colour now no longer shows the motto that it bore,
You will find the men as "Steady" as they ever were before.
Is it "Steady?" Then by God's grace we'll be steady.
"Steady, Twelfth!" the Suffolk men stand firm and true.
We'll acquit ourselves like men, for the watchword they made then
Must be passed along by chaps like me and you.

J. G. FRERE.

IN SUFFOLK

"The best men we ever had—with great hearts."
Extract from a letter of a General in France.

In Suffolk, then, the poppies fired
The yellow corn that crowned the rise;
In Suffolk, then, the lark aspired
To link my soul with Paradise:
How often Bury's hopeful spire
I saw in June's untroubled morn;
How oft I lingered to admire
And praise my Suffolk's day new-born.

In Suffolk, now, no poppies glow,
No golden grain the headland crowns;
A moaning mist is all I know;
Banished the lark by winter's frowns;
Banished the spire by winter's night;
And banished all the hopes I had—
The golden hours; the golden light—
For who will give me back my lad?

A message bring they? How he fell
One of a strong and unturn'd line;
"The best we ever had," they tell;
"Great-hearted men," and one was mine.
And one *is* mine. In Suffolk yet
A risen bird above the corn
Shall sing his song; while further set
A lifting spire shall greet the Morn!

FRANK ELIAS.

THE SUFFOLK SOLDIER TO HIS COUNTY

We come to see you—and we come to show
How we, your sons, uphold our common name,
Knowing, as we must know,
Your pride is ours, our heritage the same—
That in their turn your younger sons will go
Along the paths we tread—will bear the flame
Passed on to us by those of long ago.

The Viking spirit that our fathers brought
Lies hid beneath the peaceful toil of years,
Hating oppression, upright, fearing naught,
Yet sure and stubborn often it appears.
That spirit moves amongst us even now :
Out to the world, as fared our fathers then,
It calls from field and village—from the plough
As boys we leave you, to return as men.

So we return, like children to their home—
That homely soil whence springs the Suffolk breed—
From the far corners of the earth we roam,
Our hearts new grounded in a soldier's creed ;
Our duty ready at our country's call,
Honour and service that may be endured,
A firmer love implanted in us all
For that dear land where welcome is ensured.

J. G. Frere.

INDEX

A

Abancourt, 352
Abbasia, 17, 350
Abbeville and area, 41, 170, 353
Abbs, 2nd Lt., R.E., 274
Abeele, 223
Ablott, Sgt. A., M.M., 221
Abraham Heights, 230
Abu Qir, 155
Acquin, 89, 90
Adams, Capt. F., Chevalier O. of L., C. de G., 357
Adams, Capt. W., 343
Adams, 2nd Lt. G. H. C., 193
Adinkerke, 228
Adkins, Bandmaster H. G., 330
Agnew, Capt. J. S., 212
Agnew, 2nd Lt. V. C. W., 212
Agnew, Maj. Sir G., Bt., M.P., 362, 365, 390
Agnez-Acq., railway between, 181
Ailly-le-Clocher, 353
Ainsley, Lt., C., 77
Aird, 2nd. Lt. G. M., 268
Aire, 281
Aisne, River, 37
  Battle of, 39, 40, 41
Aisne–Oise Canal line, 269
Aivatli, 157
Albani, 2nd Lt. d', 65
Albemarle, Brig.-Gen., the Earl of, 365, 371
Albert, King of the Belgians, 59, 300, 357
Albert, Town, Area, and Sector, 92, 133, 147, 154, 170, 174, 177, 178, 186, 194, 198, 272 *sqq.*; the leaning Virgin of, 153
  Battle of, 288
  Bridge-heads, defence of, 273–4
Albert–Amiens Road, 273, 275
Albert-Arras Railway, 225
Albert–Bapaume Road, 147, 197
Albert–Millencourt Road, 273
Alderwick, 2nd Lt. E. E. G., 253
Alette, 93
Alexandria, 16 *et alibi*
Allanson, 2nd Lt. H. P., 128, 183
Allen, 2nd Lt. O. A. E., 93
Allen, Sgt. J., 54
Allenby, J.M., Viscount, G.C.B., G.C.M.G., K.C.B., 22, 179, 188, 208, 217, 226, 227, 317, 219, 350, 351; entry of, into Jerusalem, 211
Allerton, Capt. C., D.S.O., 93, 196, 198, 248
Allfrey, Maj. F. E., 323, 324, 327, 328, 330, 339, 340
Allison, 2nd. Lt. C. H., 187
Allonville, 192
Allouagne, 48, 60, 321
Allsopp, Rev. F. G., C.F., 294
Allum, Lt. W. J., 219
Allum, Pte. W. C., D.C.M., 210, 313
Almack, 2nd Lt. H., 196
Alston, 2nd Lt. A. R., 110
Alston, 2nd Lt. G. K., 102, 104
Althaus, Capt. F. R., 89, 311, 312
Ambrines, 181
American ammunition, 148
American troops, 277
Amiens, 92, 153, 261
  Battle of, 293 *seq.*
Amiens–Albert Road, 272
Amigny–Rouy, 268
Ancre, River, 146, 147, 165, 195, 197, 288
  Battle of the, 187, 276
Anderson, Pte. F., M.M., 221
Anderton, 2nd Lt. J. D., 187
Andrew, Lt. R. H., 135
Andrewes, Lt.-Col. G. L., V.D., 100, 332
Andrews, Pte. C., M.M., 244
Angier, Maj. H. A., M.C., 91, 168, 243, 246
Anley, Brig.-Gen. B. L., 298
Annequin, 47, 129, 144
Anness, 2nd Lt. W. P., 281
Annezin, 198, 267
Anstruther, Lt.-Col., J. H. F., 100
Anzac Cove, 205, 214
Anzacs, the, 106
Apilley, 231
Arbuthnot, Maj. L. C., 92, 93, 122, 149, 190, 198, 271
Arbuthnot-Leslie, Lt. G. R., 213
Argent, Sgt., M.M., 35
Argles, Capt., C. A. C., M.C., 241, 274
Arleux, Battle of, 221, 233, 234, 351
Armsby, Pte. H., 90
Armentières, 250
  Sector, 152
Armentières–Fleurbaix Line, 285
Armes, Lt.-Col. W., 102, 103, 104–5
Army of Occupation, 357, 391, 396
Army Service Corps, a tribute to, 346
Arnold, Capt. K. F. F. W., 51, 64, 69

Arras, and the Arras Sector, 85, 172, 177, 179, 181, 188–9, 221, 223, 235, 250, 251, 354–5
Two Batts. meeting in, 235
Battles of, 198, 219, 232 *seq.*, 260
Arras–Cambrai road, 261
Arrewage Sector, 297
Artois, 120
Ashton, Lt. E. M., 102, 104
Ashton, Lt. P. W. B., 106
Ashworth, Lt. F., 253
Ashworth, Lt. J. P. C., M.C., 234
Ashworth, Pte. J., M.M., 221
Ashworth, 2nd Lt. G. B., 179
Askham, 2nd Lt. S. T., 195
Athys, 26, 250
Attichy, 39
Attree, Capt., F. W. W. T., 77
Aubers Ridge, Battle of, 85 *seq.*, 321
Audruicq., 354
Auja Stream, 313, 317
Australia Gulley West, 106
Austro-Serbian War declaration, 45
Aveluy, 170, 172
Avesnes-les-Aubert, 298, 299
Aviss, Cpl. O. G., 144
Ayton, 2nd Lt. M. C., M.C., 222, 288

B

Baboon Camp, 243
Bac St. Maur, 280
Backhouse, C.S.M. H. E., 242
Backhouse, 2nd Lt. E. H. W., 22, 35
Badger, Lt., K. H. C., 217
Bagenal, Lt. N. B., 96, 174–5
Bagot, Capt. Hon. W. L., 117
Baguley, Capt. G. F. R., M.C. & Bar, 298, 299, 355, 400
Bailey, Pte. J., D.C.M., 59
Bailey, 2nd Lt. F. W., 291
Bailey, 2nd Lt. W. G., D.S.O., M.C. & two Bars, 293, 400
Bailiff Wood, 173
Bailleul, 42, 55, 81, 90, 142, 168, 171
Bailleulmont, 247
Baillie, 2nd Lt. W. A., 188
Baird, Lt.-Col. E. W. D., 116, 117, 118
Baisieux, 321
Reserve Line, 271
Baker, Pte. A/L/Cpl., M.M., 35
Baker, Capt. L. J., M.C., 140, 221, 234, 264, 266, 385
Baker, 2nd Lt. P. A., 236
Baker, Sgt. F. D., D.C.M., 259
Balaam, Cpl. S. C., D.C.M., promoted K. Sgt. on the field, 62
Balders, Capt., D. V. M., M.C., 17, 50, 52, 54, 64, 66, 69, 70, 77, 400
Baldock, 2nd Lt. F. F., 279
Baldwin, 2nd Lt. A. P., 291
Balfour of Burleigh, Lord, 394
Ballantine, 2nd Lt. W. P., 169
Balloon Wood, 77, 79
Balua Lake, 318
Bamkin, 2nd Lt. H. P., 89, 90
Bannerman, A/Capt. G. C. B., 230
Bapaume, 223, 249, 276
Battle of, 284
Bapaume–Cambrai road, 290
Barakli Dzuma, 162, 163, 164
Barastre, 223
Barber, Lt. R., M.C., 140
Barber, Sgt. B., 134
Barber, Sgt. M. R., commissioned, 325
Barclay, Capt. C. M., 112
Bargh, 2nd Lt., 65, 77
Barker, C.S.M. J., 82
Barker, Lt. G. P., 212, 213
Barlin, 199
Barly, 200
Barnard, 2nd Lt. A., 291–2
Barnard, 2nd Lt. A. W., 284
Barnardiston, Lt.-Col. S. J. B., D.S.O., 18, 22, 31, 330, 392, 393
Barne, Maj. M., D.S.O., 212, 400
Barnes, 2nd Lt. R. S., 46, 63
Barnett, 2nd Lt. G. B., 297–8
Barratt, A/Cpl. J., M.M., 162
Barrett, Cpl. D., M.M. & Bar, 282, 355
Barrett, 2nd Lt. J. W., 272
Barrett, Capt. V. W., 97, 196
Barthou, M., 92
Barton, T/Capt. R. F., 182, 222
Bartram, 2nd Lt. F., 292
Basécles, 296, 396, 401
Basse Forest, 231–2
Bavai, 23
Bayenghem-lez-Eperlecques, 300
Baylis, Lt. A. K., 267
Baylis, 2nd Lt. S. A., 210
Bayliss, 2nd Lt. H. J., 266
Bayonet Trench, 180, 234
Bazentin-le-Grand, 176, 190, 192
Bazentin-le-Grand–Montauban Line, the, 273
Bazentin-le-Petit and Wood, 175, 176, 189
Bazentin-le-Petit–Martinpuich road, 175
Bazentin Ridge, Battle of, 182 *seq.*
Beach Post, 208
Beaden, Sgt. W. G., D.C.M., M.M., 145, 400
Beaudignies, 292
Beaufort, 181
Beaumont Hamel, 179, 277
Beaurains, 179
Beaurepaire Farm, 194
Beauval, 195
Beckett, Col. E. W., 117
Bécordel, 179, 189

Bécourt, village, Château, and Wood, 75, 92, 153, 173, 174, 175, 191
Bedford House, near Ypres, 138
Bedwell, 2nd Lt. V. L. S., 191
Beer, R.S.M., 102
Beersheba, 205, 209
Capture of, 217
Beersheba–Gaza Turkish Line, 209
Beirut, 317, 318, 349
Beit Dukla, 218
Beit Hanun, Turkish rail-head, 210
Beit Iksa, 218
Beit Nabala, 211, 218, 311
Beitania–Rafal Line, 318
Belashitza positions, 308, 309
Beles positions, 309
Belgium, 23, 24, 49
Bell, C.S.M., 102
Bell, Lt. N. K., 341, 342
Bell, 2nd Lt., W. J. 91
Bellegoed Farm, 228, 230
Bellery, 287
Bellevue Farm, 174
Bellewaarde Farm, Battles of, 79, 80, 82, 133
Bellyache Wood, 84
Bemment, 2nd Lt. L. A., 299
Bence-Lambert, Lt.-Col. G. L., C.M.G., 332, 362, 263
Bendall, Pte. G. H., 387
Bennet, Maj. (Suffolk Yeo.), 114
Bennett, Philip, M.P., 113
Bennett, 2nd Lt. H. F., 288
Bennett, 2nd Lt. F. W., 280
Bennett, 2nd Lt. L. P., 194
Bennett, 2nd Lt. S. G., 183
Benson, Capt., 24
Berguette, 237
Berles-aux-Bois, 194, 208
Bermerain, 299, 352, 401
Bermeries, 23
Bernafay Wood, 166, 179, 192
Bernard, A. M., 329
Berners, Lt. Charles, 112
Berneuil, 200
Berrill, 2nd Lt. F. C., 22, 35
Bersez, M. Paul, 393
Bertrancourt, 188
Berwick, Lt. W., 294
Béthune, 47, 48, 94, 120, 129, 132, 144, 196, 199
Beugny, 223
Beuvry, 46, 47, 196
Bevan, Lt. C. B., 183
Beyts, Lt. C. F., M.C., 93, 124
Bichancourt, 231, 232, 269
Biez Farm, 85
" Big Willie " Trench, 126, 127
Biggs, Capt. A. C. B., M.C., 242
Biggs, 2nd Lt. H., 49, 50, 53, 54
Billy-sur-Ourcq, 40
Birbeck, Lt.-Col. O., 359
Bird, Capt. A. K., 96, 154
Bird, 2nd Lt. C. E., 172
Birdcage Line, Macedonia, 157, 158
Bir-el-'Abd, 204
Birley, Maj. R. F. A., 36
Bittleston, Capt. N. A., 22, 32, 33, 330
Black, Capt. D. S., M.C., 235, 273
Black Line, the, 234, 239, 249
Black Prince, the, 43
Blackburne, Rev. E. F., C.F., 248
Blackwell, Capt. W., 22
Blackwell, 2nd Lt. T., 273
Blairville, 225, 228, 259
Blanch, 2nd Lt., J. A., 248, 285
Bland, F. L., 329
Blanks, Sgt. H., M.M., 35
Blauwe Poort Farm, 52
Blencowe, Rev. J. W., C.F., 213
Blendecques, 46
Blinco, Sgt. C., D.C.M., 257
Bloomfield, Sgt. T. A., M.M., 401
Blowers, 2nd Lt. C. P., 292
Blue Line, the, 229, 232, 233, 250, 270
Bluff, the Ypres Salient, 135 *seq.*, 300, 301
Blunden, Lt. R., 97
Boardman, Capt. C., 372
Boche Trench, near Ypres, 139
Boeree, 2nd Lt. A. R., 86
Boeschepe, 70, 281
Boesenghem, 132, 243, 298
Boggis, 2nd Lt. S. J. W., 253
Bohain, 37
Bohun, Cornet George Brown, 112
Bois l'Abbé–Cachy Line, 270
Bois du Biez, 62, 86
Conference of officers at, Painting of, 61
Bois des Bœufs, 233
Bois de Boussu, 25
Bois Escardonneuse, 293, 294
Bois Gentelles, 270
Bois Grenier, 151, 152, 237
Line, 177
Sector, 285
Bois d'en Haut, 294
Boisleux, 194
Bois Marrières, 294
Bois Neuf, 247
Bois Robert, 271, 272
Bois Rosignol, 192
Bois des Tailles, 183
Bois du Vert, 222, 235
Bolingbroke, Capt. N., 231 *& n.*, 243, 271, 277
Bolingbroke, Lt. R. C., M.C., D.C.M., 124, 171, 240, 241
Bollezeele, 120
Bols, Brig.-Gen. L. J., 55, 79
Bolton, Lt., 17
Bolton, Lt. E. T., 250, 281
Bolton, 2nd Lt. C. W., 192

Bonavis Ridge, 235, 236
Bond, Col. F. G., V.D., 374
Bond, Lt. H. F., M.C., 145, 189
Bond, 2nd Lt. C. R., 224
Bond, 2nd Lt. H. M., 233
Bondues, 357
Bonney, Sgt. R. C., M.S.M., 396
Boocock, 2nd Lt. H. J., 217
Booker, Maj. W. J., 107
Boom Ravine, Battle of, 171, 243
Bornat Hill, 311
Bott, 2nd Lt. N. A., D.C.M., M.M., 128, 224, 225, 262
Bouchavesnes, 193, 200
Bouquemaison, 235
Bourlon Wood, 258, 357
Bouzincourt, 168, 237
Bowen, Capt. L. A. G., M.C., 178, 179, 180, 234–5, 237
Bowers, Cpl. F., D.C.M., 242
Bowes, Brig.-Gen. W. H., 42, 58, 59
Bowman, A/Sgt. S., M.M., 313
Box, Lt. C. H., 125
Boyelles, 227, 228, 279
Boyne, 2nd Lt. H. H., 190
Brabazon, Brig.-General, 118
Bradley, Lt. S., 50, 51, 64, 67, 68, 78, 80
Bradley, 2nd Lt. J., M.C., 140, 183
Bradon, 2nd Lt. H., 164
Bragg, Sgt. H., D.C.M., 137
Brain, 2nd Lt. P., 244
Braine, 41
Brandhoek Camp, 74, 82, 83, 84, 123, 223
Bray, 150
Bray–Albert Road, 168
Bray Dunes, 228
Bray, Lt. N. G., 292
Bray-sur-Somme, 193
Breilly, 320
Breslau Trench, 183
Bresle, 153, 154
Brett, Capt. J. H., 96, 279, 281
Brett, Lt.-Col. C. A. H., D.S.O., 18, 19, 29, 31, 32, 33, 34, 35, 38
Brettell, Lt.-Col. R. V. G., 94, 120, 121, 122, 123
Brévillers, 179
Bridges, Pte. W., D.C.M., 35
Bridewell, 2nd Lt. W. A., 246
Brielen, 73
Briggs, Maj.-Gen. C. J., 155, 188
Bright, 2nd Lt. F. H., 125
Bright, 2nd Lt. L. L., 89
Brill, Pte. B. H., D.C.M., 128
Briqueterie, the, 166
Broke, Capt. Philip Bowes, 112
Brome, Charles, Lord (Marquess Cornwallis), 111, 112
Bronfay Farm, 92
  Two Batts. meeting at, 166
Brooke, Capt. F. W., 341
Brookc, Capt. G. D., 178
Brooke, Lt. Francis, 112
Brooke, 2nd Lt. J. J., 338
Brookes, Lt., W. L., S.O., 93
Brookes, C.S.M., 173
Brown, Lt., H. M., M.C. 270
Brown, Brig.-Gen. P. W., 244, 248
Brown, Capt, E. L., M.C., 46, 86
Brown, Capt. O. H., D.S.O., 96, 174, 176, 177, 271, 355
Brown, Lt. J., 194
Brown Line, the, 220, 250
Brown, 2nd Lt. G. M., 339, 340
Brown, 2nd Lt., H. M., 46
Brown, 2nd Lt., W., M.C., 241, 242
Browne, Brig.-Gen. G. H. S., C.B., 400
Browne, 2nd Lt. A. A., 292
Bruay, 200
Brussels, 351
Brunger, Capt. R., D.S.O., 145
Bruncker, Brig.-Gen. C. M., 103
Bryant, Lt., 246
Bryant, Lt. G. F., 246, 247
Bryant, 2nd Lt. G. L., M.C., 281, 282
Bryant, Maj. T. H., 375
Bryce, Capt. A. G., R.A.M.C., 237
Buckoke, 2nd Lt. O. L., 253
Buire, 146, 147
Bulfin, Gen. Sir E. S., K.C.B., C.V.O., 49, 313, 317
Bulgar Trench, 169
Bulgaria, 108 ; Entry of, into the War, 155–6 ; Allied Entry into, 310
Bull, Maj. P. C., D.S.O., 91, 167, 168, 238, 276, 277, 353
Bullecourt, 224, 357
Bullen, 2nd Lt. F., 248
Bull's Run, near Flers, 179
Bunbury, Capt. Sir H., Bt., 367, 374
Bunbury, 2nd Lt. P. S. St., 64, 188
Burgess, 2nd Lt. W. F., 185
Burj Badawil, 318, 319
Burman, Capt. W. F., 136, 179, 290
Burnand, 2nd Lt., 32, 34
Burnett-Stuart, Maj.-Gen. J. P., 385
Burrell, Pte. J. G. L., D.C.M., 59
Burrowes, Capt. R. V., M.C., 96, 154, 252, 253
Burrows, Lt. A. G., M.C. & Bar, 400
Burrows, Sgt. E., M.M., 225
Burton, B. H., 329
Burton, R.S.M. R., M.C., 38, 58–9, 325
Burton, 2nd Lt. G. E. E., 189
Bury, Col. the Viscount, M.C., 358
Bury St. Edmunds, Suffolk Regt.'s Cenotaph at, 359
Bus Farm, 55
Bus-les-Artois, 188
Butkova Area, 305, 306, 308
Butler, Lt.-Col. Hon. L., 59
Butler, Lt.-Gen. Sir R. H. K., 293

Buxton, Capt. G. C., 116, 117, 118
Buxton, Lt. A. R., 117
Buxton, 2nd Lt. E. H., 212
Byng of Vimy, Gen. Lord, G.C.B., G.C.M.G., 222, 225, 254, 261, 273, 288
Byrne, Capt. S. H., 93, 196
Byron, 2nd Lt. L. W. H., 279

C

CACHY, 271
Cadogan, Col. G. O., Earl, 363, 375
Cadogan, Lt. Hon. E. C. C., 212, 213
Caestre, 141, 142
Cairo, 16, 17, 349, 351
Calicut, 385
Calonne-sur-la-Lys, 60, 199, 237
Cambrai, Battle of, 198, 235, 257–8, 266
Cambrai Road, 33, 232
Cambridge Road, near Ypres, 73
Cambrin, 127, 144
Campagne, 89, 296
Campbell, Brevet-Maj., J. A., D.S.O., 50, 54, 155, 158, 163, 226, 381, 400
Campbell, Brig.-Gen., J. C., 97
Campbell, Lt.-Col. W. M., D.S.O., M.C., 22, 313, 316, 395, 397, 398, 401
Campbell, 2nd Lt. D. W., 291
Canada Huts, Ypres Salient, 135
Canadian Troops, 65, 67, 68, 126, 233
Canal du Nord, Battle of, 290, 291
Canche, River, 192
Candas, 170, 192
Canning, Capt. C. V., M.C. & Bar, 244, 248, 259, 278, 280, 281, 282, 355, 400
Cape Bon, 319
Cape Helles, 380
Capon, Cpl. A., M.M., 193
Capper, Maj.-Gen. J. E., 123
Card, Capt. S. W., 91, 92, 167, 168
Cardonette, 195
Carleton, Brig.-Gen. F. M., 145, 190
Carleton Trench, 191
Carlisle, 2nd Lt., W. T., 301
Carnarvon Redoubt, 209
Carnegy, Maj.-Gen., 47
Carnoy, 149, 150, 182
Carnoy–Mametz Road, 92
Carpenter, Capt., 141
Carpenter, T/Lt.-Col. G. G., 290, 291, 292, 391
Carr, 2nd Lt. D. G., 200
Carrigan, Lt. H. C., 302, 306
Carrington, 2nd Lt. W. G., 185
Carter, C.S.M. C., 35
Carthew, Capt. P. R. W., 22, 35
Cartigny, 237
Cassel, 41, 228
Catchpole, Capt. T. J., 210
Catchpole, Lt. C., 46
Catchpole, Maj. A. H., 91, 167, 168
Catchpole, 2nd Lt., C. E., 180
Catchpole, Sgt. C. E., M.M., 168
Caterpillar Wood, 182
Valley, 183
Cator, Maj.-Gen. A. B. E., 269, 272
Causton, C.S.M. C., D.C.M., 300, 400
Cautley, Capt. H. L., 42, 82, 323
Cautley, Capt. H. M., 370
Cautley, Maj. W. O., D.S.O., 59, 323, 325
Cavalry Farm, 261
Cavan, Lt.-Gen., the Earl of, 126, 193, 196
Cavaliero, 2nd Lt., 253
Cave, L/Cpl., 176
Cayeux, 352
Cayley, 2nd Lt. K. H. E., 77
Central Keep (Loos), 127, 128
Chacrise, 40
Chalk, 2nd Lt. T. W., 178
Chalk Caves, Arras, Holy Communion in, 219
Chalk Pit, Loos, 91, 129, 130
*Chalmers, Capt. R., 73, 77
Chalmers, Lt. J. A. G., 185
Champagne, 120
Champtortel, 39
Chandler, Maj. W. G., 64, 68, 69, 182, 290, 293, 391
Channel Seaboard, the, 45
Chapelle Duvelle, 237
Chapigny, 42
Chaplin, Pte. J. H., M.M. & Bar, 271
Chaplin, 2nd Lt., 253
Chapman, 2nd Lt. J. H., 107
Charrington, 2nd Lt. L. M., 69, 70
Chase, Lt. M. S., 384
Chase, R.S.M., C. de G., 68, 77, 305
Château Segard, 241
Château Wood, 230, 240
Chaud Chapp, 243
Chauny, 231
Chelers, 188, 200
Chelmsford, Rt. Hon. Viscount, Viceroy of India, G.C.S.I., G.C.I.E., G.B.E., 351
Chequer, 2nd Lt. A. M., 301
Cherisy, 238, 254
Chesham, Brig.-Gen. Lord, 118
Cheshire Quarry, 236, 237
Chetwode, Lt.-Gen. Sir P., Bt., 205, 319
Chibnall, Lt. R. S., 91, 240, 241
Chinnery, L/Cpl. J., D.C.M., 42, 58
Chinney, Pte. H., 43
Chivres Ridge, 41
Chocques, 60, 199, 287
Christophers, Capt. R. B., 247
Church, Capt. S. W., 93, 122, 197
Churchill, Capt. H., 112

* He was the elder son of Lord Chalmers, both of whose sons were killed in the Great War.

Churchman, Capt. E. H., 338
Churchman, Lt.-Col. A. C. (Sir A. Churchman, Bt., M.P.), 335 *& n.*, 338 *n.*
Churchman, Lt.-Col. W. A., V.D., 332
Church work, 233
Cité St. Clie, 244
Cité St. Pierre, 295
Clapham Junction, Flanders, 228, 240
Clark, C.Q.M.S., 179
Clarke, Capt. F. L. Stanley, 339
Clarke, Lt.-Col. E. P., D.S.O., T.D., 46, 61, 143, 190, 332, 397, 398
Clarke, 2nd Lt. P. T., 316
Clark, 2nd Lt. S. E., 284
Clarke, 2nd Lt. W., 374
Clarke, Sgt., 363–4
Claughton, Lt. D., 96, 152
Claydon, Pte. W., 326
Clayton, Cornet John, 112
Clayton, Sgt. S., 40
Clee, Capt., C. B. B., 238, 241
Clemson, Capt. E., M.C., 161, 162, 164
Cléry-sur-Somme, 194
Clifford, Brig.-Gen. H. F. H., D.S.O., 41, 42, 49, 54, 58, 59, 64, 73, 82, 137, 185–6
Clifford, Sir Hugh, 186 *& n.*
Clutterbuck, Capt. W. E., 216
Cobb, Sgt. A., 74
Cobbold, Capt. C. A., 89, 131
Cobbold, Capt. C. J. F., 335
Cobbold, Lt. F. R. C., 93, 122, 125
Cobbold, Maj. P. W., 343
Cochrane Alley, 184, 185
Cockburn, Lt. G. P., 338
Cockburn, Capt. R., 46, 47, 62, 63
Cockell, 2nd Lt. B. W., 102
Cockerton, Pte., 176
Cockerton, 2nd Lt. C. H., 284
Cojeul River, 225, 264
  Valley, 194
Colchester Pageant, 1926, 307
Coldstream Guards, 122, 129
Coleman, Maj. W. F., 92
Coles, Capt. R. J., 299
Coles, Lt. A. E. M., M.C. & Bar, 400
*Coles, 2nd. Lt. R. J., 176
Coles, Lt.-Col. R. G., 386, 387
Coley, Lt. C., 289
Collett, Lt. H. S., 185
Collins, Col. H. A., V.D., 362, 365, 374
Collins, 2nd Lt. N. C., 179
Collinson, Maj. G. F., 340
Collis, 2nd Lt. B. H., 124
Collis, 2nd Lt. H. H., 233
Collyer, 2nd Lt. G. W., 196
Colthorpe, 2nd Lt. J. R., 198, 199
Coltman, 2nd Lt. H. E., 288
Colvin, Lt.-Col. R. B., 116, 117
Combles Valley, 197
Condren, 268
C.B., or the Christmas Bulletin of the Cyclist Battalion, 337
Congreve, Brevet.-Maj. W. La T., 137, 182, 183
Congreve, Lt.-Gen. Sir W. N., V.C., 123, 165, 182, 273
Connor, C.S.M. J., D.C.M., 282
Constantine, King of Greece, 156
Constantinople, 156
Contalmaison, 166, 178
Cook, Capt. F. W., M.C. & two Bars, D.C.M., 225, 291, 292, 400
Cook, Pte., 52
Cook, 2nd Lt. R. E., 281
Cooper, A., 116
Cooper, Brevet-Lt.-Col. F. S., D.S.O., 17, 51, 52, 181, 232, 233, 236, 326, 370, 371, 380, 386, 393, 395
Cooper, Lt. N. E., 292
Cooper, 2nd Lt. G. G., 246, 248
Cooper, Maj. E. R., 360
Cooper, 2nd Lt. R. H., 91
Cooper, 2nd Lt. W. P., 178
Copeman, Lt.-Col. H. C., D.S.O., C.M.G., 145, 189, 190, 192, 193, 194, 229, 231, 270, 271, 295, 396, 400
Corbie, 192, 198
Cornet Halte, 25
Cornish-Bowden, Maj. J. T., 39, 40
Cornwallis, Marquess, 111
Cornwell, Pte., 171
Corville, Pte. A., 141
Cory, 2nd Lt. C. W., 102, 104
Cotton, 2nd Lt. W. J. S., 228
Coulommiers, 39
Courage, Maj. H. F., 212
Courcelles, 187
Courcelles-le-Comte, 248, 288
Courcelette, 170
Courtney, 2nd Lt. A. J., 222, 289
Cousins, Rev. A. E., C.F., M.C., 181
Cowper, 2nd Lt. F. N., 180
Cowper, 2nd Lt. S. G., 186, 221
Cox, Lt. J. E., R.A.M.C., 85
Cox, Pte. G., M.M. (special), 401
Cox, 2nd Lt. D. W., 77
Cox, 2nd Lt. E. F., 178
Coxhead, Brig.-Gen. J. A., C.B., 362, 365
Coxwell, 2nd Lt. L. F., 235
Crack, C.S.M. W., M.S.M. (special), 400
Cragg, Pte. D., M.M., 144
Crandon, Capt. G. L., M.C. and Bar, 167, 238, 241, 274, 275, 277, 253, 400
Cranfield, Lt. H., 281, 341
Crawley, Lt. H. E., 116, 117
Creagh, Capt. H. T. P., M.C., 91, 149, 242, 299
Crépy-en-Valois, 37
Cretan Division, the, 308, 309

* Not killed (as stated on p. 176), but only wounded.

Crisp, Lt. J. F., 213
Crissall, R.S.M. J., D.C.M., 282
Crofton, Maj. G. H. S., 91, 341
Croisilles, 278
Croisilles-Bullecourt Sector, 258
Croisilles–Henin region, 166
Crois Barbée, 62, 142
Croix Marmuse, 63, 72
Croker, Maj.-Gen. H. L., 158, 304
Crook, 2nd Lt. H. W., 237
Crooke, Lt.-Col. C. D. Parry, 88, 89, 129, 323
Crosfield, Maj. G. R., 135, 137, 139
Crosher, 2nd Lt. H. G., 168
Cross, Maj. A. M., M.C., C. de G., 259, 283, 284, 356
Crossley, 2nd Lt. J. de B., 212
Crouy, 271
Crowther, 2nd Lt. N., 321
Crozat Canal, 269
Cruddas, Lt.-Col. H. W., 61, 62, 143
Cruickshank, Lt.-Col. F. H. G., 116
Crump, Capt. A. V., 255, 256
Cubitt, Capt. C. F., 375
Cubitt, Capt. F. S., M.C., 46, 294, 397, 400
Cuinchy, 48, 144, 146
Cunningham, Lt. J. M., 274
Curly Crescent trenches, 127, 132
Curragh, The, 18, 19, 21
Currey, Maj. V. F., 89, 130, 131, 323
Curtis, C.Q.M.S. W., 38
*Curtis, 2nd Lt. W., 176
Cutbill, Capt. A. M., 22, 31, 34, 35
Cuthbert, Brig.-Gen. C. J., C.B., 21
Cyprus, 17

D

DABAA, 216
Dabbs, 2nd Lt. J. C., 237
Dallimer, 2nd Lt. F., 227
Dalrymple-Hay, Brig.-Gen. J. M., C.B., D.S.O., 340
Daniels, A/Cpl. H. J., D.C.M., 80
Dansweiler, 391
Danvers, Rev. G. C., C.F., 219, 288
Danvers, 2nd Lt. R. W. F., 253
Daours, 92, 147
Dardanelles, the, 380
Darley, 2nd Lt., 175
Davall, 2nd Lt. C. G., 224, 267, 288
Davey, A/Cpl. G., M.M., 162
Davies, A/Lt.-Col. F. G., 92, 93, 133
Davies, Maj. H., M.C., 343
Davies, Pte. F., D.C.M., 90
Davis, 2nd Lt. J. D., 298
Davoren, Lt. V. A., 89, 131
Dawson, Brig.-Gen. Sir F. R. Douglas, G.C.V.O., K.C.B., &c., 365
Day, Cpl. S. J., V.C., 252, 355, 400
De Aar, 118
Dead Cow Farm, 60
Dealtry, Capt. C. M. E., M.C., 134, 136, 141
Dean, C.S.M. J. J., 178
Death, Pte., and his "Suffolk Death-trap," 59
de Castro, Capt. J. V. R., 84, 134
de Castro, 2nd Lt., 65
Deck, 2nd Lt. R. F., 133
de Crespigny, Capt. H. V. C. Champion, M.C., 42, 400
Deighton, Capt. G. W., M.C., 89, 131, 132, 178
Dier el Belah, 217
de Jongh, 2nd Lt. A. A., 89
de la Pryme, Lt.-Col. W. H. A., 123, 125
de Lisle, Lt.-Gen. Sir Beuvoir, K.C.B., K.C.M.G., D.S.O., 357
Delville Wood, 166, 167, 182, 183, 191
Demirhissar, 159
Dempsey, L/Cpl. J., D.C.M., 59
Denier, 188, 221, 245
Dennis, Capt. A., 102, 107
Dernancourt, 183, 192, 193, 275
de Saumarez, Lord, 387
Desert, the, 201
Desert Column, the, 205
Desert march, 203
Dessart Wood, 245, 247
Dettingen, Battle of, 43
Devas, Lt. B. W., 187
Deverell, Maj.-Gen. C. J., 188
Deversoir, 203
Devon Lane, 143
Dew, 2nd Lt. C. C., 245
Dewdrop Trench, 192
De Wet, General, 118
Dewetsdorp, 118
Dickebusch, 73, 80, 241, 301
Dikerin, 314
Dingley, 2nd Lt. K. M., 187
Dingley, 2nd Lt. W., 234
Distillery, the, 85
Ditton, 2nd Lt. G., 207
Dixey, 2nd Lt. E. H., 150, 178
Dixon's Gully, Gallipoli, 108
Diyala River, 286
Dockerill, Col.-Sgt. U., M.S.M., 331
Doiran, Lake, 156, 164, 305, 308, 310
Dolap, 304
Dollignies, 301
Domat, 270
Dominick, 2nd Lt. J. C., 91
Dooley, Maj. W., 46, 338
Dooley, 2nd Lt. W. J., 189
Doouss, 2nd Lt. F. J., M.C., 236, 301
Double, C.S.M., H. G., D.C.M., 59, 222
Double, C.Q.M.S., 102

* Not killed (as stated on p. 176), but only wounded.

Double Crassier, the, 199, 243
Douchy-les-Ayette, 228
Doué, 39
Doughty, Lt. George, 112
Doughty, Maj. E. C., D.S.O., 22, 24, 31, 34, 35, 36
Douglas, Lt. A. G., 196, 248
Doullens, 188, 192, 194, 223, 235
Dour, 25, 26
Douve, River, 42
Dowse, 2nd Lt. R. J. O., 323
Dowsett, R.S.M. E., M.M.D., M.S.M., 327, 331
Dowsing, W., 387
Dranoutre, 56, 81
Drummond, 2nd Lt. G. C., 234
Du Cane, Maj.-Gen., 285
Duck's Bill, the, 146
Duddy, 2nd Lt. G. L. A., 281
Dueidar Post, 204
Duisans, 221
Duke, Capt. H. N., 191
Duke of York's Own Loyal Suffolk Hussars, Yeomanry Cavalry, Officers of (1899), 116
Duleep Singh, Capt. Prince F. V., 116
Duncan, Maj.-Gen. F. J., 298, 354
Duncan, Maj.-Gen. J., C.B., C.M.G., C.V.O., D.S.O., 394
Duncannon, Capt. Viscount, 213
Dunn, A/Sgt. E. W., 43
Dunn, 2nd Lt. J., 259
Durham, 2nd Lt. J. C., 175
Durrands, Lt. W. B., M.C., 163, 303, 304
Durtnell, 2nd Lt. R. N., 251
Dyer, Lt.-Col. J. E. F., 146, 149

E

Eagle, 2nd Lt. G. C., 89, 180
Eardley-Wilmot, Lt.-Col. T., D.S.O., 98, 200, 283, 284
Earle, Capt. T., 212
Easterley, 2nd Lt. H. T., 294
Easy, Pte. T., M.M., 126
Eaton, 2nd Lt. C. T., 190
Ebblinghem, 230
Ecacheries, 396
Ecaillon, River, 298
Ecoust St. Mein, 289
Edgar, Cornet Mileson, 112
Edgehill Station, Flanders, 193
Edwards, L/Cpl. W. H., D.C.M., 298
Edwards, R., M.B.E., 329
Edwards, Rev. C. Pierrepont, C.F., 102, 164
Eecke, 134, 135, 230
Egypt, 15 *seq.*, 96, 110, 129, 155, 201 *seq.*, 317, 319
Egyptian Expeditionary Force, 205 *seq.*, 319
Eighteen, 2nd Lt., 49
El 'Arish, 204, 205
  Redoubt, 209, 210
El Burj, 205
Eley, Maj. D. R. A., D.S.O., 161, 163, 303, 304, 326, 398
El Ferdan, 216
Elias, Lt. F., Poem by, 337, 403
Elisan, 162, 303, 307
Eliza, the charger, 174
El Jib, 218
Elkington, B. W., 329
Elkington, 2nd Lt. T. G., 139–40
El Kubri, 216
Elliston, Capt. W., 335
El Mirr, 313
Elouges, 26
El Shatt, 216
Et Tireh, 312
Elverdinghe, 253
Elvey, 2nd Lt., C. L., 233
Emeny, 2nd Lt. F. C., 268
Emmerson, 2nd Lt., 316
Emrys-Evans, Lt. P. V., 96, 153, 175
England, Capt. R., M.C., 93, 122, 126, 248, 284
Enquin-les-Mines, 187
Enraght, Lt. E. H., 272
Ensor, Capt. L., M.C., 93, 197; gallant rescue by, 195–6
Epehy, Battle of, 295
Erquinghem, 151, 177, 298
Ervillers, 259
Es Safre, 318
Escarmain, 292
Esdud, 211
Estaires, 42, 86, 168, 243, 272, 298
Estrée Blanche, 133
Etinehem, 149
Evans, Lt. S. N., 337, 338
Evans, 2nd Lt. A. L., 183
Evans, 2nd Lt. B. S., 229
Everard, Sgt. A., M.M., 145
Everett, Lt. H. F., R.A.M.C., (T.F.), 102, 104
Eversden, 2nd Lt. R. E., 213
Everson, Sgt. A. G., M.M., 193
Everitt, Cpl., M.M. & Bar, 179
Ewing, 2nd Lt. H. E., 298

F

Facer, L/Cpl. W., M.M., 126
Fache, Maj. G. L. M., M.C. & Bar, 91, 149, 167, 241, 242, 243, 277
Fair, Capt. A., M.C., 316, 350
Falkner, Lt. H. E., 196, 248

Fallowes, Lt. J. T. C., 93, 197
Famechon, 223, 239
Farquhar, Lt.-Col. W. A., 151, 153, 175
Farren, 2nd Lt. J., 187
Faulconer-Wright, Capt. E. H., 394
Fauquissart, 42
Favières, 37, 39
Fayers, L/Cpl. S., 35
Feetham, Brig.-Gen. E., 244
Fère-en-Tardenois, 41
Ferfay, 287
Fergusson, Maj.-Gen. Sir C., Bt., C.B., M.V.O., D.S.O., 21, 23, 35, 53, 54, 59, 81, 177
Festubert, 132
Feuchy Chapel Redoubt, 233
Road, 233
Ffrench, 2nd Lt. D. M., 46
Ficheux–Mercatel Road, 225
Fiddian, 2nd Lt. W. M., 97, 174
Field, 2nd Lt. C. C., 141
Finlay, Maj. F. D., 98
Fir Lane, 84
Fish, 2nd Lt. J. L., 178
Fisher, 2nd Lt. G. W., 231
Fisher, 2nd Lt. R., 230
Fison, Capt. J. F. L., M.C., 70, 145, 191, 338
Fison, Lt. F. G. C., 146
Fison, 2nd Lt. R. C., 206
Fitch, Capt. W. F., M.C., 198, 244, 248, 254
Fitton, Brig.-Gen. H. G., 95, 151
Fitzclarence Farm, 229
Fitzgerald, Lt.-Col., 365
Fitzherbert, 2nd Lt. G. C., 107, 339
Flack, Pte. W., 24
Flanders Mud, 52, 57, 58, 187, 193, 200
Flers, 179
Flers-Courcelette, Battle of, 185, 196 *seq.*
Flesquières, 246, 290, 291
Fletcher, Cpl., 240
Flêtre, 72
Fleurbaix, 152, 237, 280, 285–6
Flint, 2nd Lt. E. C. M., 212, 213
Floringhem, 132
Foch, Marshal, 41; tribute paid by, to the Men of East Anglia, 349
Fontaine l'Etalon, 235
Fookes, R.S.M., 277
Forbes, Lt. D. K., 17, 50, 53, 54
Forceville, 168, 169, 170
Ford, Maj. S. W., 91, 166
Forsdike, Capt. J., 375
Fort Rompu, 152, 280, 286
Fortuin, 67
Forward Cottage Trenches, Ypres Salient, 123, 125, 126
Fosse, 142
Fosse 8 (Loos), 126, 128
Fosse 9 (Loos), 121
Fosseux, 233, 234
Foster, 2nd Lt. J. C., 97, 281
Foulsham, Lt. E. C., 127, 128
Foulsham, 2nd Lt. C. S., 168
Fouquereuil, 129, 133
Fournes, 321
Fowke, Lt. William, 112
Fox, Capt, L. B., M.C., 107, 207, 210, 315
Francis, Pte. R. C., D.C.M., 44, 58, 325
Francis, 2nd Lt. F. W., 185, 221
Franklin, 2nd Lt. G. F., 284
Franks, 2nd Lt. H. C., 267, 268
Franvillers, 133, 149
Fraser, Rev. D., C.F., 91
Fraser, Rev. J. B., C.F., D.S.O., 167
Fraser, Capt. G., M.C. (attd. A.O.D.), 400
Fraser, 2nd Lt. E. G., 42
Freeman, Spt. A. W., M.M., 313
Fremicourt, 223, 290
French, Capt. D. M., 295
French, Gen. Sir John, *see* Ypres, F.M. the Earl of
French, R.S.M., J. J., D.C.M., 207, 350
French Report on the gallantry of Pte. W. Waterson, 2nd Batt., 184–5
French, 2nd Lt. A. C., 179
Frere, Capt. J. G., D.S.O., M.C., 46, 60, 146, 386, 387, 400
Regimental Songs by, 402–3
Frévillers, 244
Frezenberg Ridge, the, 66, 68, 84
Battle of, 76 *seq.*
Fricker, 2nd Lt. L., 289
Fricourt, 146
Ridge, 153
Wood, 190, 191
Frid, Gen., 393
Frost, 2nd Lt. G. T., 89, 190
Frost, 2nd Lt. H. G., 93, 125
Frost, 2nd Lt. R. W., 178
Fryer, Maj. C. R., 18
Fryett, 2nd Lt. J., 257, 258
Fudge, 2nd Lt. A., 196
Fuller, Pte. R., D.C.M., 43, 58
Fuller, Signaller, 141
Furniss, Lt. L. H., 242
Fyson, Capt. C. M., 210, 350

G

GABY Glide Trench, 135
Gadd, Brevet-Maj. H. R., D.S.O., M.C., 89, 331, 391, 392
Gainsford, Lt. H. E., 179
Gallipoli, 15, 96, 102, 152, 156, 201, 213 *seq.*, 249, 310, 314, 317
Town, 380
Game, R.S.M., 95
Ganzoni, 2nd Lt. F. J. C. (Sir John Ganzoni, M.P.), 46, 60, 397

Gardham, 2nd Lt. H. P., 139, 141, 182, 185, 268
Gardiner, 2nd Lt. G. D., 196
Gardner, Lt. C. G., 197, 265
Garnett, 2nd Lt. J. E., 201
Garnett's Wood, 313
Garrett, Capt. S., 46, 62
Garrett, Lt.-Col. F., 46, 47, 61
Garrod, Sgt., 267
Garvey, 2nd Lt., 49
Gaston, Capt. J., R.A.M.C., M.C., 227, 296
Gates, 2nd Lt. C. A., D.C.M., 34, 59, 73
Gates, 2nd Lt. D. L., 127, 128
Gauntlett, Lt.-Col., V.C., 330–1
Gaudiempré, 192
Gavrelle Sector, 251
Gaza, Battles of, 205 *seq.*, 211, 217, 312
Gaza–Beersheba Line, 299
Gazelle Heights, 203
Gedge, Lt. P., 89, 131
Geese and gunnery, 109
Gendall, Rev. C. F., C.F., 146
Geneife, 201, 202
George II, 43
George III, 111
George V, H.M. the King, 22, 23, 42, 43, 47, 93, 101, 114, 115, 122, 213, 287, 294, 326, 327, 328, 344, 373, 389, 396
George, Lt. T. L., 22, 34, 35
George Street, near Delville Wood, 191
Gibbs, Capt. W., 212
Gibbs, 2nd Lt. C. C. S., 194
Gibbs, 2nd Lt. R. C., 265
Gibraltar, 157, 214
  Siege of, 36
  Two Batts. meeting at, 386, 393
Gilban, 204
Gilbert, Lt. G. A. B., 288
Gilson, Lt. R. Q., 96, 173, 174
Ginchy, 166, 197
Ginn, 2nd Lt. D. B., 213
Girbow, Pte. R. G., 43
Girdwood, Maj.-Gen. E. S., 216, 319
Givenchy, 42, 48, 132
  Sector, 146
Glanfield, Lt. B. St. J., 46, 192
Gleichen, Maj.-Gen. Lord (Edward), formerly Count Gleichen, K.C.V.O., C.M.G., D.S.O., 21
Glen, 2nd Lt. D., 227
Glencorse Wood, 229, 240
Gnoina Ridge. 157
Goat, Maj. A., 333
Goatcher, 2nd Lt. F., 170, 190
Godbolt, Lt. B., 51, 64, 68, 78, 153
Goddard, Pte. S. G., 24
Goddard, Pte. W. J., M.S.M. (special), 400
Godewaersvelde, 168, 223, 230
Godley, Lt.-Gen. Sir A. J., 215, 294
Goldsmith, Lt. H. C., M.C., 210
Goldsmith, Maj. F., 212, 213
Gomme, Capt. E. E. C., 222
Gommecourt, 192, 288
Gonneheim, 90
Gonnelieu, 247, 257, 357
Gooch, 2nd Lt. R. E., 284
Goodall, 2nd Lt. G. A. C., 190
Goody, R.S.M., A., D.C.M., M.S.M., 256, 284, 286
Goody, R.S.M., W., M.C., 276, 277
Gordon, Lt. N. M., M.C., 400
Gore, Brig.-Gen. R. C., 152, 281
Gorre, 42, 146
Goshawk, Cpl. W., M.M., 244
Goss, Capt. F. O. H., R.A.M.C., M.C. & Bar, 286
Gough, Gen. Sir H., G.C.B., G.C.M.G., 239, 253, 261
Gough, Lt. G. H., 299
Gouzeaucourt, 235, 247, 256
Gouzeaucourt–Holnon Front, 320
Gouy-en-Artois, 233
Graham, Brevet-Col. F., 91, 92
Graham, Col. V. W. H., 97
Graham, Lord Douglas Malise, A.D.C., 31
Grammont, 358
Granby, Capt. the Marquis of, 365
Grand, 2nd Lt. H. S., 177, 251
Grandéglise, 396
Grantham, Brevet-Col. C. F., 343, 344
Gravelines, 152
Gravenstafel, 65–6
Graves of the slain in Palestine and Syria, Inspection of, 350
Gray, Rev. Dr., 352
Gray, 2nd Lt. W. L., 291
"Great-hearted men," 403
Greece, 156, 158, 159
Grenadier Guards, 195
Green, Capt. A., 235, 273
Green, C.S.M., S. C., M.C., 400
Green Line, the, 239, 251
Green, Lt. D., M.C., 315, 400
Greene, Capt. E. A., 212, 213
Greene, Capt. E. J., M.C. & Bar, 238, 400
Greene, Capt. W. R., 116, 117
Greenwood, Lt.-Col. C. F. H., D.S.O., 338, 339
Greig, 2nd Lt. D. M., 84, 85, 136
Grenay, 120
Grierson, Lt.-Gen. Sir J., 22, 23
Griffiths, 2nd Lt. A. I., 257
Grimble, 2nd Lt. H., 169
Grimwade, 2nd Lt. E. L., 187
Grissell, Lt.-Col. T. De la G., M.C., 212, 213, 320, 400
Grose-Hodge, 2nd Lt., 65, 69
Grosville, 227
Grouches, 188
Grove Farm, 213
Grovetown Camp, 149

Guarbecque, 281
Guémappes, 227
  Attack on, 220
Guémappes–Noreuil Line, 282
Guendecourt, 179, 187, 197
  Attack near, 101
  Wood, 180
Guillemont, 166
Guinness, Lt. A. H., 93, 124, 195
Guinness, Maj. Hon. W. E., 117, 212, 213
Gurrey, Capt. P., 234
Guvezne, 158, 310
Gymnich, 391

H

Habershon, 2nd Lt. S. H., 248, 286
Habieta, 202, 203
Hackett, Capt. B., R.A.M.C., 89, 130
Haddock, Lt. W. T., 107, 201
Hague Convention, the, 69
Haifa, 317
Haig, F.M. Earl, 18, 22, 120, 124, 125, 140, 146, 151, 166, 170, 197, 202, 230, 236, 246, 258, 260, 269, 282, 286, 288, 339, 357
Haine, 24
Haine, River, 25
Hairpin Trenches, Loos, 130, 131, 132
Haking, Lt.-Gen. Sir R. C. B., 94
Haldane, Lt.-Gen. Sir J. A. L., G.C.M.G., K.C.B., D.S.O., 58, 136–7, 179, 188, 223, 388
Hale, 2nd Lt. W. S., 187
Hales, Pte. C., D.C.M., 124
Half-way House, near Jerusalem, 211
Hall, Capt. A. C., 89
Hall, Cpl. P., M.M. & Bar, 296
Hall, Lt. W. R., M.C., 252, 279
Hall, Maj. T. B., 248
Hall, 2nd Lt. F. E. C., 185
Hall, 2nd Lt. N. de H., 162
Halloy, 233, 298
Halloy–Pernois District, 188
Hallsmith, 2nd Lt. G., D.S.O., 257, 258, 259, 285
Hamblin, Lt. J. E., 254
Hamelincourt, 251, 258, 279, 282
Ham, 37
Ham-en-Artois, 94, 123, 172, 243
Hamet Billet, 281
Hamill, 2nd Lt. G. E., 250
Hamilton, 2nd Lt. H. F. P., 237
Hamilton, Gen. Sir Ian, 17, 103, 104
Hamlyn, 2nd Lt. W. H., 183
Hammond, Lt. G. E., 125, 344
Hammonds, 2nd Lt. E. H., 259
Hamp, 2nd Lt. W., 189
Hancock, 2nd Lt. P. H., 292
Handy, L/Cpl. A. C., M.M., 199
Hangard Wood, 270
Hannaford, 2nd Lt., 169
Hannan, 2nd Lt. G. G., 24
Hannant, 2nd Lt. E. G., 233
Hannay, Capt. H., M.C., 400
Hanun, 24, 25
Happy Valley, 185
Harber, C.S.M., 221
Harding, Lt. J. W., 292
Harding, 2nd Lt. E. J., 189
Hardy, 2nd Lt. V. I., 125
Hare, Maj.-Gen. S. W., 34, 204, 316
Hargicourt, 251
Hargrave, Lt.-Col. H. J., 102, 332–3
Harmer, Lt. J. N., 197, 251
Harp, the, 219, 220, 221
Harper, Lt. D. W., 97
Harrington, Pte. G., M.M., 162
Harris, Capt. A. J. A., 236
Harris, Capt. P. C., 51, 54, 55, 323
Harris, Col. J. E., 55
Harris, Col. Rt. Hon. Lord, 117, 362
Harris, 2nd Lt. C. A., 193
Harrison, Capt. W. E., M.C., 250, 278, 281, 282
Harrison, 2nd Lt. A., M.C., 265, 344
Hartley, 2nd Lt. G. P., 272
Hartopp, 2nd Lt. C. W. L., 131
Hartopp, 2nd Lt. R. L., 133
Harvey, Cpl. F., D.C.M., 107
Harvey, 2nd Lt. G. W., 281
Harvey, 2nd Lt. R. G. C., 27
Harwood, Pte., 387, 388
Hattam, Lt. H. C., 230
Hattersley, Lt. G. R., 174, 250
Haudricourt, 352, 353, 401
Hausburg, Capt. E. F., 42, 323
Haughton, Capt. J. W., 237
Hauteville, 188
Haverskerque–Amusoires Sector, 320
Hawkins, 2nd Lt. T., 237
Hayne, Lt. H. L., M.C., 248, 400
Haynes, 2nd Lt. F. G., 106
Haynes, 2nd Lt. W. G., 228
Hayward, Lt. R. A., 295–6
Hazebrouck, 51, 134, 150, 157
Haznatar and Alipsa, 304
Head, Lt. J. A., 91
Head, 2nd Lt. G. M. T., M.C., 246, 248
Hearne, Capt. J. S., 89, 180, 277, 331
Hearne, Pte. M., D.C.M., 286
Hébuterne, 192
Hedges, Capt. F. R., 93, 122
Heigham, Capt. C., 89, 90, 179
Heigham, Maj. M. F., 93, 122, 197, 199
Heligoland Redoubt, 173
Henderson, Lt. J. J., 321
Henencourt Château, 271
  Wood, 175
Henincourt, 133
Henen hill, 279

Henty, Maj. G. H., 131, 178, 234, 237
Hepworth, Capt. L. F., 22, 24
Herbie, 210
Herinnes, 357
Heriot-Maitland, Brig.-Gen. J. D., D.S.O., 192, 231
Hervey, Col. C. R. W., 329
Herziele, 78, 80, 243
Hester, Sgt. F., 134
Heudicourt, 237
Hewlett, 2nd Lt H. C., 234
Heycock, Col. C. T., V.D., 95
Hickie, Brig.-Gen. W. B., 91
Higgins, Lt. W. B., 185
Higginson, Brig.-Gen. H. W., 239
Highwood, 183, 185, 186, 190
High Wood, 183, 185, 186, 190
Hignett, 2nd Lt. E., 193
Hill, Lt.-Col. H. T. Coppinger, M.C., 106, 207, 211, 311, 313
Hill, Lt.-Col. G. V. W., D.S.O. & Two Bars, 149, 237, 238, 241, 243, 276, 277, 353, 392, 400
Hill, 2nd Lt. S. R., 236
Hill 60, 52, 65, 72, 73
Hill 60 in Gallipoli, 106, 107, 108, 215
Hill K.12, 319
Hill 2450, 318
Hills, 2nd Lt. C., M.C., 289
Hills, Sgt. C., D.C.M., M.M., Commission in the Field, 355
Himpson, Drummer, M.M., 168
Hindenburg Line, 172, 198, 200, 220, 226 *seq.*, 236, 245, 247, 251, 255, 256, 258, 279, 291
  Trench, 169
  Tunnel, 226, 291
Hines, Drummer, M.M., 168
Hinges, 60, 266, 267, 287
Hingette, 60
Hinnell, 2nd Lt. P. S., 102, 104
Hitchen, Pte. J., M.M., C. de G., 356
Hitchcock, 2nd Lt. C. H., 285
Hobson, 2nd Lt. H. A., 276
Hodges, 2nd Lieut. J., 320
Hodgson, Brig.-Gen. H. W., 212, 216
Hodgson, 2nd Lt., 237
Hodgson, 2nd Lt. P. K., 212
Hogg, 2nd Lt. R., 320
Hoggan, Capt., 65, 69, 78
Hohenzollern Redoubt, 126, 127, 128, 142
Hoile, 2nd Lt. W. H., 197
Hollandscheschur Farm, 59
Hollinrake, 2nd Lt. J. C., 128
Hollond, Lt. C. E., 343
Holloway, 2nd Lt. A., 268
Honours gained by the Suffolk Regt. in the Great War with the addition of some not mentioned in the text, 400
Hong Kong, 394
Hood, Lt. T., 178, 180
Hooge, 74, 82 *seq.*, 126
Hook Trench, 222
Hooper, Capt. H. R., M.C., 398
Hooper, 2nd Lt., 65
Hopkins, Lt. G., 197, 246, 248, 284
Hornby, 2nd Lt. G. P., 65, 77
Horne, Capt. G. B., M.C., 213, 320, 400
Horne, Gen. the Lord, G.C.B., K.C.M.G., 381, 396
Horton, Lt. H. F., M.C., 400
Horton, 2nd Lt. C. A. E., 107, 233
Houdain, 26
Houle, 137
Houlton, Capt. J. W., 65, 80, 303
Houplines Sector, 280
Houthulst Forest, 242, 243
Houtkerque, 126
Howell, Lt. A. H. L., 244
Howell, 2nd Lt. H. R., 233
Howes, Pte. W., M.M., 221
Howitzer Wood, 193
Howman, A/C.S.M., E., 65
Hoyland, Lt. H., 67
Hubbard, 2nd Lt. A., 172
Hudson, Lt. P., 100
Hughes, Lt. G., D.C.M., 315, 316
Hughes, Maj. Sir C., Bt., 370, 374
Hughes, 2nd Lt., 65
Hughes, 2nd Lt. R. P., 259
Hull, Capt. W. C., M.C., 238, 274, 277
Hulluch, 121, 198
  Road, 127
Hulluch–Givenchy Sector, 132
Hulluch–Lens Road, 121
Hume, Pte. W., 108
Hume, Capt. T., 179, 387, 390
Hume, Lt. R. D., M.C., 65, 69, 72, 145, 178, 191, 230
Hunt, Capt. E. D. C., M.C. & Bar, 17, 49, 50, 128, 393, 400
Hunt, C.S.M., 102, 106
Hunt, Pte. J. T., D.C.M., 259
Hunt, 2nd Lt. J. W. R., 251
Hurle, Sgt. R. F., M.S.M., 248
Hurrell, R.S.M., C. H., 92, 93, 125
Hutcherson, 2nd Lt. H. B., M.C., 269, 271
Hutchinson, Maj. E. F., *see* Hausburg

I

IDRIS Mah, 162
Igglesden, 2nd Lt. G. F., 183
Ilot, sector, 92
Imbros, 103, 214
Ince, Sgt. A., Mil. Med., 305
Infantry Hill, 222, 223, 267
Inglefield, Maj.-Gen. F. S., 103
Ingouville-Williams, Maj.-Gen., 95, 165, 175

Inskip, 2nd Lt. S. P., 79, 140
In Seirat, 205, 206, 207
" In Suffolk," poem by Lt. F. Elias, 337, 403
Intermediate Trench, 175, 176
Ipswich Crater, 145
Ireland, 392
Iremonger, Maj. E. A., 91
Isaacs, 2nd Lt. H. R., 233
Isham, Capt. J. A. R., M.C., 89, 179, 180, 181
Ismailia, 202, 203
Ives, C.S.M. S., M.M., 189

J

JACKSON, Capt. A. H. M., 98, 256
Jackson, Capt. R. M., 102
Jackson, Maj. E. A., 323, 325
Jackson, 2nd Lt., 65
Jackson, 2nd Lt. C. B. A., 213
Jackson, Sgt. A., M.M., 221
Jacob, F.M. Sir C. W., G.C.B., K.C.S.I., K.C.M.G., 170, 239, 398
James, Capt. A. L., 89, 179
James, 2nd Lt. H. P., 22
James, Maj., 97
Japanese Generals, Inspection by, 96
Jarvis, Lt.-Col. F. W., D.S.O., 116, 117, 212, 213, 400
Jeffery, Lt. A. S., 172
Jeffrey, Sgt. H. E., C. de G., 300
Jenkin, 2nd Lt. C. O. F., 97, 175
Jenks, 2nd Lt. H. W., 340
Jermynn, Sgt. W., awarded Italian Bronze Medal for gallantry, 194
Jerusalem, 218, 311, 316
  Allenby's entry into, 211
  Surrender of, 218
Jeudwine, Lt.-Gen. Sir H., K.C.B., K.B.E., 398
Jewitt, 2nd Lt. R. J. C., 201
Joffre, Marshal, 151
Johnson, Capt. A. A., M.C., 187, 293, 381
Johnson, C.S.M., M.S.M., 353
Johnson, Lt. D. B., M.C., 282
Johnson, Maj. H. H., 333
Johnson, 2nd Lt. A., 286
Johnson, 2nd Lt. O. B. G., 250
Johnson, 2nd Lt. R. A., 182
Johnson, 2nd Lt. S., 183
Joicey, Lt.-Col. Hon. H. E., 129, 155, 304, 306, 380
Jolly, 2nd Lt. L. B., 65, 79
Jones, C.S.M. J. H., M.M., D.C.M., 259
Jones, Drummer L., 38
Jones, Pte. L., D.C.M., 59
Jones, Rev. E., C.F., 237
Jones, 2nd Lt. H. A., 198
Jones, Sgt. H. G., M.M. & Bar, 223
Joscelyne, 2nd Lt. C. P., 253
Joseph Trench, 169
Josselyn, Lt.-Col. J., D.S.O., 400
Joubert, Gen., 42
Jourdain, Capt. E. N., 17, 50, 53, 54, 55
Joyce, 2nd Lt. E. G., 193
Jubbulpore, 381

K

KAIAJIK Aghala, 106
Kamberli, 305
Karajakoi Bala, 160
  Zir, 160
Karakol Dagh, 103, 105
Katia Oasis, 204
Katoomba Post, 202
Kavak Tepe, 103
Kay, Lt.-Col. R. C., 342
Kean, Capt., 277
Keary, Maj.-Gen. H. D'O., 60, 86
Keats, 2nd Lt. F. T., 91, 148 *seq.*
Keats, Capt. J. R., 91, 146, 168, 172
Keats' Redan, 148
Keefer, Lt. P. W., 309
Keen, 2nd Lt. B. A., 102
Keen, 2nd Lt. M. H., 128
Kefr Kassim, 316
Keightley, 2nd Lt. G. S., 281
Keir, Lt.-Gen. Sir J., 123
Kell, Lt. W. F. S., 208
Kelley, 2nd Lt. E. C., 178
Kelly, Maj.-Gen. F. H., C.B., 332
Kelsey, 2nd Lt. S., 124
Kemble, Lt. H. N., 183
Kemble, 2nd Lt. A. F., 78, 84
Kemmel and Area, 55, 81, 142
Kemmel Ridge, Battles of, 281
Kemmel–Ypres Road, 43
Kemp, Col. Sir Kenneth, Bt., 344
Kendle, Maj. R. H., T.W., 102, 104
Kendle, 2nd Lt. E. J., 102, 106
Kendrick, Lt.-Col. E. H., D.S.O., 177, 249, 250, 254, 355
Kenny, 2nd Lt. L. H., 156
Kendrick, Brig-Gen. R. J., 184, 186
Kenyon-Stow, Rev. L. D., 116
Kerrison, Lt. R. O., 116, 117
Khan Yunus, 205
Khartoum, 16, 17, 18, 41, 49
Khirba, 204
Khurbet Kesfa, 315
Kiazim Pasha, 109
Kilner, Capt. G., 102, 107, 316
Kilner, 2nd Lt. T. U., 162
Kincard-Smith, 2nd Lt., 65
Kinder, Capt. T. H., 89, 178
King, 2nd Lt. E. F., 323

King, 2nd Lt. G., 199
King, 2nd Lt. R. W., 274
King George's Road, 61
King Street, near Ypres, 139
Kiretch Tepe Sirt, 105
Kitchener of Khartoum, F.-M. Earl, 81, 88, 93, 118, 362, 364
Klinderbelk, 286
Kluck, General von, 393
Knight, Capt. C., M.C., 238
Knight, C.Q.M.S., 179
Knights, L/Cpl. A. J., D.C.M., 168
Knights, Sgt. J., M.M., Méd. Mil., 304, 305
Knowles, 2nd Lt. L. H., M.C., 256, 259, 284
Knox, Capt., 24
Knox, Capt. R. U. E., 91, 166
Kodzagoria Wood, 308, 309
Kopriva, 304
Kortabeele Farm, 253
Kortepyp Camp, 230
Kottakkal, 384
Kovno, 81
Kressenstein, Gen. Kress von, 210
Kruisstraat, 54, 73, 85
Kubeibeh, 211, 318
Kuchik Anafarta Ova, 103
Kumli, 163, 303, 307
Kuprï, 303
Kustendil, 310

L

La Bassée, 47, 48, 165, 266
  Canal, 120, 266
  Road, 144
  Sector, 198
La Beuvrière, 199
La Boisselle, 92, 147, 153, 172, 173, 175, 178
Labourse, 91, 198
La Breuviette, 200
La Brique, 71
Lacey, Sgt. C., D.C.M., 259
Lack, Capt. J. W., 91, 168
La Clytte, 51, 59, 73, 142
  Two Batts. meeting at, 58
Lacouture, 42, 60, 62
Ladell, Lt. E. E., 235, 350
La Folie, 298
La Fortelle, 268
La Gorgue, 86, 347
La Houssoye, 153
Lake, Capt., 229, 230
Lake, Cornet Francis G. Y., 112
Lake, Maj. E. L. D., 390
Lala Baba, 105
La Limon, 40
La Longueville, 293, 391, 401
Lambres, 47
Lambton, Capt. Hon. G., 374
Lancashire Reserve Trenches, Loos, 127, 129
Landguard, 111
Landon, Maj.-Gen. H. J. S., 144
Landrécies, 22
Langemarch, 68, 259
Langman, Maj. H. C., 333
La Panne, 228
La Pannerie, 267
Larkins, 2nd Lt. R. T., 179
La Rolanderie Farm, 280
Larwood, Cpl. A. W., D.C.M., 259
Last, Sgt., M.M., 244
La Targette, 292
Lateau Wood, 235, 236
Latham, Lt.-Col. F., D.S.O., 198, 245, 248
La Tourelle, 85
Latron, 218
Lattre, 321
Lattre St. Quentin, 181, 221
La Vacquerie, 255, 357
Law, Capt. H. F., 93, 122
Law, 2nd Lt. C. L. Q., 134
Lawes, 2nd Lt. T. E., 222
Laws, Sgt. W., 35
Lawler, Lt. R. J. A., 238
Lawrence, Lt.-Col., 102, 106–7, 201, 203
Lawson, Col. Hon. W., 118
Layard, Lt. P. C., 288
Layer Stream, 63
Leach, 2nd Lt. J. R., 224
Leach, Capt. R. W., 17, 51, 52
Leader, Pte., M.M., 168
Leader, 2nd Lt. S. B., 233
Lebeau, M. Sylvère, 393
Lebucquière, 248
Le Carrier, 41
Le Cateau, 22, 26, 27, 324
  Battles of, 23, 31 *seq.*, 73, 313, 326, 329
    Foreword on, by Lt.-Gen. Sir H. Smith-Dorrien, 28
  War Memorial at, 393
Le Cateau–Cambrai Road, 33
Le Cauroy Area, 235, 254
Le Cornet Bourdois, 94
Le Cornet Malo, 81
Le Cheminant, 2nd Lt. C., 235
Ledward, Capt. E. F., 146, 233
Ledward, Capt. G. W., 102, 104
Lee, L/Cpl., 271
Lee, Lt. J. V., M.C., 247, 248
Lee, Maj.-Gen. R. R., 171
Lee, 2nd Lt. H. V., 163, 164
Lee, 2nd Lt. R., 131
Leeman, 2nd Lt. F. W., 258
Leembruggen, Lt., R.A.M.C., 266
Leeming, Capt. H., M.C., 256, 301, 302
Lees, Capt. F. C., R.A.M.C., 248
Lees, Lt.-Col. R. L., D.S.O., T.D., 343
Le Feuvre, Capt. F., 340

Leggett, L/Cpl. W. Z., M.M. & Bar, 296
Leigh, 2nd Lt. S. P., 107
Leighton, 2nd Lt. S. E., 289
Leinster Regt., 384 *& n*
Leith-Hay-Clark, Maj. N., 17, 51, 180–1, 254, 387
Lembet, 156, 157
Lens Area, 199, 244
Le Préol, 198
Le Quesnoy, 132
Le Sart, 297
Les Bœufs, 192, 196, 197
Les Brebis, 200, 244, 266
Les Celestins Wood, 182
Les Choquaux, 132
Les Fosses Farm, 220
Lestrem, 61, 63, 268
Le Touret, 60
Levita, Maj. H. P., 116
Lewin, Lt. G. F. A., 233
Lewin, 2nd Lt. H. J., 221
Lewis, 2nd Lt. G. S., 298
l'Homme Mort, 282
Lightbody, 2nd Lt. G. K., 80
Likeman, Lt.-Col. J. L., 223, 225, 262, 387
Likovan, 158
Lille, 24, 321
  Canal, 321
Lillers, 48, 132, 199, 245, 272
Lindenhoek, 55, 142
Lindsay, Maj. J. H., 237
Ling, Capt. H. F., 46, 191
Ling, 2nd Lt. G. A., 234
Lingley, Sgt. E. H., D.C.M., 400
Little Bitter Lake, Egypt, 202, 203
"Little Willie" Trench, 126, 127, 128
Liverpool Street Station, War Memorial at, to Men of East Anglia, 349
Llarena, 2nd Lt. E. F., 82
Llewellyn, Bvt.-Maj., 331
Llewellyn, 2nd Lt. W. L., 42
Lloyd, Brig-Gen. S. E. Massy, C.B.E., 323, 325, 327, 389, 390, 400
Lloyd, Lt.-Col. L., D.S.O., & Two Bars, 97, 259, 284, 285, 286, 301, 302, 340, 400
Lloyd, 2nd Lt. G. T., 281
Lloyd, 2nd Lt. J. S. D., 49, 51, 69
Locke, 2nd Lt. R. S., 139
Locket, 2nd Lt. G. E., 79, 80
Locre, 42, 81
Locre-Scherpenberg Road, 42
Lodge, Pte. J., M.M., 225
Logan, Capt. C. R., 89, 178
London, the Lord Mayor of, Tribute paid by, to the Men of East Anglia, 349
  Peace Procession, 1919, Colours of 5th Batt. carried in, 351, 387
Long, Lt.-Col. G. H., 333
Long, Maj. A. de L., 221
Long, 2nd Lt. G. S., 169
Long, Sgt. H., M.M., 162
Longley, Lt.-Col., 24
Longpré, 193
Long Trench, 222
Longueau, 269
Longueval, 166, 167, 182, 183
  Ridge, 183
Long Valley, 174
Lonsdale, Col. the Earl of, 117
Lonsdale, 2nd Lt. H., 142
Loos, Battle of, 81, 91, 120 *seq.*, 133, 142 *seq.*, 149, 326
  Sector, 185, 198, 200
Louvencourt, 195
Lovell, Sgt. J. F., 256
Lowry-Corry, Col. Hon. H. W., D.L., 329
Lowther, Lt. A. J. B., 64, 73
Luard, Maj -Gen. C. C., C.B., C.M.G., 394
Lucas, Lt.-Col. A. G., 114, 116, 117
Lucheux, 257
Lucienne of Armentières, 349
Ludd, 211, 311, 314, 319
Lummis, A/Capt. W. M., M.C., 140, 288, 290,[291
Lushington, Lt.-Col. E. C. M., 92
Lygon, Lt. Hon. H., 212
Lynn, Sgt. F., D.C.M., 59, 182
Lyons, Maj. J. G., 307
Lys River, 249, 286, 296
  Battles of the, 266, 280, 281, 301, 351

M

Maadan, 204
Macandrew, Brig.-Gen. H. J., 147, 149
McCracken, Maj.-Gen. F. W. N., 144
McCrae, Lt.-Col. Sir G., 174
McDonagh, 2nd Lt. P., 42
Madonald, Lt. D. K., 195, 196
Macedonia, 15
Macey, R.S.M., C. W., D.C.M., 256
McGain, 2nd Lt. A. W., 97, 172
McGough, C.S.M. A., D.C.M., 58, 82
Mack, Capt. I. A., 96, 174
Mack, Lt.-Col. A. P., 93, 125, 195, 196, 197
McKelvie, 2nd Lt. A. C., 213
Mackenzie, Maj.-Gen. C. J., 281
Mackinnon, Lt. N. A., 316
McLean, 2nd Lt. A. A., 174
McMahon, Sgt. J., D.C.M., 257
McNicol, Capt. J. H., R.A.M.C., M.C., 51, 64, 68–9, 78, 80, 159
Macpherson, Mr., Deputy Sec. of State for War, 371
Madeleine Redoubt, 225
Madras, 381
Mafeking, 118
Mahalesi, 162

Mailly-Maillet Wood, 195
Maison Rouge, 232
Major, Capt. A. W. C., M.C. & Bar, 224, 265, 400
Malabar Field Force, 382 *seq.*
Malakoff Farm, 251, 252
Malappuram, 384, 385
Maltby, 2nd Lt. C. T., 274
Maltby, 2nd Lt. P., 274
Maltz Horn Farm, 184
Mametz, 92, 189
  Wood, 166, 175, 176, 190
Mann, C.Q.M.S. H. E., M.M., D.C.M., 300, 381
Mann, Pte. J. W., D.C.M., 124
Mann, 2nd Lt. W. L. K., 292
Mansura, 206
  Escarpment, 206
Maple Copse, 34, 85
Marchant, 2nd Lt. S. T., 274
Marcoing, 246
Marden, Maj. T. O., 244, 245, 248, 255
Marichuk, 395
Maricourt, 149, 290, 294, 320
  Wood, 148
Maris, Capt. A. A., 106, 311, 312
Markes, Maj. J. C., 167
Marne, River, 37, 40
  Battle of the, 56
Maroc Sector, 200
  Trenches, 199, 295
Marriott, Lt.-Col. C., 100
Marriott, Lt. H. S., 100, 375
Marshall, Capt. J. D., R.A.M.C., D.S.O., 183, 221
Marshall, Lt.-Gen. Sir W., 385
Marshall, 2nd Lt. W. R., 180
Martin, Capt. E. K., R.A.M.C., 91
Martin, Pte. C., M.M. & Bar, 193, 230
Martin, Pte. C., M.M. & Bar, 230
Martin, R.S.M. J., 89
Martin, 2nd Lt. A., 288
Martlesham Heath, 212
Martyn-Sinnington, 2nd Lt. A. L., 213, 217
Mason, C.S.M. H., 244
Mason, Lt. G. H., 100
Mason, Lt.-Col. M. F., D.S.O., 46, 66, 400
Mason, 2nd Lt. A. C., 176
Mason, 2nd Lt. K. R., 86
Mason, 2nd Lt. S. H., 169
Mason, 2nd Lt. V. K., 176
Mason, Sgt. J., M.M., 168, 240
Mathew, Lt. H. C., M.C., 258, 284
Matthews, Capt. J. C. G., M.C. & Bar, 91, 235, 400
Matthews, Sgt. W. J., D.C.M., M.M., (commission in the Field), 201, 282, 355
Mauquissart, 142
Maurepas and Area, 193, 200
Mawer, 2nd Lt., 136
Maxse, Maj.-Gen. F. I., 91, 165
Maxwell, Lt. R. H., 392
Maxwell, Lt.-Gen. Sir R., 151
Maxwell, Lt.-Gen. Sir J. G., 201, 203
Maxwell, Maj. A. C., 151
Maxwell, 2nd Lt. J. D., 176, 253
Maxwell-Lawford, 2nd Lt. F., 253
May, Lt. E. C., 51, 54
Maycock, Maj., D.S.O., 78, 79, 80
Maynard, Capt., 112
Mazar, 204
Mazingarbe, 133, 185, 198
  Two Batts. meeting at, 186
Mazirko, 161, 162
Mead, C.S.M., S. W., D.C.M., M.M., 282
Meadows, R.S.M. F., D.C.M., M.S.M., 282, 327, 331
Mealand, 2nd Lt. T., M.C., 289
Meaulte, 191, 192, 193
Meautys, Capt. P. R., M.C., 239
Medway Trench, 168, 169
Mee, Capt. J. T. M., 291
Meen, C.Q.M.S., M.M. and Bar, 102, 291
Megiddo, Battles of, 314 *seq.*
Mellish, Rev. E. W., C.F., V.C., M.C., 141 *& n*
Mendur–to the Sea Line, 207
Menin Area, 59
  Road, 73, 74, 82, 239, 240, 301
Méricourt l'Abbé, 195, 243
  Two Batts. meeting at, 183–4, 190
Merisen, Capt. C. W., M.C., 400
Merris, 51, 52, 90, 230
  Two Batts. neighbours near, 58
Merville Area, 285, 297
Méteren Area, 177, 228, 230
Methuen, F.M. Lord, 118
Mezeirah, 314
Michael, 2nd Lt. G. E. M., 267
Middleton, Lt. H. S., music by, 337
Miers, Lt.-Col. H. J., 107, 201
Milburn, 2nd Lt. L. E., 46, 86
Milburn, 2nd Lt. W. H., 189
Miller, Lt. C. H., M.C., 244, 245
Miller, Lt. D. M., 251
Miller, Lt. E. B., 340
Miller, 2nd Lt. G., 258
Mills, Sgt. W., 82
Milne, Lt.-Gen., 304
Minden, Battle of, and Minden Day, 36, 80, 183, 202, 223, 371
Mingay, Pte. A., 246
Miraumont, Action of, 170, 171, 243
Miskin, Capt. F., M.C., 200, 256, 257, 259
Mitchell, Capt. H. D., 46, 62, 228, 342, 343
Mitchell, 2nd Lt. C. W., 299
Mitchell, 2nd Lt. O. C., 231

Moascar, 202, 203
Moat Farm, 74, 83, 84
Mogg's Hole, 142
Molembaix, 302, 401
Molineaux, Sgt., 33
Monastir, 160, 163, 164
Monchy-le-Preux, 220, 221, 222, 223
Sector, 234
Monier-Williams, Capt. H. B., M.C. & Bar, 381, 386, 398, 400
Monro, Gen. Sir C., Bt., G.C.B., 146, 381
Mons, 24, 73
Retreat from, 22, 25 *seq.*, 325
Mons–Condé Canal, 24, 25
Mons–Le Cateau Road, 293
Montauban, 166
Alley, 191
Montauban–Carnoy Road, 193
Montay, 26, 27
Spur, 33
Montreuil, 40, 93
Moody, C.Q.M.S., 102
Moorson, 2nd Lt. A. E., 189
Moplah Outbreak, 382 *seq.*
Morbecque, 151, 152
Morbey, Capt. C. F. W., 89, 235
Morgan, Capt. C. L., 96, 174
Morgan, 2nd Lt. J. B., 22, 35
Mormal Forest, 23, 26
Morland, Gen. Sir T., K.C.B., K.C.M.G., D.S.O., A.D.C., Colonel of the Suffolk Regiment, 386
Morisson, Lt., 315
Morton, Brig.-Gen. E., 341
Morton, Maj. P. F., 151, 174, 196
Morval, 196
Battle of, 197–8
Mory, 259
Copse, 284
Moseley, Capt. G. K., 281, 338
Moss, 2nd Lt. C. J., 185
Mossop, 2nd Lt. N. R., 133
Mouflers, 200
Moulin-des-Roches, 40, 41
Moulton-Barrett, Lt.-Col. E. M., 68, 250
Mound, 235
Mount Lofty, 203
Mount Pleasant Wood, 251
Moury-Muset, M., 393, 394
Mowatt, 2nd Lt. C. F. R., 302
Mowbray, Capt. C. H., 41
Mowbray, 2nd Lt. K. J. W., 220
Moyenville, and Area, 275, 290
Moysey, Capt. F., M.C. (special), 17, 50, 54, 401
Mudd, 2nd Lt. W. A., 251
Mudros, 103, 109, 110, 214, 215, 216
Muhammadiya, 204
Mumford, 2nd Lt., 49
Munday, 2nd Lt. G. C., M.C., 137, 140
Murray, Lt.-Gen. Sir A., 204–5
Murray, 2nd Lt. W., 320
Musker, 2nd Lt. H., 212, 213
Musketry Successes, 401–2
Myddleton, 2nd Lt. E. G., 22, 33, 35

N

Nagle, Capt. W. J., D.S.O., M.C., 268, 289, 290
Nanteuil, 37
Napoleon I, 211
Neal, L-Cpl., Belg. Dec., 396
Nebi Samwil, Battle of, 218
Needham, Capt., 80
Needham, Lt., 137
Needham, Maj. R. M. B., D.S.O., 80, 158, 400
Neely, 2nd Lt. H. B., 65, 69
Negus, Sgt. J. P., D.C.M., M.M. & Bar, 176, 252, 355
Neuve Chapelle, 41, 42, 321
Area, 86
Battle of, 61 *seq.*, 142
Sector, 70, 72
Neuve Église, 42, 238
Neuville-Vitasse, 226, 238, 263, 265
Nevoljen, 160
New Bedford Road Gully, Gallipoli, 214
New Cut Alley, 142
Newell, 2nd Lt. E. P., 224
Newport and Brecon saps, 143, 244
Nicholls, Capt. D. W. A., M.C., 233
Nicholls, Lt. D. W. A., M.C., 178
Nicholls, 2nd Lt. P. C., 22
Nichols, Maj. C. B., M.C., 225
Nichols, 2nd Lt. P. B. B., 89, 132
Nicholson, Lt. C. J. H., 91
Nicholson, Lt.-Col. W. N., C.M.G., D.S.O. 387, 388, 400
Nicholson, Maj.-Gen. Sir C. L., 175, 254, 278, 280, 397
Nilgiri Hills, 382
Nisbet, Brig.-Gen. F. C., 307
Nisbet, Capt. C. A., 97, 199
Nixon, C.S.M., 102
Nobbs, 2nd Lt. G. F. P., 271
Noble, Capt., B. B., R.A.M.C., 192
Nœux-les-Mines, 143, 144, 196, 245
Noonan, C.S.M., 53
Nord Departement, M. le Préfet de, 393, 394
Noreuil, 289
Norfolk, Henry, 7th Duke of, 15
Norfolk Lodge, 85
Norfolk Post, 31
Norfolk Street, Gallipoli, 215
Norfolk Trench, Gallipoli, 85, 106, 107
Northbécourt, 142, 152

North Belah, 209
Northcote, Lt. O. S. I., 91, 146
Northen, Capt. E., 212
Norton, L/Sgt. G. H., M.M., 126
Norton, 2nd Lt. C. J., 107, 207
Norton, 2nd Lt. E., 191
Norrent Fontes, 132
Nowell, 2nd Lt. E. H., 81
Noyelles, 320
Noyelles-les-Vermelles, 126, 130, 132, 247, 320
Nunn, Pte. J., 144
Nunn, Pte. W., 52–3
Nunn, R.Q.M.S. H. F., M.S.M., 305
Nunn, Sgt.-Maj., A/R.S.M., 155
Nurlu, 295, 320
Nutter, Capt. H. C., 222

O

"O" TRENCH, Ypres Salient, 53, 54
Oakes, Cornet Orbell Ray, 112
Oakes, Capt. N. B., 22, 37, 39, 64, 303, 307, 394
Oakey, 2nd Lt. F. G., 253
Oakley, 2nd Lt. F., 110
Observation Hill, 315
O'Donnell, Maj. J., 213
Officers of the Suffolk Regiment killed in the Great War while serving with other Regiments, List of, 399
Oldham Post, Suez Canal, 202
Olga House, 253
Oliver, Capt. C. M., 102
Oliver, Lt. G. G., 107, 108, 315
Oliver, Maj. B. E., 102, 351
Oliver, 2nd Lt. C. M., 192
Olley, Sgt. W. F., M.S.M., 390
Oppy, 192
Orange Hill, 233
Orange Lane, 234
Orbell, Pte. J. A., D.C.M., 90
Orcq., 371
Ord, Col. J. T., 114
Orfano, Gulf of, 157
Orford, Maj. E. E., 22, 32, 35, 394
Orljak Ravine, and Ridge, 160, 161, 162, 304
Ormanli, 304
Ory, Lt. V. W., 124
Ost Dunkerke, 228
Otapara Signal station, 384
Ouderdom, 53, 70, 72, 85, 141
Ourcq, River, 40
Ovillers-la-Boisselle, 148, 165, 178
Owen, Brig.-Gen. Cunliffe, 327
Owen, Capt. I. G., 127, 161, 160, 308
Oxford Street Trench, 83
Oxlade, Capt. H. J. W., 107, 207

P

PACKARD, Capt. C. T., M.C., 93, 122, 124
Packard, 2nd Lt. T., 79, 80, 325
Packard, 2nd Lt. W. H., 189
Packer, 2nd Lt. B. F., 245
Page, Cpl. G. M., 24
Page, 2nd Lt. A. H., 168
Page, 2nd Lt. H. D. S., 281
Pageant produced by 1st Batt., 388
Pain, Lt. J. W., 46, 72
Palestine, 15, 217
Palestine Campaign, 204 *seq.*
Palfrey, Pte., 52
Palmer, 2nd Lt., 163
Palmer, 2nd Lt. C. W. B., 235
Palmer, 2nd Lt. F. N., 244
Palmer, 2nd Lt. L. C., 230
Palmer, 2nd Lt. W. C. M., 236
Panton, 2nd Lt. H. A., 286
Paprat, 305
Pargiter, 2nd Lt. R. A., 65, 77
Paris, 37, 38
  Allied Victory March through, 380
Parker, Capt. A. Hyde, 365
Parker, Lt. A. S., 102, 104
Parker, 2nd Lt. W. H., 97, 152, 178
Parker, 2nd Lt. W. S. Hyde, 212
Parkinson, Pte., 287
Parkinson, Sgt.-Maj. O. W., M.C., 59
Parmenter, Pte. S., 141
Parry, Capt. R. A., D.S.O., 46, 72
Parry-Crooke, Lt.-Col. C. P., 294, 400
Parry-Jones, Capt. O. G., R.A.M.C., 169
Parsons, C.S.M. J. C., D.C.M., 400
Parsons, Lt. J. C., 50, 127, 160
Pas-de-Calais, 354
Passchendaele, 231
Passchendaele–Becelaere Road, 65
Passman, Lt. K. G., 289
Pateman, C.S.M. J., M.S.M., 286
Paterson. Lt. E. W., 212
Patten, 2nd Lt. A. G. B., 144, 183
Patterson, Drummer E., 92
Pattisson, Lt. W. H. M., 190
Pawsey, 2nd Lt. H. C., 191
Payne, Capt. L. G. S., M.C., 50, 53, 54, 400
Payne, 2nd Lt. G. H., 22
Pearce, 2nd Lt. K., 258
Pearson, Capt. E. E., 22
Pearson, Sgt. J. W., D.C.M., 216, 313
Peart, Capt. C. H., 142, 367
Pear Tree Bluff, 84
Peck, 2nd Lt., M.C., 238
Pedrick, 2nd Lt. C. R., 284
Peebles, Maj. A. S., D.S.O., 22, 23–4, 25, 31, 32, 33, 35, 368, 391, 392, 394
Peizière, 235, 295
Pemberton, Capt. R. O. W., 212, 213, 320
Pendle, Sgt. A. E., D.C.M., 62, 86

Percy, Lt. J. M. V., 185, 297
Pereira, Brig.-Gen. G., 300, 301
Pereira, 2nd Lt. F. V. C., 22
Péronne, 200, 235, 251, 252, 320
Perry Post, 202
Peter's Peak, 202
Petit Audenarde, 357
Petit Bois, 43, 294
Petit Miraumont, 171, 172
Petit Morin, 39
Petre, Capt. Hon. J., 116, 117
Pettitt, Sgt. W., D.C.M., 62, 86
Pheasant Farm, 242
Phelan, Capt. E. C., R.A.M.C., M.C., 22, 35, 85
Phillips, 2nd Lt. S. H., 244, 248, 281
Phillips, 2nd Lt. V. M. G., 22, 24
Philosophe, 198
Pickard-Cambridge, Lt. E. A., 64, 182, 306
Pickard-Cambridge, Lt. T. D., M.C., 84, 183, 331
Piccardy, 268 *seq.*
Pichon, M., 92
Pickles, Capt. A., 342
Picton, Gen. Sir Thomas, 17
Pidcock, 2nd Lt. T. R., 292
Pigott, Lt.-Col. R. E. P., 97, 98, 200
Pilckem Ridge, Battle of, 239, 240, 241
Pilkington, 2nd Lt. D. H., 189
Pinceboom, 141
Pinney, Maj.-Gen. R. J., 192, 193, 225
Pizzey, L/Sgt. C. A., M.M., 144, 193
Place, Sgt., 43
Plateau Post, 202
Platts, Capt. A. L., 183
Platts, Lt. J. C., 96
Pledger, Lt. B. E., 258
Plessis St. Avoye, 39
Ploegsteert, 55, 90
Plumer, F.M. Lord., G.C.B., G.C.M.G., G.B.E., 56, 124, 300
Pocklington, 2nd Lt. G. R., 236
Podd, Sgt. J., M.M., 193
Poelcapelle, 242
Poincaré, Raymond, President of the French, 41
Pollock-Hodsoll, Lt. G. B., 323
Polygon Wood, Battle of, 223–4, 230
Pommerœuil–Thulin Road, 25
Pond, 2nd Lt. E. R., M.C., 289
Ponsonby, Lt.Col. A. E. V., 381
Ponsonby, Maj.-Gen. J., Colonel of the Suffolk Regiment, 258, 381 *n*, 385, 388, 389, 390
Pont Fixe, 48
Pont du Hem, 86
Pontoise, 37
Pont des Quatre Vaux, 27, 31
Pont Riquel, 86
Pont Street, Somme Area, 183
Pont à Vaches, 23
Pooley, Sgt.-Master-Cook, 85
Poperinghe, 64, 78, 123, 125 *seq.*, 137, 144, 165, 281
Poroi Railway Station, 306
Upper and Lower, 306, 307
Port Arthur (Flanders), 86
Port Sudan, 17, 49
Porter, Brig.-Gen. C. L., 186, 288
Postlethwaite, Lt. C. J., 259
Postlethwaite, 2nd Lt. C. T., 235
Potijze, 71, 230
Potter, C.S.M. F., D.C.M., 244
Potter, Maj. J. T., 323, 327
Potter, 2nd Lt. A., 269
Poulter, 2nd Lt. C. G., 237
Power, 2nd Lt. E. V., 187
Pozières, Battle of, 177, 179
Pratt, Capt., R.A.M.C., M.C., 167
Pratt, Pte. W., D.C.M., 257
Prentice, 2nd Lt. J. R., 82
Prestidge, Lt. J. V. FitzG., 80, 251
Pretty, Capt. H., 46, 146, 189
Pretty, Lt. D., 86
Pretty, Lt.-Col. F., T.D., D.L., 46, 72, 190, 295, 298, 334, 397
Pretty, 2nd Lt. D., 46
Price, 2nd Lt., 197
Priel Wood, 251
Prieska, 118
Princes Street, Longueval, 166–7
Pritchard, Lt. R. G., 65, 68, 69
Proctor, Capt. A. M. W., M.C., 259
Proctor-Beauchamp, Col. Sir H., Bt., C.B., 104
Proven, 123, 253
Pryke, 2nd Lt. A., 221
Pryor, Lt. E., 112
Pullinger, 2nd Lt. A. F., 91, 149
Pulleyn, 2nd Lt. F. F., 250
Pulteney, Lt.-Gen. Sir W. P., 165, 172, 373
Pulverman, 2nd Lt. O. P., 81
Putley, C.S.M. O. T., 124
Pye, C.S.M. F., 79
Pym, Maj. C. E., 212, 213
Pym, 2nd Lt. E. I. L., 86
Pyramids, the, 201

Q

QUADRILATERAL, the, 195, 196, 197
Quantrill, Sgt. H., D.C.M., 54, 381
Quarries, the, Loos, 130, 131, 132, 320
Quarries Sector, Hulluch, 198
Queensland Camp, 228
Querrieu, 153, 294
Quessy, 268, 269
Quilter, Capt. E. C., 332

R

RAE, 2nd Lt. R. L. C., 198, 241
Rahm Allah, 318
Railway Triangle, 234
 Wood, 73–4, 82
Raimbert, 142, 143
Ramleh, 110, 211
Ramsay, Maj.-Gen. F. W., 272
Ramsay, Maj.-Gen. Sir J. G., 94
Ranby, Lt. H., 235
Rancourt, 193, 200, 294
Randolph, Lt.-Col. A. F., D.S.O., 400
Ransford, R.Q.M.S., 277
Rantieh, 312, 314
Ras-az-Zamby, 318
Ras-el-Ain, 313, 316, 317
Rash, Capt. J. C., 227
Rash, 2nd Lt. K. R., 180
Raven, Lt. H. V., 292
Raven-Hart, Lt. R. J. M., 340
Rawes, 2nd Lt. V. N., 168, 172
Rawlinson, Gen. Lord, 165, 170, 293, 382, 385
Rawson, Capt. N. R., R.A.M.C., 93, 124, 196
Raymond, Sgt. P. R., M.M., 35
Reed, C.S.M., T/R.S.M., W. A., M.S.M. (special), 400
Read, Lt. C. L., 100
Read, Pte. F. J., D.C.M., 240, 242
Read, 2nd Lt. R. S., 222
Recruiting March of 1st Batt., 1927, 388
Red House Wood, 314
Red Line, the, 239, 252
Redding, Capt., H. A., M.C. & Two Bars, 200, 259, 286, 400
Reed, Lt. C. C., 207, 312
Reed, Pte. G., 141
Reed, 2nd Lt. H. A., M.C., 281, 282, 400
Regina Trench, 170
Reid, Capt. E. H., 22
Reid, Capt. G. F., M.C., 278, 279, 282
Rendlesham, Lt.-Col. F. A. T. Lord, 114, 362, 365, 375
Renescure, 150, 151
Reninghelst, 71, 138, 141, 228, 239
Rennison, Rev. E. D., C.F., 203, 350
Repington, Col. A'Court, 367
Resurrection Trench, 172
Reumont, 31
Reynolds, Lt. T. W., 22
Rhine, River, 391
Rhododendron Spur, Gallipoli, 106
Rhonelle, River, 299
Ribécourt, 246
Richards, Capt. L. J., M.C., 231, 294
Richards, Lt. M. F., M.C., 259
Richards, 2nd Lt., 46
Richardson, Lt.-Col. M. E., D.S.O., 254, 255
Richebourg l'Avoné, 60
Richebourg St. Vaast, 60, 62
Richmond, Sgt. E., M.M., 225
Ride, Lt. R., 112
Riddlestone, Pte. F., D.C.M., 35
Ridge Wood and Cemetery, 80
Ridley, Capt. R. M., M.C., 91, 277, 353, 400
Rifle Trench, 234
Rigby, 2nd Lt. B. C., 227
Ritz Street Area, 241
Rivière, 227
Rix, Lt. F. W., 141 *& n.*
Roach, C.S.M., W., 146
Roberts, Brevet-Col. H. R., 340, 341
Roberts, F.M., Earl, 47
Roberts, Lt. J., 140, 340
Roberts, Maj. L. S., 198
Roberts, Pte. H. H., M.M., 289
Roberts, 2nd Lt. J. R. T., 59
Roberts, 2nd Lt. S. C., 230
Robertson, F.M. Sir W., 329, 338–9, 392, 396
Robertson, 2nd Lt. J. A., 274
Robins, 2nd Lt. R. T., M.C. & Bar, 257, 400
Robinson, Lt. H. W., 200, 258
Robinson, Lt.-Col. J. H., 393
Robins, Sgt. G., 90
Robinson, Pte. F., M.M., 225
Robson, Lt., 174
Roclincourt, 177, 249
Rodwell, Capt., 280
Rodwell, Capt. E. J., 46
Rodwell, Maj. F. J., O.B.E., T.D., 62, 278, 280, 281, 282, 333, 339 *& n.*
Roe, 2nd Lt. C. C., 323
Roe, Sgt. L. K., M.S.M., 396
Rolph, Lt. C. H., 200
Rolph, 2nd Lt. H. B., M.C., 292, 293
Rolt, Brig.-Gen. S. P., C.B., 21, 31, 32
Romani, 202, 204
Romeries, 292
Rond d'Orléans, 269
Rongy, 295
Rooke, Lt. N., 102, 104
Roper, Lt.-Col. S. D., 339
Rose, L/Cpl. W., D.C.M., 125
Rose Trench, 242
Rosenhill Huts, 70, 72, 80
Rosling, L/Cpl. A. M., D.C.M., 210, 313
Ross, Maj.-Gen. C., 195, 244
Roubaix, 357
Rouen, Peace Review at, 11th Batt. in, 354
Rœux, 234, 251, 296
Rouez Wood, 231
Rougeville, 39
Roulers Railway, 73, 83
Round Hill Post, 202, 203
Rous, Capt. Sir John, Bt., 112

Rousbrugge, 243
Rouville, 37
Row, 2nd Lt. H. A., 46, 62
Rowbotham, 2nd Lt. J. C., 93, 248, 249
Rowe, 2nd Lt. H. E., 281
Rowland, 2nd Lt. J., 279
Rowley, Capt. J. R., 102, 210
Roxbrough, 2nd Lt. W. H., M.C., 281, 282
Roxby, Capt. F. M., 78, 79
Rubrouch, 241
Rucker, 2nd Lt. A. N., 256
Rudd, Pte. L., M.M. (special), 401
Rue d'Aire, Béthune, 121
Rue des Berceaux, 61
Rue du Bois, 60, 61, 85
Rue de l'Épinette, 60
Rue de Temple, Arras, 189
Ruggles-Brise, Maj.-Gen. H. G., 97–8, 257
Rumbelow, L/Cpl. E., 35
Rumbelow, Lt. A. G., M.B.E., 388
Rumégies, 296
Rumilly, 291
Rundle, Lt.-Gen. 118
Rupel, Fort, 159
  Pass, 160, 164, 304
Rupprecht, Crown Prince of Bavaria, 56
Rush, 2nd Lt. E. W., 234
Rush, Sgt., 39
Rushbrooke, Capt. B. D., 50, 77, 78, 79
Russell, Capt. V. C., D.S.O., M.C. & Bar, 183, 185, 221, 222, 264, 291, 400
Russian General, Inspection by a, 96
Rutter, Sgt. J., M.M., 193
Ryley, Lt. H. B., 312

S

Saacy, 39, 40
Sadd, Lt. A. H., 374
Sailly, 152
Sailly-Labourse, 122, 126, 132
  Two Batts. meeting at, 123
Sailly Laurette, 194, 294
Sailly-le-Sec, 200, 293
Sailly-sur-la-Lys, 298
St. Amand, 192
St. Eloi, 80, 140
  Fighting near, 55
St. Floris and Sector, 60, 281, 296
St. Hilaire, 296
St. Jan ter Biezen, 242, 300
St. Jean, 71, 72, 123, 124, 125
St. Julien, 67, 223
  Battle of, 69, 72, 80
St. Julien-Poelcappelle Road, 65
St. Léger, 278, 282
St. Léger-Mory-Ecoust Road Line, 287
St. Martin, 298
St. Martin's Hill, 150
St. Omer, 41, 46, 47, 142, 150, 167, 182, 296
St. Ouen, 39
St. Quentin, 36, 37, 40
  Battle of, 320
St. Quentin–Le Cateau–Landrecies Railway, 32
St. Sauveur, 149
St. Venant, 320
St. Waast, 23, 24, 26
St. Marguerite, 41
Salford Post, Suez Canal, 202
Salmana, 204
Salonika, 155, 156, 157, 158, 305
Salonika–Constantinople Railway, 309
Salonika–Seres Road, 159, 160
Salt Lake, Gallipoli, 103, 105
Samson's Ridge, 208
Samuel, Capt. W. G., 338
Sanctuary, Capt. C. L., 9, 168, 169
Sanctuary, 2nd Lt. W. T., 91
Sanctuary Wood, 83, 84, 126, 133, 134, 240
Sandpit Area, 195
Sarakli, 308
Sarrail, Gen., 304, 307
Saul, 2nd Lt. H. L., 299
Saunders, 2nd Lt. C. J., 128
Saunders, Sgt. A. F., V.C., 122, 400
Savage, L/Cpl. W., D.C.M., 171–2
Savage, 2nd Lt., 241
Savoy Trench, 191
Sawyer, C.Q.M.S., 43
Sawyer, 2nd Lt. H., 180
Scarborough, the Earl of, G.B.E., K.C.B., 367, 372
Scarpe, River, 233
  Battles of the, 221, 226, 233, 238, 249 *seq.*, 264
Scheldt Canal, 236
Scheldt, River, 301, 302, 321
Scherpenberg Hill, 42, 81
Scherpenberg Ridge, Battle of, 201
Schiff, Capt., 257
Scholefield, Capt. L. C., 199
Schreiber, Lt.-Col., 100
Schroder, Lt. F. T., 59
Scoggings, Pte. H. J., D.C.M., 59
Scoggins, C.M.S., H. R., M.M., 189
Scorpion Camp, 317
Scots Redoubt, 174
Scott, Capt. G. Lacey, 102, 105, 107
Scott, Maj.-Gen. Sir A. B., 232, 236
Scott, 2nd Lt. L., 284
Scott, 2nd Lt. R. T., 197
Scott-Walker, 2nd Lt. K., 177
Scrimgeour, Capt. S., M.C. & Bar, 229, 230, 295, 400
Scrimgeour, 2nd Lt. H., 189
Scudamore, Capt. P. L., 93, 248
Schwaben Redoubt, 168 *seq.*
Seal, Sgt. W. G., 134

Searies, 2nd Lt. A., M.C., 302
Searle, L/Cpl. H., D.C.M., M.M. & Bar, 90, 202, 355
Seddon, Capt. A. E., 96, 176
Seddon, Lt. G. N., 90, 174
Seddon, 2nd Lt. E. J., 198
Selby, Lt. H. P., 55
Selle, Battle of the, 298, 299
Semmens, 2nd Lt. C. S., 274
Sensée River and Valley, 226, 228, 255
Senussi, the, 216
Seranvillers, 292
Serapeum, 202, 203
Serbia, 156, 310
Serbia, Crown Prince of, 162
Serches, 40, 41
Seres Road, 157, 158, 304
Serre River, Battle of the (Battle of the Ancre), 187
Sector, 187, 188, 219, 223
Setques, 230
Shanghai, 394
Sharp, 2nd Lt. W. F. F., 253
Sharpe, C.S.M. C., 132
Sharta, 217
Shaw, 2nd Lt. F. C., 175
Shaw, 2nd Lt. H. A., 96, 176
Shears, 2nd Lt. A. C., 178
Sheen, 2nd Lt. C., 251
Sheikh Abbas, 205, 206, 207
Ridge, 207
Sheik Hassan, 209, 210
Sheikh Zuwa'id, 205
Shell Valley, 189, 190
Shepherd, L/Cpl. E., M.M., 193
Shepherd, 2nd Lt. R. S., 281
Sheria, 217
Wadi, 218
Shewen, Brig.-Gen. M. T., 94, 120
Short, Capt. H. A., M.C., 178, 234
Shrapnel Corner, 73, 230
Trench, 221
Shushe, 211
Shuttleworth, 2nd Lt., 230
Sidi Bishr, 110, 216
Siegburg, 396
Signal Grec Avance Sector, 308, 309
Sills, C.Q.M.S., 102
Silver, Capt. S. W. H., 91, 92
Silver, Lt. W. L. C., 91
Simkin, Pte. B. J., D.C.M., 193
Simmons, 2nd Lt. J. A., 248, 281
Simoncourt, 234
Simpson, Capt. W. L., M.M., 222, 264, 264–5
Simpson, Sgt. H., M.M., 193
Sixteen Roads, 170
Skinner, Maj.-Gen. P. C. B., 300
Smee, Capt. A. A., M.C. & Bar, 286
Smee, 2nd Lt. J. C., 299
Smith, A/C.S.M. G., 222
Smith, Capt. E. C., 134
Smith, Cpl., Belg. Dec., 396
Smith, Cpl. L., M.M., 193
Smith, L/Sgt. H., M.M., 225
Smith, L/Sgt. W., D.C.M., 62, 88
Smith, Lt. C. F. B., 17, 50, 53, 54, 55, 286
Smith, Lt. G., 112
Smith, Lt.-Col. d'Arch, 17, 133, 135, 140, 182
Smith, Pte. H. J., 245
Smith, 2nd Lt. C. F., 286
Smith, 2nd Lt. D. C., 131
Smith, 2nd Lt. D. C. W., 106
Smith, 2nd Lt. E. M., 291
Smith, 2nd Lt. G., 251
Smith, 2nd Lt. J. L. H., 85
Smith, 2nd Lt. N. H., 189
Smith, 2nd Lt. R. G. P., 197
Smith, 2nd Lt. S. B., 224
Smith, 2nd Lt. S. N., 235
Smith, Sgt. A. C., D.C.M., 286
Smith-Dorrien, Gen. Sir H., 23, 31, 37, 42, 56, 59, 363, 393, 394
Foreword by, on the Battle of Le Cateau, 28
Smith-Rewse, Capt. H. G., 343
Smyth, Maj.-Gen. N. M., 272
Sneesby, 2nd Lt. C., 245
Snelson, 2nd Lt. B. G., 181
Snow, Lt.-Gen. Sir T. D'O., 226
Soghanli Dere, Fort, 380
Sokolovo, 305
Solbe, Lt.-Col. C. E. De L., 92
Solly-Flood, Brig.-Gen. A., 132, 181
Somerset, Lt.-Col. C. W., M.V.O., C.M.G., 95, 96, 177, 355, 400
Somme, River, and Area, 146, 149, 153, 197, 200, 219, 228, 294, 352
Battles of the, 57, 133, 150, 165, 182 *seq.*, 194 *seq.*, 288, 333
Sones, Pte. P. E., D.C.M., 62, 86
Sorel-le-Grand, 235
Sorley, Capt. C., 89, 90, 130 *& n.*, 131
Souastre, Two Batts. meeting at, 239
South African War, the, 23, 29, 37, 43, 55, 100, 116, 130, 231 *n.*
Southgate, Pte. H. A., D.C.M., 141
Spalding, C.S.M. E., D.C.M. & Bar, 282, 355, 400
Spall, R.Q.M.S., 102
Sparks, Capt. H. P., M.C., 59, 64, 382, 390
Spens, Maj.-Gen., 89
Speyer, 2nd Lt. F. W. H., 222
Sphinx, the, 201
Sphinx Post, 202, 203
Spion Kop, 117
Spoilbank, 84, 85
Spong, 2nd Lt. J. S., 133
Spooner, Brig.-Gen. A. H., 297
Spragge, Lt.-Col. E. B., 212

Spriggs, M.G. Sgt., D.C.M., 33, 35
Spurgeon, 2nd Lt., 237
Squirl-Dawson, Capt. W. B., 42
" Stabilis," a Suffolk Regimental Song, by Capt. J. G. Frere, 402–3
Stace, Capt. H. W., 96, 153
Staden, Cpl. S. F., M.M., 299
Staddon, Capt. H. K., 268, 269
Stallard, 2nd Lt. W. W., 233
Stambruges, 396
Stanford, Capt. H. C., 93, 248
Stanley, Lt.-Col. A. W., 95, 341
Stannard, C.S.M. A., M.C., 59
Stantial, 2nd Lt. F. E., 70, 325–6
Stapley, 2nd Lt. L. d'A., 180
Starling, Capt. R., 92, 93, 248, 249
Stebbings, 2nd Lt. G. W., 46, 86
Steel, A/Capt. D. G., M.C., 185, 187
Steele, Capt. G., 343
Steenwoorde, 228, 239
Sterry, Pte. W., 141
Stevens, Lt. T. T., 93, 122
Stevens, Lt.-Col., 36
Steward, Capt. G. B., M.C., 93, 124
Stewart, Lt.-Col. A. F., C.M.C., O.B.E., 380
Stirling Castle, Flanders, 229
Stokes, 2nd Lt. A. L., 298
Stone, Rev. F., C.F., 146
Stone Heaps Hill, 312
Stonehouse, 2nd Lt. D. U., 266
Stork, Lt. E. S., 212
Stotherd, Maj. S. B., 89, 132
Stovell, 2nd Lt. L. A., 65, 69
Stoyle, 2nd Lt. A. H., 248
Stracey, Maj. E. H. D., 93, 94
Stradbroke, Col., the Earl of, 102
Strategy, Chinese dictum on, 163
Stray Farm, 253
Strazeele, 51
Strickland, Lt.-Gen. Sir E. P., K.C.B., K.B.E., C.M.G., D.S.O., 48, 60, 62, 144, 145, 397
Strong, 2nd Lt. W. E., 320
Struma River, Plain, and Valley, 158, 159, 160, 162, 164, 304, 307
Stuart, Capt. C. E., 337–8
Stuart, Maj. G. R. C., C.B., D.S., 329
Stubbings, Capt. T., 161, 163
Stubbs, Lt.-Col. G. C., C.M.G., D.S.O. & Bar, 18, 141, 182, 184, 185, 222, 223, 287, 289, 290, 396, 400
Sturdy, Lt. J. R., M.C., 162, 303
Stutfield, 2nd Lt. H. B., 91
Suez Canal, 201, 202, 216
" Suffolk Death Trap," the, 59
Suffolk Prisoners of War Fund Committee, 329–30
Suffolk Regt., Cenotaph of, 359
Suffolk Regimental Songs, 402 *seq.*
Suffolk Sector, 146
" Suffolk Soldier, The, to his County," by Capt. J. F. Frere, 404
Suffolk Volunteers, the, 360 *seq.*
Sunken Road, 142
Surafend, 314
Surbiton Villa Line, 240
" Surrounding," by a Bantam, 226 *& n.*
Sus-St. Léger, 192, 257, 287
Suttle, 2nd Lt. J. T., 257
Suttle, 2nd Lt. N. E., 191
Suvla Bay, 103, 104
Suzanne, 193, 200
Swan, Cpl. G., 168
Switch Trench, 189
Sworder, 2nd Lt. C. F., 178
Sykes, Lt. A. H. H., 27

T

TAILBY, Lt., 249
Tait, Capt. W. I., 102
Talbot, 2nd Lt. H. P., 265
Tallon, 2nd Lt. M., 176
Talus Bois, 185
Tamlyn, 2nd Lt. J. R., 235
Tamplin, Maj. H. R., 362, 364
Tann, R.S.M. J., 344
Tayler, Lt. E. W. N., 245, 246, 342
Taylor, Capt., 213
Taylor, Capt. G. H. R., 237
Taylor, C.M.S., 221
Taylor, Lt. A. C. J., 246, 247
Taylor, Lt. A. F., 178, 179
Taylor, Lt. A. T. C., 80
Taylor, Lt. T. O., 210
Taylor, Maj. A. C., 63, 163
Taylor, Pte., 176
Taylor, Pte., 365
Taylor, 2nd Lt. A. C., 183
Taylor, 2nd Lt. G. T., 285
Taylor, 2nd Lt. J. N., 220
Taylor, Sgt. W. D., D.C.M., 282
Taylor, T/Lt.-Col. A. G., 323, 394
Teager, 2nd Lt. W. E., 237
Teke Tepe, 103
Tel Asur, Actions of, 313
Telfer, 2nd Lt. A. C., 97
Tempest, Lt. F. L., 96, 176
Temple, Capt. A. H. W., 42, 43, 323, 324
Temple, 2nd Lt. H. J., 106
Templeux-la Fosse and Gurlu Wood Trenches, 320
Tergnier, 268, 269
Terry, Maj. W. J., 30, 89
Teverson, Lt. H. G., M.C., M.M., 288, 290, 291, 400
Thacker, 2nd Lt. G. D. W., 281
Theobald, C.S.M. M. G. W., D.C.M., 136
Theobald, Cornet John Meadows, 112

Theobald, Lt. R., M.C., 250, 281
Thiepval, Battle of, 170, 243
Thill, Lt. J. J., 134
Thistle Alley Trench, 190
Thomas, Capt. H. G., 17, 49, 50
Thomas, Capt. L. G., 199
Thomas, Lt. T. M. Chitty, 89, 131, 132
Thomas, Maj., 140–1
Thomas, Maj. E. A., 343
Thomas, 2nd Lt. S., 174
Thompson, C.S.M., 113
Thompson, Pte., M.M., 287
Thompson, Pte. W., 141
Thomson, Capt. G. A. L., 323
Thomson, Maj. Sinclair, 80, 128, 129, 313, 316, 392
Thomson, 2nd Lt. H., 237
Thorn, 2nd Lt. D. O., 220
Thornhill, T. A. C., 339
Throssell, 2nd Lt. H. C. S., 199
Thurlow, Pte., M.M., 168
Thursby, Lt. F. D. V., 292
Tillard, Maj. E. C., 333
Tillett, Pte., 372
Tilloy, 221
Tillul, 204
Tingley, Pte. W., D.C.M., C. de G., 302, 356
Tirur, 382, 384
Titch, Pte. M., 141
Todd, 2nd Lt. H. G. W., 89, 186
Tollemache, Capt. Hon. D. A., 116
Tollemache, Capt. Hon. M. G., 194
Tomkin, Maj. V. W. R., 212, 213
Tomkins, 2nd Lt. A., 289
Tomlinson, 2nd Lt. T. F., 107
Tool Trench, 222
Tournai, 321, 401
Tournant, 38
Toussoum, 203
Toutencourt, 276
Tower Hamlets, Ypres Area, 223
Townley, Capt. C. E., 96
Transloy, Battle of, 180
Transvaal, Western, 118
Trask, 2nd Lt. S. R., 179
Treves, Sir F., Bt., 116
"Triangle," the, 47
Tribe, Pte. G., M.M., 221
Tricker, 2nd Lt. R., 257, 284
Trimble, T/Lt.-Col. J. B. O., 199
Troisdorf, 391, 396
Trollope, Capt. H. C. M., D.S.O., M.C., 64, 82, 140, 185, 392
Trônes Wood, 184, 192
Trounce, 2nd Lt., 238
Truscott, Lt. F. G., M.C., 336, 338
Tuck, Lt.-Col. G. L. J., C.M.G., L. of H., D.S.O. & Bar, 95, 96, 175, 177, 250, 251, 253, 255, 280, 282, 297, 354, 355, 400
Tuck, 2nd Lt. W. H., 280
Turcoing, 356
Tunnel Trench, 258
Turkey Trot Trench, 109
Turner, Capt. H. K., 62, 189
Turner, Capt. M. A., 189
Turner, Capt. S. W., M.C. & Bar, 190, 230, 299, 355, 400
Turner, C.S.M., G., D.C.M. 282
Turner, Lt., 277
Turner, Lt. G., M.C., 300
Turner, Lt. K. W., 144, 191
Turner, Lt. M. A., 46
Turner, Lt.-Col. F. W., 46, 71, 72, 144, 145, 333, 338
Turner, Maj. C. H., 83–4, 89, 134
Turner, 2nd Lt. E. L., 284
Tuttle, 2nd Lt. E. W., 213
Tuttle, Capt. A. E., 374
Twiddy, 2nd Lt., 265
Tyler, A/Sgt. R., D.C.M. & Bar, 400

U

ULLSWATER, Rt. Hon. Viscount, 73
Ulster Crisis, 18 *seq.*
Umbrella Hill, 208, 209
Uniacke, Maj.-Gen. H. C. E., C.B., C.M.G., 353
Unwin, Maj. R. B., 330, 331
Unwin, Pte. F., 101
Urakuth Mala (hill), 384, 385
Usher, Capt. T., 91, 168
Uskub, 310
Usna-Tara Ridge, 154

V

VALENCIENNES, Battle of, 299
Valentia, Col. Viscount, 117
Van Straubenzee, Brig.-Gen. C. H. C., C.B., 18, 89, 400
Vardar, River, 156, 164
Varesnes, 269
Vendegies, 298
Vendin, 60
Vendin-le-Viel, 129
Venizel, 40
Venning, Capt. E. G., 78, 79, 80
Verbrandenmolen and Sector, 52, 53
Verlorenhoek, 66, 68
Vermelles, 121, 122, 127, 143
Vesquin, 142
Verry, 2nd Lt. F. T., 258
Vesey, 2nd Lt., 64
V.C.'s gained during the War, 122, 141, 252, 400

Vielle Chapelle, 41, 42, 47, 60, 61, 63
Vierstraat Area, 56, 58 *seq.*, 72
Cross-roads, 73
Switch, 142
Vieux Berquin, 151
Vignacourt, 133
Ville-sur-Ancre, 197
Villers-sous-Ailly, 193
Villers Bocage, 293
Villers Cotterêts, 269, 270
Villers Plouich, 255
Vittora Camp, 297, 298
Vincent, Brig.-Gen. B., 181
Vinden, Capt. H. F., 223
Vlamertinghe, 52, 65, 79, 85, 134
Vraucourt Switch, 290

W

WADI-EL-'ARISH, 204
Wadi-el-Ayun, 315, 316
Wadi Ghuzze, 205, 206, 217
Wadi Saba, 217
Wadi Sheria, 218
Wadi Union, 217
Wainwright, A/Capt. G. H., 267, 289
Wales, H.R.H. the Prince of, 43, 47, 202
Walford, Lt. A. E., 185
Walford, Maj. G. H., 18, 65, 185
Walker, Capt. K. M., 224, 296
Walker, Capt. P. S., 51
Walker, C.S.M. W., D.C.M., 189
Walker, Lt. G. H., 242
Walker, Maj. P. S., 237
Walker, 2nd Lt. F. C., 147
Walker's Pier, Anzac Cove, 214
Wallace, Lt.-Col. H. R., D.S.O., 343
Wallace, Lt.-Col. W. B., C.M.G., 50, 52, 64, 66, 67, 70, 77, 325, 400
Waller, Pte. R. C., M.M. (special), 400
Waller, 2nd Lt. S. H. C., 107
Walne, 2nd Lt. H. G., 221
Walters, 2nd Lt. L. H., 172, 242
Wancourt, Battle of, 261 *seq.*
Back-to-back fighting in, 266
Wancourt–Guémappe Sector, 225
Wanquetin, 188, 233
War Memorials
Bury St. Edmunds, 359
Le Cateau, 393
Liverpool Street Station, 349
Ward, Brig.-Gen. T., 311, 314
Ward, 2nd Lt. A. N., 266
Warloy, 175
Warlus, 228
Warner, Hon. Col. Sir C., Bt., Lord-Lt., 362, 363, 375, 389, 390, 393
Warnes, Capt. G. C., 102, 104, 311
Warwick Huts, Somme Area, 171
Wasmes, 25
Waterloo, Battle of, 112
Waters, Capt. G. T., 274
Waters, Pte., 326
Waterson, Pte. W., D.C.M., French report on his gallantry, 184–5
Watkins, Sgt. J. H. W., D.C.M., 400
Watkiss, Lt.-Gen., 47
Watou, 223
Watten, 228
Watts, C.S.M. W., 179
Wavrin, 321
Wayman, 2nd Lt. C., 193, 196
Webb, C.S.M. W., D.C.M., M.C., 59, 225
Webb, L/Cpl. G., M.M., 145
Webb, 2nd Lt. B., M.C., 295, 396
Webber, C.S.M., A., 72
Weir, Brig.-Gen. G. A., 157, 304
Weli Sheikh Nuran, 205
Wellington, Nilgiri Hills, 381, 382, 384
Wellington Camp, 228
Wellington Caves (Barracks), Arras, 188
Wellington Crescent, Ypres Salient, 239
Wellington Huts, Aveluy, 172
Wells, Capt. J. D., R.A.M.C., 46
Wells, C.S.M. D., M.M., 242
Wells, Pte. S. G., M.M., 313
Wells, 2nd Lt. A. J., 285
Wepener, 118
Wervicq, 301
West, Lt., 81
Westhoek, 230
Weston, 2nd Lt. J. D., 175
Weston, Maj. W. V., 341
Westoutre, 42, 43, 60
Meeting at, of 1st and 2nd Batts., 44, 64, 65, 72
Westwood, 2nd Lt. W. P., 230, 338
Whalley, Cpl., 228
Whatling, 2nd Lt. H. W., 150
Whatman, Capt. A. D., 72
Wheeler, 2nd Lt. J. D., 241
Whillier, Lt. L. A., 197
White City, Trenches near, 179
White, L/Sgt. G. E., D.C.M., 124–5
White, Lt.-Col. F. A., D.S.O., 50, 52, 80, 123, 127, 128, 129, 142, 344
White, Lt.-Col. R. E., V.D., 342, 343
White, 2nd Lt. H. J. F., 65, 70
White, 2nd Lt. H. W., 266
Whitehead, Capt. T. H., 172
White Hill, Jerusalem, 318
White House, the, 42
Whiting, L/Cpl. G., MM. & Bar, 229, 230, 271
Whitmore, Capt. G. F., 100
Whitson, Maj. W. R., 247
Whymark, 2nd Lt. W. E., 258
Wiers, 296
Wiggett, A/C.S.M. C. G., M.M. & Bar, 290

Wilder, 2nd Lt. R. C. P., 42, 323
Wilding, Cpl. G. H., M.M. & Bar, 355
Wiles, 2nd Lt. J. D., 161, 162
Wilhelma, 211, 312, 314
Wilkinson, Lt. E. J. G., 299
Wilkinson, Maj.-Gen. Sir P., 186
Willcocks, Lt.-Gen. Sir J., 47, 62
William II, ex-Kaiser, 58, 137
Williams, Capt. E. C. T. B., 32, 58, 59, 64, 66
Williams, C.Q.M.S., 40
Williams, Lt. H. A., 276
Williams, R.Q.M.S., F. C., 97
Williams, 2nd Lt. D. R., 166
Williams, 2nd Lt. H., M.C., 257
Williams, 2nd Lt. L. C. M.C., 286
Williams, 2nd Lt. S. C., 227
Williamson, 2nd Lt. A., 93, 124
Willis, Capt. M. H. S., D.S.O., 400
Wills, Lt. A. J., 102
Willson, 2nd Lt. H. H., 170
Wilmot-Johnson, Capt. L., 93, 125, 248
Wilson, A. Maitland, D. L., 329
Wilson, Capt. C. S., 49, 50, 54, 327, 330
Wilson, Capt. F. M., 338
Wilson, Capt. T., 400
Wilson, Lt. J. B. M., 253
Wilson, Lt. P., 102
Wilson, Lt.-Col. F. T. D., 22, 31, 32, 328, 331, 381, 384, 386, 387, 391, 392, 394
Wilson, Lt.-Gen. Sir H. F. M., 380
Wilson, Pte., D.C.M., 381
Wilson, 2nd Lt. F., 197
Wilson, 2nd Lt. G. M., 222
Wilson, 2nd Lt. W., 198
Windsor, Lt. L. St. L., 74
Windy Corner, 61
Wing, Maj.-Gen. F. D. V., 89, 130
Wingsway, 143
Winkworth, 2nd Lt. K. J., 241
Winn, Capt. A., 39, 40
Winton, Lt. H. G. D., 73
Wintour, Brig.-Gen. F., 55
Witle Poort Farm, 78, 79
Wolfe, General, 17
Wollaston, Lt.-Col. F. H. A., D.S.O., 202, 311, 312, 313
Wolseley, F. M., Viscount, 17, 75
Wolton, Capt. E. D., 102, 107, 211
Wolton, Capt. H. C., M.C. 102, 210, 311, 350
Wolton, 2nd Lt. O. B., 102, 104
Wolton, 2nd Lt. W. R., 227
Wombwell, L/Sgt. R. B., 42
W.A.A.C.'s, 328–9
Wood Alley, 174
Wood, Capt. A., 91, 167, 168
Wood, Capt. O. I., 17, 49, 50, 51, 64, 68, 128
Wood Lane Trench, 190, 191, 192
Wood, Lt., 54
Wood, Lt. G. D., 89, 131
Wood, Maj.-Gen. P. R., 230
Wood, 2nd Lt. W. A., 217
Woodcock, Brig.-Gen. W. J., 281
Woodgate, A/Lt. A. H., 250
Woodhouse, 2nd Lt. R. P., 213
Wood-Martin, Capt. F. W., 17, 50, 53, 54, 55
Woods, Lt. C. H., 248
Woods, Lt. T. C. H., 279
Woods, 2nd Lt. E. H. T., 189
Woods, 2nd Lt. H. W., 227
Woods, 2nd Lt. W. J. P., 178
Woodward, Sgt. J., M.M., 145
Woodward, 2nd Lt. W. T., 222
Woollcombe, Lt.-Gen. Sir C. L., 223, 258
Wootton, Capt. J. W., 96, 174, 253
Wormald, Capt. O. E., 107
Wortley, 2nd Lt. M. L., 128
Wright, C.M.S., 102
Wright, Lt.-Col. C. F., 332
Wright, Maj. A. B., M.C. & Bar, 97, 174, 252, 254, 280, 282, 355
Wright, 2nd Lt. C. F., 128
Wright, 2nd Lt. E. S., 178
Wright, 2nd Lt. H. W., 142, 187
Wrinch, 2nd Lt. S., 77
Wrixon, 2nd Lt. A. H., 153–4
Wulverghem, 42, 55, 301
Wynn, Capt. T. S., M.C., 133, 136, 264, 265
Wytschaete Area, 56
  Ridge, 73

Y

Y Wood, 82
Yates, 2nd Lt. S., 230
Yeatman, Capt. C. D., 307
Yebrud, 319
Yehudieh Trenches, 311
Yenikoi, 160, 161
York, H.R.H. the Duke of, (George V), Hon. Colonel, Suffolk Yeomanry, 114, 115
Young, Maj. T. S., 340, 341
Y.M.C.A. tents, 348
Young, Sgt., 313
Ypres, 52, 53, 55, 65, 68, 70, 71, 72, 73, 76, 77, 83, 84, 86, 137, 223, 230
  Battles of, 65 *seq.*, 72, 73, 76 *seq.*, 190, 239 *seq.*
Ypres, F.M. the Earl of (Gen. Sir John French), 37, 41, 45, 48, 51, 63, 94, 120, 133, 336, 365
Ypres Salient, 52, 65, 66, 70, 73, 74, 76, *seq.*, 123 *seq.*, 135, 185, 186, 194, 223 *seq.*, 231, 253, 256
Ypres–Comines Canal, 52, 78 84, 135, 136, 300, 301

Ypres–Comines Railway, 65
Ypres–La Bassée Sector, 56
Ypres–Roulers Railway, 226, 242
Ypres–St. Eloi Road, 138
Ypres–Zonnebeke Road, 66, 300

Z

ZEERUST, 118
Zeifizfiyeh Hill, 211, 311
Zeitun, 350
Zillebeke, 78, 239
  Lake, 300
Zillebeke-Zandvoorde Road, 239
Zouave Wood, 74, 83
Zollern Redoubt, 172
  Trench, 168, 169
Zonnebeke, 65, 66, 223, 224
  Road, 71
Zudrove, 228

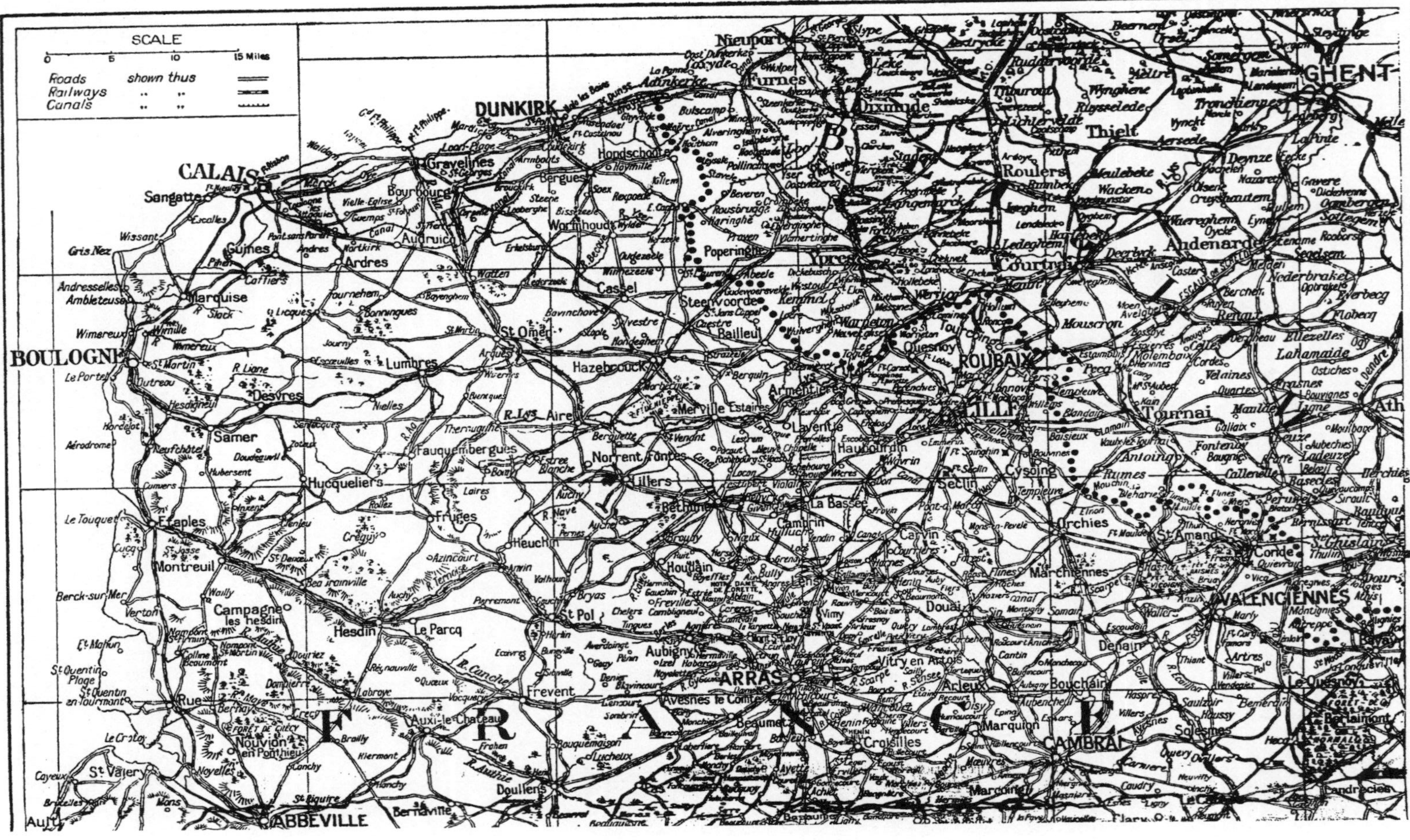
SCALE
0 5 10 15 Miles
Roads shown thus
Railways " "
Canals " "
DUNKIRK
CALAIS
BOULOGNE
ABBEVILLE
GHENT
Nieuport
Furnes
Dixmude
Thielt
Roulers
Ypres
Poperinghe
Courtrai
Audenarde
Gravelines
Bergues
Hondschoote
Cassel
St Omer
Hazebrouck
Armentières
Lille
Roubaix
Tourcoing
Tournai
Bailleul
Steenvoorde
Aire
Merville
Estaires
Béthune
La Bassée
Lens
Arras
Douai
Cambrai
Valenciennes
Orchies
Seclin
Marchiennes
St Amand
Condé
Denain
Bapaume
Doullens
Frevent
St Pol
Hesdin
Montreuil
Etaples
Le Touquet
Samer
Desvres
Lumbres
Ardres
Guines
Marquise
Wimereux
Le Portel
Rue
St Valery
Le Quesnoy
Landrecies
Solesmes
Ath
Renaix
Mouscron
Lillers
Fruges
Hucqueliers
Fauquembergues
Crécy
B
E
F
R
A
N
C
E

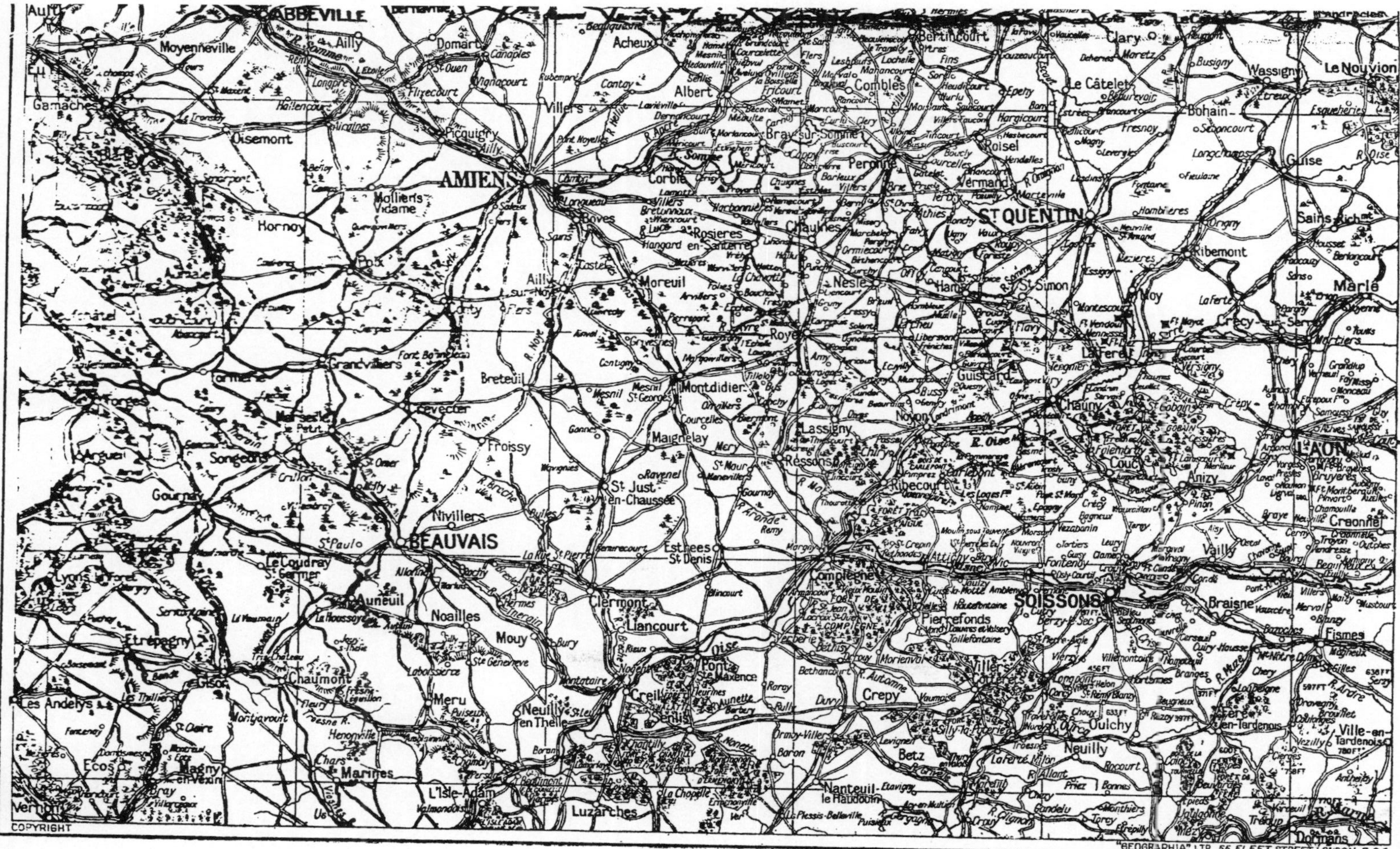

ABBEVILLE
Aily
Moyenneville
Domart
Canaples
Acheux
Albert
Bertincourt
Clary
Le Câtelet
Wassigny
Le Nouvion
Gamache
Oisemont
Picquigny
AMIENS
Combles
Bohain
Guise
Molliens Vidame
Hornoy
Corbie
Bray sur Somme
Peronne
Roisel
Vermand
ST QUENTIN
Boves
Rosieres
Chaulnes
Ribemont
Marle
Poix
Moreuil
Nesle
Ham
St Simon
Moy
Conty
Roye
La Fere
Grandvilliers
Breteuil
Montdidier
Guiscard
Chauny
Crecy-sur-Serre
Froissy
Maignelay
Lassigny
Noyon
LAON
Songeons
Ressons
Ribecourt
Coucy
Anizy
Gournay
St Just en-Chaussee
Nivillers
BEAUVAIS
Estrees St Denis
Compiegne
Vailly
Craonne
Le Coudray St Germer
Auneuil
Noailles
Clermont
Liancourt
SOISSONS
Braisne
Fismes
Mouy
Pierrefonds
Etrepagny
Gisors
Chaumont
Pont St Maxence
Villers Cotterets
Les Andelys
Meru
Neuilly en Thelle
Creil
Senlis
Crepy
Oulchy
Fere en-Tardenois
Ville-en-Tardenois
Ecos
Magny en Vexin
Marines
L'Isle-Adam
Luzarches
Betz
Nanteuil le Haudouin
Neuilly
Vernon
Dormans
COPYRIGHT
"GEOGRAPHIA" LTD 55 FLEET STREET, LONDON. E.C.4.